THE
UFO
VERDICT
EXAMINING THE EVIDENCE

THE
UFO
VERDICT

EXAMINING THE EVIDENCE

ROBERT SHEAFFER

PROMETHEUS BOOKS

Buffalo, New York 14215

Published 1986 by Prometheus Books
700 East Amherst Street, Buffalo, New York 14215

90 89 88 87 86   4 3 2 1

Library of Congress Catalog Number: 80-84406

ISBN 0-87975-338-2

Printed in the United States of America

To Kenneth
whose birth delayed this book at least
six months — and who made
me not even care!

CONTENTS

FOREWORD

How can the "UFO question" ever be solved? The claim that there must be some extraordinary stimulus behind at least *some* UFO reports is, in the final analysis, immune from disproof. No matter how many cases are found to have prosaic explanations, there are always more to be researched.

Robert Sheaffer quite correctly puts the question in a scientific framework: After a third of a century of UFO reports, UFO books, newsletters, magazines, and conferences—of believers, disbelievers, unbelievers, contactees, and abductees—have the UFO proponents succeeded in making a case for the existence of that extraordinary stimulus? The UFO proponents must carry the burden of proof and overcome the "shadow of a doubt," although, in a topsy-turvy view of the scientific method, they often assign this responsibility to the "skeptics," claiming that it is the UFO nonbelievers who must disprove the existence of "true UFOs."

Sheaffer is a scrapper, and an effective one. He is a dogged researcher, chasing after clues and piercing misinformation with inspired intuition—as some of his classic research papers show (see the chapters on the Betty Hill case, the Jimmy Carter UFO, and the great Ohio police chase). More than that, Sheaffer is an insightful theorist; he puts the "UFO question" into the perspective of the history of scientific thought. And the "UFO Verdict" (a title I am proud to say I proposed) is now in.

Prominent UFO spokesmen have often given lip service to the idea that they welcome criticism and debate. For example, leading UFO theorist Dr. Jacques Vallee has written: "I make an appeal to skeptics . . . They could do much to raise the standards of research . . . The most serious obstacle to the progress of research is not the lack of government funding for some Flying Saucer Institute, but simply the absence of informed, interested, and intelligent skeptics. Such an intervention by critical minds . . . is essential if we are to survive tomorrow's mythological immersion."

Robert Sheaffer is an "informed, interested, and intelligent" skeptic. Although it remains to be seen whether the UFO movement will respond in the positive way foreseen by Vallee, for the rest of the public Sheaffer's presentation of the UFO evidence and the scientific verdict based on that evidence will be enlightening and useful.

James Oberg

James Oberg is a space specialist at NASA's Mission Control in Houston and the UFO columnist for Omni *magazine. In October 1979 in London he was awarded the Cutty Sark prize for the best scientific paper on UFOs.*

ACKNOWLEDGMENTS

Gathering the information required for a book of this scope is far more than any one person could ever hope to accomplish. Without the assistance of the many people who willingly shared their ideas, their materials, and their sense of humor about the whole UFO question, this book would not have been possible.

Special acknowledgments are due Philip J. Klass, Paul Kurtz, Martin Gardner, and James E. Oberg for their invaluable and extremely generous assistance. Many others have also generously provided materials, assistance, and ideas: Jack Acuff, Gray Barker, Tom Bearden, Jerome Clark, Daniel Cohen, Tom Comella ("Peter Kor"), Doris Doyle, J. Dan Duke, Fred Durant, George Earley, George Fawcett, Kendrick Frazier, Les Gaver, Allen H. Greenfield, Richard Greenwell, Don Henshaw, Hayden C. Hewes, Betty Hill, Michael Hutchinson, John Keel, Martin S. Kottmeyer, Elmer Kral, Willard F. McIntyre, Bruce S. Maccabee, the late Donald H. Menzel, James W. Moseley, William Moulton, Early J. Neff, Mark Plummer, Gary P. Posner, James ("The Amazing") Randi, Ian Ridpath, Robert Schiller, David A. Schroth, William H. Spaulding, Ernest H. Taves, Marcello Truzzi, Hans Van Kampen, Colman Von Keviczky, Joseph Wittemer, and, of course, Mr. X.

Not everyone named will agree with everything I have written. If I have inadvertently forgotten anyone, he or she has my sincere apologies.

A large debt of gratitude is owed to Cynthia Dwyer for her skillful copy editing and many helpful suggestions. Immediately after finishing work on this manuscript, Cynthia went to Iran as a free-lance journalist, where she was arrested by the Revolutionary Guards and charged with spying for the CIA. As this book goes to press, she is still being held. To Cynthia go my most sincere wishes for a safe and speedy return home.

1

THE UFO VERDICT: EXAMINING THE EVIDENCE

I must premise, that this being matter of Fact is only capable of the evidence of authority and sense. —Joseph Glanvill, philosopher of science and member of the Royal Society, 1666[1]

Flying saucers, also known as Unidentified Flying Objects or UFOs, have been in the news more or less continuously since 1947, when the famous June 24 sighting by pilot Kenneth Arnold, alleging that a formation of strange disks was zipping up and down Washington's Mt. Ranier, burst into the headlines. That certainly seems like a long time ago. Hundreds of books, thousands of articles, and millions of words have been written on the subject, and an end to the controversy is still nowhere in sight.

There are many who claim that UFOs can only be explained as extra-terrestrial spaceships or even more exotic phenomena: interpenetrating universes, "alternate realities," and the like. There are many people who claim to have actually *met* the alleged occupants of flying saucers, and even to have taken rides in the craft. The late George Adamski was the best known of these so-called "contactees": he claimed to have held lengthy discussions with people from Venus.

Others claim to have been "kidnapped" or abducted aboard a strange craft by alien beings, where they were subjected to a bizarre medical-type examination, and afterward set free with their conscious memories of the incident erased. There are many reports on file of "close encounters" with a mysterious craft, whose description seems to rule out any known object. Mancuvers are often reported that would be plainly impossible for any device of human construction.

If reports such as these are accurate, there can be little doubt that our planet is under surveillance by intelligent beings from some unknown place or time. We must stress the word *if,* however, because there is not yet any indisputable proof that such reports have any foundation in reality. Nonetheless, the UFO phenomenon does indeed *seem* to promise an enormous potential for scientific advancement, *if* the reports of UFO encounters are indeed accurate descriptions of some real phenomenon.

This book is titled *The UFO Verdict: Examining the Evidence,* because in scientific matters the most solid evidence possible is required. Scientific questions can be settled by nothing less than a strict adherence to the scientific method, which demands that we examine the matter in a dispassionate and objective manner. Whatever personal feelings we may have on the subject and whatever hopes or fears we may secretly harbor must be cast aside the moment we claim for ourselves the title "scientific investigator" of UFOs. We have all no doubt heard dozens of intriguing and exotic tales about flying saucers, many of them stories we might like to believe. But in science, hearsay and speculation simply will not do. If we are to create a genuine *science* of the study of Unidentified Flying Objects—a most commendable effort, a goal to which nearly all major UFO groups claim to be committed—then UFO reports must be subjected to the same relentless scrutiny that physicists, biochemists, geologists, and all other true scientists routinely give their data.

In this book I shall examine some of the best UFO evidence on record, because our ultimate conclusion about UFOs must be based not on our wishes or on preconceived ideas but on the evidence. Some of the most famous UFO cases will be examined: the alleged "UFO abduction" of Betty and Barney Hill, the sightings at Exeter, the UFO report by Jimmy Carter. All of the facts presented in this book are the result of painstaking research, and references are cited for all of the major sources.

An attitude of healthy skepticism is to be encouraged, for the overall standard of accuracy in writings in the UFO field is dismally low. *No* UFO author's unsubstantiated assertions are to be taken as fact, no matter how provocative or seemingly authentic a particular statement may be. The great majority of writings on UFOs have been filled with what we must bluntly label hokum or wild flights of fancy. The only statements worthy of consideration by serious readers are those that can be fully substantiated. It is my sincere intention and belief that the statements in this book fall into that category. I welcome challenges should there be any that do not.

It is my hope that after reading this book and carefully weighing the evidence discussed herein, the reader will come away with a more accurate and rational perspective on UFOs and will be better able to evaluate the merit of the many claims made almost daily on this highly controversial subject. The single element most seriously lacking in the field of UFOlogy is critical thinking. If this book in any way assists or encourages the reader in that regard, I shall consider my effort to have been a success.

NOTE

1. Joseph Glanvill, *Saducismus Triumphatus* (London, 1666, 1668, 1681, 1689, and later printings), p. 67.

2

CLOSE ENCOUNTER OF THE FIRST KIND: JIMMY CARTER

Contrary to what some people believe, not everyone who files a UFO report is obscure and unreliable. UFOs have been reported by people in all walks of life. More often than not, the supposed UFO witness seems to be a sober and sensible individual and does not appear to be suffering from any mental derangement. Sometimes he or she is a person of high standing in the community. Scientists, engineers, military and commercial pilots, as well as policemen, are among those who have reported seeing UFOs. One cannot say that all these people are lying or that they all suffered from some temporary aberration. Their narratives appear to be as sincere as human testimony can possibly be, and it is indeed difficult to listen to them without feeling a powerful emotional urge to believe what they are saying.

No one seriously questions these facts. But the important question to be answered is: Do these reports by seemingly reliable persons establish the real existence of UFOs, or do they rather serve as a warning that even the most sober and reliable persons can be led astray by unconscious errors in perception? To attempt to resolve the question, let us examine the UFO sighting reported by a well-known man from Georgia. Ten other people are said to have joined him in experiencing a Close Encounter of the First Kind—that is, one in which the UFO reportedly comes within a few hundred yards of the witness.

By June of 1976, Jimmy Carter of Georgia was the undisputed front-runner for the Democratic Party's nomination for president. In its issue of June 8, the supermarket tabloid *National Enquirer* carried the headline "Jimmy Carter: The Night I Saw a UFO." It was with this story that my investigation began. The article is based upon an extremely brief interview with Mr. Carter, who said, "I am convinced that UFOs exist because I have

4

seen one . . . It was a very peculiar aberration, but about twenty people saw it . . . It was the darndest thing I've ever seen. It was big, it was very bright, it changed colors and it was about the size of the moon. We watched it for ten minutes, but none of us could figure out what it was." The sighting took place in Thomaston, Georgia, according to the *Enquirer,* in 1973 following a late-evening speech Mr. Carter gave to the local Lions Club.

The *Enquirer* goes on to quote Mr. W. Asbury Stembridge, of Macon, Georgia, who not only had reportedly discussed the sighting with Mr. Carter but had also supposedly said, "My wife Charlotte saw the same UFO." While the Carter family was of course not willing to discuss the sighting, even if they could be reached, I did reach Mr. and Mrs. Stembridge by telephone, only to learn that the statements attributed to them were not at all accurate. Mrs. Stembridge explained in exasperation that she had told the *Enquirer* reporter "over and over" about the details of her own reported UFO sighting (which occurred when Mr. Carter was *not* present) but that they proceeded to write her up as a corroborating witness nonetheless. Mr. Stembridge happened to remark that, while Carter had only briefly mentioned the UFO incident to him years before, "my recollection doesn't put him in Thomaston at all" on the night of the sighting.

Milton Jones, a Columbus, Georgia, attorney, was quoted in the *Enquirer* story saying, "I vividly remember Jimmy telling me about spotting the UFO." But when I reached Mr. Jones by telephone, he too remarked on the inaccuracy of the *Enquirer* account; he had told the reporter that his recollection of the UFO discussion was not at all "vivid" but quite vague. Carter had once mentioned the incident in his presence, several years before, but Mr. Jones was unable to recall any specifics about it. When I mentioned that the *Enquirer* account placed the incident at a Lions Club speech in Thomaston, Mr. Jones replied, "The speech to the Lions Club rings a bell, but Thomaston very definitely does not ring a bell." He seemed to recall that it had been somewhere "down in south Georgia."

Bill Heule works for radio station WSFT in Thomaston. He had long been active in local Lions Club affairs. After the *Enquirer* story appeared, Mr. Heule queried his friends in the club: not one of them had any recollection of such an incident on the night Jimmy Carter came to Thomaston. Mr. Heule told me that he found it difficult to believe that the supposed UFO sighting could have taken place at the Thomaston Lions Club without his hearing of it.

Three Georgians who had known Jimmy Carter for years told me they doubted that the sighting occurred in Thomaston. My investigation had reached a standstill: I now had no remaining thread to pursue.

I began making inquiries of various UFO researchers, looking for someone who might be able to provide some facts on the case. Finally, someone suggested that I contact Hayden Hewes, director of the International UFO Bureau, who had written a brief piece on the Carter sighting for *Argosy*

UFO.[1] I reached Mr. Hewes by telephone at his home in Oklahoma City, and it was he who provided the first significant lead. When brief press reports appeared during the big UFO flap of 1973 to the effect that then-Governor Carter had previously spotted a UFO, the International UFO Bureau mailed a UFO sighting report form to Carter at the State Capitol in Atlanta. Carter apparently filled out the form in some haste, his handwritten replies being brief and not easily legible. He then mailed it back to Oklahoma. Mr. Hewes was kind enough to lend me a photographic transparency of the 1973 report in Carter's own handwriting (plate 1).

As I suspected, the event did not occur in Thomaston. Carter's account named Leary, Georgia, a very small town in the southwest corner of the state. Mr. Carter did not specify the exact date of the incident, but he estimated it to have been in October, 1969, and not in 1973 as the *National Enquirer* had reported. The time of the sighting was given as 7:15 PM, a time apparently known because Carter was "outside waiting for a meeting to begin at 7:30 PM." (The *Enquirer* story places the incident *after* the meeting.) The object was "bluish at first — then reddish," it "seemed to move toward us from a distance, stop, move partially away, return then depart." It appeared to be in the west, at about 30° elevation. Mr. Carter states that "10 members of Leary, Ga., Lions Club" also witnessed the object, but he fails to list any of their names or addresses, as requested. Not all questions were answered.

Describing the angular size of the object, Governor Carter judged it to be "about same as moon maybe a little smaller [*sic*]. Varied from brighter/larger than planet to apparent size of moon . . . at one time, as bright as moon." When given the option of requesting anonymity, Carter boldly checked the box declaring "You may use my name."

Having determined the correct locale of the sighting, it would be necessary to learn the exact date before it would be possible to attempt to identify the object. I sent off a letter addressed to the director of the Leary Lions Club, seeking additional information. The letter was returned to me unopened; across the envelope, someone had written, "No Lions Club active." Information on this case was not going to come easily!

Since the Lions Club angle appeared to be getting nowhere, I decided to begin by simply calling *somebody* in the town of Leary. Presumably Leary would be typical of an old-fashioned American town, where almost everyone would know everyone else. It was. I began with the mayor's office. The woman who answered the telephone was friendly and helpful, as were all the Leary residents I eventually spoke with. She did remember the day that Mr. Carter came to Leary, but could not remember exactly when that was or what night of the week the Lions Club meetings might have been. And she had not heard *anything* about a sighting of a UFO on that occasion.

She suggested that I might contact Marshall Jordan, owner of Jordan's store, for further information. Mr. Jordan explained to me that the Lions

Club in Leary had not been active for a number of years; the former leader of the club, Frank Lunsford, is now deceased. Mr. Jordan likewise remembered Jimmy Carter's visit to Leary, although he had been unable to attend the Lions Club meeting that night. He did not know exactly when this was. And no, he had not heard about any UFO being sighted the night Jimmy Carter was in town.

Mr. Jordan suggested I call Fred Hart, another former member of the now-defunct club. Mr. Hart recalled that the meetings were on Monday nights, but he, too, was unable to determine the exact date of Carter's visit. As an officer, Mr. Hart had kept some Lions Club records in his house that might have revealed the exact date of the sighting, but unfortunately the records were destroyed in a fire. Did he recall anything about a UFO sighting during Carter's visit? He did not, he began to say; he and Carter had driven all over town, spending the afternoon together, but he didn't remember seeing anything. I pointed out that the sighting was supposed to have occurred during the evening, just before the meeting. This jogged his memory: "It seems like there was a little—like a blue light or something or other in the sky that night [pause] like some kind of weather balloon they send out or something . . . it had been pretty far back in my mind!" Here at last was the first lead in Leary! Mr. Hart, however, was not exactly overwhelmed by the sighting, as Mr. Carter appears to have been; indeed, he barely recalled the incident at all. He did not believe the object to be anything out of the ordinary. (By contrast, Jimmy Carter told the *Atlanta Constitution* that after the UFO sighting he immediately went to a tape recorder and dictated a description of what he remembered as a "very remarkable sight."[2]

At Mr. Hart's suggestion, I telephoned Stanley Shepard, owner of the Shepard Oil Company. By now news of my interest in the incident had spread all over town; it seemed that the Carter UFO sighting had become the favorite topic of discussion over the cracker barrel. Like the others, Mr. Shepard remembered Jimmy Carter's visit to Leary, though he did not know when it was, and he did *not* recall anything about a UFO sighting. The Lions Club, he explained, used to hold its meetings at the town swimming pool. Mr. Shepard generously offered to borrow a key to the now-abandoned swimming pool building and examine the club records left in storage there. (The Leary investigation certainly helped this Yankee to understand the meaning of "southern hospitality.")

When I called Mr. Shepard back, he explained that the files were in a state of total disarray. He found a few club records, but none for 1969. Numerous other calls turned up few leads. The only Leary newspaper, the *Calhoun County Courier,* did not keep any issues going back as far as 1969. Jack Perryman and Herman Balliet, also former members, were unable to add any more details.

Meanwhile, suspecting that the object might be a balloon, I attempted to determine the source of any balloon that might have been sighted in Leary during October of 1969. Astronomical objects were ruled out because no brilliant planets were visible in the western sky that month after sunset. Nor was the bright star Arcturus a likely explanation, even though it was well placed, because the sky would have been far too bright for Acturus to be easily visible at 7:15 PM.

However, balloons at sunset can be a striking sight, high in the atmosphere in direct sunlight after the sun has set for ground observers. Unfortunately, I was unable to pinpoint any balloon launches that might have been visible from Leary. While this does not prove that no balloons would have been visible, it does not allow us to state with any certainty that the object *was* a balloon. There is no central registry of balloon launches; one must attempt to contact every possible balloon launch site. Since some balloons can cross a continent or an ocean, it is impossible to eliminate all possible sources for balloon launches.

I contacted three of the major research balloon-launching facilities in the United States, but none of them had any balloons over Georgia during October 1969. It is possible that balloons may have been launched from other places, but tracking them down would be a nearly impossible task.

Smaller weather balloons must also be taken into account. These balloons at launch are about three feet in diameter and expand as they ascend to approximately 30,000 feet altitude to test the winds. But there are no regular weather-balloon launch sites within a hundred miles of Leary. However, I learned through a most improbable accident—telephoning a science professor at a local Georgia college when a certain student just happened to be in his office—that in 1969 the Navy was operating a now-defunct air station in Albany, Georgia, just twenty-five miles from Leary. This airfield regularly sent up lighted balloons to test the winds. (Since the solution to a UFO case can often depend upon stumbling across information of this nature, it is not surprising that so many UFO incidents appear to have no solution.)

However, I found that Navy balloons apparently do *not* provide the solution to the Carter UFO sighting. The standard balloon launch times for weather readings are 0 hours and 12 hours Greenwich Mean Time, and weather observers with whom I have spoken say that these times are fairly strictly observed; only rarely does a balloon go up more than a few minutes early or late. Occasionally additional balloons are launched at 6 hours and 18 hours GMT. But the Carter UFO sighting (assuming it was in October) corresponded to 23:15 GMT. Unless a balloon were launched an hour or more ahead of schedule, it would not have been visible in Leary at that time.

Mrs. Frank Lunsford is the elderly widow of the man who was described as the "backbone" of the Lions Club in Leary. She did indeed recall the night Carter came to Leary, but did not know the date and did not recall any UFO being sighted. The club meetings were always on Tuesday nights, she recalled. The Leary Lions Club had disbanded, she said, just a few weeks after her husband's death (a statement with which all Lions Club members seemed to agree). Mrs. Lunsford said that while she had no letters or other documents that might contain the date of Carter's visit, she knew that it was just a matter of weeks before her husband's death. When did Mr. Lunsford pass away? "February 17, 1969," she replied immediately. *If what Mrs. Lunsford told me was correct, the sighting could not possibly have taken place in October 1969* as Carter had stated. Her recollections suggested that the incident took place in either January or February of 1969.

Judge Peggy Cowart at the county courthouse suggested that I might call Mrs. Schramm, a reporter for the *Calhoun County Courier* who lives in nearby Edison. While Mrs. Schramm was unable to add anything new, her husband, a leading member of the still-active Lions Club in Edison, put me in touch with Mr. Charles Mask, long-time secretary of the Edison chapter, who is a veritable repository of accurate information concerning Lions Club activities. He pinpointed Carter's term as district governor of the Club— ending in June 1969 — *which also appeared to rule out October 1969 as the correct date*. Looking in a back issue of the Official Directory of the Lions Club International, he ascertained that the Leary Club had met on the first and third Mondays of each month, at 7:30 PM. Most important of all, Mr. Mask was able to refer me to the place where all Lions Club records are permanently stored: the Lions International Headquarters in Oakbrook, Illinois. I had assumed all along that local club records would be stored locally, or not at all. But Mr. Mask pointed out that Carter, as district governor, was required to turn in a visitation report for each local club he visited, and these reports might still be available.

After thanking Mr. Mask, I dialed the Lions Club International Headquarters, where I was put in contact with Mr. Al Webb. When I called back the following day, he had found the long-sought information: a copy of Jimmy Carter's district governor visitation report for his trip to Leary. It bore the date of Monday, January 6, 1969. Mrs. Lunsford was right: Carter's visit had indeed occurred just six weeks before her husband's death. Carter did not make any mention of a UFO sighting in his Lions Club report.

Al Webb explained that it was only through a fortunate accident that this report was preserved, since normally all such records are destroyed after about seven years. But seven years after Jimmy Carter's term as district governor, he was a candidate for president of the United States. Fortunately, the Lions Club employee handling the matter recognized that a collection of papers written by a man who might soon be president might have historical value, so he preserved the file. Had this employee not been so alert, it is highly improbable that any solution to the Carter UFO sighting could ever have been found.

The actual date of Carter's speech in Leary, January 6, 1969, was nine months earlier than Mr. Carter's recollection had placed it. This not only invalidated all of the research I had done looking for balloon launches, but totally changed the positions of all astronomical objects. When I computed the positions of the planets during the month of January, I found that *Venus was a conspicuous evening star, nearing its maximum brilliance.* Venus was to be found in the west-southwest at 7:15 PM, at about 25° elevation, *in virtually the exact position that Carter reported his UFO.* When I obtained the weather records from the nearby Albany airfield, they revealed that the weather was cold and clear, although a few scattered clouds were present that evening. In fact, the morning of the day of the sighting saw the coldest temperature readings of the entire winter. It is in crisp, cold, transparent air such as this that planets and stars seem especially large and brilliant.

Mr. Carter is in good company in misinterpreting Venus as a UFO. No other single object is responsible for so many UFO sightings. Every time Venus reaches its peak brilliance in the evening sky, hundreds of such "UFO sightings" are made. No other celestial object except the sun and moon ever achieves such brilliance. Indeed, Venus is so brilliant that it can often be seen before the sun has set, or even in full daylight, if one knows exactly where to look. On several occasions I have gone outside at noontime to see if Venus would be visible without optical aid; every time that the sky was clear enough (and that planet was near its peak brilliance), I was able to discern it plainly, after determining exactly where to look. Plate 2 shows Venus and the moon seen together at noontime, captured by a modest telephoto lens, without the aid of any filters or special processing. Even the ardent UFO believer Jacques Vallee has written: "No single object has been misinterpreted as a 'flying saucer' more often than the planet Venus. The study of these mistakes proves quite instructive, for it shows beyond all possible dispute the limitations of sensory perception and the weakness of accounts relating shapes and motions of point sources or objects with small apparent diameters."[3]

During World War II, many rounds of ammunition were wasted firing at Venus, believing it to be an enemy aircraft. U.S. bomber crews over Japan reported that they were being "followed" by a "ball of fire," which they believed to be an airplane attempting to shine a searchlight on them for the benefit of Japanese gunners. This "aircraft" was, of course, the planet Venus. Yet for weeks these experienced flight crews continued to mistake that brilliant yet distant planet for a new enemy weapon.[4]

Nor is Jimmy Carter the only political figure to mistake a bright planet for a UFO. In October 1973, Governor John Gilligan of Ohio reported that he and his wife had observed a UFO while driving back from a weekend trip. The object was said to have "a vertical beam of light, amber colored," and it was observed to remain in the south-southeast. Governor Gilligan's UFO coincides with the position of the planet Mars, which was especially brilliant that month due to its close proximity to Earth.

It is most instructive to note the many false leads and faulty recollections that often make the solution to a UFO sighting difficult to obtain. Mr. Carter recalled the date as being nine months later than it actually was. If it had not been possible to correct this error by referring to written records, the solution to the sighting would never have been found. The press had widely misreported both the time and the location of the incident and the circumstances of the sighting as well. Witnesses' memories of the incident deteriorated with time, and spurious "facts" began to creep in, such as a widespread mistake recalling the night of the week on which the meetings were held.

Carter's recollection that the object "came close, then moved away" does not, of course, describe the actual motions of the planet Venus. Such statements, however, are commonly encountered in descriptions of bright planets reported as UFOs; they show the fallacy of according too much weight to unsubstantiated subjective impressions. Venus is not as bright as the moon, nor is its angular size as great as that of the moon, as Carter also reported. (In virtually every instance, the inaccuracy tends to make the object seem more brilliant and more mysterious.) Mr. Carter's distance estimate, which had the object hovering from 300 to 1,000 yards away, is thus thirty million miles or so short of the actual distance to Venus. One can only speculate how many other "close encounters" actually involve distant airplane lights, or far more distant celestial objects. Plainly, not every nocturnal object that is judged to be close to the observer is in fact nearby.

What would have been the outcome of this investigation if the records of Carter's Lions Club visitation had not been preserved at Lions International? What if Jimmy Carter had not filed a UFO report in 1973? What if the object had in fact been a balloon, but that I remained unaware of the now-defunct Navy airfield in nearby Albany, or if the object were a big "Skyhook" balloon launched by some research facility that is no longer launching balloons and whose records are unavailable? In each of these quite plausible scenarios, the correct explanation of the incident could never have been established. When viewed with this in mind, it is not at all surprising that there remain some UFO sightings for which explanations have not yet been conclusively established. Indeed, the amazing thing is that, despite all the difficulties, such a large number *have* been satisfactorily explained.

Allan Hendry, managing editor of the Center for UFO Studies' *International UFO Reporter,* who is certainly no UFO debunker, has remarked on "the thin veil that can exist between UFOs and IFOs" (identified flying objects). Investigating a UFO reported in Las Vegas, Nevada, in 1977, Hendry was unable to suggest any reasonable explanation. However, by a lucky accident he was referred to a local office of the Environmental Protection Agency (EPA), which had sent up a lighted balloon to make pollution readings. Hendry remarks, "If I hadn't the sheer luck of being put in touch with the EPA, do you think I would have contrived a solution like 'illuminated balloon on a half-mile of string'?"[5] Would anyone have believed him if he had?

I confess to having oversimplified my investigation of the Jimmy Carter UFO, for I did not include the many telephone interviews that led nowhere. It takes just a few minutes to report a UFO sighting, yet it may take months to find the solution. If Carter had not been a candidate for president, no one would have invested the time and money required to obtain the solution to his UFO sighting. It would have remained forever in the column of "unexplained" UFO reports, which are said to constitute the "evidence" for UFOs. If a similar amount of time and effort were invested in other "unexplained" cases, how many of them would still be without explanation at the close of the investigation?

Yet despite the fact that my solution to the Carter UFO incident appeared in publications with nationwide circulation as early as 1977, UFO proponents continue to exploit this case. Numerous radio and television commentators continue to uncritically repeat "Jimmy Carter has seen a UFO." A 1978 "completely factual" documentary sound-recording directed by the well-known UFO researcher Dr. J. Allen Hynek trumpets the Carter UFO sighting without even a hint that the incident has been fully solved. The Carter UFO incident provides us with a litmus test for evaluating the reliability of UFO authors and researchers; anyone who continues to uncritically state that Jimmy Carter has seen a UFO has in effect warned the listener that little or no effort has been made to get the facts straight.

NOTES

1. Hayden C. Hewes, " 'I Have Seen a UFO!' Admits Jimmy Carter," *Argosy UFO,* November 1976, p. 8.
2. *Atlanta Constitution,* September 14, 1973, p. 1D.
3. Jacques and Janine Vallee, *Challenge to Science* (Chicago: Regnery, 1966), p. 110.
4. Philip J. Klass, *UFOs Explained* (New York: Random House, 1974), p. 90.
5. Center for UFO Studies, *International UFO Reporter* 2, no. 4 (April 1977):8.
6. See *International UFO Reporter* 4, no. 3 (September/October 1979):19.

3

THE UFO MOVEMENT: GALILEOS, HATFIELDS, AND McCOYS

Scientific is the sixty-four-dollar word in UFOlogy today. Every investigator, every group, pays homage to the name of science, and each claims to be working toward making the study of UFOs a respectable scientific field. These people harbor little doubt that the "science" of "UFOlogy" will someday take its supposedly rightful place alongside geology and biology.

Such claims of lofty intention would, however, carry more weight with the outside observer if the "science" of UFOlogy were slowly converging toward some generally accepted hypothesis about UFOs, or at least assembling a body of unambiguous data. But instead of converging, the various factions that make up the UFO movement appear to be growing steadily farther apart, through feuds and schisms. Indeed, the more UFOs are studied, the less there is upon which the various groups can agree.

The term "UFO movement" is increasingly used today, even by UFO buffs themselves, and the term is not inappropriate. Like the women's movement, the antiwar movement, and other social movements that have sprouted on the American scene in recent years the UFO movement is composed of people who zealously pursue a common goal: the recognition of the "reality" of UFOs by society at large, and by scientists in particular. Perhaps the best comparison might be made with one of the many small religious movements now gaining in popularity, because, although there is little else that the subsects of the UFO movement agree upon, all are firmly convinced that *when* (not *if*) the full truth about UFOs becomes known, it not only will revolutionize science but will also enrich our everyday lives beyond our wildest dreams.

The present-day UFO movement can be broadly divided into two major factions: those who believe that UFOs are nuts-and-bolts spacecraft built by some extraterrestrial intelligence (ETI), and the "new wave," who view UFOs not as spacecraft but as a paranormal phenomenon related to ghosts, telepathy, fairies, and psychic healing. The notion of UFOs as ETI is firmly implanted in the public mind. (Indeed, as is evident to anyone who deals with the public on this subject, the question of UFOs is *inseparable* from the question of extraterrestrial life by the public at large.) While the nuts-and-bolts faction probably still holds the upper hand in the UFO movement, the "new wave" is advancing rapidly, having won over some of the key people in the movement. Those who believe UFOs to be alien spacecraft consider the "new wave" to be insufferably frivolous and mystical, and fear that they threaten the prospects for the "science" of UFOlogy at least as much as the skeptics do. The "new wave," for their part, view the nuts-and-bolts faction as hopelessly reactionary and unimaginative, fixated forever in the 1950s world view that is now outdated. Present trends suggest that the "new wave" may someday gain the upper hand.

The very first organization on the UFO scene was the United States Air Force. When the first wave of sightings took place in June and July of 1947, the military was quite naturally concerned, for it was feared that the "flying disks" might be a new weapon of some foreign power. The Cold War climate caused many to fear that perhaps the Soviets, using captured German rocket scientists, had succeeded in putting into production radically new aircraft that the Nazis might have had under development at the end of the war in Europe. But after the Air Force had investigated UFOs for several years, under Project Sign, then Project Grudge, and later Project Blue Book, it became apparent that the entire investigation was leading nowhere. Nothing of substance had come out of any case, and no report investigated indicated any threat to the national security—which was, after all, the Air Force's only concern about UFOs.

Unfortunately for the Air Force, by the time it had its fill of UFOs, it was into the controversy up to its neck. UFO buffs lambasted the Air Force daily for its supposedly excessive skepticism, for being so blind as to fail to see the overwhelming evidence of visitors from space. Several pro-UFO congressmen, including House Minority Leader Gerald R. Ford, began to pressure the Air Force into devoting more money and manpower to UFOs— and hence, presumably, to come up with a more acceptable (that is, a more pro-UFO) conclusion. The Air Force's chief astronomical consultant on UFOs, J. Allen Hynek of Northwestern University, had by the late 1960s changed from a UFO skeptic to a moderate UFO believer (to become less and less moderate with each passing year). He, too, began openly disagreeing with the Air Force's skeptical position. The Air Force found it politically impossible to get out from under the UFO controversy.

Finally, in the wake of the big UFO flap of 1965–66, the Air Force, wishing to be rid of the burden once and for all, contracted with the University of Colorado for a major new $500,000 Scientific Study of Unidentified

Flying Objects, headed by the noted physicist Edward U. Condon. When the Condon Committee formally released its skeptical report in January 1969, concluding that the "study of UFO reports is not likely to advance science," the Air Force found justification for closing down its UFO investigations, which were formally ended on December 17, 1969. The *Condon Report* has been severely criticized by UFO believers, and not without reason. They point to the 39 percent of incidents investigated that are not conclusively solved in the final report. However, all of the reports left "unidentified" by Dr. Condon's team have subsequently been explained in the writings of Klass, Menzel, Taves, and Oberg, a fact that most UFOlogists prefer to simply ignore.[1]

UFOlogy in the United States today is dominated by a relatively few names. There are the familiar "big four" groups: APRO, CUFOS, MUFON, and NICAP, with their well-known directors and researchers. There are also a handful of big-name independent UFO personalities: Stanton Friedman, John Keel, Brad Steiger, and Jacques Vallee. Some of those on the outside of this little circle (and who, one might deduce, would like to see the circle redrawn) term their work "middle UFOlogy," and heap a great deal of criticism upon what they perceive as the country-club exclusiveness and conservatism of the "establishment" UFO groups.

APRO—the Aerial Phenomena Research Organization—is the oldest surviving UFO group in the United States. Founded in 1952 by Coral and James Lorenzen, APRO now boasts a formidable array of Ph.D. consultants in every subject from aeronautics to zoology. Mrs. Lorenzen became quite interested in UFOs after several reported sightings. Her studies of the UFO phenomenon convinced her that "the objects were painstakingly mapping the geographical features of the country . . . progressing from mountain ranges to rivers, coastlines, and eventually lakes. In 1948 they began their disturbing visits to military installations. Doubtless no major military base was overlooked."[2]

Mrs. Lorenzen observes that flying saucers apparently turned their attention to South America in 1954 and 1955, and APRO did likewise. A wave of UFO landings and occupant sightings erupted in South America in the mid 1950s, but APRO was the only major American UFO group to take these stories seriously. Most UFO believers at that time wrote off occupant sightings (now known as "close encounters of the third kind") as wild and woolly tales. But the willingness to believe on the part of the UFO movement has steadily grown with each passing year, and today the mainstream of UFOlogy has expanded its credulity far enough to encompass APRO's belief in occupant sightings and UFO abductions.

NICAP—the National Investigations Committee of Aerial Phenomena—is perhaps the best-known of all American UFO groups, and it still claims to retain the largest membership. Founded in 1956, NICAP's star blazed brightest from 1957 to 1969, when Major Donald E. Keyhoe, U.S. Marine

Corps (Retired), served as its director. NICAP was firmly convinced of the existence of an Air Force conspiracy to cover up "the truth" about UFOs, and Keyhoe's crusade to force the government to release its supposed UFO secrets was little short of an obsession. In the 1960s, NICAP's far-flung sub-chapters were so numerous and well organized that that group "staked a claim," as it were, to a number of cases that became major "classics" in UFOlogy: the Hill "abduction" (1961), the Heflin photos (1965), the Portage County, Ohio, police UFO chase (1966). (UFO groups presume to establish something akin to *property rights* by being first on the scene for a given case. Should another group muscle in on "their" case, as MUFON accused APRO of doing on the Kentucky "abduction" case of 1976,[3] UFOlogical warfare begins in earnest.)

While NICAP remained convinced that UFOs are spaceships piloted by beings from another world, for years they rejected out of hand any report of UFO creatures being sighted. (Yet if NICAP truly believed its own credo, such reports should not be difficult to accept.) NICAP suffered a severe financial loss in 1969–70, and Keyhoe was eased into retirement. Today the group's financial footing is still precarious, and the flame of zeal that once burned so brightly has all but burned out. Many of NICAP's leading members have either lost interest in UFOs or become active in other groups.

MUFON was founded by Walt Andrus in 1969, as an offshoot of APRO. Originally known as the Midwest UFO Network, MUFON soon went nationwide as the Mutual UFO Network, and is now headquartered in Seguin, Texas, near San Antonio. The rapid rise of MUFON was due in part to the torrent of long-time UFOlogists who defected from NICAP in the early 1970s; most of those who disassociated themselves from the failing NICAP are now MUFON members.

In 1973, former Air Force UFO consultant Dr. J. Allen Hynek founded the Center for UFO Studies. CUFOS differs from the other groups in that membership is said to be limited to scientists of established professional reputation. CUFOS is happy, however, to accept fifteen dollars a year from anyone who wishes a subscription to its monthly *International UFO Reporter*; and since the only tangible benefit conferred by membership in *any* UFO organization is receipt of that group's monthly newsletter, CUFOS' exclusivity of membership is at best an academic distinction. Since CUFOS does not have a widespread network of UFO investigators, it has worked out an arrangement making MUFON's field investigators available to do CUFOS' legwork.

A smaller group that has been receiving a great deal of publicity of late is Ground Saucer Watch (GSW), organized in 1957 by William H. Spaulding and his brother J. A. Spaulding, who now serve as directors of "western operations" and "eastern operations," respectively. Not until the group was almost twenty years old, however, did GSW have any noticeable impact on saucerdom. Today GSW's chief claim to fame is its computer enhancement of supposed UFO photographs, which I'll examine in detail in a later chapter. By means of "pixels" and "profiles," GSW's photo analysts claim to be able to tell an *authentic* UFO photograph from a bogus one. Their conclusions thus far show 95 percent are fraudulent. But the photos that the UFO buffs like to emphasize are the 5 percent that "the computer" (as if it were some sort of latter-day oracle) is said to have pronounced authentic. GSW is also receiving attention for taking legal action against the Air Force and the CIA, seeking freedom-of-information release of supposed "UFO secrets" many groups claim the government is withholding.

Many smaller UFO groups abound. Some are contactee-oriented: they take seriously certain individuals' claims of frequent and continuing contact with the "Space Brothers." Contactees usually portray the UFO people as identical in appearance and mannerisms to earthlings, except that they are supremely wise and benevolent, urging mankind to end all wars, abolish poverty, distrust, and atomic energy, adopt socialism, and live in perfect harmony. George Adamski, whom we will hear more of later, is the best-known of the "classic" UFO contactees. Of course, the Space Brothers never land openly in front of the United Nations to proclaim their platitudes to all mankind; they invariably select as their mouthpiece some obscure individual, often with a long history of involvement in mystical sects. The UFO establishment in general has *not* placed much credence in the contactees' tales (although, reflecting the climate of ever-increasing credulity, in recent years several prominent UFOlogists have expressed the opinion that "there must have been at least some grain of truth in Adamski's stories").[4] Most UFOlogists feel that the contactees' wild tales are prejudicing both the public and the scientific community against the supposedly "serious" aspect of UFOlogy, such as abductions, psychic effects, and the relationship between UFOs and fairies.

While UFO believers have been well organized for many years, until recently those of a more skeptical orientation have been neither vocal nor well organized. For many years the leading UFO skeptic was the noted Harvard astrophysicist Donald H. Menzel (1901–1976). Indeed, his was for a time almost the only voice outside the government raised in opposition to widespread popular misinformation on "flying saucers," as they were then universally called. The author of three books on the subject of UFOs,[5] as well as numerous popular and scholarly works on astronomy, Dr. Menzel made many enemies in UFOdom with his hard-nosed skepticism and irascible temperament. For many years Menzel performed an indispensable role in almost single-handedly challenging the claims of the True Believers, although in many instances his reliance on elaborate explanations involving extraordinary and implausible mirage phenomena seriously weakened the credibility of all attempts at rational analysis of UFO sightings. The only other active UFO skeptic during the 1950s and early 1960s was J. Allen Hynek, who has now become the spiritual leader of the pro-UFO movement.

Not until 1966–68, when Philip J. Klass became active in UFOlogy, was the title of "No. 1 UFO Skeptic" lifted from Dr. Menzel's weary shoulders.

In 1976 the American Humanist Association sponsored the creation of the Committee for the Scientific Investigation of Claims of the Paranormal (CSICOP), a group of scientists, philosophers, educators, writers, and magicians who share a common concern about the rising tide of uncritical acceptance of claims about such alleged phenomena as ESP, astrology, pyramid energy, and UFOs. "Perhaps we ought not to assume that the scientific enlightenment will continue indefinitely," Chairman Paul Kurtz said in announcing the committee's formation. "For all we know, like the Hellenic civilization, it may be overwhelmed by irrationalism, subjectivism, and obscurantism. Perhaps antiscientific and pseudoscientific irrationalism is only a passing fashion; yet one of the best ways to deal with it is for the scientific and educational community to respond—in a responsible manner—to its alarming growth."[6] Among the founding members of the CSICOP were noted science-fiction writer Isaac Asimov, psychologist B. F. Skinner, astronomer Carl Sagan, Martin Gardner of the *Scientific American,* and James ("The Amazing") Randi, noted magician and escape artist.

The following year, 1977, a UFO subcommittee of the CSICOP was formed to examine claims of UFO encounters. Founding members of the subcommittee were Philip J. Klass, senior editor of *Aviation Week & Space Technology* and author of *UFOs Explained*; James E. Oberg, noted aerospace writer, whose numerous articles have appeared in *Omni, Astronomy, Spaceflight, Analog, Science Digest,* and many other publications; and this writer. Other members include Daniel Cohen, author of *Myths of the Space Age,* and Ernest H. Taves, coauthor with Menzel of *The UFO Enigma.* The UFO Subcommittee is the first and thus far the only UFO organization made up of persons who are not inclined toward belief in the literal truth of UFO claims.

While it might seem likely that the UFO believers' groups would soon be at war with the CSICOP, in actuality they often prefer to pretend that the skeptics simply do not exist, and to fight instead with each other. No matter that each group professes to be totally devoted to applying scientific methodology to UFOs: whenever devotees of the various groups and factions get together, the fur soon begins to fly.

APRO has been mad at NICAP for many years over NICAP's refusal to accept stories of UFO occupant sightings, a feud made worse by intense organizational rivalries as well as by personality clashes between the Lorenzens and Keyhoe. So deeply did the bitterness run that, when in 1968 pro-NICAP writer John G. Fuller's article "Flying Saucer Fiasco" appeared in *Look* magazine, mercilessly roasting the Condon Committee for its negative opinions about UFOs, the *APRO Bulletin* countered with James Lorenzen's editorial titled "A Fiasco Has Two Sides." In it APRO actually defended the anti-UFO Condon group against many of the criticisms made by NICAP.

Apparently APRO's displeasure with UFO skeptics was not as keen as the deep animosity it must have felt for its chief rival among the pro-UFO groups.[7]

Today, after NICAP's near total demise, the old controversies continue. APRO's Coral Lorenzen speaks of NICAP with contempt: "While we were doing research, outfits like NICAP had their public-relations teams working overtime." As for APRO's attitudes toward MUFON, its chief rival today, writer Jesse Kornbluth observes that "it's MUFON that brings the passion to Coral Lorenzen's voice; MUFON that preoccupies her more than any saucer report." Mrs. Lorenzen laments that "MUFON is a carbon copy of APRO; Walt Andrus was one of our state directors. He attacked us and took our people away. He didn't step into the spotlight until 1969, when it was safe. What use is there in starting a new organization when APRO is already in existence?" To which MUFON's Andrus replies that there would be no need for a MUFON "if the right people ran APRO."[8]

As for her other coworkers in the UFO field, Mrs. Lorenzen says, "The government has failed the people. It knows that there's evidence that these things are dangerous if you get too close—and Dr. Hynek is too concerned about image to acknowledge that these things happen, so we'll have to do the dirty work for him. Stanton Friedman? He's too busy lecturing; he hasn't worked at his field in years."[9]

The hostilities and personality conflicts that have always existed in the realm of UFOlogy were intensified still further by the hotly debated "UFO abduction" incident involving Travis Walton, which took place on November 5, 1975. According to the story told by young Travis and five fellow woodcutters, they happened to see a UFO hovering not far off the ground as they returned home after a day's work in a forest near Snowflake, Arizona. Travis had previously expressed his desire to take a ride aboard a UFO; he and his brother had made a pact that, if one of them should ever be "abducted" by aliens, the abductee would try to arrange for the UFO to go back and pick up the other. Travis's wish had come true! He claimed to have run directly beneath the UFO, where he was reportedly zapped by a powerful beam. Travis's friends returned to town and reported him missing. Five days later, Travis reportedly turned up in a telephone booth in a nearby town.

GSW's investigators were among the first on the scene, interviewing Travis's brother Duane while Travis was still supposedly missing. GSW's suspicions were aroused by the remarkable lack of concern on the part of Travis's brother and mother, even though Travis might presumably never return. After Travis had rematerialized, GSW's Bill Spaulding reports that Duane Walton "accused us of being negative after we questioned him about a couple of holes in the story," and took Travis away.[10] GSW pulled out of the case, publicly proclaiming it to be a hoax. CUFOS' Hynek, who was eager to fly to Arizona to interview Travis, was rebuffed, and told to wait in line.

But what GSW scorned, APRO prized, especially since Coral Lorenzen was then planning a book about UFO abductions.[11] APRO and the tabloid *National Enquirer* soon began to champion the Walton "abduction." In February 1976, Travis passed a polygraph test administered by George J. Pfeifer of Ezell & Associates in Phoenix. A few months later, the *Enquirer's* "blue ribbon" panel of Ph.D. UFO "experts," dominated by APRO consultants, selected the Walton incident as the best UFO case of 1975. They awarded the woodcutters a $5,000 prize, with half of it going to Travis. The Walton "abduction" looked extremely good. APRO was positively ecstatic. MUFON was beginning to embrace the case, and GSW was regarded as an outcast by the other UFO groups for being so negative about a case that, in the words of one UFO newsletter, *"may be the most iron-clad UFO case in history"* (emphasis in original).[12]

But in July 1976, UFO skeptic Philip J. Klass dropped a bombshell. Klass revealed that APRO and the *National Enquirer* had arranged an earlier secret polygraph test for Travis with John J. McCarthy, the most experienced polygraph examiner in the state of Arizona. McCarthy found Travis to be attempting "gross deception," and pronounced the abduction story a hoax. APRO and the *National Enquirer* "deep-sixed" this damaging evidence, while continuing to publicly boost the case as the ultimate UFO abduction. Klass also found that the less-experienced polygraph examiner who had passed Travis was repudiated by his employer, who disagreed with the interpretation of the test results.

NICAP published Klass's detailed findings on the case, which further exacerbated the near total break between NICAP and APRO.[13] Meanwhile, GSW was rescued by the revelation of APRO's Watergate-style cover-up of embarrassing facts. GSW, which had been in a state of near panic when it found itself on what appeared to be the wrong side of the "case of the century," now proudly boasted that it had been right all along.

In the end, the credulity explosion now under way within the UFO movement proved itself adequate to swallow the Walton "abduction," inconsistencies and all. APRO has successfully stonewalled the crisis, since the vast majority of UFO investigators are inclined to believe "UFO abduction" tales. Establishment UFOlogists today generally incline toward believing Travis. Hynek has vacillated back toward acceptance in spite of his initial skepticism, stating "Walton's story seems more consistent than that of his detractors," as if Klass were the one who *perpetrated* the cover-up, rather than the one who revealed it. (Hynek is not noted for stating a position clearly. In the words of "new wave" UFOlogist John Keel, "Hynek has established a record of increasing vagueness and indecision . . . he has alternately come out for and against every possible theory and avenue of approach.")[14]

APRO's Lorenzens and GSW's Spaulding, who are in close agreement about the nature of UFOs, remain deeply divided by animosities and mutual accusations concerning the Walton case. But Spaulding and Klass, who disagree fundamentally as to whether UFOs are "real," have a cordial working relationship despite their differences. GSW has even gone so far as to announce its support of the CSICOP's UFO Subcommittee "in its attempt to separate fact from fiction." If today's UFOlogy really were a *science,* as its supporters endlessly proclaim, such broad-minded cooperation would not be a unique exception, but the rule.

Outside the major UFO groups is a loose, ill-defined movement calling itself "middle UFOlogy." These people generally tend to be young and often have attitudes grounded in the 1960s counterculture. One highly vocal spokesman for "middle UFOlogy" is Allen H. Greenfield, moddish, young, and articulate. Greenfield criticized fast-rising UFO groups such as MUFON for being too establishment: "MUFON, like NICAP before it, was in essence a middle American UFO organization that incorporated the middle American work ethic and social conservatism into the framework of a UFO group . . . MUFON, having developed during the Viet Nam war, developed less of the para-military right-wing flavour that, until recent years, so characterized NICAP." (Arch-egalitarian Greenfield, for unknown reasons, always writes his attacks on the establishment using status-ridden British rules of spelling.) Greenfield has even gone so far as to propose that "a Task Force on Racism in UFOlogy should be established to assess the extent of racism, sexism, and agism involved in the practices of present and future organizations and conventions. If necessary, this should be followed by a joint committee to increase participation in ufology by minority groups and women."[15]

Those within the UFO movement ceaselessly proclaim themselves to be the Galileos of a brave new science. Yet their never-ending internal squabbles are suggestive not of Galileo and the Church, but of the Hatfields and McCoys. A fledgling science is relatively unified internally through its application of scientific methodology, resulting in a broad consensus on the subject matter. Its debates and quarrels are largely directed at opponents *outside* the movement, whom it seeks to convert, or at least to defeat. But the present-day movement of "scientific" UFOlogy is often unwilling to meet its challengers in open and fair debate, resorting to name-calling and character assassination of UFO skeptics — when it chooses to recognize their existence at all.

Much of the rationale for the proliferation of UFO groups can be explained by the observation that, if all Indian tribes were to unite under one teepee, there would be a lot of grumbling, unhappy ex-chiefs. The leaders of major UFO groups are typically the kind of people who would otherwise live rather humdrum lives: engineers, accountants, middle-level managers. But as leaders in internationally known organizations of UFO "experts," they are suddenly catapulted beyond the ordinary. Radio and TV stations clamor for interviews. Newspapers seek their opinions on various

UFO cases. The "experts" travel across the country and even around the world to give lectures and to meet with other UFOlogists: they are treated as VIPs everywhere. Their books sell many thousands of copies, enhancing their reputations among believers and bringing in substantial royalties.

APRO's co-founder Coral Lorenzen belittles her rival groups with the question: "What use is there in starting a new organization when APRO is already in existence?" It strikes me as odd that anyone in her position should find it necessary to ask.

NOTES

1. Philip J. Klass, *UFOs Explained* (New York: Random House, 1974), chapters 15, 16, 19, 20, 21; Donald H. Menzel and Ernest H. Taves, *The UFO Enigma* (New York: Doubleday, 1977), chapter 8; James E. Oberg, *Space World* (February 1977).

2. Coral E. Lorenzen, *Flying Saucers—The Startling Evidence of Invasion from Outer Space* (New York: Signet, 1966), p. 21.

3. *APRO Bulletin* (October 1976):4

4. Statements of at least partial acceptance of Adamski's claims: James McCampbell, *UFOlogy* (Jaymac, 1973), p. 116; Ray Stanford (interview), *UFO Report* (August 1978).

5. Donald H. Menzel's UFO books are *Flying Saucers* (Cambridge, Mass.: Harvard University Press, 1953), *The World of Flying Saucers* (New York: Doubleday, 1963; Lyle G. Boyd, coauthor), and *The UFO Enigma* (New York: Doubleday, 1977; Ernest H. Taves, coauthor).

6. *The Humanist,* (May/June 1976): 28. For more on the CSICOP, see *Time,* December 12, 1977; *New York Times,* August 10, 1977, A11; *Smithsonian,* March 1978; *Washington Post,* June 11, 1978, F1; *Reader's Digest,* July 1978.

7. John G. Fuller, *Look* (May 14, 1968):58; James Lorenzen, *APRO Bulletin* (May/June 1968):2.

8. Jesse Kornbluth, "The UFOlogist Establishment," *Oui* (November 1976):121, 124.

9. Ibid., p. 56.

10. *Arizona Daily Star,* Tucson, November 13, 1975.

11. Kornbluth, p. 56.

12. Allen H. Greenfield, ed., *UFOlogy Notebook* 3/1 (1976).

13. *NICAP UFO Investigator* (June 1976).

14. J. Allen Hynek, *International UFO Reporter* 3, no. 5 (May 1978); John Keel, *UFO Report* (June 1977):12.

15. Greenfield, *Saucers and Saucerers* (privately published, 1976), p. 59; Greenfield, ed., *UFOlogy Notebook* 3/6 (May 1977).

4

CLOSE ENCOUNTER OF THE
SECOND KIND: EVIDENCE

Close Encounters of the Second Kind bear a special importance, for when it is reported that a UFO left tangible evidence of its presence, here is clearly the area in which to begin digging for "scientific paydirt." . . . It is in this category of UFO reports that we find the real challenge to scientific inquiry. —J. Allen Hynek[1]

While reports of "close encounters of the first kind" can indeed be exciting and dramatic, it is not until we examine the reports of so-called close encounters of the second kind that we are dealing with anything tangible. According to the categorization set forth by J. Allen Hynek in *The UFO Experience,* a CE-II case is one in which a physical effect from or interaction with a UFO is reported. We may divide CE-II cases into two major categories: "soft" evidence, where a UFO incident reportedly produces impressions on the ground or other physical effects, and "hard" evidence, in which we reportedly have artifacts or fragments from the UFO itself.

Perhaps the best-known of the "soft" evidence CE-II cases is the famous Delphos, Kansas, "UFO landing" of November 2, 1971, chosen by the *National Enquirer*'s "blue ribbon" panel of Ph.D. UFOlogists as the most scientifically valuable UFO case of that year. A ring was to be seen on the ground, allegedly under the spot where the craft hovered. Dr. Hynek, acting as spokesman for the *Enquirer* panel, stated: "This ring of soil differed markedly from its immediate surroundings, not only in chemical composition but in appearance. The soil was dried out and powdery. For more than a year after the sighting, the soil would not accept water, nor could anything be grown in it."[2]

Philip J. Klass obtained some photographs from the witnesses, the Johnson family, showing the ring allegedly glowing. The source of illumination was readily apparent: a flashbulb on the camera, and not any intrinsic luminosity, since the brightness of everything in the photograph falls off in proportion to its distance from the camera. The existence of the ring itself, however, was held by UFO proponents to be powerful evidence that a strange craft did indeed hover a foot or two off the ground at that spot.

Then in 1975, Jacques Vallee somewhat apologetically wrote that the composition of this seemingly mysterious ring had at last been unambiguously identified by a French laboratory: it was a natural growth of a funguslike organism of the family Actinomycetaceae, genus Nocardia. While this might seem to the casual reader to have resolved the mystery, Vallee suggests that "high energy stimulation" from a UFO "might have triggered the spectacular growth of the Nocardia." The Johnson family also blamed the UFO ring for various other alleged physical effects: temporary blindness, temporary numbness of fingertips, and virgin births among animals on the farm. (We shall examine Ronald Johnson's subsequent sighting of the Wolf Girl in chapter 18.) In a telephone interview, Durel Johnson claimed to have a photo showing the "little man" from the UFO, but he was unwilling to send me a copy unless I promised him a percentage of the royalties from this book.[3]

Rings on the ground such as the one at Delphos are among the most commonly reported supposed physical effects from UFOs. In earlier ages, such circles on the ground were widely known as "fairy rings," it being supposed that such a feature, discovered in the woods, indicated that the wee folk had chosen that spot for a midnight revel. But neither UFOs nor fairies need be postulated to account for reports of this genre, because the forces of nature quite suffice to produce such artifacts. Mushrooms and other fungi often grow in a nearly circular ring, from a few inches to fifty feet or more in diameter, according to an authoritative work on lawn diseases. A ring of dark green, fast-growing grass often outlines the fairy ring, and after heavy rain mushrooms often quickly sprout up, defining the ring.[4] It should come as no surprise that hundreds of fairy rings are reported worldwide and that people often attempt to tie them to reports of UFO sightings.

The other commonly occurring physical effect reported to be caused by UFO sightings is the stalling of automobile engines, sometimes allegedly accompanied by the unexplained dimming of headlights. Unfortunately, while this alleged effect certainly is tangible—*if* it in fact exists—we are forced once again to fall back upon unsubstantiated eyewitness testimony, because in no instance is there any *lasting* physical evidence of the supposed effect of UFOs upon automobiles. In every case, when the supposed UFO vanishes, the alleged malfunction of the automobile vanishes as well, leaving nothing to investigate. It is impossible to say whether the reported effect was the result of a genuinely mysterious phenomenon, of inaccurate reporting, or if the overexcited driver stalled or turned off the engine when he imagined a UFO to be close. Thus we see that many reported close encounters of the second kind turn out to be of the one-and-a-half kind, at best; for, although physical effects are indeed reported, they make as clean a getaway as the flying saucer itself.

One well-known case of an automobile reportedly stalling in the vicinity of a UFO is found in the Air Force Project Blue Book files. At about 8:30 AM on January 23, 1965, in the vicinity of Williamsburg, Virginia, a motorist reported that his late-model automobile stalled near a major intersection. Almost immediately, he reported, he saw an object shaped like a mushroom, at least seventy-five feet in height, hovering a few feet above a nearby field, giving off a noise similar to that of a vacuum cleaner. Although the road was jammed with rush-hour traffic, not only were there no other cars reportedly stalled by the presence of this gigantic UFO, but no one else seems even to have noticed it. Hynek examines this factor, and finds nothing incredible about it. "One might wonder why there weren't more witnesses to the event; but as we have already noted, one of the chief characteristics of UFO sightings seems to be their isolation in time and space. This is, of course, a highly puzzling feature and has contributed greatly to attempts to discredit the phenomenon."[5]

Investigators who produced the much-reviled *Condon Report* examined two automobiles that had reportedly been stalled in the course of a close encounter of the second kind. After a careful examination, no abnormal radiation was found, and the magnetic "signature" of the metal (formed by the earth's magnetic field when the metal is stamped) was found to be identical with that of other automobiles of the same model and year that had *not* had any supposed encounters with UFOs. It was also determined by direct experimentation that while a one-kilogauss magnetic field was sufficient to make a lasting and easily detectable magnetic imprint on an automobile, an automobile's ignition system continues to operate normally in magnetic fields of twenty kilogauss or more. Thus the effects of any magnetic field strong enough to interfere with an automobile ignition system should be easily detectable months, or even years, afterward. The Condon investigators also note that during World War II in England, when radar was a military secret, some local people of Burnham-on-Crouch were convinced that the mysterious radar antennae recently erected near their town were somehow causing passing automobiles to stall. When the purpose of the radar apparatus later became known, the mysterious automobile stallings apparently ceased.[6]

Far more dramatic, and potentially more probative, than the "soft" physical evidence for UFOs described are reports of "hard" evidence: actual UFO fragments or artifacts. Probably the best known of these is the alleged saucer fragment originating in Ubatuba, Brazil, in 1957. The society columnist for a prominent Rio de Janeiro newspaper received a letter from a supposed admirer, along with some metal fragments allegedly from a UFO that was said to have exploded above a beach where some men were fishing. The signature of the supposed admirer was illegible, and it was never determined why he sent his supposed UFO fragments to the society columnist instead of to a science writer, to a UFO group, or to military authorities. Thus nothing whatever is known concerning the credibility—or lack thereof—of the person who allegedly saw a UFO explode and retrieved the fragments.

The late Olavo T. Fontes, M.D., APRO's chief investigator in Latin America, contacted the newspaper columnist, examined the pieces, and arranged for a supposedly expert spectrographic analysis of the metal. "The conclusion was that the magnesium in the sample was of unusual purity, with no detectable inclusion of other elements," Fontes stated. Several other tests of the magnesium reportedly revealed that it "represents something outside the range of present-day technological development in earth science. In fact, the metal was of such fantastic purity that even to see it symbolized on paper is unbelievable." Dr. Fontes concluded that "on the basis of this evidence, it is highly probable the metallic chunks picked up on the beach near Ubatuba, in Sao Paulo, Brazil, are extraterrestrial in origin." APRO's co-founder, Coral Lorenzen, considered Dr. Fontes's report to be so significant that she included it as a chapter in her UFO book titled *Flying Saucers: The Startling Evidence of the Invasion from Outer Space.*[7]

The Condon investigators, however, reached a dramatically different conclusion in their 1969 report. They obtained samples of the metal from APRO (whose willingness to risk learning unpleasant facts about their "evidence" is certainly commendable). A high-sensitivity neutron-activation analysis was performed, revealing that the supposedly absolutely pure UFO fragment contained seven times more manganese, four times more chromium, ten times more copper, and a hundred times more zinc than a highly refined sample of magnesium produced by the Dow Chemical Company in the 1940s. "The analytical results presented above show that the claimed UFO fragment is not nearly as pure as magnesium produced by known earthly technology prior to 1957, the year of the UFO report," the Condon researchers concluded. Yet as recently as 1977, eight years after the Condon study, APRO's director of research, Dr. James Harder, argued that, since the Dow magnesium sample contained a detectable amount of mercury and the Ubatuba fragment does not, "we can say it is an authentic fragment, beyond any reasonable doubt, of a UFO."[8]

Among the most pertinent, the most tantalizing, and certainly the most dramatic of all reports of "hard evidence" are the ever-present rumors of one or more UFOs reportedly having crashed in the southwestern United States. The Air Force reportedly maintains an elite corps of "Blue Berets," whose job it is to intercept all fragments of crashed saucers and whisk them off to a vault at the Wright-Patterson Air Force Base in Ohio.

The crashed-saucer stories first began to circulate in 1950, when a mysterious figure delivered a lecture to an undergraduate science class at the University of Denver. He regaled his audience with tales of a crashed saucer that reportedly had been examined in minute detail by U.S. officials. Theatrical writer Frank Scully very quickly put together a book on the incident titled *Beyond the Flying Saucers,* creating a nationwide sensation. In the Scully book, we read that government scientists have learned that saucers utilize "magnetic" propulsion and derive their energy from following "magnetic lines of force" (an absurdity, say physicists), and that all of the saucer's dimensions were evenly divisible by nine (but apparently only when measured by the English system of inches, feet, and yards). The bodies of the craft's occupants, looking very much like earthly midgets, were said to have been dressed in 1890-style clothing. Scully identified the anonymous lecturer as Silas M. Newton, a supposed oil millionaire, and Newton's mysterious "scientific" source, "Dr. Gee," who was later identified as Leo A. Ge Bauer. Both Newton and Ge Bauer were indicted two years later for a scheme in which they allegedly tried to swindle an unsuspecting investor into buying a worthless device for "detecting oil."[9]

For many years, Scully's yarns were given scant credence by "scientific" UFOlogists, although the rumors did not die out completely. However, it was not until the mid-1970s that the credulity explosion now taking place in the UFO movement reached such proportions as to allow the crashed-saucer tales to be swallowed by the mainstream of UFOlogy. The stories were revived in 1974 by Dr. Robert S. Carr and soon afterward by Leonard H. Stringfield, active in UFOlogy since 1949 and currently an investigator for CUFOS as well as a member of the Board of Directors of MUFON. Stringfield states that "on several occasions in the past 30 years UFOs have crashed and the bodies of dead entities have been taken from them . . . what I have been getting lately are growing numbers of reports from reliable military people who claim to have seen all this firsthand. . . . There's a 1948 crash, another from 1951 or 1952, something in 1953, one in 1958, and two incidents in the 70's." Stringfield has also claimed that there was at least one close encounter of a military kind between UFOs and U.S. forces during the spring of 1977, with casualties on both sides. The aliens possess, he says, a certain physical feature that is so startling he could not reveal its nature. When this statement triggered a question about the aliens' sexual organs, Stringfield replied that their "sex organs were very sensitive," but refused to go into further details.[10]

In the weeks prior to the MUFON International UFO Symposium in Dayton on July 29, 1978, Stringfield generated intense excitement and anticipation by promising to break "the story of the century" about crashed saucers. "What I have is literally a bombshell," he stated. "The first part concerns the recovery of crashed UFOs with the occupants held in military custody and the second part concerns the retrieval of the UFOs" by what

Stringfield terms the "Blue Berets." "I will also present information on the autopsies of the aliens, which were humanoids, but not human, ranging from 3½ to 4½ feet tall. Some of the bodies are still around, having been placed in deep freeze for preservation."[11]

Unfortunately, when the time arrived for Stringfield to deliver on his bold promises at the MUFON conference in Dayton, the verdict was almost uniformly negative. The *Dayton Journal Herald* reported that "there were hazy intergalactic tales, lots of claims, but no *corpus delicti*." "No starship wreckage was displayed, no preserved bodies were shown and no sources were named," that paper reported. "It was more conjecture than proof."[12] Backing up Stringfield's crashed-saucer claims at Dayton was Robert H. Barry of the 20th-Century UFO Bureau (chapter 12), who believes that some UFOs are piloted by angels defending the state of Israel.

Another well-known "crashed saucer" advocate is W. Todd Zechel, director of research of GSW and founder of a now-defunct group called Citizens Against UFO Secrecy (CAUS). Despite his wild claims, Zechel was for a time taken quite seriously by the mainstream of UFOlogy; the *International UFO Reporter,* of which Allan Hendry is managing editor, ran an in-depth interview with Zechel, supposedly for purposes of acquainting its readers with "progress in the UFO scene." *Fate* magazine's Jerome Clark has said of Zechel, "At this moment in history, it's distinctly possible that W. Todd Zechel is UFOlogy's major figure."[13]

Zechel claims to have information from former military personnel (whose names are never mentioned, and hence whose credibility cannot be judged) alleging personal involvement in UFO crashes. "The spacecraft was described as metallic," Zechel stated, "with the typical disc or saucer shape, and some 90 feet in diameter. There was one dead space being on board. He—or it— was described as small, about four feet, six inches tall. The most noticeable features about it were that it was completely hairless, and its hands had no thumbs. All the troops involved were warned that if they said a word about the incident, they would be the 'sorriest people around.'" Asked by *International UFO Reporter* whether or not he believed such stories, Zechel replied, "I have every indication that it is legitimate." Zechel wrote in the *MUFON UFO Journal:* "There is enough evidence to warrant a lawsuit to force disclosure of records [from the government] related to the recovery of an extraterrestrial vehicle with occupant. By compelling military officers and government officials to testify under oath about their knowledge of such an incident, CAUS submits that the reality of UFOs will be irrefutably established."[14]

Zechel claims to have worked for the National Security Agency (NSA)— the high-security intelligence agency headquartered at Fort Meade, Maryland, near the Baltimore–Washington Airport—and to have left intelligence work to pursue UFO research after "10 years of distinguished service." "It wasn't until after I went to work for the National Security Agency that I was forced to confront the reality of UFOs," Zechel states. But Philip J. Klass charges that Zechel is not being truthful about his background. Zechel *never* worked for the NSA, Klass charges, and he spent only three years, not ten, in the Army Security Agency, which sometimes works as a support service for the NSA. The most convincing refutation of Zechel's supposed intelligence background was the article he wrote for *UFO Report* under the transparent pseudonym "Ted Zachary" (note the initials "TZ"). In it he carelessly lets it slip out that he is director of research of Ground Saucer Watch, a position occupied by no one else.[15] Nobody who had *really* completed a distinguished career in intelligence work would ever make such a laughable blunder. (Zechel blames an unnamed supposed co-author for the gaff.)

As for the seven years "missing" between Zechel's claimed vs. confirmed intelligence career, Klass charges that Zechel was actually working as a fireman and then as a carpenter in Baraboo, Wisconsin, and later moved to Milwaukee, where he managed a pornographic book store. Klass further charges that, during this interval, Zechel "borrowed," and has never returned, one automobile, a portable tape-recorder, and over $800 in cash from two individuals, while at the same time running up approximately $2,000 in unpaid telephone bills. "At this moment in history, it's distinctly possible that W. Todd Zechel is UFOlogy's major figure." Thus did Jerome Clark deliver the UFO establishment's solemn verdict.[16] Within a year, Clark had come to view Zechel in much the same terms as Klass does, but refused to explain publicly what had happened to change his views.

Stringfield and Zechel are not the only UFOlogists who take seriously those tales about the Air Force concealing crashed flying saucers and keeping the bodies of little green men in pickle jars. APRO's James Lorenzen told a 1977 UFO conference in Chicago: "A type of evidence that we'd like to see, that we hear about and haven't seen, is the rumored crashed disk with the little bodies. That's the one we'd like to see. We haven't found it yet. We have hopes, and we have promises, but there are many obstacles in the way. I'd like to lay this out for you first: if anyone here has information on the crashed disk, *I want to hear about it.*" Lorenzen assured his listeners that APRO would respect the confidentiality of anyone who might reveal to them the location of those pickle jars.

Another dramatic claim of a retrieval of a UFO fragment was published in Timothy Green Beckley's tabloid *UFO Review.* "Alien artifact uncovered from UFO crash site," it proclaims. Beckley, the self-styled "Mr. UFO," describes how the alleged UFO artifact was found in a desert region of California by John Peele, a vegetarian and physical fitness enthusiast who was on a ninety-one-day jogging trip across the United States. While heading toward a distant mountain peak, Peele reportedly felt something "very odd" in the air. He then reportedly sighted what was apparently the partially buried wreckage from the crash of an unknown aircraft. He claims to have squirreled away in a cave for safekeeping a number of peculiar artifacts, including a lightweight piece of metal similar to aluminum, but which could not be bent, and some strange blue glass that was too dark to see through. (Peele is now unfortunately unable to locate his hoard.) All he took with him was a small, burned, astronaut-style "alien" glove, much smaller than one manufactured for a normal-sized adult. Beckley explains: "Without a doubt the strangest feature is the stamping of the word "Large" in English on the innermost layer of material. Almost immediately one would assume that this would rule out the glove being of extraterrestrial origin. But the fact remains that no pressurized glove of this size would ever be marked "Large" if it were manufactured by our military." The glove has reportedly been examined by aerospace experts who cannot identify it, causing Beckley to conclude that Peele's discovery "may" be the proof that everyone has been waiting for.[17]

But perhaps the most dramatic and potentially significant incident involving physical remains from a UFO was the famous incident in Carbondale, Pennsylvania, a modest-sized town in the northeast corner of the state, not far from Scranton. On the evening of Saturday, November 9, 1974, three teenage boys reportedly heard a noise in the sky and looked up to see a red ball of light coming at them from over a nearby mountain. They reported that it plunged into a small pond. (One local newspaper described this body of water as a "cesspool which the media was courteous enough to label a "pond.") After receiving several other reports of a bright object flashing across the sky, the Carbondale police decided to investigate. A light could be seen glowing faintly from the depths of the "pond." Perhaps the boys *were* telling the truth about seeing a flying saucer plunge into the water!

Thus began a two-day vigil by the side of the "pond" involving the police, both the Carbondale and Scranton Civil Air Patrols, reporters, the local citizenry, and a number of UFO believers, some of whom had traveled as far as several hundred miles to witness the great event firsthand. Robert Barry of the 20th Century UFO Bureau traveled to Carbondale, stating, "I don't think it's a hoax," citing as corroboration other Pennsylvania UFO reports over the previous few days. An investigator representing Hynek's CUFOS also arrived on the scene. One police officer drew his service revolver and fired several shots at the glowing submerged object. But since this officer almost certainly did *not* allow for the differing refractive indexes of water and air when taking aim, his bullet apparently did not strike the mysterious glowing entity.

An attempt to fish the object out using poles and a net apparently snagged something, but whatever it was it fell back to the bottom of the pond. The police made an ill-advised attempt to remove reporters and spectators from the vicinity, which served only to increase suspicion that something truly dramatic was being hushed up. The three boys who originally reported the supposed landing in the pond alleged that they also saw a scuba diver enter the pond on Sunday afternoon. He allegedly emerged "white faced" and "gestured a size with his arms." Apparently he had seen a crashed saucer down there, of gargantuan proportions! The boys claim, however, that the diver was quickly silenced by law-enforcement officers,[18] no doubt participating in the worldwide cover-up of startling UFO facts.

Finally, one determined scuba diver, Mark Stamey of Auburn, New York, convinced the local officials to permit him to dive into the so-called "cesspool." A boat carying a geiger counter preceded him, to ascertain that the object that allegedly crashed was not dangerously radioactive, perhaps the remnant of some nuclear-powered space vehicle. Within five minutes, Stamey returned from the murky depths (all of ten feet), carrying a totally unexpected, self-luminous object, obviously the product of some highly advanced technology: a battery-powered railroad lantern. It was never determined who had thrown it into the pond.

The aftermath of the Carbondale UFO-fragment retrieval unfolded just as one might expect. When the lantern was retrieved, the Carbondale Police Department announced that its involvement in the matter was ended. But local UFO proponents suggested that the lantern was just a clever ploy, planted in the pond to provide a convenient excuse for the UFO cover-up to continue. If nothing is found in the pond, it can be argued that the object either dematerialized, burrowed into the earth, slipped into the fourth dimension, or else was secretly removed. However, if a mundane object is retrieved, it will obviously have been planted there by government agents as part of a sinister cover-up. Nothing short of the retrieval of an alien craft, bearing Alpha Centauri license plates, will suffice to satisfy the dedicated UFO proponents.

There have, of course, been many other reported instances of "soft" as well as "hard" physical evidence of a UFO encounter. What these cases all have in common is this: as soon as the alleged UFO incident has ended, either there is no physical evidence remaining (as in the case of the alleged interference with automobiles and other machinery) or else the alleged evidence is easily attributable to perfectly ordinary causes. Not *one* piece of UFO evidence, either soft or hard, has yet been presented that could not easily be produced by prosaic earthly natural forces or technology. No one has yet stepped forward with an extraterrestrial calculating machine, a space helmet designed for a spherical head, the body of an unknown creature, a high-technology device of unknown purpose and design, or a sample of an obviously artificial chemical element unknown to earth, having an atomic number of, say, 150. (Although APRO's James Harder claims to have detected the presence of such an element in the center of an "alien" sphere, whose owners unfortunately will not let it be torn apart in the interest of science. But Harder is unwilling to undertake this even if he could, since he is convinced that, if disturbed, the alien object would "go critical" and cause a nuclear explosion.[19])

Until such tangible and definitely unearthly UFO evidence turns up, one is forced to conclude that *there are no close encounters that are truly of the second kind.* At best, they are just close encounters of the first kind (in other words, unsubstantiated reports) with interesting but nonetheless unverifiable embellishments.

NOTES

1. J. Allen Hynek, *The UFO Experience* (Chicago: Regnery, 1972), chapter 9.

2. *National Enquirer,* May 27, 1973, quoted by Philip J. Klass in *UFOs Explained* (New York: Random House, 1974), p. 314.

3. Jacques Vallee, *The Invisible College* (New York: Dutton, 1975), chapter 1; telephone interview with Mr. and Mrs. Durel Johnson, May 6, 1980.

4. Shurtleff and Randell, *Lawn Diseases and Pests,* quoted in *International UFO Reporter* 3, no. 7 (July 1978).

5. J. Allen Hynek, *The Hynek UFO Report* (New York: Dell, 1977), pp. 177–78.

6. Edward U. Condon, ed., *Scientific Study of Unidentified Flying Objects* (New York: Bantam, 1969), pp. 100, 282 (case 12); 380 (case 39); 749.

7. Coral E. Lorenzen, *Flying Saucers: The Startling Evidence of the Invasion from Outer Space* (New York: Signet, 1962), chapter 9.

8. Condon, pp. 94–96; James Harder speech titled "The Hard Evidence for UFOs," presented at *Fate* magazine's Chicago UFO Conference, June 24, 1977.

9. Frank Scully, *Behind the Flying Saucers* (New York: Holt, 1950), pp. 129–35; Roland Gelatt, *Saturday Review,* December 6, 1952, p. 31.

10. Leonard H. Stringfield, interviewed in *UFO Report,* July 1978; Stringfield's talk at the picnic of the UFO Study Group of St. Louis, reported in the *Centralia* (Ill.) *Sentinel,* June 27, 1978.

11. UPI story, *San Diego Tribune,* June 29, 1978; *Centralia Sentinel,* June 27, 1978.

12. Joni Johns, *Dayton* (Ohio) *Journal Herald,* July 31, 1978.

13. *International UFO Reporter* 3, no. 5 (May 1978); Clark in *UFO Report,* August 1978.

14. *Midnight/Globe,* January 24, 1978, 23; *International UFO Reporter,* May 1978; *MUFON UFO Journal,* August 1978.

15. Scotia-American Films press release, written by W. Todd Zechel; "Ted Zachary," writing in *UFO Report,* August 1977.

16. Philip J. Klass, "Will the Real W. Todd Zechel Please Stand Up" (privately published paper, 1978); Jerome Clark, *UFO Report,* August 1978.

17. Timothy Green Beckley, *UFO Review* 4 (June 1979):3.

18. *The Miner* (Carbondale, Pa.), November 14, 1974, 4; *Carbondale News,* November 14, 1974, 1.

19. James Harder, Chicago speech, 1977.

5

CLOSE ENCOUNTER OF THE THIRD KIND: ABDUCTION!

"Close encounters of the third kind" is the name Hynek has given to those cases in which occupants of a UFO are reportedly sighted. There are many such claims in UFO literature. Typically the witness is alone (or with one or two companions) in some deserted spot late at night when a glowing, mysterious craft is said to swoop down from the sky and land nearby. From it one or more humanoid aliens, most frequently described as dwarfish with large heads, are reported to disembark. They appear to be busily gathering up samples, or perhaps making adjustments to their craft. When they realize they have been spotted, they typically scamper back into their craft and fly away.

Such reports are certainly dramatic enough to excite anyone's imagination. Yet remarkable as they are, reports of mere *sightings* of UFO occupants are eclipsed by the even more astonishing and bizarre reports of UFO abductions, in which the witness claims to have been forcibly taken aboard a UFO and given some kind of examination by alien beings before being released. Usually the witness claims to have no conscious memory of the "abduction" and discloses his or her story for the first time under hypnosis. UFO abduction stories were practically unknown before 1965, except for one report from South America. In recent years, however (especially since 1975), the number of reported UFO abductions has risen dramatically, and today nearly every "scientific" UFO investigator will vehemently defend the authenticity of at least a few of the best-known abduction cases. Let us concentrate our examination of CE-III cases on the most highly regarded abduction stories, since these are the ones that are said to provide the strongest evidence of the reality of UFO occupants. We will begin with what is perhaps the most famous UFO incident of all time: the "abduction" of Barney and Betty Hill.

If we were to ask a dozen leading UFOlogists to name the most complex, the most puzzling, the most inexplicable of all reported UFO encounters, the consensus would probably be "the Hill UFO abduction." The Hills' story is widely known (and believed) throughout UFOdom, having been the subject of John G. Fuller's highly successful 1966 book *The Interrupted Journey,* which was serialized in *Look* magazine. More recently, the Hill story was dramatized in a popular made-for-TV movie *The UFO Incident* (NBC–TV, October 20, 1975, and repeated several times). Betty Hill has appeared on numerous radio and TV talk shows, and is a frequent lecturer at UFO conferences and at colleges. Barney Hill died in 1969. The popular account of this famous incident is as follows:

Barney and Betty Hill were returning to their home in Portsmouth, New Hampshire, about midnight on September 19–20, 1961, after a vacation trip to Montreal. As they drove through a deserted area in the White Mountains of New Hampshire, they reportedly saw a starlike object that seemed to follow their car. When the object appeared to come closer, Barney Hill, getting out of the car to observe it through binoculars, believed that he saw alien faces peering at him through a row of windows. He ran back to the car, shouting to his wife that they were about to be captured; they drove off, frightened and confused, and arrived home late.

After they had been home for several days, Betty Hill began to have a series of dreams in which she envisioned that she and Barney had been taken aboard the supposed craft and given a physical examination by strange-looking humanoid creatures. Several years later, when the Hills were undergoing psychiatric treatment, under hypnosis they each told of being "abducted" by alien beings during two supposedly "lost hours" in their journey—exactly as Betty had envisioned in her dreams. Official records reportedly have shown that numerous radar installations throughout New England tracked an unknown object landing and taking off at exactly the times stated in the Hills' account. Finally, under post-hypnotic suggestion, Betty Hill drew a so-called star map, which she supposedly saw aboard the flying saucer. Reportedly these stars have all been identified by UFO researcher Marjorie Fish, and all turned out to be stars capable of supporting planets with life.

This is the Hill story as UFO proponents tell it. But let us examine it more closely, to determine whether or not the account of this fascinating incident, as popularly given, is actually correct.

Between 10:00 PM and midnight on September 19, 1961, the Hills were driving south along Route 3, nearing New Hampshire's White Mountains. The witnesses report that the sky was perfectly clear. A gibbous moon (more than half full) was shining brightly low in the southwest. As they passed the town of Lancaster, Betty reported seeing a "star" or planet below the moon. Soon afterward, she reportedly spotted a second object, which she described as a bigger or brighter star, above the first object. This was the object that she believed to be a UFO.

They watched this object, or "craft," for at least thirty minutes. It appeared to be following their car. Barney believed it to be an ordinary object, perhaps a satellite or airplane; but Betty quickly decided that it must be a flying saucer, and she fervently attempted to convince her husband that it was. "Barney! You've got to stop!" she shouted. "Stop the car, Barney, and look at it. It's amazing."[1] Her near-hysterical excitement proved contagious. Barney stopped the car to get out for a better look, while Betty remained inside ("flopping in the front seat," according to Barney[2]). He looked at the object through binoculars and fancied that he could see a row of lighted windows with alien faces peering out. The aliens appeared to be busily engaged in pulling levers and quickly turned their backs to him, except for the "leader." Barney was horrified to see that the leader of the aliens appeared to be a "Nazi," as he described it.[3] Now he, too, was terrified. He got back into the car and drove off. Betty described him as "in a hysterical condition, laughing and repeating that they were going to capture us."[4] It was at about this point that the supposed "two lost hours" are said to begin.

Is it possible to identify the "star" that Mrs. Hill reported seeing below the moon that night? The moon was then near the constellation borders of Sagittarius and Capricornus, a region void of any conspicuously bright stars. The planet Saturn, however, was a highly conspicuous first-magnitude object almost directly below the moon, as seen from the White Mountains. But there was a second planet present—Jupiter, two and a half magnitudes (twelve times) more brilliant than Saturn, looking "like a star, a bigger star, up over this one,"[5] which parallels Betty Hill's description of the UFO. The Hills reported seeing two starlike objects, one of them the UFO. But two starlike objects were near the moon that evening—Jupiter and Saturn; Mrs. Hill's description of the relative positions and brightness of the objects almost perfectly describes the two planets. *If a genuine UFO had been present, there would have been three objects near the moon that night: Jupiter, Saturn, and the UFO.* Yet they reported seeing only two. The conclusion is inescapable: no unusual object was present. What Mrs. Hill was calling a "UFO" was in fact the brilliant planet Jupiter.

To some it will seem incredible that any sane person could misperceive a distant (if brilliant) planet as a close-in structured craft, complete with portholes and alien faces peering out. But the examples of numerous other UFO cases prove conclusively that this does indeed happen. In *UFOs Explained,* Philip J. Klass documents how three educated adults, including the mayor of a large city, observing the reentry of a piece of space debris nearly a hundred miles over their heads, described it as a mysterious craft, with square "portholes," passing less than a thousand feet overhead. Allan Hendry's data compiled at the Center for UFO Studies shows that well over half of all so-called close encounters of the first kind can be attributed to either advertising aircraft or stars, with one "third-kind" encounter—an alleged occupant sighting—attributed to each of them.[6] It should be noted that Betty Hill did not claim to have seen the object at its alleged close approach. She remained in the car when Barney got out with binoculars to confront the object. Betty's description sounds much more like a brilliant point-source of light such as Jupiter: "Even when it was coming in, it still looked like a star. It was a solid-light type of thing . . . you couldn't see it too clearly without the binoculars."[7]

A further calibration of the accuracy of the witnesses' descriptions can be made by comparing their description of the weather conditions at the time of the incident (one of their few observations that *can* be checked) with official weather records. *This comparison reveals that the Hills' recollection is seriously in error.* In their report to the Air Force and in their discussions with John Fuller while he was working on *The Interrupted Journey,* the Hills stated that the sky was perfectly clear at the time of the sighting. Yet the official weather station atop nearby Mt. Washington, tallest of the White Mountains, recorded that high, thin cirrus clouds covered more than half the sky at the time of the incident, and this is confirmed by the records of other weather stations throughout New England. Such clouds, while thin and wispy, would be extremely conspicuous in the bright moonlight. Thus we see that one of the few statements in the Hills' account that *can* be verified turns out to be totally inaccurate.

The two "lost hours" were said to begin when the Hills drove off after Barney's terrifying look at a Nazi spaceman. A short series of beeping or buzzing sounds were heard, apparently coming from the rear of the car. In the "official" version of the story, the first set of beeping sounds caused the Hills to lose consciousness, while the second caused their conscious recollection to return roughly thirty-five miles down the road. However, Barney Hill told APRO in 1963 that the beeping sounds *began* at that time and *kept up* for approximately thirty-five miles until they reached Ashland, where the sounds ceased as suddenly as they had commenced.[8] (Apparently Barney's memory of this interval of the journey was not entirely lost.) Each beep caused the car to vibrate. One possible explanation for the "hypnotic beeps" would be some kind of flaw or corrugation in the pavement, such as often is encountered in construction zones or before reaching a toll booth.

Even after the Hills had returned home, it was not evident to them that two hours had been "lost." Not until several weeks afterward, after they had been subjected to intense cross-examinations lasting up to twelve hours by dedicated UFO proponents seeking to squeeze the last drop of recollection from the witnesses, was it concluded from their inability to account accurately for every minute of the evening that two hours were mysteriously "missing."

But the Hills' account of that evening's timetable has never been fully consistent. In their report to the Air Force (their earliest account) they gave the time of the reported close encounter as between midnight and 1:00 AM.

In *The Interrupted Journey,* we read that it took place not long after 11:00 PM. In *The Edge of Reality,* a book by Hynek and Vallee, there is a transcript of a conversation from a radio show, in which Betty Hill says, "We estimated the UFO started to move in close to us right around 3:00 AM."[9] Which of these times is correct? It is obviously impossible to establish the existence of two lost hours when we have this uncertainty ranging over nearly four hours. If Betty Hill herself is unable to give an accurate chronological account of the night's events (Barney Hill is now deceased), how can anyone else hope to do so?

A few other facts will help us view the question of the "lost hours" in perspective. Under hypnosis, Barney explained that, as the UFO seemed to be moving in closer, "I became slower in my driving . . . I must have been driving five miles an hour, because I had to put the car in low gear so it would not stall."[10] Barney also relates sitting in the car, motionless, watching an orange light that presumably was the moon setting (moonset was at about 1:50 AM). He says, "I just wasn't driving ahead at this time."[11] He does not recall how long they sat there, or why he had stopped in the first place. Also, the Hills tell of leaving the main road and driving down some back roads in a dazed condition, where they reportedly encountered UFO aliens — although it is difficult to say how much of that part of their story is fact and how much is fantasy. But one thing is clear from the above: the Hills appear to have used up a great deal of time doing things other than driving directly home.

What about the hypnosis testimony itself? When Dr. Benjamin Simon, a prominent Boston psychiatrist, placed Barney and Betty Hill under hypnosis separately, they each told of being "abducted" by alien creatures and then being released with no conscious memories of the incident. This is considered by many to be the strongest evidence supporting the reality of the alleged UFO encounter. After all, how could each of them tell very similar stories unless it all really happened? And since the experience was related under hypnosis, doesn't that *prove* the story to be authentic?

Unfortunately, the answer is no. Psychologists generally agree that what a person says while under hypnosis need not necessarily be actual fact but rather represents what the person *believes* to have happened. Hypnosis is of little value in separating fact from fantasy.

How did they each come to tell essentially the same story? Shortly after the alleged UFO incident, Betty began having a series of dreams about being abducted by the supposed UFO occupants. She wrote down these dreams and discussed them with anyone who wanted to listen (there were many who did). Barney had heard these accounts many times. *The "abduction" story told under hypnosis was simply a retelling of these dreams.* Under hypnosis, Barney admitted to Dr. Simon that Betty had told him "a great many details of the dreams." This prompted Dr. Simon to ask why it was that Barney knew nothing about what had supposedly happened to Betty aboard the

UFO, yet Betty seemed to know everything that supposedly had happened to Barney.[12] If Barney was in fact just repeating the dreams his wife had described, she would of course be able to supply far more details than he.

But the most significant fact to to be noted about the hypnosis testimony is that *Dr. Simon himself does not believe it.* A careful reading of *The Interrupted Journey* clearly reveals Dr. Simon's skepticism. In chapter 12, Dr. Simon indicates what he believes to be the most tenable explanation for the "abduction" story: the dreams of Mrs. Hill had "assumed the quality of a fantasied experience." When he appeared on the NBC-TV "Today" show on the morning of the day that the Hill TV movie was shown, Dr. Simon reaffirmed his opinion: "It was a fantasy . . . in other words, it was a dream. The abduction did not happen."[13] Dr. Simon expressed this same opinion to Philip J. Klass, who quotes him in two UFO books.[14] Dr. Simon is a man eminently qualified to distinguish between fantasized and real events, since that is one of the principal tasks of the analyst.

The believers in the Hill story have a ready answer for this. They say that Dr. Simon's opinions on UFOs are unimportant, because he doesn't know a thing about UFOs. This may be true. But he certainly knows something about psychiatry, and in his professional opinion the celebrated "abduction" story is a dream, not a real event.

Another often-cited "proof" of the Hill incident is the supposed "radar confirmation" of the sighting. The existence of these radar reports has supposedly been revealed recently by the Air Force, reportedly proving that an unknown craft did indeed take off at the very time of the supposed UFO abduction. Betty Hill herself has repeatedly made this claim, which has now become widely accepted in UFO circles.

Appearing on the Lou Gordon show in Detroit (WKBD-TV, November 9, 1975), Mrs. Hill alleged, "When the UFO was coming in around midnight, it was picked up on seven different radars, all along the New England coast." Very impressive, if true. In another TV appearance, on the NBC-TV "Today" show (October 20, 1975), Betty Hill once again claimed that seven different radars had seen the object land about midnight, and she added, "The Air Force in our area released a radar report of it being seen leaving the area at 2:14 AM," which appears to confirm beyond any doubt the reality of the alleged abduction. Unfortunately, with just one exception, all the records alleged to support this truly remarkable claim have accidentally been lost.

I am indebted to Philip J. Klass for his assistance in tracking down the claims about radar. Klass was also a guest on the Lou Gordon show when Betty Hill repeated her claims about the radar sighting. He asked her if she could provide him with a copy of the documents that are alleged to support them. She readily agreed to do so, but said regretfully that she had only the documents pertaining to one of the radar sightings in her own file—the Air Force radar that reportedly showed the object leaving the area—and that a newspaper reporter had the others. A few weeks later, she informed Klass that the newspaper reporter was unable to provide *any* documentation supporting any of the seven alleged radar sightings, because records of them had all reportedly been "lost."

The only piece of evidence in existence that in any way supports the supposed radar confirmation of the sighting is the brief paragraph from Pease Air Force Base in Portsmouth, New Hampshire, that is contained in the Air Force report on the Hill case: "0614Z observed unidentified A/C come on PAR 4 miles out. A/C made approach and pulled up at ½ mile. Shortly afterward observed weak target on downwind, then radar CTC lost. TWR was advised of the A/C when it was on final, then when it made low approach. TWR unable to see any A/C at any time."

Translating the official jargon, the report says: "At 2:14 AM E.D.T., an unidentified target was observed on the Precision Approach Radar 4 miles out." (This is a type of radar that sends out its signals in a narrow beam, directly down the runway. It has an extremely narrow field of vision, seeing only those objects that are in a direct line of sight with the runway.) "The object appeared to approach the runway, but left the beam of the radar when it was about one-half mile away. Shortly afterward, another, weaker false target was observed, then nothing more was seen. The control tower was twice told about the object, but they were never able to see it."

One highly significant factor is missing from this account—the Airport Surveillance Radar. This is the wide-angle radar that scans the entire region around the airport, keeping track of all airplanes in the area; the Precision Approach Radar merely guides the aircraft onto the runway once the Airport Surveillance Radar has steered it into the general area. As far as the USAF records indicate, *the Airport Surveillance Radar saw no unidentified objects at any time.* This suggests that the other radar unit was not detecting an actual aircraft when it briefly showed an unknown target. (Sometimes even birds and insects are registered as targets on radars such as the PAR.) The second false target, weaker than the first, confirms the suspicion that the PAR was not detecting any actual craft. Radar "angels," as these false targets are called, give rise to many spurious UFO reports.

Even if we stretch a point to grant that the Pease radar sighting did indeed represent a genuine UFO (this sighting occurred near Portsmouth, New Hampshire, along the Atlantic Ocean), there is no reason to connect it with the UFO reportedly seen in the White Mountains, many miles away, two hours earlier. Why didn't the observers in the control tower see the UFO if it approached within one-half of a mile? Even more puzzling, why would a UFO enter the runway approach pattern of the Pease Air Force Base, imitating an aircraft about to land?

What does the now-famous "star map" prove? Much attention has been focused on this supposed star pattern, which Betty Hill claims to have seen aboard the UFO and subsequently sketched by post-hypnotic suggestion (plate 4). The reason for all this attention has been the work of Miss Marjorie Fish, former third-grade teacher at the Oak Harbor Elementary School in Ohio. Using colored beads strung out on a 3-D frame, she claims to have matched the "stars" drawn by Betty Hill with a group of nearby stars that are all similar to the sun, and which appear to be likely places to find habitable planets. Miss Fish utilized the most accurate astronomical reference work currently available, and the basic accuracy of her star positions has been established.

One of the biggest boosters of the Fish map has been Stanton Friedman, a well-known professional UFO lecturer who bills himself as "The Flying Saucer Physicist." When he and Betty Hill appeared together on the Tom Snyder Show on NBC–TV (October 22–23, 1975), Friedman made it sound as if the stars of the Fish map, alone among all the stars in the universe, matched the "stars" of Betty Hill's sketch like an apple fits its skin.

All fifteen of the stars on the Hill sketch were identified by Miss Fish, according to Friedman, and all of them are the kind of stars that are likely to have habitable planets. Since this is true of only about 5 percent of the stars in our part of the galaxy, Friedman went on to say: "The chances that the Fish map would grab fifteen and come up with the right kind are, well, . . . astronomical." "Every one of the stars on the map are the right kind of stars, and all the right kind of stars in the neighborhood are part of the map," he told an amazed Tom Snyder.

Another well-known proponent of the Fish map is Dr. David Saunders, a psychologist formerly of the University of Colorado and the University of Chicago, who was a dissident member of the Condon Committee. Dr. Saunders, a specialist in statistics, has estimated that the odds against a random pattern of stars matching Betty's sketch as well as the Fish map is "at least 1000-to-1."[15]

The only problem with statements such as these is that they are incorrect and misleading. All fifteen stars have been identified, according to Friedman, but he neglects to mention that Betty's original sketch contains twenty-six stars, not just fifteen. Why doesn't the Fish map identify the remaining eleven? Three of Betty's background stars (unconnected by lines) are included in the Fish map, because they fit nicely, but the other eleven are ignored. This is hardly a valid scientific procedure.

As for the claim that all the stars that fit the pattern are exactly the right kind for supporting planets with life, Friedman neglected to tell us that Fish excluded other stars on theoretical grounds, as being unsuitable for supporting life-bearing planets.

Betty Hill shows a star between the points represented on the Fish map by Tau Ceti and Gliese 86, but Fish does not. Zeta 1 and Zeta 2 Reticuli on the Fish map (the supposed home base of the UFOnauts) are shown as giant globes on Betty's sketch, supposedly because they are high above the rest of the map in the third dimension and hence appear larger. Yet other stars on the map, such as Tau 1 Eridani and Gliese 95, are equally high above the rest of the stars, but they appear as tiny dots, not as giant globes. Furthermore, although the globes in Betty Hill's sketch are widely separated, on the Fish map Zeta 1 and Zeta 2 Reticuli are so close as to be inseparable without a magnifying glass (though of course they are never drawn that way).

Another investigator of the Hill star-map is Charles W. Atterberg of Elgin, Illinois. He has made an interesting finding concerning these two principal stars on the Fish map. Generating a mathematical representation of the Fish map, which is far more accurate than stringing up beads, Atterberg found that the orientation of Zeta 1 and Zeta 2 Reticuli, as given in the star catalogs, is totally out of line with the corresponding giant globes of the Hill sketch. The lines connecting Betty's globes slant northwest and southeast, but a line through the two Zetas actually slant northeast and southwest (although the distinction is largely academic, since magnification would be required to even see Zeta 1 and Zeta 2 as separate objects were the Fish map drawn accurately). Thus on the two most critical points of the map, the supposed "home base" stars of the UFOnauts, the Fish map is totally wrong in the orientation and separation of these stars.

As Cornell University astronomers Steven Soter and Carl Sagan point out,[16] the only reason that there appears to be any resemblance at all between the Hill sketch and the Fish stars is because of the way the lines have been drawn. View the two patterns simply as dots, without any lines to help the reader visualize the resemblance, and the two patterns look about as different as can be.

Not only is the resemblance between the Fish map and the Hill sketch questionable, but more than one pattern of stars has been found that appears to match the sketch. As I have noted elsewhere,[17] at least two other such "identifications" of the Hill sketch have thus far been documented.

In 1965 a map of the constellation Pegasus appeared in the *New York Times*, showing a location of a strange astronomical object designated CTA-102, which a Russian radio astronomer claimed was an artificial radio beacon in space. Upon seeing the map, Betty Hill noted a striking resemblance between the stars of the constellation Pegasus and the stars she had drawn on her sketch. She then proceeded to fill into her sketch the corresponding star names from the *New York Times* map. (Of course, these are entirely different stars from the ones on the Fish map.) The supposedly artificial radio source, CTA-102, appeared very near the UFOnauts' supposed home base, the star Zeta Pegasi. Was it a beacon to guide the UFOs home from their explorations?

This Pegasus map so impressed author John Fuller that he included it in *The Interrupted Journey*. It appeared to provide strong evidence in support of Mrs. Hill's story. But the case for the Pegasus map quickly fell apart. Other astronomers soon refuted the sensationalist claims that had been made about CTA-102. This supposedly artificial object turned out to be simply another quasar (whatever *that* may someday turn out to be), and that was the end of the Pegasus map.

The third supposed identification of the star map of Betty Hill was proposed by Atterberg. He computed the patterns made by certain groups of stars when viewed from various perspectives in space. After much labor, Atterberg discovered that there exists a point in space, along the southern boundary of the constellation Ophiuchus, from which the stars in the sun's vicinity appear to match almost exactly the pattern of the Hill sketch. The Atterberg map fits the sketch much more closely than does the Fish map, identifying twenty-five of Hill's twenty-six stars, instead of just fifteen. Atterberg did not restrict himself to just the stars favorable for life. He started out by plotting all the stars in the sun's vicinity, which makes it all the more remarkable that the majority of the stars supposedly visited by the aliens (according to this map) are quite favorable for life. Of the eleven stars supposedly visited by aliens (not counting the sun), seven of them are listed in Stephen H. Dole's Rand Corporation study, *Habitable Planets for Man*, as stars "that could have habitable planets." Not a bad percentage for stars selected at random from the solar neighborhood!

Even more surprising is the fact that the three stars that form the heart of the Atterberg map—Epsilon Eridani, Epsilon Indi, and Tau Ceti—which are connected by lines supposedly representing the major trade routes of the UFOnauts, have been described by Carl Sagan as "the three nearest stars of potential biological interest."[18] Surely this is more remarkable than any of the evidence supporting the Fish map.

The purpose of this discussion is not to convince you that Atterberg has found the home star of Betty Hill's abductors, but to show that an impressive-sounding case can be made for more than one map. If I had to choose one of these three maps, I'd pick the Atterberg map as being the most impressive—it is, after all, the closest to Betty Hill's sketch. Even Miss Fish concedes that the Atterberg map is accurate, though she goes on to argue that her own map is better. But "better" is not the issue here: *there are simply too many star patterns that fit Betty Hill's sketch.* Random star positions, when rotated, sorted, and manipulated, can be made to match nearly any pre-established pattern, as long as we are willing to expend enough time and effort to obtain a match. Atterberg illustrated this point nicely when he showed his map to a friend who had not previously seen the Hill sketch. He reports that his friend quickly replied that he knew exactly what the map represented: "It's the neighborhood I live in. This is my house. That is the house on the corner. And if we angle up this way, this takes me down Devon Street, and there's the gas station."

If twelve more people, each as intelligent and as dedicated as Marjorie Fish or Charles Atterberg, were freely to devote months or even years of their spare time to a painstaking analysis of the existing star catalogs, in due time we would have a dozen more of these maps, each closely resembling the pattern sketched by Betty Hill, and each one boasting of some amazing feature that simply cannot be explained unless we accept the map as having been drawn from something Mrs. Hill saw aboard a UFO.

Recent developments in the Hill case are straining even the almost boundless credulity of the UFO establishment. About 1977, Betty Hill began talking about a "UFO landing spot" in southern New Hampshire, where she goes as often as three times a week to watch UFOs. Its exact location is a loosely kept secret, as numerous reporters and UFO watchers have accompanied her to the site. Mrs. Hill claims that Close Encounters are such frequent events at this site that she has made up names for some of the more frequently appearing UFOs: one she calls "the military" because of its allegedly hostile activity, and another is "the working model."[19] Betty Hill explains that "the 'new' UFOs aren't friendly as the 'old' ones were. Whereas before they would buzz cars, flying over the roofs and behaving almost playfully, now they sometimes shoot beams, and dart at cars in menacing fashion . . . once they even blistered the paint on my car."[20] Mrs. Hill also has asserted that the aliens sometimes get out and do calisthenics before taking off again.[21]

In a long, three-part article by APRO's Dr. Berthold E. Schwartz, a New Jersey psychiatrist, numerous alleged paranormal events experienced by Betty Hill are related. She reportedly has encountered a "Pumpkin Head" form that glides beside her car as a UFO hovers above. Afterwards, she is "filled with electricity," setting off airport security devices and resetting electric clocks. She has also performed babysitting chores for a troublesome ghost named Hannah, to give her sister a respite from a long and tedious haunting. After the ghost had reportedly settled in at Betty's home in Portsmouth, "Hannah would walk in the room, cough, and you'd see the rocking chair rock but nobody was in it," Mrs. Hill stated.[22]

John Oswald, a field investigator for CUFOS, accompanied Mrs. Hill on a vigil at her now-famous UFO landing spot. He reported that "obviously Mrs. Hill isn't seeing eight UFOs a night. She is seeing things that are not UFOs and calling them UFOs." On one occasion, he reports, Mrs. Hill was unable to "distinguish between a landed UFO and a streetlight."[23] Nonetheless, Oswald still believes that Betty Hill was abducted by aliens in 1961 because "we can't break the case or disprove it."

In view of all these things, it must be painfully evident to even the staunchest UFO believer that the credibility of the one "true" classic CE-III case, the Hill "UFO abduction," is essentially nil. Yet I cannot name a single prominent member of a pro-UFO group who has publicly disassociated himself or herself from the Hill case because of its many absurdities. In fact, the "true believers" seem to cling to it as tightly as ever, afraid that if they are seen backing down from even one classic abduction case because of its lack of credibility they would find themselves back-pedaling on the proverbial "slippery slope" to outright skepticism. Acceptance of the Hill story is a litmus test of abject credulity, an indication of willingness to utterly discard all remnants of critical thinking in order to immerse oneself in a universe of exciting if unverified entities. For all that the reading public knows, the UFO establishment still stands foursquare behind Betty Hill—her landing spot, Pumpkin Head, ghost, and UFO laser beam notwithstanding. If a "scientific UFOlogy" actually existed, it would have repudiated the Hill case long ago.

Prior to about 1966, when the Hill abduction story became well known to the public, accounts of "UFO abductions" were virtually unknown. (A 1957 case involving Brazilian farmer Antonio Villas Boas, who claimed to have been abducted by UFO creatures and then seduced by an alluring, nude extraterrestrial female, produced more snickers than converts. But it is more generally believed today.) The Hill case, with its seemingly high degree of credibility, broke new ground in terms of its acceptability to the UFO movement. It was the first claim of face-to-face contact with UFO aliens that was embraced by the mainstream of the UFO movement, and it turned out in retrospect to have been a watershed event, opening the floodgates for a torrent of subsequent "UFO abduction" claims, contributing significantly to the climate of ever-increasing credulity that has characterized the recent UFO scene.

A flood of "abduction" stories followed in the wake of the NBC–TV telecast of the movie dramatization of the Hill case on October 20, 1975. A minor "UFO flap" in certain areas of the country occurred as well.

A significant portion of the book *Abducted* (1977), by APRO's James and Coral Lorenzen, consists of spin-off cases generated in the wake of the movie. Some of them represent alleged sightings from a few months earlier, whose "missing hours" and "abduction" aspects were only recognized after the supposed abductee watched *The UFO Incident* on October 20. The Lorenzens write that "the summer and fall months of 1975 appear to have been a busy time for whoever and whatever was generating the reports of abduction."[24] That the TV movie may have been the reason seems not to have occurred to them.

The best-known of these spin-off cases occurred on August 26, 1975. Mrs. Sandra Larson of Fargo, North Dakota, along with her daughter and a friend, reportedly had a UFO close encounter at about 4:00 AM along a deserted stretch of Interstate 94 in her home state. They reportedly saw from eight to ten round, glowing objects, whose descriptions suggest that they might have been a brilliant metor that exploded in the earth's atmosphere. After watching the NBC–TV movie on October 20, Mrs. Larson began to "squarely" face up to the supposedly "lost hour" from her trip, and after suitable hypnotic regression by APRO's Dr. Leo Sprinkle, a psychologist at the University of Wyoming, a minor "classic" abduction case was born, earning endorsement from the Lorenzens, Sprinkle, and Jerome Clark. Mrs. Larson asserts that when they were allegedly abducted aboard the craft, the aliens had all three of the abductees "dissected like frogs," but somehow managed to put them back together again, none the worse for the experience.[25]

In Norway, Maine, two young men, David Stephens and a friend who does not want his name published, reported a "UFO abduction" that occurred on October 27, 1975, precisely one week after the Hill TV movie. This case is somewhat unusual in that it involves not missing hours, but *surplus* minutes; they reportedly traversed a road in dramatically *less* time than would have been required if no UFO were present. Presumably the UFO aliens picked them up, examined them, erased their memories, and released them *before* they had even been abducted! David claims to have been examined by "creatures" in a room like an operating room. The Lorenzens do not say whether or not the young men had watched *The UFO Incident* one week before. One APRO investigator knowledgeable about astronomy was with David Stephens on another night when the latter claimed to see more UFOs; they were readily identifiable as the planets Jupiter and Mars and the star Betelgeuse. The Lorenzens concede that the witnesses' "lack of knowledge of the heavens" may account for some of the weird phenomena they reported *after* the "abduction," but the supposed abduction itself is not questioned.[26]

The celebrated Travis Walton abduction case (chapter 3) occurred on November 5, 1975, less than three weeks after *The UFO Incident* was telecast. In Walton's obviously ghost-written account of the incident, he asserts that neither he nor any other member of his woodcutter's crew had watched the movie. But this is contradicted by Dr. Jean Rosenbaum, a psychiatrist who spoke with Travis at length after the incident, and about whom Travis has always spoken approvingly (even though Dr. Rosenbaum believes Travis's story to be rooted in psychological factors, and not a real event). In an article written by Rodney Barker, who evidently had the full cooperation of Dr. Rosenbaum, it is noted that Travis had indeed watched *The UFO Incident*. Dr. Rosenbaum interprets this to mean that Travis had probably assimilated the details of the Hill abduction and worked these into his own account.[27]

Judy Kendall, a legal secretary who lives in northern California, claims to have had a "UFO abduction" experience in the early 1970s involving four "lost hours." Her first inkling that she and her car had been floated off the ground came during 1975, in a movie theater, when she watched a vehicle float off into the air in Walt Disney's *Escape to Witch Mountain*. A few months later, she saw the Hill movie and decided to undergo regressive hypnosis. Under hypnosis, she told of undergoing a painful physical examination by creatures with "grasshopper eyes."[28]

In addition to the spate of "abduction" cases, the Hill movie seems to have triggered a respectable, if not overwhelming, flap of UFO sightings. A Defense Department memo, dated November 11, 1975, declassified under a Freedom of Information Act request (chapter 14) reads, "Since 28 OCT 75 numerous reports of suspicious objects have been received at the NORAD COC (Combat Operations Center) . . ."[29] The reports originated from military personnel at bases in the northeastern United States and adjacent regions of Canada. Note that the "flap" began exactly eight days after the Hill movie was shown. In the period of November 4-9, a UFO "flap" reportedly associated with cattle mutilations broke out in Wisconsin, and a police sighting was reported in Ohio. One cannot, of course, *prove* that this spate of UFO sightings was caused by the TV movie, but the timing is indeed suggestive.

There have been numerous other UFO abduction stories in recent years, far too many to discuss here, and the pace appears to be quickening. While each case has its own unique aspects, a typical scenario runs: sighting of an unidentified object, wondering about a possible abduction, regressive hypnosis leading to "discovery" of a previously forgotten physical examination aboard a UFO by alien beings, subsequent experience of paranormal events. The debt to the Hill case is obvious. Several major "abduction" cases were reported before the Hill movie was telecast, but after the case had been widely disseminated in print. Patty Price first believed she may have been abducted after reading a *Saga* magazine article on UFOs. Sgt. Charles I. Moody first speculated he may have been abducted after happening upon a copy of *Official UFO* magazine.[30]

APRO's Dr. Sprinkle, one of the most prolific discoverers, through regressive hypnosis, of hetetofore unknown "abduction" cases, observes that, as a general rule, a two-stage pattern is developing. The first stage is the abduction story itself; the second stage is the development of supposedly psychic powers. "The victims suddenly find they possess altogether new psychic powers and have developed strangely superior knowledge . . . without exception, they all felt their experiences were not just one time things," Sprinkle stated.[31] Jacques Vallee discusses this same idea in considerable detail in his book *The Invisible College*.[32] Thus Betty Hill believes herself to be receiving telepathic messages from her alien abductors;[33] David Stephens reports seeing an ashtray levitate a foot into the air;[34] Sandy Larson reports a return of the UFO entities several months later, who "magnetized" her as she lay in her own bed and "floated" her through the wall to a nearby waiting UFO.[35] It should be emphasized that the UFO movement does *not* view such wild stories as in any way discrediting the abduction tales they accompany; on the other hand, they are widely seen as further proof that some truly deep mystery has occurred. Thus, given UFOlogy's near-boundless credulity, the wild tales continue to escalate—and to be believed.

The most significant recent development in the "abduction" realm—and perhaps in all UFOdom—is the research on "imaginary" abductees by Dr. Alvin H. Lawson, professor of English at California State University at Long Beach, in collaboration with Dr. W. C. McCall and John De Herrera. Lawson and his colleagues selected a group of individuals who had no significant interest in or knowledge of UFOs and caused them to undergo regressive hypnosis, where they were asked to envision a purely imaginary "UFO abduction" experience. Their accounts were compared with those of supposedly "real" abductees.

Although major dissimilarities were expected, Lawson was surprised to find that "an averaged comparison of data from four imaginary and four "real" abduction narratives showed no substantive differences." The researchers were also surprised to learn that many presumably obscure patterns and details from abduction accounts in the UFO literature also turned up in the imaginary narratives (leading them to speculate that some form of ESP was used to draw this information from the minds of the researchers). Some "imaginary" subjects developed what seemed to be conscious memories of a UFO encounter, where none had ever occurred. Lawson observes that the details of both "real" and "imaginary" abductees' supposed physical examinations by UFO entities *often parallel events in that person's own medical history*: surgery, catheterization, and so forth.[36] This implies that the alleged physical examinations by UFO beings do not describe real events.

Lawson further observes that the visual imagery and other patterns reported by "real" and "imaginary" abductees are overwhelmingly similar and that both differ little from those frequently reported in drug-induced hallucinations and in the "death narratives" of persons supposedly at death's door. This suggests that all such phenomena originate from the same unconscious, hallucinatory wellspring. Lawson goes on to note certain differences between "real" and "imaginary" abductions, which he terms "crucial." For example, "imaginary" subjects usually control their emotions and report no physical effects, while "real" abductees are often frightened and emotional, and usually allege some kind of physical or physiological effect from the incident.

But CUFOS' Allan Hendry has shown through numerous examples that the degree of a witness's emotional reaction does not in any way establish the authenticity of an alleged sighting, and James Oberg has noted that the very factors that Lawson says distinguish the "real" abductees operate as selection factors in favor of "discovering" an alleged abduction.[37] Witnesses to "real" UFO sightings who do not display those disturbing symptoms — amnesia, nightmares, severe emotional upsets — almost never undergo the regressive hypnosis that enables them to "discover" the supposed abduction experience. In any case, the hypnosis experiments indicate, in Lawson's own words, that "the imaginations of individual witnesses may be the source of much if not all the data we have about alleged abductions."

Yet, no matter how much doubt has been raised about the Hill "abduction" case and the many similar cases that followed in its wake, UFO "abduction" cases remain the most highly publicized incidents and the most highly valued "cases" to UFO proponents. APRO views such cases not only as a golden opportunity to learn more about the inside of the craft (the Lorenzens urge that any "abductee" who has detailed recollection of dials or gauges consult with an aerospace engineer at once), but also as a great hazard as well, especially if UFO skeptics succeed in convincing the public that UFO abduction stories are all nonsense. "How many youngsters," the Lorenzens ask, "complacent" in the belief that UFO abduction claims have no basis in fact, will innocently venture into "lovers' lanes or isolated areas for camping trips and fall prey to the things described in this book?" (They apparently feel that if the public were adequately forewarned about this matter, amorous teenagers would avoid venturing into isolated areas for fear of being snatched up by a UFO.) The Lorenzens strongly feel that the public should have a choice: "to be abducted or not to be abducted." All right-minded citizens must agree. But because of the supposed unwillingness on the part of the authorities to admit that they are unable to deal with the problem, the Lorenzens warn that "each and every inhabitant of this earth is a potential victim."[38]

Somehow I can't place that very high on my worry list.

NOTES

1. John G. Fuller, *The Interrupted Journey* (New York: Dell, 1966), chapter 7.

2. Ibid., chapter 6.

3. Ibid., chapter 5.

4. From Betty Hill's letter to NICAP's Major Keyhoe, published in *The Interrupted Journey,* chapter 2.

5. *Interrupted Journey,* chapter 7.

6. Philip J. Klass, *UFOs Explained* (New York: Random House, 1974), p. 9; Allan Hendry, *The UFO Handbook* (New York: Doubleday, 1979), chapters 5, 7.

7. *Interrupted Journey,* chapter 7.

8. *APRO Bulletin,* March 1963, p. 7.

9. J. Allen Hynek and Jacques Vallee, *The Edge of Reality* (Chicago: Regnery, 1975), chapter 4.

10. *Interrupted Journey,* chapter 6.

11. Ibid., chapter 10.

12. Ibid., chapter 8.

13. NBC–TV's "Today," October 20, 1975.

14. *UFOs Explained,* pp. 252–54; *UFOs Identified* (New York: Random House, 1968), p. 229.

15. David Saunders, *Astronomy,* August 1975.

16. Steven Soter and Carl Sagan, *Astronomy,* July 1975.

17. Robert Sheaffer, *Astronomy,* July 1975; *Official UFO,* August 1976.

18. Carl Sagan and I. S. Shklovskii, *Intelligent Life in the Universe* (San Francisco: Holden-Day, 1966), p. 349.

19. *Boston Herald American,* October 10, 1977.

20. Jerome Clark, interview with Betty Hill, *UFO Report,* January 1978, p. 40.

21. Betty Hill's UFO lecture, reported in *Centralia* (Ill.) *Sentinel,* June 27, 1978.

22. Berthold E. Schwartz, *Flying Saucer Review* 23, nos. 2, 3, 4 (1977); see no. 3 (October 1977):12, 14.

23. *Foster's Daily Democrat,* Dover, N.H., October 15, 1977; John Oswald, personal communication, March 19, 1979.

24. James and Coral Lorenzen, *Abducted! Confrontations with Beings from Outer Space* (Berkley, New York, 1970), p. 70.

25. Ibid., chapter 5; UPI, February 12, 1976.

26. *Abducted!,* chapter 6.

27. "Walton," *The Walton Experience* (New York: Berkley, 1978), p. 143; Rodney Barker, *Argosy UFO,* July 1976.

28. B. Ann Slate, "Against Her Will," *UFO Report* (1979).

29. *New York Times Magazine,* October 14, 1979.

30. *Abducted!,* pp. 10, 40.

31. *The Globe,* December 25, 1979.

32. Jacques Vallee, *The Invisible College* (New York: Dutton, 1975), chapter 1.

33. Raymond Fowler, *Official UFO,* January 1976, p. 14.

34. Alex Evans, *UFO Report,* September 1978, p. 22.

35. *Abducted!,* p. 64.

36. Alvin H. Lawson, *MUFON UFO Journal,* November and December 1977; CUFOS' *Journal of UFO Studies* 1, no. 1 (1979).

37. Hendry, *The UFO Handbook,* chapter 8; James Oberg, personal communication, 1979.

38. *Abducted!,* pp. 159, 210.

6

UFOs: THE PHOTOGRAPHIC EVIDENCE

One of the strongest factors persuading many people of the reality of UFOs is the existence of hundreds of photographs of supposed UFOs. Although many of these photos show little more than featureless blobs, some of them do indeed clearly depict structured objects that cannot in any way represent any known phenomenon. Since most people tend to accept, whether consciously or not, the old maxim that "seeing is believing," the UFO skeptic inevitably encounters many individuals whose faith in the reality of UFOs rests primarily on the photographs they have seen of supposed UFOs. "But what about the photos taken at such-and-such a place?" these people will ask. "They're so clear that they couldn't possibly be fakes!"

The average person, having only a nodding acquaintance with photography, does not realize how easy it is to create impressive-looking hoax UFO photos using only modest equipment. Plate 10 shows a dramatic close-up UFO photograph, which is known beyond a doubt to be a fake: it was taken by the author. While appearing to constitute a compelling photographic record of a nocturnal close encounter of the first kind, it is in fact nothing more than a banana-split ice-cream dish hanging from a slender thread in a darkened basement. The illumination is provided by a flashlight. The flat top of the inverted dish is rounded off with modeling clay, with a toothpick stuck in the top to serve as a convincing antenna. Adhesive black dots pressed onto the side give the illusion of portholes. Although the mind's eye perceives this UFO as a giant structured craft, it is in fact no more than six inches in diameter. An example such as this serves to remind us that a photograph carries little or no information that would enable a person to determine the actual size of the object; a large, distant object looks much the same as a small one nearby. Hence there is no reason to conclude that we are seeing a photograph of a "genuine" UFO merely because the object *looks* large.

In plate 11, we see another apparently large structured object, this one in daylight. This UFO was fabricated by the author from an aluminum pie plate and a cottage-cheese container. It is about eight inches in diameter. Hemispheres of Ping Pong balls serve as its landing gear, connected by strips of black electrical tape. Black dots again make convincing portholes. Supposed UFO contactees such as George Adamski have given us many photographs of this type, usually accompanied by exciting tales of conversations with the Space Brothers. While many people are persuaded by such photographs that there must be some truth in the UFO contactees' stories, anyone with an adjustable camera can easily produce a photograph like this. For many years it was speculated that the celebrated Adamski UFO photos actually depict a chicken brooder; a more recent analysis by Ed Rogers of the British UFO Society suggests that Adamski photographed the lid of a soft-drink vending machine.[1] Whatever the object may have been, there is little reason to doubt that photographs of this type, showing a structured UFO with no foreground or background objects, can easily be produced from small-model "UFOs," using no special equipment, techniques, or genuine flying saucers whatsoever.

Plate 12 shows two glowing elliptical UFOs hovering over a row of suburban houses. This is a multiple exposure. The author fabricated an elliptical light source by shining the diffused beam of a flashlight through the hole of a 45-RPM record, viewed at an angle. The "UFO" was photographed alone twice in a darkened basement. The camera was then carried outdoors to record the background. Great care had to be taken to ensure that the UFO did not "fall" upon some rooftop! Perhaps it is worries such as this that account for the peculiar fact that we generally do not learn about supposed UFO sightings in which photographs were taken until *after* the photographs have been developed and found to be convincing enough to report.

The last of the author's UFO fabrications included here is seen in plate 13. We see what appears to be a glowing, structured craft hovering in the vicinity of the moon. The method of fabrication of this photograph is somewhat novel, and hence were it to be submitted to a believers' UFO organization, accompanied by a suitably convincing narrative, it might well have become one of the all-time "classic" UFO photos, an imposing pillar of the "UFO evidence." An electronic strobe flash was attached to the camera. This device produces a brilliant flash of light of exceedingly brief duration, typically less than 1/1000 second. The shutter speed was one-half second, more than enough to record the image of the full moon. The model "UFO," fabricated from two aluminum plates, was tossed in the air. When it appeared to be in the vicinity of the moon, the camera shutter was released, triggering the flash. The brief burst of the flash "froze" the rapidly moving model, which afterward sailed invisibly out of the field, while the shutter remained open to record the moon.

Do I mean to imply that all supposed UFO photographs are deliberate hoaxes? Not at all, because there are many odd-looking objects a sincere photographer might capture on film. For example, processing defects can sometimes cause odd-shaped, saucerlike objects to unexpectedly appear on film. These can be the result of a crease in the negative, which often results in a thin crescent-shaped object, or a drop of a developing chemical that has splattered in the wrong place, creating a round or saucer-shaped object. Police Chief Buchert's photograph of the crescent-shaped "Floyd" UFO (chapter 19) turned out to be nothing more than a crease in the film.

Another frequently encountered type of UFO is a large, oddly shaped luminous object, peculiar yet geometrized, which unexpectedly appears in a photograph. This is caused by a lens flare, when an especially brilliant source of light—usually the sun—results in light being reflected several times off the different elements inside the lens, and onto the film. Plate 14 shows the sometimes spectacular effects produced by lens flares. When the photographer says something like "I didn't see anything unusual at the time, but when I had the pictures developed, this UFO mysteriously appeared!" we may be reasonably confident that we are probably dealing with either a processing defect or a lens flare. While neither of these two types of UFOs are likely to withstand scrutiny by experienced photographers (although a few have proved most puzzling indeed), the popular press is nonetheless flooded with such UFO photographs.

All manner of objects turn up in supposed UFO photographs. Often one or more interior lights, reflected in a window, serve to make convincing UFOs, as in the celebrated photo of four UFOs from the Coast Guard Station in Salem, Massachusetts.[2] Other published UFO photographs depict star trails, the crescent moon rising alongside Venus, distant birds or airplanes that appear as tiny dots, a rotating color-filter wheel for a Christmas Tree, and numerous featureless blobs of all shapes and sizes. (How anyone can become excited about a blob of light showing absolutely no shape or details, and nothing in the background, it utterly incomprehensible to me, but a significant percentage of supposed UFO photographs fall into this category. In 1975 NICAP selected two such blobs to be among the "four of the best [UFO] photo cases available."[3]) Unusually shaped clouds are also sometimes captured by an enthusiastic photographer who believes he is seeing a UFO. Distant aircraft, when seen at certain angles, can look remarkably disklike, especially when sunlight is reflected directly back toward the viewer. Many photographs of distant, relatively featureless daylight UFOs are probably aircraft.

While hundreds of purported UFO photographs have been published, even many leading UFO believers concede that in general these photos are of little worth. Even as dedicated a UFO proponent as J. Allen Hynek has recently written, "The adage 'a picture is worth a thousand words' simply does not apply when it comes to proving the reality of UFOs based on photographs in the Blue Book files . . . the most positive statement that one can make about such photographs is that, while the probability is quite high that they are genuine, the physical reality of the UFO[s] photographed cannot be established with absolute certainty. There are no cases in the Blue Book files that meet the above stringent conditions." Hynek believes that there are, however, a few Blue Book photos that nearly meet his requirements for authenticity.[4] William H. Spaulding of Ground Saucer Watch (GSW) has published the results of a series of computerized enhancements that are intended to authenticate supposed UFO photographs. GSW is not a UFO debunking organization; they believe that a government conspiracy exists that hides much significant UFO evidence from the public. Yet Spaulding believes that 595 out of 626 of the supposed UFO photos he has examined (95 percent) have been shown to be not authentic.[5]

The value of the photographic evidence for UFOs can only be determined by a careful examination of the best UFO photos, as selected by the various UFO believers' organizations. If reliable photographic evidence for the existence of UFOs is to be found anywhere, it must be among the "classic" photos, as selected by the UFO proponents themselves.

Two unrelated series of photographs from Brazil rank high on the list of UFO classics. One was taken from the deck of the Brazilian Navy ship *Almirante Saldanha* by a professional photographer, near the island of Trindade in January 1958. Dr. Menzel labels this photograph "the most famous of all purported photographs of a UFO," and it is included among NICAP's "four best" UFO photos (plate 15). The *Almirante Saldanha* was participating in scientific research for the International Geophysical Year. According to published reports, at about noontime on January 16, Captain Viegas of the Brazilian Air Force suddenly shouted that he saw a flying saucer. Almiro Barauna, the photographer, was fortunate enough to happen to be on deck with his equipment ready and snapped four pictures of the UFO. "At least twelve of the crew (including the ship's commander) and staff are known witnesses," asserts NICAP. Barauna was said to have been accompanied by an officer to the ship's darkroom, where he developed the UFO photos under strict supervision. Later the photos were released to the press by no less a person than the president of Brazil. The Trindade Island UFO photos certainly seem upon first examination to be impressive evidence indeed.

There is, however, an embarrassing fact seldom noted in the believers' literature. The fortunate photographer, Almiro Barauna, *was a specialist in trick photography.* He had previously published fabricated photographs of UFOs to illustrate a supposedly humorous article he had written, titled "A Flying Saucer Hunted Me at Home." He had also published trick photographs of supposed treasure chests lying on the ocean floor. What an extraordinary coincidence that a man with such inclinations should be present when a genuine UFO happens to fly by! Another embarrassing fact emerged when newsmen finally had an opportunity to interview the crew of the *Almirante Saldanha* several weeks later. Although the deck had been crowded with sailors, not one of the crew had actually seen the object! It also was learned that the officer supervising Barauna in the darkroom was none other than his friend Viegas, who had first raised the cry of flying saucer. Even had Barauna been under close supervision, he could easily have prepared the film in advance to contain the image of the UFO. This "classic" photo is so weak that even Hynek gives it only a lukewarm endorsement. Yet Stanton Friedman, NICAP, and others continue to rate it very high.[6]

The other "classic" Brazilian UFO photos were taken from the Ilha Dos Amores, the Island of Lovers, by two photographers from *O Cruziero* magazine (which also published the Trindade UFO photos). Sent to the island in May 1952 to obtain photographs of amorous couples, they returned instead with five photographs of a supposed UFO. Upon closer examination, the UFO is clearly seen to be fraudulent. While trees and mountains in the foreground cast shadows to the left, the dome of the flying saucer casts its shadow to the right. (But perhaps a sufficiently advanced technology can cause shadows from the sun to fall on the left and the right at the same time? Maybe the clever UFO people deliberately cast an inconsistent shadow, in order to discredit the phenomenon?) According to Hynek, the two reporters, returning with the photos that they swore to be genuine, asked for $25,000 for the five negatives; they found no takers. As weak as these photographs are, Ralph Blum included them in his book *Beyond Earth* as presumably authentic. Hynek is skeptical of the photos, but APRO's Coral Lorenzen pronounces them to be "the first authentic UFO photographs," and APRO's consultant, the late Dr. Olavo Fontes of Brazil, claimed that they provide "absolute photographic evidence . . . that 'flying saucers' are real."[7]

One proposed means for sorting out the hoax UFO photos from the supposedly authentic ones is the computer enhancement performed by GSW. Because GSW has pronounced 95 percent of the UFO photos it has examined to be not authentic, the group has come under a great deal of criticism from the other pro-UFO organizations. While some have accepted GSW's conclusions unhesitatingly, others reject its analyses out of hand, unwilling to believe that any technique that says that such-and-such a "classic" photo is a hoax could possibly have any value whatsoever. Both of these reactions are unreasonable. The computer has a reputation in some circles today as something of an oracle, an all-knowing electronic wizard whose pronouncements cannot be challenged. Others view computers as unreliable. Those of us who work with digital computers in our daily jobs know that neither view is correct. A computer is the most efficient, most reliable machine for processing information yet devised by man. *But the conclusions said to have been reached by the computer are in fact human conclusions.* The systems analyst who designed the logic flow, or who directed the interpretation of the ones-and-zeroes output to emerge from the computer, has in fact rendered the conclusion—not the machine itself. It is important to keep this point in mind.

The value of computer enhancement in bringing out otherwise invisible details in photographs is well established. These techniques have been used extensively by NASA to enhance blurry spacecraft photos of celestial objects. Some of the interpretations by GSW, however, are not so universally accepted. For example, when entering a photographic image into the computer's memory, the image is broken down into an array of 512 horizontal columns and 480 vertical rows, creating a total of 245,760 picture elements, or "pixels." These numbers are of course arbitrary; the more pixels, the better the resolution of the computer's image of the photograph. A pixel is an arbitrary, dimensionless point, each one assigned a value depending on its brightness, from zero for pure black to 255 for pure white. The pixel is as arbitrary and fictional a construct as the "number line" that mathematicians mentally construct to represent real numbers. Yet GSW pronounces UFO photos to be authentic or not depending on whether their pixels have "sharp" or "fuzzy" edges. This is like a student failing in mathematics because the "number line" in his imagination was too wavy. It is difficult to understand why GSW believes its analysis of a movie film of a supposed Bigfoot creature could ever hope to tell the difference between a "real" monster and a man in a monkey suit.[8] Thus many people, myself included, consider many of GSW's conclusions to be unsupported by their data.

There are, on the other hand, some aspects of the GSW photo analysis that are clearly of value. In bringing out otherwise invisible details, sometimes a string supporting the "UFO" seems to leap into view! Also valuable is the profile that can be drawn from the shadows (or lack thereof) on the object. The eye can distinguish between "flat" objects in a photograph and three-dimensional ones, and the computer can make the same distinction with greater precision. The results of GSW's enhancement of supposed UFO photos can, if critically evaluated, often be a valuable addition to our knowledge about the case.

GSW recently became embroiled in a controversy concerning one of the most highly regarded series of "classic" UFO photos of all time. Two major articles in *Flying Saucer Review* proclaim their authenticity, and pro-UFO newsman Frank Edwards considered them to be "bona fide photos of an unknown object."[9] On August 3, 1965, highway investigator Rex Heflin of the Orange County (California) Highway Department was in his truck on Myford Road south of Santa Ana, just off the crowded Santa Ana Freeway, inspecting overhanging growth along the roadside. Facing northeast, he reportedly spotted a UFO that moved toward him from the left and hovered in front of him. It was said to be "silvery or metallic," shaped somewhat like a straw hat. Heflin grabbed the Polaroid camera that he always kept in his truck to use in his work and reportedly snapped three clear pictures of the object before it disappeared into the distance ahead of him (plate 16). This object supposedly flew directly over the Santa Ana Freeway, which Heflin's photograph reveals to be filled with traffic, as usual. The UFO flew almost to the perimeter of the U.S. Marine Corps Air Facility at Santa Ana, above which several helicopters were airborne at the time of Heflin's sighting. The object would have had to fly in the vicinity of the San Diego Freeway, the Newport Beach Freeway, the Orange County Airport, and many nearby residences and office buildings in this populous Los Angeles suburban area. Yet the only person who reported seeing the UFO on that bright, sunny afternoon was Rex Heflin.

Heflin reported that his two-way radio went dead just before the UFO appeared, although the FCC facility at Santa Ana reported no VHF or UHF radio interference at that time. Strangely enough, when Heflin regained the use of his radio, he did not report that he had just sighted a giant Unidentified Flying Object and that he had the Polaroid instant pictures to prove it. Instead, he said absolutely nothing about the incident to his coworkers or to anyone over the radio, waiting until he returned to the office later that day, when he began showing his three UFO pictures to his friends. One friend suggested to Heflin that they "should try to sell the photographs to *Life* magazine." The friend called the Los Angeles office of *Life* that same afternoon. *Life* expressed interest and advised sending the photos to New York, but the photos were not published in *Life* and were returned two weeks later.

Heflin's UFO photos were first published in a local newspaper, the *Santa Ana Register,* and soon attracted nationwide attention. He was interviewed by investigators from the U.S. Air Force Project Blue Book and the nearby El Toro Marine Corps Air Station. According to the Marine Corps report, "Heflin stated that he would be willing to submit to a polygraph examination only if the *Register* or someone put up $1,500 with no results guaranteed." The reason for his reluctance to face the lie detector was said to be that Heflin knows "from his experience as an investigator" that the polygraph machine "is not reliable enough" and was concerned that "if the examination turned out negative, it would endanger his job." But were someone to put up $1,500, he apparently was willing to take that risk.

Several weeks after Rex Heflin first began showing around his three photographs of a supposed UFO, he produced a fourth photograph, allegedly taken at the same time, which no one had previously seen or heard about. The fourth photo shows a "smoke ring," which was supposedly left behind by the UFO as it disappeared. Unlike the other three photographs, which show the sky to be hazy but clear, this one shows a sky covered by thick clouds, raising serious doubts as to whether it could actually have been taken just minutes afterward, as the witness claimed. When asked why he kept the fourth photograph a secret for so long, even during several in-depth interrogations about his experience, Heflin explained that "three [UFO photos] were enough for one day," and that he felt his story was already incredible enough.[10]

The Air Force concluded that the Heflin UFO incident was a "hoax" and that the object depicted was small and close to the camera. Among the reasons for suspecting a hoax is that while details of distant objects are softened by haze (it was a smoggy Los Angeles day), or even hidden completely, the UFO is sharp and distinct, as if there were no haze whatsoever between it and the camera.

Unfortunately, the original Polaroid prints of these UFO photos will never be subjected to careful scrutiny, because Heflin claims that just two days after the incident was first reported in the newspapers he gave the originals to a man (he subsequently claimed "two men") claiming to represent NORAD (North American Air Defense Command). No such person had ever been sent by NORAD, and the original prints have never been located. GSW performed its computer enhancement on the best set of duplicate prints available and concluded that the incident was a hoax. They note that in the first of the three UFO photos, which shows the object at its minimum distance from the camera, the object is not in focus, as it is in the other two. Distant objects, however, are in focus in all three. This strongly suggests that the object was small and extremely close to the camera. GSW's "pixels" also supposedly show the object to be small and close in the two photos that are in focus. Most significant of all, GSW's enhancement reveals, in the two photos showing the UFO sharply in focus, what appears to be a thread supporting the UFO! Upon publication of these findings, a torrent of abuse was heaped upon GSW by the other pro-UFO groups, for the sin of having questioned such a "classic" photograph, and thereby calling into doubt a crucial pillar of the "UFO evidence." The MUFON director for Southern California, Idabel Epperson, in an open letter accused GSW's William Spaulding of pursuing a "relentless campaign of publicly defaming Rex Heflin's character." Spaulding has been denounced by many others, both in public and in private, but he has not wavered under the intense pressure. The Heflin photos remain today a pillar of the "UFO evidence."

Jorma Viita is a young Danish shipyard worker who is amazingly prolific in the production of UFO photographs. He claims to have obtained UFOtos on no less than sixteen difference occasions during 1974 alone! Several of Mr. Viita's UFOs look remarkably like salad bowls and baking pans tossed into the air. Others are clearly double exposures, while one looks exactly like a button, sporting a buttonlike rim and five precisely spaced holes in the center (plate 17). Viita says that he became interested in UFOs in 1966, after reading a book by George Adamski.

For some inexplicable reason, the UFOs always seem to turn up when Viita is quite alone: "At these sightings I have always, with the exception of once, been alone and without any witness. Or, I have often been out with my wife and my children, e.g. on holidays, but then we have never observed anything. Why it is so I do not know." Viita concedes, "I realize that it could be easy to fake these pictures, but being without support of any witness I cannot do else than assure that these pictures are genuine." The prolific Dane, who has produced more than one hundred UFO photos, is taken very much at his word throughout UFOdom. MUFON used one of Viita's photos on its 1976 UFO calendar, with a statement by photo consultant Adrian Vance endorsing its authenticity. Major Colman S. Von Keviczky, director of ICUFON (Intercontinental UFO Galactic Spacecraft Research and Analytic Network), has no reservations whatsoever in proclaiming these photos to be authentic. During a radio debate with the "Flying Saucer Physicist," Stanton T. Friedman, he challenged me to refute the UFOtos of Jorma Viita, if I could. And in a 1976 symposium sponsored by the Center for UFO Studies, one researcher used one of the Viita photographs as a standard of authenticity against which he evaluated another UFO photograph. GSW's computer analysis has, however, rejected Viita's photos as hoaxes, having determined by methods that are not exactly clear that the object in one of the photos appears to have a "skin texture of plastic or painted wood."[11]

Another classic UFO photograph is the one taken in Tulsa, Oklahoma, on August 2, 1965, the day before the Heflin photos. (A major UFO "flap" was then in progress.) Alan Smith, age 14, says that he was standing in the back yard of his parents' home, near the Tulsa International Airport, at about 1:45 AM when a strange multicolored craft flew over. No one at the airport, or anywhere else in Tulsa, was able to snap a picture of this low-flying object, even though it was said to have remained in the area long enough for young Alan to run into the house, grab his camera, and take its picture. Four relatives and neighbors were with him at the time of the sighting. But when the photo was developed, all of them agreed that the object they saw in the sky—"just a blob of light"—did not look anything like the object in the photo. According to one published account, Alan had previously expressed on several occasions his desire to take a photograph of a UFO, and he received a substantial sum of money—$1,000—for his photo from the *Oklahoma Journal*. Other sources claim, however, that he received only $15 for it.[12]

The object in the photo looks very much like a close-up, out-of-focus image of the type of three-color filter wheel used to illuminate artificial Christmas trees. We see a large floodlight-type bulb, an opaque filter wheel, with openings covered by yellow and blue filters, partially covering the bulb (the uncovered portion being pure white). We can also see the outline of the base of the bulb. GSW, however, has analyzed the Smith photo, and has declared it to be authentic. The object supposedly is "a solid disc shape," and "somewhere between thirty and forty feet in diameter," this conclusion being based upon the finding that the "individual pixels" were "broken and wavy." This supposedly establishes that the object is about a mile away. That the object might be too close to the camera to be in sharp focus does not appear to have been considered by GSW's computer. Ralph Rankow, a NICAP photo analyst who has strongly endorsed the Heflin photos, agrees that the Smith UFO photo shows nothing but a Christmas tree floodlight. He believes, however, that Alan Smith did sight a genuine UFO, and attempted to snap its picture. But upon finding that the picture did not come out, Rankow explains, Smith must have been so disappointed that he fabricated a convincing-looking UFO, using a tricolored floodlight, in order to corroborate his story.[13]

The tadpole-shaped blob of light in plate 18 is from a sequence of motion-picture film taken by astronaut James McDivitt aboard the Gemini 4 spacecraft on June 4, 1965. It was selected by NICAP as one of the "four best photo cases available," even though the object shows no discernible shape or features whatsoever, shows nothing in the background, and, in NICAP's words, "does not depict with accuracy the shape of the object described by McDivitt." (In fact, McDivitt has flatly stated that this photo does not depict the object he reportedly saw out the window of his spacecraft; he explained that the "UFO" in the photo is just sunlight reflecting off the head of a bolt, seen against a dirty window glass.) James E. Oberg makes a convincing case that the cylindrical object that McDivitt failed to recognize was in fact his own Titan booster rocket in a nearby orbit, which he had previously had difficulty identifying. Oberg's identification is strengthened by the fact that McDivitt was complaining to the flight surgeon during this phase of the flight about his eyesight, because of an accidental massive urine spill inside the cabin; it is further substantiated by McDivitt's statement shortly after the flight that the object "looked a lot like the upper stage of a booster." That NICAP has selected a featherweight UFO case such as this, out of dozens of supposed UFOtos in their files, as one of the "four best available," is perhaps the most convincing demonstration of the weakness of the photographic "evidence" for UFOs.[14]

The third of the NICAP "four best" UFO photos shows only a featureless blob of light, taken by a TV cameraman in Manchester, Georgia, in 1973. Nothing is visible in the background.

The remaining one of the four was taken by Mr. and Mrs. Paul Trent of McMinnville, Oregon, on May 11, 1950, "a date never to be forgotten by . . . researchers of UFO phenomena," says NICAP. "The Trent photograph is probably the best recording of a UFO, because the prints contain so much information" (plate 19). According to Hynek, a recent analysis of the Trent photos by physicist Bruce Maccabee showed that "the strange object had to be at a considerable distance from the camera" and hence could not possibly be a hoax. Dr. William K. Hartmann, chief photo analyst for the ever-so-skeptical *Condon Report*, wrote that "this is one of the few UFO reports in which all factors investigated, geometric, psychological, and physical, appear to be consistent with the assertion that an extraordinary flying object, silvery, metallic, disk-shaped, tens of meters in diameter, and evidently artificial, flew within sight of two witnesses."[15] Many UFOlogists rate this case as *the* strongest photo case on record.

"It was getting along toward evening — about a quarter to eight," Mrs. Trent explained. "We'd been out in the back yard. *Both of us saw the object at the same time*" [emphasis added].[16] Her husband ran into the house to get the camera, which was loaded with film. He reportedly managed to snap two pictures of the object before it disappeared. Mrs. Trent meanwhile ran into the house to call her mother-in-law, who lived just down the road and presumably might also be able to see the UFO. However, there was no answer, and Mrs. Trent reportedly returned outside just in time to see the object disappear toward the west.

While the photos certainly depict a clearly structured object of artificial construction, there are strong reasons for doubting that it is an "authentic" UFO. While Mrs. Trent says in the interview quoted above that they were *both* outside and spotted the object at the same time, and that her husband ran inside to fetch the camera, in another interview a few days afterward she stated that she had been *alone* outside at the time and that, when her husband failed to come outside after she called him, *she had to run in to get him and the camera*. It is difficult to believe that a person describing a real event, within a span of just a few days, could reconstruct it so differently. Another reason for suspicion is that the Trents did not hasten to tell anyone about their experience or immediately send the photos off to be developed. Instead, the film containing the invaluable UFO photos was left in the camera until Mother's Day, so that a few unexposed frames would not be wasted. After the photos had been developed, clearly showing the image of a supposedly real flying saucer, a reporter who came to interview the Trents found the irreplaceable negatives lying "on the floor under the davenport where the Trent children had been playing with them." What a curious way to treat the negatives of the first authentic photographs of a flying saucer from outer space!

Another gross discrepancy in the Trents' narrative is in the time of day at which the photos were supposedly taken. The witnesses claim that it was in the evening, just after sunset. Yet there appears to be direct sunlight in the foreground (although a good deal of haze is apparent, either in the atmosphere or because of smudges on the lens, or both). We see a highlight of direct sunlight on the metallic oil tank and distinct shadows of the eaves on the garage wall, as well as on a distant house. In an unpublished paper written in 1969, I did an analysis of the size of the shadows on the garage wall which, based upon plausible estimates of the size and shape of the boards and upon technical considerations of the size and luminosity of the source of illumination in the photos, conclusively establishes that the shadows were cast by the sun and could not have been indirect lighting from any source.

This enables us to determine the precise time of day that the photos were taken, since we know that the garage wall faces due east. The time works out to be approximately 7:30 AM Pacific Standard Time, or *twelve hours earlier than the witnesses had claimed in their narrative!* Either the witnesses are not telling the truth about the circumstances of the photographs or else they are unable to distinguish morning from night. In neither case is their testimony very credible. When presented with the findings in my paper, Dr. Hartmann reversed his earlier favorable appraisal of the McMinnville photos and has publicly stated his opinion that the photos are a hoax.[17]

Yet another weak point in the credibility of the McMinnville photos is the fact that the witnesses are "repeaters": persons who claim to have sighted UFOs on several occasions. Many pro-UFO researchers consider it prudent to take the testimony of repeaters with a giant grain of salt, and NICAP has stated that a criterion for rejection of a UFO photo should be "pictures taken by individuals with a history of UFO sightings." This describes the Trents exactly. Mrs. Trent told the Portland *Oregonian* that she had spotted UFOs along the coast on three different occasions, but until the photos were taken "no one would believe me." In a 1967 follow-up interview in the same newspaper, Mrs. Trent stated, "We've seen quite a few since then [1950], but we didn't get any pictures, they disappeared too fast."[18]

Even though Hartmann tended to accept the McMinnville UFO as genuinely distant, he did identify what appeared to be the most plausible means for producing such photos as a hoax. In both photos, the object appears to be under a pair of telephone wires. Furthermore, the object apparently is under the *same* point in the wires in both photos, even though the camera has moved a considerable distance. Also tending to raise suspicion is Hartmann's observation that, as the camera was carried away from the wires, the UFO decreased in size by approximately the same percentage as did the wires. In short, *it appears as if the UFO is a small model hanging on threads from the overhead telephone wires.* Indeed, a careful inspection of photo No. 1, shown in plate 19, reveals some ill-defined object—perhaps a tangle of threads—atop the wire where one of the hypothetical threads would be expected to meet the wire. Free-standing telephone wires do not often carry suspicious objects delicately balanced on top! Another geometrical factor that argues against authenticity is that the object is asymmetrical, its left side having a different shape than its right, and that the antenna on top is plainly off center and leaning to the left. One would expect that an advanced, space-faring civilization could at least manage to stick an antenna on straight!

Why are the McMinnville photos, with all their inconsistencies and implausibilities, considered by many to be the most impressive series of UFO photos on record? Because of a single densitometric measurement taken on a small region of one of the two negatives: the underside of the UFO. As we know, the more distant an object becomes, the more scattering of light by the atmosphere takes place between the viewer and the object. Hence a non-self-luminous object becomes progressively brighter as the distance increases. At the maximum limit of visibility, the brightness of the object reaches the brightness of the horizon sky, and the object is no longer visible. This effect is familiar to everyone who has ever seen a distant mountain or tall building which was almost invisible because the contrast between it and the sky was quite small. In the McMinnville photos we see the distant hills becoming progressively lighter due to atmospheric scattering.

The object in the McMinnville photos looks pale and washed out, especially in photo No. 2 (not shown), as if it were at a great distance. To attempt to determine the distance to the object, Hartmann made a series of plausible assumptions, and after carefully measuring the negatives with a densitometer (the McMinnville photos are among the few "classic" UFO photos for which the original negatives are still around to be measured), he determined that the underside of the UFO was too bright to be a shaded, nonluminous object close to the camera, even if its color were pure white. Attributing the excess brightness to atmospheric scattering of light between the object and the camera, Hartmann tentatively concluded that the object seemed to be at a distance of a mile or more. If so, it would be at least ninety feet in diameter, and hence could not possibly be a hoax.

In my 1969 paper, I suggested an alternative explanation for the excess brightness of the underside of the object: veiling glare, the "spilling over" of light due to optical imperfections, from the bright sky to the adjacent dark image of the UFO. By a series of test exposures using an increasingly smudged lens, I was able to show that light from surrounding bright areas, such as the sky, does indeed "spill over" into small, isolated dark areas, such as a small-model UFO seen against a bright sky.

In 1975 the photometric aspects of the photos were further studied by Dr. Bruce S. Maccabee, a physicist who works at the Naval Surface Weapons Center in Silver Spring, Maryland. Dr. Maccabee, who is affiliated with NICAP, MUFON, and CUFOS, did the most in-depth investigation to date of the McMinnville UFO and one of the most detailed studies of any UFO photograph anywhere. He supported my contention that there is a significant amount of veiling glare in the photos, a factor that Hartmann's analysis did not take into account. Maccabee also found several other highly significant factors previously overlooked, such as the fact that no optical system disperses light evenly across the film plane (the brightness falls off away from the center) and that a horizontal shaded surface will differ from a vertical one. Hence Hartmann's analysis of the object's distance was completely invalidated (although Hynek thinks that Maccabee "fully substantiated" Hartmann's work).[19]

However, taking into account all of these new factors, Maccabee also reached the conclusion that the object appears to be distant, based upon the unusually bright underside of the UFO. Does this measurement rule out that the object may be small and close? Maccabee was careful to title the paper presenting his findings "On the Possibility That the McMinnville Photos Show a Distant Unidentified Object." His analysis required him to push back the frontiers of the science of photography in several areas, and scientists understand that pioneering research is seldom definitive. Dr. Maccabee concurs that not until this type of analysis has been repeated and explored in depth by other researchers can any degree of confidence be placed in the findings.

Even if it is confirmed, however, that the brightness of the underside of the object is indeed anomalous, the existence of an "authentic UFO" is not thereby established. Maccabee points out that there is one simple alternative explanation: the model UFO was made of translucent plastic, and hence light from the sky could pass through the object and cause it to appear brighter than a shaded, opaque object could possibly be. The Dutch science writer and UFO skeptic Hans Van Kampen has suggested that sunlight reflecting off the metal oil tank might account for the brightness of the object's underside. Another prosaic and entirely plausible explanation is that the Trents had a flashbulb mounted on their camera when the picture was taken. Portrait photographers often use a "fill-in flash" for daylight shots, to soften harsh shadows. If the Trents, for whatever reason, had an ordinary flash bulb attached to their camera, it would cause the bottom of the object to appear far brighter than expected. (A flashbulb would also explain the washed-out appearance of the object in the other photo.)

Occam's Razor is the principle that directs scientists to avoid embracing exotic or speculative hypotheses when prosaic ones will do just as well. Since there are plausible prosaic explanations for the densitometric measurements made on this photo, these measurements are of no value in establishing the existence of an extraordinary flying object.

Maccabee sent the negatives of the McMinnville photos to GSW, which agreed that the object was distant because its computer enhancement showed the "pixels" to be wavy. Since the edges of the UFO image are furthermore shown to be not sharp, but ragged, this is interpreted by GSW as indicating great distance. Yet certain nearby telephone wires, whose edges show poor contrast (like the UFO), are also seen to be "wavy." Can the nearby wire be miles away? Stranger yet, one of the distant hills, among the most distant objects visible in the photographs, is shown by GSW's computer to have edges as sharp as razor blades! Is this tree-covered hill a hoax, made of cardboard and set up in the foreground? Something is very wrong with GSW's attempts to determine distances in this manner.

GSW's pretensions of being able to distinguish "true" UFO photos from hoaxes were dealt a fatal blow by CUFOS' Allan Hendry. At different times, Hendry sent GSW two nearly identical photographs of a supposed UFO, taken by the same photographer on the same roll of film just minutes apart. One was proclaimed to be genuine; the other was called "the crudest attempt at a hoax that we have ever seen."[20]

The "classic" UFO photos described above are the *best* photographic evidence for UFOs, as selected by the UFO proponents themselves. The great majority of UFO photographs are weaker still. Upon the official release of the Air Force Blue Book records in 1976, Philip J. Klass and I spent a long and, as it turned out, monotonous evening in the National Archives in Washington looking over the complete collection of UFO photographs. While neither of us had high expectations of encountering anything that would cause us to revise our opinions about UFOs, we were both genuinely surprised at the extremely low overall quality of the collection. Most of the UFOs in Blue Book's photographic collection have no structure whatsoever: a blip, a dot, a blur, a line. There were at best just a handful that might be termed even moderately clever hoaxes; most of the rest were so indistinct as to be utterly laughable.

Owing to the relatively poor photographic quality of the microfilm rolls, there were a sizable number of "UFO photos" in the Blue Book collection on which we were unable to discern any image whatsoever! Billions of photographs have been taken by Americans for each of the thirty-three years since the advent of the UFO era, hundreds of UFOs are reportedly sighted each year, and yet no one is able to get better UFO pictures than that? The only reasonable explanation for such a curious state of affairs is that there are no genuine UFOs to be photographed.

NOTES

1. See *New York Post,* September 22, 1975, p. 20.
2. *Hynek UFO Report* (New York: Dell, 1977), caption under Salem UFO photo.
3. *NICAP UFO Investigator,* October 1975, p. 3.
4. *Hynek UFO Report,* p. 234.
5. *Phoenix Gazette,* March 30, 1977, Bl.
6. Menzel and Boyd, *The World of Flying Saucers* (New York: Doubleday, 1963), pp. 206–16; *The Hynek UFO Report,* pp. 246–51; Friedman on the Ed Busch Show, KNBR Radio, San Francisco, December 19, 1975.
7. Menzel and Boyd, p. 206; Hynek, caption under photograph; Lorenzen, *Flying Saucers: The Startling Evidence of the Invasion from Outer Space* (New York: Signet, 1962), p. 112; Fontes, quoted in *Condon Report,* case 48.
8. "Computer Analysis Proves Creature's Existence," *UFO Report,* January 1978, p. 37.
9. Ralph Rankow, article in *Flying Saucer Review* 14, no. 1 (January/February 1968); John R. Gray, article in *FSR* 15, no. 1 (March/April 1969); Frank Edwards, *Flying Saucers— Serious Business* (New York: Lyle Stuart, 1966), chapter 13.
10. U.S. Air Force Blue Book files; *Condon Report,* case 52.
11. The Viita quotations are from *UFO Kontakt,* IGAP Journal Special Report, Fraternity of Cosmic Sons and Daughters, Denmark (1975); 1976 MUFON Skylook Calendar; Colman S. Von Keviczky, personal correspondence; Friedman, KNBR Radio, December 19, 1975; CUFOS, *Proceedings of the 1976 UFO Conference*; GSW, *MUFON Skylook,* March 1976.
12. Tulsa, Oklahoma, UFO sighting, *Journal of Occult Studies* 1, no. 2 (August 1977): 186–203, especially pp. 201, 202.
13. *Journal of Occult Studies* 1, no. 2; *Official UFO,* April, 1976, p. 16.

14. NICAP *UFO Investigator,* October 1975; NICAP *Photograph Descriptions* (1975); James E. Oberg, "Astronauts and UFOs," *Space World,* February 1977, p. 4.

15. NICAP *Photograph Descriptions* (1975); Hynek, *The Zetetic* 1, no. 2 (Spring/Summer 1977): 77-79; William K. Hartmann, *Condon Report,* case 46.

16. McMinnville, Oregon, *Telephone Register,* June 8, 1950.

17. Hartmann, "Historical Perspectives: Photos of UFO's," in *UFO's: A Scientific Debate,* ed., Sagan and Page (Ithaca, N.Y.: Cornell University Press, 1972).

18. Quoted by Klass in *UFOs Explained* (New York: Random House, 1974).

19. Bruce S. Maccabee, "On the Possibility That the McMinnville Photos Show a Distant Unidentified Object," in CUFOS' *Proceedings of the 1976 UFO Conference; Hynek UFO Report,* p. 245.

20. Allan Hendry, *The UFO Handbook* (New York: Doubleday, 1979), chapter 16.

7

THE SCIENTIFIC STUDY
OF WITCHCRAFT

We have the attestation of thousands of Eye and Ear-witnesses, and those not of the easily-deceivable and vulgar only, but of wise and grave discerners; and that, when no interest could oblige them to agree together in a common Lye. —Joseph Glanvill, 1668.

It is the strange fortune of some men to be immortalized by their follies rather than by their virtues. —Ferris Greenslet, Glanvill's biographer.

UFOs are not the only supposedly mysterious phenomenon to have been investigated "scientifically." Nor is our twentieth century the only age in which supposedly scientific investigations of such phenomena have taken place. More than three hundred years ago, some of the finest scientific and philosophical minds of the late seventeenth century devoted their efforts to a "scientific" investigation of witchcraft. They investigated *only* those reports of bewitchings and demon sightings that came from sober, credible persons, whose testimony would be accepted in any court of law. The "signal" was carefully separated from the "noise." What was left was believed to be a small but significant residue of reliably witnessed instances of human beings changing into animals and of women giving birth to serpents and toads. Hearsay and legends were considered of no account, because these researchers were in every sense *scientific* as we understand that word today, dedicated to observation, not rumor or speculation. Their efforts were rewarded by what appeared to be an overwhelming abundance of evidence that, in at least *some* reported instances of witchcraft, human beings had gained supernatural powers by entering into pacts with the so-called Powers of Darkness.

The seventeenth century was one of the most progressive and momentous eras in human history. Not only did science waken from the stupor into which it had fallen many centuries before, but the fundamental alteration of mankind's world-view that took place during this century has prompted most historians to regard it as the intellectual transition between the Middle Ages and the modern world. It was the century that produced the thought of Francis Bacon, the astronomy of Galileo and Johannes Kepler, the political philosophy of Thomas Hobbes and John Locke, the science of Robert Boyle, William Harvey, and Sir Isaac Newton, the mathematics of Descartes and Leibniz, and the skepticism of Pierre Bayle and Bernard Fontenelle. It was also the age that planted the seeds of some great ideas that blossomed in the following century in the works of Voltaire, Diderot, Hume, Franklin, and Jefferson. In 1600, the fossilized doctrines of the medieval schoolmen held sway throughout the academic world, and the writings of Aristotle were the object of near-religious veneration. By 1700, however, the leading centers of learning throughout Europe turned not to antiquity for answers, but to Newton, Galileo, or the latest issue of the Philosophical Transactions of the Royal Society.

The cornerstone of this great intellectual revolution was the recognition of the value of the empirical method in science. Philosophical disputes (which we today refer to as scientific questions) were no longer to be settled by quoting from Aristotle or by deductions from self-evident principles both necessary and complete, but by carefully recorded observations relating to a theory expressed in mathematical form. The scientific method, as we understand it today, is largely a seventeenth-century invention. Freed from the dogmas of Aristotle and Ptolemy and propagated by the great scientific societies that sprang up across Europe, the infant prodigy became known as "the New Science," and a new science it truly was, as different from the old science as the predictions of Halley are from the prophecies of Nostradamus.

One of the leading champions of the New Science was Joseph Glanvill (plate 21), born in Plymouth, England, in 1636. He studied at Oxford and Lincoln College, earning the degree of master of arts, and was ordained into the ministry of the Anglican Church. But Glanvill never worked full-time at the ministry, because he was interested in too many other things. He published some sermons that are read to this day by people who read such things, but he achieved recognition during his lifetime primarily for his strong advocacy and clear exposition of the philosophy of the New Science.[1]

In 1664 Glanvill published *Sceptis Scientifica or, Confest Ignorance the Way to Science in an Essay of the Vanity of Dogmatizing, and Confident Opinions,* which received a great deal of attention in the small but growing scientific community. Glanvill presented a copy of this book to the Royal Society, the leading scientific body in Europe at that time, and it was so well received that Glanvill was soon elected a member.

In *The Vanity of Dogmatizing* we find a surprisingly modern exposition of the methodology of science, clearly showing that Glanvill and his colleagues intended to make a clean break with the dogmas of the past. "We look with a superstitious reverence upon the accounts of praeterlapsed ages," he wrote. "We reverence gray-headed Doctrines, though feeble, decrepit, and within a step of dust. We cannot gain a true assurance of any [theory], but by suspending our assent from all, till the deserts of each, discover'd by a strict enquiry, claim it . . . a *Scepticism,* that's the only way to science." Glanvill proclaimed: "Authorities alone with me make no number, unless Evidence of Reason stand before them.[2]

The Vanity of Dogmatizing shows that Glanvill had little use for the superstitious doctrines that were so prevalent in his time. He derides those who gave credence to the supposed astrological significance of celestial phenomena: "We need not be appal'd at Blazing Stars, and a Comet is no more ground for Astrological presage than a flaming Chimney."[3] (Glanvill was far more enlightened on this subject in 1664 than are millions of college-educated intellectualoids today.) He expresses sentiments so clearly modern that they must have seemed to many of his contemporaries to be seditious if not downright heretical.

Indeed, some of Glanvill's thinking on religion is quite liberal, even by the standards of many fundamentalist groups of today. He contends that what passes for true piety is often just indoctrination.[4] By asserting that "the Scripture is not all Allegory," he clearly implies that much of it *is*.[5] Glanvill even goes so far as to suggest that challenging religious teachings is *desirable*. Authority and Dogma meant so little to him who warned us of the "vanity of dogmatizing" that some of his religious colleagues went so far as to call him "atheist." Glanvill was no atheist, as his writings show, but he was a man of truly liberal persuasions, firmly committed to the empirical method in science and fully in favor of free and open debate on both religious and scientific questions.

But one realm in which Glanvill was convinced that exciting new discoveries awaited was in the scientific study of witchcraft. Glanvill played a key role in getting many learned men interested in studying this supposedly real phenomenon. He devoted an entire book to the subject: *Saducismus Triumphatus* (1666; revised, 1668, 1681, 1688, 1689), taking its name from the Hebrew Sadducees, who denied the reality of spirits and angels—the "triumph of the denial of spirits" was what Glanvill felt the supposedly excessive skepticism about witchcraft on the part of some of his colleagues was leading up to. Hence he set out to prove, *empirically,* that witches and apparitions unquestionably do exist.

"We have the attestation of thousands of Eye and Ear-witnesses, and those not of the easily-deceivable vulgar only, but of wise and grave discerners; and that, when no interest could oblige them to agree together in a common Lye," he observes. "For not only the melancholick and the fanciful, but the grave and the sober, whose judgements we have no reason to suspect to be tainted by their imaginations, have from their own knowledge and experience made reports of this nature."[6] In short, credible persons reporting incredible things.

Glanvill was anything but naively credulous: "I allow that the great body of Mankind is very credulous, and in this matter [witchcraft] so, that they do believe vain impossible things in relation to it," such as "carnal Copulation with the Devil, and real Transmutation of Men and Women into other creatures" (such transformations were held to be a type of unknown illusion). He admits further that "there are Ten thousand silly lying Stories of Witchcraft and Apparitions among the vulgar." (IFOs far outnumber true UFOs, as all scientific UFOlogists are aware.) "That infinite such have been occasioned by Cheats and Popish Superstitions . . . [that] Melancholy and Imagination have very great force, and can beget strange perswasions. And that many stories of Witchcraft and Apparitions have been but Melancholy fancies." He was careful to note that "there are many strange natural Diseases that have odd Symptoms . . . and that such are sometimes falsely ascribed to Witchcraft."[7]

But even after discounting all of these *false* reports of witchcraft, there still remains, he asserts, a hard-core residue of incidents that cannot be explained by any natural phenomenon. He instructs us that "a single relation for an Affirmative, sufficiently confirmed and attested, is worth a thousand tales of forgery and imposture, from whence an universal Negative cannot be concluded." ("It takes only one white crow to prove that not all crows are black" is how UFOlogists most commonly state this point.) Glanvill chastises those who consider themselves scientists to bear in mind that "to affirm that those evil spirits cannot do that which we conceit impossible, is boldly to stint the powers of Creatures, whose natures and faculties we know not; and to measure the world of Spirits by the narrow rules of our own impotent beings." ("The 'U' in UFO stands for 'unidentified'"; "There are more things in Heaven and Earth, Horatio, than are dreamed of in your philosophy.") The existence of witchcraft is, he says, an empirical fact: "Matters of fact well-proven ought not to be denied, because we cannot conceive how they can be performed. Nor is it a reasonable method of inference, first to presume the thing impossible, and thence to conclude, that the fact cannot be proved."[8] ("The Air Force's hypothesis about UFOs was, 'it can't be, therefore it isn't.'")

Just as today's UFOlogists hold that it will remain for the science of future centuries to fully explain UFOs, Glanvill admitted that there were many aspects of witchcraft for which his age had no explanation. For example, he had no explanation at all for the supposedly established fact that demon familiars (devils in the form of small animals, such as toads or cats) suck witches' milk from some unusual mark on a witch's body (usually a wart or mole). But this aspect of the phenomenon, no more puzzling than the UFOs' reported ability to defy gravity, did not trouble him unduly. "I say that we know so little of the nature of Daemons and Spirits, that 'tis no wonder we cannot certainly divine the reason of so strange an action."[9]

Saducismus Triumphatus, subtitled "Full and Plain Evidence Concerning Witches and Apparitions," is divided into two parts: "The first treating of their Possibility; the second of their Real Existence." The second part consists of a collection of more than three dozen carefully selected, reliably witnessed incidents of witchcraft and related phenomena, all from the recent past. (Some of the testimony had been gathered by Glanvill's associates after his sudden death in 1680 at age 44, to be included in the edition of 1689.) Only *recent* instances of witchcraft, in England or neighboring countries, were considered to be significant, because "things remote, or long past, are either not believed, or forgotten: whereas these being fresh and near, and attended with all the circumstances of credibility, it may be expected that they should have the more success upon the obstinacy of the Unbelievers."[10] Most of the witnesses to the events described were still alive at the time of publication. Upon such testimony Glanvill rested his entire case for the reality of the witchcraft phenomenon.

> In order to the proof that there have been, and are unlawful confederacies with evil spirits, by vertue of which the hellish accomplices perform things above their natural power; I must premise that this being matter of Fact, is only capable of evidence of authority and sense; and by both of these, the being of Witches and Diabolical contracts, is most abundantly confirm'd. All Histories are full of the exploits of these Instruments of darkness; and the testimony of all ages, not only of the rude and barbarous, but of the most civiliz'd and polish'd World, bring tidings of their strange performances.[11]

How convincing was the "evidence" assembled in support of witchcraft? Was it as impressive as the "evidence" presented for UFOs?

Julian Cox, an old woman about seventy years old, was indicted at Taunton in Somersetshire in 1663 (just three years before the first edition of *Saducismus Triumphatus*) on the charge of having bewitched a young maid whose body languished. The case was heard before Judge Archer. Four credible persons, all solid citizens (their names are withheld to ensure privacy, as is often done in UFO cases), gave sworn testimony as follows:

• Witness No. 1 was in the forest hunting, his hounds pursuing a hare. The animal was becoming exhausted and ran towards a large bush. When the witness reached the bush just seconds later, instead of a hare, he found Julian Cox lying in the bush! She was so out of breath that she was unable to speak. (Witches were frequently reported to change their shape from human to animal and back again.)

• Witness No. 2 was inside the witch's house and encountered a toad, which he tried to kill, believing it to be just an unwelcome pest. But he was reportedly unable to harm it: the toad could not be crushed, beaten, cut, or burned! Before his eyes, it reportedly vanished into nothingness, just as UFOs are reported to do. The witness assumed this "toad" to be the witch's demon familiar!

• Witness No. 3 was milking his cows one day when Julian Cox happened by; she remained in the vicinity for a short time. During the time she was near, the cows reportedly reacted violently to her presence. "His cattle ran mad, and some ran their heads against the trees, and most of them died speedily"—certainly a most astonishing way for animals as docile as cows to react to anyone! In UFO cases, incidents of reported animal reactions to the presence of UFOs are considered to be among the strongest possible proofs of the reality of the incident. We must accord the same weight to animal reactions in establishing the reality of the witchcraft phenomenon.

• Witness No. 4 reportedly saw Julian Cox fly in her chamber window.

The proof of the bewitching was established by testimony equally impressive. After Julian Cox became angry at the maiden, the girl fell ill, and saw visions of Cox and a black man tormenting her. This vision of Cox was stabbed in the leg with a knife blade—and the real woman was discovered to have a fresh wound in her leg, in exactly the same place! The maiden imagined that the witch was forcing her to swallow great pins. Soon large swellings formed upon her body, and several great pins were clearly seen to pass out of them. Let the skeptics try to explain that! After her arrest, Julian Cox testified that she had been recruited into witchcraft by three persons who came up to her, riding on broomsticks.

In the County of Cork, in 1661, the servant girl Mary Longdon had done something to annoy the alleged witch Florence Newton. About a week later, in an act of apparent reconciliation, Florence kissed her and said, "Mary, I pray thee, let thee and I be friends." But a few weeks afterward, Mary began to have sudden and violent fits, so powerful that "three or four Men could not hold her." In the course of these fits, she would often vomit up "Needles, Pins, Horse-nails, Stubbs, Wooll, and Straw." Before the onset of a fit, many small stones would reportedly rain upon her, following her wherever she went. "She and several others would see them both fall upon her and the ground," and then mysteriously vanish.

In her fits she reportedly saw Florence Newton tormenting her with pins. In alleged instances of levitation that dramatically foretell many UFO and psychokinesis reports of our present age, Mary was said to have been transported "to the top of the House laid on a board betwixt two Sollar Beams, sometimes put into a chest, sometimes under a parcel of Wooll, sometimes betwixt two Feather-beds." When Mary tried to read the Bible, the Good Book was mysteriously torn from her hands with such force that two persons couldn't hold it. These effects were confirmed in court by the testimony of John Pyne, Mary's employer, by Nicholas Pyne, and other witnesses. Mary recovered as soon as Florence was imprisoned at Youghall, but shortly thereafter the witch was moved to Cork and the girl became as ill as ever. It was then ascertained that the witch was no longer restrained in bolts. She was placed in bolts once again, and the girl's illness ceased.

In Stoke Trister, Somerset, in 1664, thirteen-year-old Elizabeth Hill was reported to have been bewitched by one Elizabeth Style. Credible persons reported that while the girl was seized by fits she would rise three or four feet out of her chair. Holes were then said to mysteriously appear in her hands, face, and neck; she said that the witch was pricking her with thorns. Affidavits were sworn by eight persons declaring that they personally witnessed these events.

In 1669, reports reached the Swedish king concerning a large-scale outbreak of witchcraft in the village of Mohra. The king dispatched some commissioners, both lay and clergy, "to examine the whole business." They found that the devil had apparently drawn hundreds of the village's children into his grasp and had even been seen "in a visible shape." After a careful investigation, they found no fewer than seventy adult witches in the village, who had managed to seduce about three hundred children into the practice of black magic.

The commissioners interviewed each of the children separately ("serious" UFO investigators believe that testimony given separately is reliable—even if the witnesses have had many months to swap their stories). The commissioners found that "all of them, except some very little ones" told stories that were highly consistent. They stated that they were supernaturally carried away to the witches' fest, riding through the air on the backs of animals. Far more witnesses gave testimony concerning supernatural effects at the Mohra witches' fest than concerning the famous 1959 close encounter in Boianai, New Guinea, which many regard as the most convincing UFO incident on record.[12] Forty-eight adults and children were executed for witchcraft in connection with this incident, "the day being bright and glorious, and the Sun shining, and some thousands of people being present at the Spectacle." Just before they were executed, the witches reported that the devil had appeared to them once again, "with Claws on his Hands and Feet, and with Horns on his Head, and a long Tail behind, and shewed to them a Pit burning." Certainly for the citizens of the village of Mohra to send dozens of its citizens, including children, to their deaths in this manner, the evidence of witchcraft must have appeared overpowering and irrefutable.

This has been a brief summary of some of the more remarkable accounts of witchcraft from the 1689 edition of *Saducismus*. Other books were being written at this time by empirical investigators of the phenomenon. In 1684 Richard Bovet, a graduate of Oxford, brought out *Pandaemonium, or The Devil's Cloyster Being a further blow to Modern Sadduceism, Proving the Existence of Witches and Spirits*. Bovet decries those "Saducists" who, "having deluded themselves & endeavouring to delude others into an opinion, that *because there is such a thing in the World as a Lye; therefore it is impossible there should be any Truth.* " (It doesn't matter how many UFO reports turn out to be lies or mistakes—only *true* UFOs are significant.) Bovet was obviously much influenced by Glanvill, and in truth he does not appear to have been an original thinker. His book does contain, however, a collection of reliably witnessed accounts of witchcraft and related phenomena that are independent of Glanvill. Bovet was careful to include only "Credible Modern Relations, most of which have happened within these [past] Few years, and will be attested by persons of Unquestionable Worth and Reputation now alive amongst us." Some selections:

• Mrs. J. H. Seavington, in the County of Somerset, had offended an old woman who was said to be a witch. Falling into fits, she would vomit up great numbers of pins and needles. Animals were also affected by the witch, especially chickens and cats.

• The falconer at the estate of "Sir J.F." near Shirbourn, in Dorsetshire, was said to have inadvertently raised "the Devil." Borrowing a book from the chaplain, he was reading it aloud in his room at night when a "frightful Goblin" reportedly appeared at his bedside. He called for the chaplain, who came and helped him get rid of it.

• The "Daemon of Spraitor" in the County of Devon, 1682, and another ghost were reported not only to attempt to strangle people with their own neckties, but also, taking a shoestring out of a shoe, they caused it to crawl about like a worm.

The Bovet book also includes two excellent reports of close encounters with fairies, including one with physical effects (a fairy encounter of the second kind?).

Other leading intellectuals of the seventeenth century joined Glanvill's crusade to establish the scientific respectability of the witchcraft phenomenon. Doctor Henry More, of Cambridge University, was one of the leading English philosophers of his day. He devoted much effort in attempting to convince his colleagues that the New Science was not incompatible with Christianity, and he was an early advocate of religious toleration. In 1652, More published *An Antidote Against Atheism,* which contains a great deal of testimony from reliable witnesses asserting the reality of witchcraft and apparitions. He fully supported Glanvill's methods and conclusions, and after Glanvill's death More contributed several additional relations of witchcraft to the posthumous editions of *Saducismus.*

Another member of the Royal Society, Robert Boyle (1627–1691), author of *The Sceptical Chemist* (1661), was one of the founding fathers of modern chemistry. He studied the properties of air and discovered the gas laws that today bear his name. He was the first to show that the pressure exerted by a gas is inversely proportional to its volume. He also did significant research on specific gravity, refraction, electricity, hydrostatics, and other subjects. Unlike many scientists whose names have become associated with the "paranormal," Boyle was a true scientific superstar, an intellect of the first magnitude. But Boyle supported Glanvill's research on witchcraft. He wrote:

> We live in an age, and a place, wherein all stories of witchcrafts, or other magical feats, are by many, even of the wise, suspected; and by too many that would pass for wits, derided and exploded . . . I scarcely believe one of twenty [reports] to be true, looking upon the other nineteen, as either false or suspicious . . . I doubt not, but one circumstantial narrative, fully verified . . . will be preferred by the curious and the judicious, to a hundred improbable, and slightly attested ones.[13]

In the cultural milieu of seventeenth-century England, even a scientist of Boyle's stature could believe that after we separate the credible accounts of witchcraft from the fanciful ones we are left with a hard-core residue of witchcraft cases for which there is no explanation. It seems likely that scientists of future ages will look back upon the UFO beliefs of our late twentieth century with similar amusement.

The name of Pierre Bayle was, during his lifetime (1647–1706), almost synonymous with the word "skeptic." This noted French philosopher took courageous stands against the prevailing doctrines of his day, whether scientific, religious, or political. In 1686, he made many enemies by issuing a highly controversial plea that religious freedom—a radical idea at that time—*be extended even to atheists.* Bayle asserted that one could still have a sense of morality even if one had no religion: "There are greater errors than to deny Providence." The political and religious commentaries in Bayle's famous encyclopedic dictionary[14] are described in the *Encyclopedia Britannica* as nothing less than "subversive criticism," "cleverly designed to undo whatever effect of orthodoxy the articles may have."

In 1682 Bayle hit equally hard at prevailing "scientific" beliefs in his discourse upon the great comet of 1680, which, like all comets, caused considerable panic among learned people and simple folk alike. Many scholars of that day believed comets to be of great astrological significance, a sign of divine displeasure portending great calamity for mankind. Bayle wrote a reasoned refutation of such beliefs. Many believed that "exhalations" from a comet caused harm to mankind. But Bayle demanded to see proof that such "exhalations" ever reached the earth. Comets merely reflect sunlight, he explained; what harmful effect is this supposed to have? Even if the influence of comets *did* reach the earth, he argued, there was no reason to believe their influence would not be *beneficial* rather than harmful. He pointed out that certain years in which comets were sighted turned out to be, on the whole, rather good years, free of any major calamities.[15]

But he felt that the strongest argument to be raised against the supposed influence of comets was "that Astrology, which is the foundation of predictions from Comets, is the most ridiculous thing in the world." Bayle did not mince words when denouncing astrology:

The particulars of the presage of Comets, resting solely upon the principles of Astrology, could be nothing but ludicrous, because there has never been anything more impertinent, never anything more chimerical than Astrology, nothing more ignominious to human nature, the disgrace of which it shall always be proper to proclaim, that there have been men base enough to cheat others upon the pretext of knowing the affairs of the heavens, & men foolish enough to give credence to them, even to the point of raising the Astrologer to an official position, & to never dare to buy new clothes, or plant a tree, without his approval.

If only the average citizen of today could be as rational on this subject as Bayle was three centuries ago. Indeed, were he to come to life again, even our own sophisticated age would find the irreverent, satirical tongue of a Pierre Bayle a mite too sharp for comfort.

But Pierre Bayle believed in the reality of the witchcraft phenomenon. He knew, as did Glanvill, that the great majority of the reports—nineteen out of twenty, in Robert Boyle's estimate—were but "melancholy and imagination."[16] Bayle fully understood the means whereby sincere but fanatical witchcraft investigators could influence a witness's testimony through asking leading questions: "It is very possible for a woman to become convinced someone has placed the Devil in her. All one needs to do is to ask her, when she believes she has been bewitched, if the supposed sorcerer made faces over her, and mumbled some words which serve as preliminaries for invoking the Demon he would set upon her."[17] (This perceptive observation is totally ignored by those who today investigate close encounters of the third kind, asking the witness leading questions about "classic" effects from such a supposed encounter, effects which the investigator helpfully spells out in detail. Much significance is then attached when the reply is in the affirmative.)

But even discounting such obviously fraudulent witchcraft cases, the superskeptical Bayle felt that the residue of reliably witnessed incidents of bewitchings could not be easily dismissed: "It seems that so far the question of witchcraft has only been considered by persons either too skeptical, or too credulous. Both are ill-fitted for success, & are most of the time guilty of the same mistakes, that is to make one's mind up to deny, or to believe, without looking into the matter."[18]

In view of Bayle's extraordinary forward-looking intellect and his many positive achievements, one cannot fault him too greatly for having been on the wrong side of this one question.

The subject of witchcraft was not the only one on which such independent thinkers as Glanvill, Boyle, Bayle, and More were wrong (and whatever their foibles, these heroic men played important roles in the struggle for science, rationality, and religious freedom). Glanvill's interest in the New Science, which was then making exciting discoveries in chemistry, astronomy, medicine, and other fields, led him to believe that entirely new vistas would soon be opened up in fields as yet completely unexplored. (UFO believers assert that UFOlogy is one such exciting vista awaiting us today.) Glanvill predicted that science might someday enable men to travel even to the moon.[19] This is the kind of prediction that everyone likes to remember! But somewhat less prescient was Glanvill's firm conviction that great discoveries were waiting to be made in the scientific study of sympathetic magic. This is the type of "science" practiced by a witch doctor who sticks pins in a doll hoping to thereby injure the victim, whom the doll resembles. Glanvill predicted that wounds would someday be healed by treating the weapon that caused them and that long-distance communication could be achieved using needles "impregnated" by the same magnet, or using "sympathized hands." (One wonders if the "future science" of UFOlogy is akin to Glanvill's "future science" of sympathetic magic?)

Another of Glanvill's predictions that was wildly off base was that future telescopes would be so powerful that they would be able to reveal whether or not other planets are inhabited. There is a fundamental limitation to optical performance—the result of the wave nature of light—which was totally unknown to science in the seventeenth century. Hence Glanvill had no way of knowing that any such limitation existed, and he naively assumed that telescope progress would continue indefinitely at the pace it did during his century.

Glanvill was not alone in making such gaffes. Robert Boyle wrote in 1675 a treatise titled "Some Physico-theological Considerations About the Possibility of the Resurrection." In it, he explained how the newly explored field of chemical transformations suggested the possibility of the resurrection of the flesh. Here was a glorious vista soon to open to future science! Even the noted philosopher and mathematician René Descartes (1596–1650) was no better at predicting future scientific achievements. He felt that the transmutation of elements—a principal claim of the pseudoscience of alchemy—did in fact actually occur, and he attempted to provide a plausible explanation of how it worked.[20] No doubt he felt that future generations would remember him not only as a mathematician and philosopher but as the Galileo of alchemy as well.

Those who today predict that absolutely *anything* will be possible in the future—to lend credence to the plausibility of present-day UFO visitations— would do well to consider whether there may not exist other equally fundamental limitations that will be faced by advanced technological civilizations, limits we know absolutely nothing of today. "Any sufficiently advanced technology will be indistinguishable from magic," Arthur C. Clarke has written. But from this it does *not* follow that all reports of magic represent artifacts of some advanced technology. It is next to impossible to predict what kinds of things will, or will not, be possible to future ages. In making his predictions, Glanvill was wrong more often than he was right.

Those who today make sweeping predictions about the capabilities of supposed UFO technologies should bear this in mind.

Where did Glanvill and others go wrong in their conclusions about witchcraft? They were careful to limit themselves to cases in or near their own country from the recent past. They eliminated from consideration all reports except those emanating from highly reliable sources, from individuals whose testimony would be accepted in any court of law. Their methodology was that of science, not superstition. Yet they reached a conclusion that is obviously untenable, a *reductio ad absurdum* that nullifies not only their own conclusions but those of researchers of all other supposed phenomena whose methodologies are analogous. How did this happen?

The seventeenth-century "scientific" investigators of witchcraft made no allowances for the inherent inaccuracies in human testimony: the fact that in a small but relatively fixed percentage of instances, whether through excessive belief and hysteria or outright fraud, gross misrepresentations and inaccuracies will creep into the narrative. It is a corollary of the Second Law of Thermodynamics: information cannot be transmitted and retained with perfect accuracy, and the level of accuracy will diminish with time. As every information scientist and every communications engineer is well aware, a certain amount of noise is going to work its way into every transmission. If this noise is great enough, the original message will be so garbled as to be unrecognizable. Just as the universal law of entropy dictates that physical objects such as automobiles, buildings, and human bodies must slowly but inexorably fall apart, each transmission of information—each human narrative—must just as inevitably suffer the same fate. When a sufficient amount of "noise" has been introduced into the narrative we are left with a spurious residue of "unexplained" cases.

Glanvill and the other seventeenth-century intellectuals knew nothing of entropy and information theory. They had no organized studies of human psychology available to establish beyond all doubt the fallibility of uncorroborated human testimony. Nor were they likely to be aware of what Oberg terms the fallacy of the "zero residue": that the explanation rate must be a perfect 100 percent. In any type of investigation, whether missing person, criminal, or cause-of-accident, there always remains a small percentage of cases in which, because of incomplete information or misleading testimony, no definitive solution is ever obtained. This does *not* imply, however, that some mysterious forces are kidnapping persons, committing crimes, and causing accidents. We recognize that perfection and omniscience are not human attributes and adjust our expectations accordingly. A police force might well take pride in solving 96 percent of the crimes reported to it. Some investigators of witchcraft and UFOs, however, would interpret an explanation rate of 96 percent as signifying the existence of mysterious forces at work in 4 percent of the cases.

Ignorance of all these factors is fully understandable for individuals living three hundred years ago. It is *not,* however, so easily excused when such ignorance is found rampant among UFO investigators of the present day.

Those who advocate the "scientific" study of UFOs compliment themselves on being the Galileos of a glorious new age. But Galileos they are not. They are the Glanvills of the present day, destined to be remembered for "their follies rather than [for] their virtues," if indeed they are to be remembered at all. (How many readers knew anything of Glanvill before picking up this book? And will anyone outside a small, specialized circle of historians recognize the names of the leaders of the pro-UFO movement three hundred years hence?)

It is doubtful whether future historians will on the whole be as charitable toward today's UFO believers as they are toward the scientific investigators of witchcraft. For whatever their faults, Glanvill, More, and their associates were forward-thinking individuals who truly represented the beginning of a new age, an age of reason, science, and liberty. But the world-view of today's UFO believers represents a throwback to the almost boundless credulity of the prescientific era, when practically *any* tale of the miraculous was accepted so long as it fit with other stories that were being reported. These people personify the type of thinking that the New Science was rebelling against. Such attitudes may have been understandable in the seventeenth century when the New Science was young, frail, and not yet in complete control of the academic world. But as we now prepare to enter the twenty-first century, such naive and unscientific attitudes are a clear identification of one who wishes to turn back the clock, longing for the uncritical, miraculous universe of the Middle Ages.

NOTES

1. For biographies of Glanvill see Ferris Greenslet, *Joseph Glanvill* (New York: Columbia University Press, 1900); Moody Prior, "Joseph Glanvill, Witchcraft, and Seventeenth-Century Science," *Modern Philology* 30, no. 2 (1932).

2. Glanvill, *The Vanity of Dogmatizing* (1664 edition), pp. 137, 143.

3. *Vanity of Dogmatizing,* p. 175.

4. *Vanity of Dogmatizing,* p. 128.

5. Glanvill, *Saducismus Triumphatus* (1689 edition), p. 273.

6. *Saducismus,* pp. 67, 84.

7. *Saducismus,* p. 272.

8. *Saducismus,* pp. 72, 73, 87.

9. *Saducismus,* p. 75.

10. *Saducismus,* p. 63.

11. *Saducismus,* p. 67.

12. For the account of a close encounter in New Guinea see Philip J. Klass, *UFOs Explained* (New York: Random House, 1974), chapter 22.

13. Robert Boyle, letter to Glanvill, September 18, 1677, from *Works of the Honourable Robert Boyle, in Six Volumes,* London, 1772.

14. Pierre Bayle, *Dictionnaire Historique et Critique,* 1697.

15. Bayle, *Pensées Diverse Sur la Comete Qui Parut au Mois de December MDCLXXX,* *1682.*

16. Saducismus, p. 272.

17. Bayle, "Response aux Questions d'un Provencial," *Oeuvres Diverses,* a la Haye, 1727, Tome Troisième, Deuxième Partie, p. 559.

18. Bayle, *Oeuvres Diverses,* Tome Premier, p. 616.

19. *Vanity of Dogmatizing,* p. 181.

20. René Descartes, Letter to P. Mesland, February 9, 1645, *Oeuvres,* IV.

8

GOSSAMER GAMBOLLERS

Who taught me to curl myself inside a buttercup? Iolanthe! Who taught me to swing upon a cobweb? Iolanthe! Who taught me to dive into a dewdrop — to nestle in a nutshell — to gambol upon gossamer? Iolanthe! — The Queen of the Fairies, in Gilbert and Sullivan's *Iolanthe.*

We often use the phrase "fairy tale" to refer to some story that we consider to be absolutely unworthy of belief. The implication is that nothing could possibly be more absurd or foolish than a tale that describes the activities of "fairies," the quaint, charming little creatures that are said to populate the moors and glens. But not many people are aware that there is a significant collection of highly reliable eyewitness testimony, and even actual photographs, that suggest that stories that tell of fairies are not so totally absurd as one might at first imagine.

Some UFO investigators have noted the similarity between the fairy stories of previous ages and the UFO occupant sightings reported today. Dr. Jacques Vallee has been especially interested in this relationship, and he has written extensively on the subject. Vallee has gone so far as to suggest that the phenomena are probably one and the same; that whatever the "little people" of old may have been, and whatever the "UFO occupants" of today may be, they represent the same thing, as described by different cultures.[1]

What many people do not realize about fairy stories is that there exists a sizable body of eyewitness testimony from our own twentieth century from people who claim to have seen tiny winged fairies, people whose testimony would be accepted in any court of law. None of these people appear to be unbalanced or untrustworthy in any manner, nor is there any conceivable motive for them to fabricate their testimony. Even more remarkable, a series of photographs were obtained that show a number of tiny winged fairies frolicking in the forest. *These photographs were submitted to seemingly expert scrutiny, and have been pronounced authentic.* In short, the evidence for the existence of tiny winged fairies is hardly less impressive than the evidence produced in support of the UFO phenomenon. Where is the fairy evidence to be found?

The modern era of scientific fairy investigations was ushered in by a man whose name remains a household word even today: Sir Arthur Conan Doyle. Everyone is familiar with Doyle as the creator of Sherlock Holmes, the legendary detective whose popularity as the single most famous detective in literature has never been challenged. But Doyle was also noted for his investigations of the supernatural and the occult. Doyle's son had been killed in World War I, and like so many other bereaved parents he turned to spiritualism as a means of assuaging his grief.

Doyle became the recognized leader of the spiritualist movement in England. He claimed to have spoken to his deceased son no fewer than six times, as well as to a ghostly host of other departed friends and relatives. Although skeptical researchers had shown one "authentic" medium after another to have been fraudulent, Sir Arthur's faith in the authenticity of at least *some* manifestations was never shaken. He remained convinced that there was a signal buried in the noise, and no amount of rational persuasion, no possible revelation of shocking chicanery and fraud, could ever shake his naive faith.

Doyle's close friend Harry Houdini, the legendary magician and escape artist, was a complete skeptic regarding spiritualist phenomena, and he considered Doyle excessively credulous in this matter. As the unchallenged master conjuror of our century, Houdini was not fooled by the sleight-of-hand trickery of those who called themselves "mediums." But Doyle, who was not only less aware of magicians' tricks but also had some compelling personal reasons to believe, was bamboozled by virtually every self-styled spiritualist he encountered. The friendship between Doyle and Houdini became severely strained by this fundamental difference in outlook; in time it was ended completely. In fairness to Doyle, it should be noted that many scientists of the very highest reputation, among them Sir Oliver Lodge and Sir William Crookes, were just as easily fooled by the phony spiritualists that a magician like Houdini found so transparent. (The same scenario is repeated today in the celebrated "Geller phenomenon": top magicians cry "Fraud!" while any number of all-too-credulous scientists are ready and eager to believe.)

Once Doyle's mind had been "opened" to the possibility of a totally new and unsuspected realm of existence beyond the physical, he began to consider that other nonphysical creatures in addition to spirits might populate the universe. What other kinds of creatures do we find in literature and in legend, but whose existence is discounted by modern science? One such legendary creature immediate comes to mind: the fairy. "Victorian science would have left the world hard and clean and bare, like a landscape in the moon," Doyle wrote, seeking to roll back the frontiers of materialism far enough to admit not just spirits but fairies as well.[2]

Doyle began a fresh examination of the evidence for the existence of fairies, and he found it to be most impressive. Reliable persons, not only in forgotten ages but in the twentieth century as well, testify that they have seen, at close range, tiny winged creatures no more than a few inches high. No conceivable motive can be suggested as to why these people might fabricate their testimony; indeed, first-hand testimony such as this would be accepted by any court of law. So convincing was the evidence he obtained that Sir Arthur began writing an article for *Strand* magazine titled "The Evidence for Fairies." Among the cases Doyle cited were the following:

• The Reverend S. Baring-Gould, a noted authority on folklore, reports that in the year 1838, when he was four years old, he was riding on the box of a carriage one hot summer day, when he was astonished to see "legions of dwarfs about two feet high running along beside the horses." The boy's father saw nothing, and quickly placed his son inside the carriage to get him out of the sun. Since Jacques Vallee has written on the UFOlogical significance of sightings of the Red and Black Meu, which only Vallee's four-year-old daughter was able to see, it is clear that scientific UFOlogists should take accounts like the one given by Baring-Gould very seriously indeed.

• Baring-Gould also reports that when his wife was a girl of fifteen, she was walking down a lane in Yorkshire between green hedges, when she chanced to look down into the hedges and see "a little green man, perfectly well made, who looked at her with his beady black eyes." She was so frightened that she ran home. Doyle observes that "a girl of fifteen is old enough to be a good witness, and her flight and the clear detail of her memory point to a real experience." Yet another member of Baring-Gould's family, his son, relates seeing "a little man wearing a red cap, a green jacket, and brown knee-breeches" hiding among the pea-pods in the garden.

• Mrs. Violet Tweedale related to Doyle an experience she had some five years earlier, around 1915. One summer afternoon, while she was walking along the Avenue of Lupton House in Devonshire, she spotted a leaf of wild iris that was reportedly swinging and bending wildly. "Expecting to see a field mouse astride it, I stepped very softly up to it. What was my delight to see a tiny green man. He was about five inches long . . . I had a vision of a merry little face and something red in the form of a cap on the head. For a full minute he remained in view, swinging on the leaf. Then he vanished." Mrs. Tweedale's description of the color of the fairy's cap and jacket exactly matches that described independently by Baring-Gould's son! Hence we find independent witnesses agreeing on significant details—the kind of evidence that no UFOlogist can afford to ignore! Doyle also observes that "in the bending of the iris we have something objective . . . which cannot easily be explained away as a cerebral hallucination . . . an impressive piece of evidence." Tangible physical effects such as the bending of the iris suggest that this incident must be adjudged a "fairy encounter of the second kind."

• One Mrs. H., who requested that her name not be disclosed, gives the following account: "My only sight of a fairy was in a large wood in West Sussex, about nine years ago. He was a little creature about half a foot high, dressed in leaves." Again, the sighting took place in the summer, and the fairy was wearing green! Surely this remarkable agreement on details cannot be due to coincidence.

• Mr. Lonsdale, of Bournemouth, England, reports the following fairy sighting, occurring as he sat very still in the garden of the Branksome Park estate. "Suddenly I was conscious of a movement on the edge of the lawn . . . I saw several little figures dressed in brown peering through the bushes . . . in a few seconds a dozen or more small people about two feet in height, in bright clothes and with radiant faces, ran on to the lawn, dancing hither and thither . . . . this continued for four or five minutes." His companion, Mr. Turvey, corroborated his story. The fairies remained, one of them swinging round and round on a croquet hoop, until they were frightened away by a servant bringing tea.

Other such reports follow. Doyle points out:

> These numerous testimonies come from people who are very solid and practical and successful in the affairs of life. One is a distinguished writer, another an ophthalmic authority, a fourth a lady engaged on public service, and so on. To waive aside the evidence of such people on the ground that it does not correspond with our own experience is an act of mental arrogance which no wise man will commit.[3]

In short, credible persons reporting incredible things, to use the UFOlogists' favorite phrase. The evidence for fairies cannot be lightly dismissed unless we are likewise prepared to dismiss the same kind of testimony about UFOs.

"By a curious coincidence, if it be indeed a coincidence," explains Arthur Conan Doyle—he had just finished writing the article from which the above is taken—unexpectedly, fully conclusive evidence "for the actual existence of fairies was brought to my notice." Through the assistance of several friends and acquaintances who were members of the Theosophical Society (a mystical sect claiming esoteric wisdom, one of whose beliefs is in the reality of fairies), Doyle obtained copies of two photographs that were purported to be authentic pictures of fairies.

The photos were said to have been taken, without assistance, by two young girls of the village of Cottingley in Yorkshire. Miss Elsie Wright was thirteen years old in 1917, when the photographs were taken, and her cousin Frances Griffiths was ten. Frances was living with the Wrights while her father was with the British forces on the Continent.

Doyle obtained copies of the fairy photographs through the courtesy of Edward L. Gardner, a member of the executive committee of the

Theosophical Society. By an astonishing coincidence, Mrs. Wright, Elsie's mother, was also "a reader of theosophical teachings and had gained spiritual good from them." (We recall that Theosophist teachings proclaim that fairies are real.) These facts alone should have warned Doyle to be especially wary of the supposed fairy photographs, since they so conveniently happened to confirm the teachings of the people who were promoting them. "I have never quite lost sight of the fact that it is a curious coincidence that so unique an event should have happened in a family some members of which were already inclined to occult study," Doyle observed.[4] Yet he saw no reason at all to be suspicious about this.

The two girls claimed that practically every time they went outside they played with fairies, a claim their parents did not believe (although a student of theosophy like Mrs. Wright should have found nothing unbelievable about that). According to the Wrights' story, one day Elsie finally persuaded her father to let them borrow his new camera, so they could prove that there really *were* fairies in the Cottingley beck and glen. (Unfortunately for science, the fairies were very selective about to whom they would appear. The fairies would never show up if any strangers were present, nor if one of the two girls was away.) After being briefly instructed in the use of the camera (an old-fashioned one, holding just a single glass plate at a time), the girls reportedly returned soon afterwards with a photograph, which, when developed in Mr. Wright's darkroom, revealed the image entitled "Frances and the Fairies" (plate 22). A few weeks later, the girls reportedly obtained a second photograph, this one depicting "Elsie and the Gnome" (plate 23). In it we see a tiny, winged creature less than a foot high, sporting an Elizabethan collar, a little pointed hat, and carrying a Pan's pipe. It has never been explained why, after obtaining two supposedly authentic photographs of fairies in two attempts, the girls did not obtain dozens more, to crush by sheer volume the inevitable future criticism that the photos were carefully posed, painstakingly produced studio fakes.

Doyle found the photographic evidence for fairies to be quite persuasive. He introduced them to the world in an article in the Christmas 1920 issue of *Strand* magazine, in which he argued for their authenticity. The photos created an immediate sensation in England and abroad. Most people were, of course, skeptical of the photos. Critics pointed out that Elsie had worked for several months in a photographer's studio in Bradford and hence would have had ample opportunity to learn camera trickery. It was also noted that in the photo Frances is not looking at the fairies, but is staring directly into the camera instead. Gardner, however, had a ready answer for this objection: while Frances had seen fairies nearly every day, this was the first time she had seen a camera used up close, and hence, "for her, cameras were much more novel than fairies."[5]

Doyle is to be given credit for his sense of honesty and fair play, for unlike most UFOlogists, he devotes much space in his book *The Coming of the Fairies* (1921) to presenting and analyzing the skeptics' arguments *against* the fairy evidence. UFO proponents, on the other hand, will generally go to almost any lengths to prevent the research of skeptical UFOlogists from being presented to the public (such as not listing skeptical books in their UFO bibliographies, while including the books of irresponsible UFO proponents).

Doyle urged Gardner to get the two girls to attempt to obtain additional fairy photographs. This seemed to pose some difficulties, as the girls were no longer living together and no fairies could supposedly be seen unless both of them were present. Due to the girls' respective family and school obligations, the only time they could be together during that year (1920) was during the latter half of August. This should, however, have provided plenty of time for the girls to have obtained dozens, or hundreds, of additional fairy photographs. After all, they claimed to see fairies nearly every day! Gardner supplied Elsie and Frances with two good-quality cameras and twenty-four plates. He then departed. Asked why he did not remain in the vicinity to witness this extraordinary phenomenon, Gardner explained that "the fairy life will not 'come out' from the shrubs and plants around unless the human visitor is of a sympathetic quality."[6] (It is, of course, difficult to imagine anyone more sympathetic to the fairy phenomenon than he was.)

The girls, however, did not obtain two dozen fairy photographs in this two-week period. They obtained exactly three. One shows "Frances and the Leaping Fairy." A second depicts a "Fairy Offering a Posy of Hare Bells to Elsie." Once again the girl is not looking directly at the fairy; Gardner explains that if the "sprite" is "motionless and aware of being gazed at then the nature spirit will usually withdraw and apparently vanish." (See chapter 16 on jealous phenomena.) The third photo purports to show "Fairies and Their Sun-Bath," which Doyle found to be totally convincing: "Any doubts which had remained in my mind as to honesty were completely overcome," stated the man who created Sherlock Holmes, "for it was clear that these pictures, specially the ones of the fairies in the bush [the "magnetic" sunbath], were altogether beyond the possibility of fake."[7]

The reason that only three fairy photos were obtained during a full two-week interval was, according to Gardner, that "during that second fortnight in August, 1920, it rained almost continuously throughout the country. The papers reported the rain as general. . . . [the girls] had been able to go up to the glen only on two occasions when, in the afternoon of two days, the sun had shone."[8]

However, Gardner's statements are not confirmed by meteorological records. *British Rainfall, 1920,* a publication of His Majesty's Stationary Office, states that "Anticyclonic conditions [that is, fair weather] prevailed during the middle and latter part of the month and the weather, though cool, was on the whole dry." The weather station in Bradford, near

Cottingley, reports that rainfall for August 1920 was 38 percent below normal, and similar readings were obtained throughout the region.[9] It is difficult to imagine where Gardner found all those newspaper stories reporting a deluge.

The original materials pertaining to the incident at Cottingley today rest in a library at the University of Leeds in England, where they are accessible to researchers.[10] The final blow to the authenticity of the Cottingley photographs was dealt by the British psychical researcher Fred Gettings. In a children's book of stories and poems titled *Princess Mary's Gift Book,* published in 1915, he found a drawing containing dancing female figures in flowing robes, whose appearance almost precisely matches that of Frances's fairies, sans wings. The poem is about conjuring up fairies and refers to their "azure wings." The poses are so astonishingly similar as to leave no reasonable doubt that three of the four fairies in "Frances and the Fairies" were taken from this book. Gettings suggests that the girls copied the drawings, added wings, stuck the fairy figures in the grass, and photographed them.[11]

After the story of the Cottingley fairies was published in *Strand,* a wave of fairy sightings rippled across England. Soon sightings also began to roll in from countries around the world. Doyle set up what was in essence a "clearing-house" for reliably witnessed fairy encounters, to which persons could report their experiences without fear of unwanted publicity. As was the case in the wake of the release of the motion picture *Close Encounters of the Third Kind* some fifty-seven years later, relatively few *new* fairy sightings were generated by Doyle's controversial article. Instead, a significant number of *old* fairy sightings "came out of the closet," now that there was at last someone to whom they could be reported without fear of ridicule.

• From the Isle of Man, the Reverend Arnold J. Holmes reported the following sighting, occurring on a deserted road one night: "My horse—a spirited one—suddenly stopped dead, and looking ahead I saw . . . what appeared to be a small army of indistinct figures—very small, clad in gossamer garments . . . I watched spellbound, my horse half mad with fear . . . one 'little man' of larger stature than the rest, about fourteen inches high, stood at attention until all had passed him dancing, singing with happy abandon, across the Valley fields towards St. John's Mount."[12] In this instance the horse reportedly reacted to the fairies' presence, which would seem to rule out the possibility that these creatures were merely illusory. UFO investigators consider reports of animal reactions to UFOs to be a powerful indication that a sighting is authentic. Animals do not hallucinate, as the UFO buffs are fond of reminding us! Hence we must find animal reactions equally convincing when examining fairy evidence.

• From the Maori districts of New Zealand, Mrs. Hardy reported: "One evening when it was getting dusk I went into the yard to hang the tea-towels on the clothesline. As I stepped off the veranda, I heard a soft galloping coming from the direction of the orchard . . . suddenly a little figure, riding a tiny pony, rode right under my uplifted arms. I looked round, to see that I was surrounded by eight or ten tiny figures on tiny ponies . . . at the sound of my voice they all rode through the rose trellis across the drive . . . I heard the soft galloping dying away into the distance."

• Mrs. Rose of Southend-on-Sea reported: "I see them constantly here in the shrubbery by the sea . . . the gnomes are like little old men, with little green caps, and their clothes are generally neutral green . . . I have seen the gnomes arranging a sort of moss bed for the fairies."[13]

In the most remarkable of the subsequent fairy encounters, Elsie and Frances returned to the fairy glen in August of 1921 in the company of Geoffery L. Hodson, a Theosophist writer. All three of them claim to have witnessed a wide range of manifestations of fairy phenomena:

• *Water nymph:* "In the beck [brook] itself . . . an entirely nude female figure with long fair hair . . . I was not sure whether it had any feet or not . . . it did not detatch itself from the surroundings in which it was in some way merged."

• *Wood elves:* "Two tiny wood elves came racing over the ground past us as we sat on a fallen tree trunk . . . As Frances came up and sat within a foot of them they withdrew, as if in alarm, a distance of eight feet or so."

• *A brownie:* "He is rather taller then the normal, say eight inches . . . bag-shaped cap, almost conical, knee breeches, stockings, thin ankles, and large pointed feet—like gnomes' feet."

• *Goblins:* "A group of goblins came running towards us from the wood to within fifteen feet of us. They differ somewhat from the wood elves."

• "All three of us keep seeing weird creatures as of elemental essence."[14]

What we have, in short, are credible people reporting incredible things. How significant it must be that three persons reporting seeing this astonishing manifestation of fairy-related phenomena. Surely three sane persons cannot all share the same hallucination. If testimony of this caliber were offered in support of a UFO sighting, many UFO groups would accept the account as gospel. Indeed, the supposed evidence for fairies—which we have but briefly highlighted here—is remarkably similar in character to the evidence offered in support of UFOs. While it is true that the sheer volume of UFO reports far exceeds that of fairy sightings, since little men from space appeal a great deal more to the public's current fancy than do little men in the forest, the very same kind of evidence is being offered in support of both; we have many sightings, a few photographs, but a complete dearth of tangible evidence for either fairies or UFOs. It is difficult to see how one can accept the existence of UFOs and yet remain skeptical about fairies.

Should the reader think that the preceding comment is merely facetious, we need only observe that a number of prominent "new wave" UFOlogists are beginning to take sightings of fairies very seriously. A few have even gone so far as to endorse the reality of the Cottingley photographs. Some examples:

• Jacques Vallee has written at length in *Passport to Magonia* on the parallels between the UFO and fairy phenomena. Both reportedly leave behind rings on the ground, both are said sometimes to kidnap unsuspecting humans, both involve strange diminutive humanoid creatures, both appear to involve "another dimension" of existence, and so forth. Vallee scrutinizes reports from previous centuries (although he does not seem to be aware of the incident at Cottingley). *Passport to Magonia,* published in 1969, was to exert great influence on the direction of the UFO movement, perhaps more so than any book written after the 1950s. Its influence is still felt today; this book, more than any other, is responsible for the "new wave" of "para-normal" UFOlogy (that is, UFOs are thought to be real, but not "visitors from space").

• Jerome Clark devoted an entire chapter in his popular book *The Unidentified* to credible accounts of "fairyland," which he later tied in with the UFO phenomenon. Six pages are given to the Cottingley incident, the authenticity of which he was inclined to accept. But he stopped just short of a firm endorsement of the photographs showing fairies leaping into the air and relaxing in a magnetic sunbath; he stated "whatever one's personal reservations may be (and we admit that we are not free of them), for the time being, at least, the Cottingley photographs will have to take their place in the case for the reality of the fairy folk." As a result of recent evidence *against* the Cottingley photos, summed up in this chapter, Clark revised his views and now agrees that these "fairies" are hoaxes, claiming "I have never "believed" in the Cottingley photographs." Yet as recently as the February 1977 issue of *Fate* magazine, Clark stated: "It now remains for the skeptics to explain (1) how Elsie and Frances could have faked the pictures in the first place and (2) why they continue to insist they did not, long after they have no reason to lie."[15]

• John Keel, in a highly successful book, *UFOs: Operation Trojan Horse,* seems to harbor fewer reservations than did Clark about the reality of the Cottingley incident. Keel writes, "Sir Arthur Conan Doyle performed a lengthy investigation into one set of photos of fairies taken in England by a couple of children. Apparently they were authentic."[16]

• In Brad Steiger's popular and influential UFO book *Gods of Aquarius,* modestly subtitled *UFOs and the Transformation of Man,* we find a description of the author's own fairy encounter of the third kind: "When I was a child, I saw what was commonly referred to as an elf. I believe that I must have surprised him as much as he did me . . . I have never forgotten that smile or his merry, compelling eyes, and I have walked many a strange path and turned many a bizarre corner in the hope that I might once again meet my multidimensional friend."[17]

"These numerous testimonies come from people who are very solid and successful in the affairs of life," wrote Conan Doyle. "To waive aside the evidence of such people on the ground that it does not correspond with our own experience is an act of mental arrogance which no wise man will commit." His point is well taken. How can one disregard the evidence for fairies unless one is likewise prepared to toss aside every reported UFO sighting on record?

The next time the reader hears someone refer to a tall story as a "fairy tale," remember that Galileo was once laughed at too. Will future generations look back at the long-suffering Sir Arthur Conan Doyle for his pioneering work in making fairy research a legitimate scientific field? Perhaps he will be respectfully remembered as the Galileo of Fairy Studies.

NOTES

1. Jacques Vallee, *Passport to Magonia* (Chicago: Regnery, 1969).

2. Arthur Conan Doyle, *The Coming of Fairies* (1921, reprinted 1975 by Samuel Weiser, Inc., New York), p. 125. The entire book is devoted to presenting evidence for the reality of fairies.

3. Doyle, pp. 140–41.

4. Doyle, pp. 44, 95.

5. Doyle, pp. 65, 91.

6. Edward L. Gardner, *Fairies: The Cottingley Photos and Their Sequel* (London: Theosophical Publishing House, 1945), p. 25.

7. Gardner, p. 28; Doyle, p. 94.

8. Gardner, pp. 25–26.

9. *British Rainfall, 1920,* issued by authority of the Meteorological Committee, London, 1921, p. 100, table 3.

10. The original negatives and prints of the Cottingley photos, as well as of the correspondence, clippings, and other related materials from Gardner's collection were donated to the University of Leeds after his death. The Cottingley materials are now the property of the Institute of Dialect and Folk Life Studies, Brotherton Collection, the Brotherton Library, University of Leeds, Leeds LS2 9JT, England.

11. Jerome Clark, *Fate,* November 1978, p. 68; see also Robert Sheaffer, *Fate,* June 1978, p. 76.

12. Doyle, pp. 156–57.

13. Doyle, pp. 155–68.

14. Doyle, pp. 108–22.

15. Jerome Clark and Loren Coleman, *The Unidentified* (New York: Warner Paperbacks, 1975), pp. 80–87.

16. John Keel, *UFOs: Operation Trojan Horse* (New York: Putnam, 1970), chapter 12 (paperback titled *Why UFOs?* [Manor, 1976, p. 215]).

17. Brad Steiger, *Gods of Aquarius* (New York: Harcourt, Brace, Jovanovich, 1976), p. 11.

9

A REAL UFO EXPERIENCE

A single relation for an affirmative, sufficiently confirmed and attested, is worth a thousand tales of forgery and imposture, from whence an universal negative cannot be concluded. — Joseph Glanvill, 1666.

"The UFO Center has been established for those who wish to see positive scientific action taken to end a quarter century of misrepresentation and buffoonery."[1] With these words, the newly organized Center for UFO Studies announced the reason for its existence. No longer would investigations of UFO sightings be carried out in an amateurish, haphazard manner. A "UFO Central" had at long last been established to act as a clearinghouse for UFO sightings, to coordinate scientists' efforts to solve the UFO enigma.

The organizer and director of the Center for UFO Studies, Dr. J. Allen Hynek, is perhaps the best known of all UFO investigators. Hynek served for fifteen years as chairman of the Department of Astronomy at Northwestern University in Evanston, Illinois, directing both the Dearborn Observatory and the Lindheimer Astronomical Research Center. He was also the chief astronomical consultant to the Air Force in its UFO investigations from 1948 until the Air Force ended its research on unidentified flying objects in 1969. Hynek has played such a prominent role in the history of the UFO phenomenon that *Newsweek* magazine dubbed him "Mr. UFO." (UFO publisher, promoter, and entrepreneur Timothy Green Beckley has recently tried to usurp that title for himself, but thus far it seems to have fallen flat—like Beckley's claims about a secret UFO base at the bottom of one of the Great Lakes—having appeared only in his own promotional literature.)

Hynek has often spoken of the existence of an "Invisible College" of scientists who approach the subject of UFOs without ridicule. Some of them have carried out independent investigations into the nature of the phenomenon. The UFO Center was founded to bring together people such as these.

To achieve the aim of receiving as much significant UFO information as possible and storing it in a Central Data Bank, the Center has established a toll-free telephone service, UFO Central, which operates around the clock, twenty-four hours a day, seven days a week. This makes it possible for the Center to receive notification of significant UFO sightings without delay, almost as soon as they occur. In 1967 Hynek wrote that if a nationwide telephone "hotline" were carried out for a full year by a UFO investigative organization and yielded nothing, it would be "of great negative significance." "Then we could go back to the 'real, commonsense world' of pre-UFO days—shrugging it all off with, 'There must have been a virus going around.'"[2] Now that a nationwide "hotline" has been in operation for more than six years and has yielded nothing, Hynek has not made any more such statements.

The hotline's toll-free number, however, is never released to the Center's investigators and contributors; it is reserved for the exclusive use of "law enforcement and other responsible agencies." A similar hotline, however, was initiated by APRO, for use by its general membership. APRO openly printed its UFO Alert number in its bulletin—something that the UFO Center has never done. Even the UFO Center's generous fellows and patrons are kept in the dark. Apparently more confident of its supporters, APRO instructed the caller to call collect and to "have your facts before you," so that the call can be kept under three minutes in length.[3]

One would assume, from all of the Center's publications, that any UFO sighting reported by a law-enforcement agency to the Center for UFO Studies would be, if it is deemed significant, subjected to *the most rigorous and thorough investigation possible under present-day science.* The Center has outlined its research program, which includes "laboratory analysis of residues," "theoretical studies of dynamic and luminescent properties of UFO's," "credibility of witnesses," and "photographic and spectrographic analysis,"[4] each carried out by a trained professional utilizing the full capabilities of the laboratory or university with which he is associated. Should any UFO sighting stand up under such expert scrutiny, especially if a photograph or other tangible corroborative evidence is involved, it must presumably represent an extraordinary instance of a high credibility witness presenting convincing evidence for the existence of phenomenon that lies totally beyond the horizons of modern science. But how well does CUFOS' scrutiny actually work?

May, 1974: An officer of the Lincolnshire, Illinois, Police Department called the secret number of the UFO Center's toll-free hotline to report a local sighting. Two young boys in Lincolnshire, an upper-income suburb about twenty-five miles north of Chicago and less than an hour's drive from

UFO Central in Evanston, reported sighting a UFO on the afternoon of May 5, and produced six color photographs to corroborate their story (plates 24–29).

The boy with the camera was eleven-year-old David Dorn, a fifth-grader. He and his friend (a year younger) reported that they had been playing basketball outdoors on the afternoon of Sunday, May 5, 1974, at about 5:30 PM. David said he brought his camera along, intending for each of them to snap pictures of the other shooting baskets, when a mysterious craftlike object reportedly appeared beneath the clouds. The boys allegedly watched it move rapidly across the sky for about a minute and then disappear up through the clouds. There were no other witnesses. Each of the six photographs clearly shows a craftlike object against a background of clouds, and in three of them the tops of some trees are visible. The call from the Lincolnshire Police Department was duly recorded by the hot-line operator, who relayed it to UFO Central, where it was included in the catalog of recent hot-line calls published in the July 1974 bulletin of the UFO Center:

MAY
05   Lincolnshire, IL*

*indicates case under investigation[5]

The investigator who handled this case was the director of the Center for UFO Studies, Dr. Hynek himself. Hynek brought both boys to his office in the Dearborn Observatory on the Northwestern campus, where he interviewed each of them separately, as well as together, and found no inconsistencies in the boys' stories. Hynek was impressed by the fact that both boys reenacted the sighting in about the same amount of time, approximately fifty seconds, and, according to a local newspaper, he concluded that both boys were reliable witnesses.[6]

The Dorn case was selected by Hynek for inclusion in an NBC-TV documentary titled *UFOs—Do You Believe?* which was broadcast on the evening of December 15, 1974. Hynek, appearing alone with David Dorn, has David re-create the incident before the TV cameras. They discuss the case and examine the photos. David's mother appears, vouching for her son's credibility as a witness, and then we hear Hynek's analysis of the case: "The Dorn case, I would say, has a reasonably high credibility and strangeness. I found no reason to believe that they were hoaxing or lying, and the photographs are very similar to photographs of daylight disks we've had from many parts of the world for many years."

One fact revealed in the broadcast that should immediately cause us to suspect a hoax was that *the negatives of the UFO photos were quickly "lost," supposedly by accident.* When a UFO witness so conveniently "loses" the critical evidence, it strongly suggests that he has something to hide. Yet Hynek was not at all suspicious of this part of the boys' story. When he asked David in front of the TV cameras about the negatives, David replied, "Well, those were accidentally lost by . . . ah . . . my fault. I . . . ah . . . was so excited about the results of the pictures, they turned out so good, that I just threw everything away and they went out with the trash the other night."

Very convenient, and also very difficult to believe, unless you happen to be the director of the world's foremost scientific UFO organization. While Hynek did acknowledge that "somebody may" suspect that the boy had deliberately destroyed the evidence, he himself was not at all inclined to doubt David's story. In fact, Hynek affirmed, "I believe you. I would probably do the same thing myself. In my excitement to see the pictures I might throw the envelope away, and there go the films." Hynek here is plainly ignoring his own advice, written in 1967, that, following what he feels to be the proper procedure for a cautious UFO investigator, he "simply will not take a photograph seriously" unless he can, among other things, "have access to the original negative."[7]

Some weeks after the broadcast, I attempted to reach David Dorn by telephone. When I first called David was not in, and I spoke briefly with his sister. She revealed that David had previously been strongly interested in UFOs, that he had been keeping a scrapbook about them, and that he was now very pleased that he had finally had the opportunity to see one. This significant prior interest in UFOs should serve as a warning to every UFO investigator, and it seems odd that Hynek either did not see it, or ignored it if he did. Although people who are ardent UFO enthusiasts make up only a tiny fraction of the population, they generate a disproportionately high number of UFO reports. Many UFO investigators who are themselves sincere-but-cautious "believers" will, upon learning that a certain UFO witness had a strong prior interest in UFOs, drop their investigation of the case immediately.

When I finally got through to David, he and I talked at some length about the sighting. What he told me was entirely consistent with what he had said on the NBC-TV documentary, and with what his sister had told me earlier. David was obviously a highly intelligent youngster who seemed unusually mature for a boy of his age, and he likewise displayed a most agreeable personality. David is the kind of boy who is easy to talk to, easy to like, and who will no doubt go far in later years. We discussed the incident itself, as well as the events that preceded and followed it. One point that David brought up at least four times in our initial talk was the rainy, inclement weather at the time of the incident. The rain had just ended, he said, and thus no one else happened to be outdoors to witness the object's appearance.

When I asked David where he sent his pictures to have them developed, I was surprised to learn that he didn't know anything about it. Although he mentioned on several occasions that he enjoyed taking pictures with his own camera (a Kodak Instamatic, Model X-15), and that he always sent the film off to some photo lab for development, he was totally unable to recall the name of the lab or its supposed location. A week later, after thinking it over, he "remembered" the name of a nearby photo lab that I had earlier suggested, trying to jog his memory.

I felt frustrated by the lack of substantive detail in every part of David's story. Each attempt to extract further information from him, which such a bright, talkative youngster should easily be able to recall, succeeded only in triggering a retelling of the meager story I had already heard.

Immediately after my initial phone call to David, I called his friend, thus giving the boys no opportunity to cross-reference their stories. This boy seemed somewhat confused when I spoke in terms of David "getting his pictures back." He told me that David's father is a photographer, and had developed the pictures for him. When I expressed surprise at this revelation, he quickly backtracked, and said that he wasn't at all sure who had in fact developed the pictures. We'll call this other boy "Joe," which is not his real name, since he has never sought or received any publicity concerning the incident and his involvement in it was in fact quite minimal.

Joe seemed unable to say anything much about the sighting they had supposedly shared, except some variation on the theme "we were just shooting baskets." If David's account of the incident was surprisingly short on detail, Joe's meager repertoire of statements concerning the alleged sighting clearly revealed that, *if* the incident was indeed a hoax, Joe most certainly was not the mastermind behind it. This impression was further strengthened when I later interviewed the boys in person. While David and I stood on the celebrated basketball court, quietly discussing the alleged sighting, Joe dribbled the ball in dizzying circles around us, whizzing around the driveway like a junior pro. Try as I might to get additional information out of Joe, he kept replying that I'd just have to "ask David."

How could I ever prove my suspicion that the boys were not telling the truth? For a time it seemed that the case would forever remain inconclusive. The negatives were lost—David's story, though meager and implausible, was consistent, and Joe was unlikely to carelessly blurt out anything again, now that the boys had had ample time to correlate their responses. David seemed extremely careful to never volunteer any information beyond the simplest, most direct answer to whatever question I posed, nearly always qualifying his answer by some phrase like "I think" or "I'm really not sure." All Joe would say was, "Ask David."

One of the few points I could check was their characterization of the rainy, dismal weather that had reportedly kept all other potential UFO witnesses indoors. I obtained the official U.S. Weather Bureau records from the Glenview Naval Air Station, only ten miles from Lincolnshire, and also those from Chicago's O'Hare Field, less than twenty miles distant. *These records clearly revealed that the boys were not telling the truth about the weather conditions.* Far from depicting a gloomy, rainy weather pattern, the records from Glenview show that, although a meager 0.04 inches of rain had indeed fallen that morning, *no precipitation whatsoever had fallen for more than four hours* prior to the time of the alleged sighting. Nor was the afternoon sky uniformly overcast and dismal. At 4 PM, clouds covered only 30 percent of the sky, indicating a considerable amount of sunshine. During the hour of the sighting, the "total opaque sky cover" ranged from 50 to 60 percent, the temperature was a comfortable 62°, and the wind was in the moderate 8–12 mph range. In short, the Glenview records indicate *a very pleasant, mild spring afternoon.* The weather records from O'Hare Field were in complete agreement with those of Glenview.

It is not difficult to see why the boys wanted me to believe that inclement weather had kept everyone else indoors. Not only did the incident take place in a populated suburban area, where one would expect a large number of persons to witness such an incident if it had indeed occurred, but Lake County, Illinois, which contains Lincolnshire, is a popular recreation area close to Chicago. The region is dotted with dozens of small lakes and has beaches on Lake Michigan as well. Its lakes, parks, and rivers are among the favorite weekend recreation areas for Chicagoans and are usually well-attended when the weather is nice. Yet no other witnesses to the alleged incident ever turned up.

In September of 1975, sixteen months after the incident, I happened to be in Chicago for a few days and arranged to meet with David to examine his photographs and visit the site where they had been taken. We stood outside for approximately thirty minutes, during which our discussion was interrupted more than a half-dozen times by the noise of low-flying aircraft. Private planes flying out of nearby Chicagoland Airport and Pal-Waukee Airport, as well as larger Navy planes from Glenview, regularly fly over Lincolnshire. Yet no airborne sighting of a UFO was reported on that date. Nor did any of these airports report an unidentified craft, capable of performing extraordinary maneuvers, intruding into its already crowded airspace.

David and Joe reenacted for me the alleged sighting, and retold their familiar tale:

JOE: I think it was sprinkling a little.

DAVID: Oh, it *was,* remember when we went into the garage, waitin' for it [waiting for the rain to stop, he later explained], then we went back to your house? It was just pouring! You can see, I think, that in one of the pictures, I think you might be able to see the street [not true].

SHEAFFER: I don't remember seeing that.

DAVID: Well, it *really was* wet!

Yet just a few minutes earlier, the habitually vague David had told me that he wasn't really certain that it had rained prior to the incident!

Returning to David's house, I asked him to recount exactly what had happened when the photographs reportedly "came back" in the mail. David explained that, when the mail arrived, he was away at school. His mother did not open the envelope containing the photos; she left them downstairs for him. When David returned from school, did he immediately tear open the envelope to look at his pictures of the UFO? No, he told me, he was anxious to see them, but he calmly carried the unopened envelope upstairs and set it down on the bed. He claims that he had to go to the doctor that afternoon and was only home for fifteen minutes or a half-hour, which left him just enough time to change his clothes, with not a second to spare to rip open the envelope and look at his pictures of a genuine flying saucer. David didn't even bring the pictures with him to the doctor's office, to look at while in the car or in the waiting room. He admits to being most anxious to see his photos, yet when they reportedly arrived he seems to have been remarkably disinterested.

His excitement over his UFO photos, however, was not entirely lost. It was simply a little delayed, because David says that as soon as he got home he immediately *ran* up the stairs, *ripped* open the envelope, and threw away the negatives! His curiosity and excitement, so strangely absent just an hour before, appears to have burst forth with such frenzy that all the negatives, the only evidence that might ultimately establish the authenticity of the photos, were gone forever. Even more astonishing is the fact that, although the negatives reportedly sat in the trash for nearly twenty-four hours before the trash was picked up, neither David nor his father seemed to notice that they were missing. David's father is an avid amateur photographer who has his own darkroom in the basement (although he develops only black-and-white film at home, according to David). Furthermore, David told me that he often assists his father in developing films and enlarging negatives. Thus both father and son are thoroughly familiar with the procedures for enlarging prints from a negative, both of them studied the prints while the UFO negatives were still reportedly sitting upstairs in the trash basket, and yet neither of them ever thought to ask, "Where are the negatives?" I find this difficult to believe.

Not until the pictures had supposedly "come back" from the photo lab did David's mother call her friend, who is a reporter for the local paper, the *Vernon Review,* to come over to write up the story. And the police were not notified of the incident until David walked up to a parked police cruiser, pictures in hand, nearly two weeks after the incident. Prudent UFO investigators consider a case much more convincing if the UFO witness reports his sighting to the authorities *before* he has seen the results of his own photography.

Exactly how were these six color photographs produced? Only the negatives could ultimately settle that question. The prints, only three and one-fourth inches square, have a matte surface which, when magnified, breaks down into a tiny pattern of dots, making a detailed examination impossible. The prints certainly look as if they came from a commercial processing lab, although they could likewise have been produced at home by an advanced amateur. (As I did not myself see the Dorns' home darkroom, I have only David's word that they do not have the equipment to do color processing.) Another more likely possibility is that the UFO negatives were "doctored" at home and then sent out for commercial processing.

I find it most significant that *five of the six UFO pictures appear to show a UFO that is only two-dimensional and shows no sign of any motion.* The object in these photos looks like a flat cardboard cutout, displaying only an outline and lacking any depth whatsoever. The sixth photo depicts a UFO that is plainly a three-dimensional object, and it appears that this object was in motion at the time of the exposure. The photo of the 3-D object could easily have been produced by simply tossing a small fabricated "craft" into the air.

As for the other photographs, I find it remarkably strange that *each of the five flat, two-dimensional UFOs has a slightly different shape.* Accepting these photographs as authentic may well lead the Center for UFO Studies to conclude that the UFO entities have taken to building their craft out of Silly Putty, perhaps to better enable them to slip away before the evidence becomes too convincing. One photo shows a UFO that is slightly concave on the bottom, while on another the bottom is seen to be convex. Some are "fatter" than others—the proportions vary considerably—yet all of them lack a third dimension.

Putting all of these clues together, the most likely explanation seems to be that a UFO was painted on the negative, using an opaque fluid, to create each of the five flat two-dimensional UFOs. This would explain why the UFOs are so unnaturally dark. (One popular publication has dubbed photos of this type "light-absorbing UFOs"—a physical impossibility, since no substance can absorb more than 100 percent of the light falling on it, including the light scattered by the atmosphere between the camera and the object.) This also explains why the shapes in the different frames are inconsistent. Perhaps it is for this very reason that David Dorn's UFO negatives will never be examined.

Just before this book went to press, five years after the photos were taken, I telephoned David once again. His voice had become much deeper in the interim. He still maintained with apparently great sincerity that the UFO photos were authentic. He is now finishing high school, planning to go to college, and then on to law school. I asked him about the rain that he said had been falling but that the Weather Bureau said was not. He insisted that it *had* been raining, despite what the weather records said. I asked him why the UFO had a different shape in each of the six photos. It must have been taken at different angles, he replied. David still retains his keen interest in

UFOs and claimed to have had another sighting a few months before. He reminded me that his photos had been carefully scrutinized by Hynek and the other experts at the Center for UFO Studies and that they found no reason to doubt them.

"There exists a growing number of scientists, engineers, and other professionals generally associated with universities, laboratories, and industry, who have contemplated the possible significance of the UFO phenomenon . . . the Center provides an avenue whereby the interests and talents of these scientists and other professionals can be focused and brought to bear on this challenging problem."[8] One wonders how these universities and laboratories continue to function at all while employing the caliber of investigation demonstrated by the Center for UFO Studies in the Dorn case.

Today, that small but vocal segment of the scientific community that is active in promoting UFO "research" still stands firmly behind its leader, Dr. J. Allen Hynek, director of the Center for UFO Studies and the nation's best-known UFO expert. By all indications, these scientists concurred with Dr. Hynek when he, at the close of his investigations, presented young David with a copy of his book,[9] autographed with the inscription, "To David Dorn who had a real UFO Experience."[10]

NOTES

1. *The Center for UFO Studies* (4-page introductory booklet, 1973).
2. J. Allen Hynek, "The UFO Gap," *Playboy,* December 1967, p. 271.
3. *APRO Bulletin,* January–February 1975.
4. The Center for UFO Studies introductory booklet, 1973.
5. *Center for UFO Studies Bulletin,* July 1974, p. 2.
6. *Vernon Review* (Deerfield, Ill.), May 23, 1974, p. 35.
7. Hynek, "The UFO Gap," op. cit., p. 270.
8. The Center for UFO Studies, 1973.
9. Hynek, *The UFO Experience* (Chicago: Regnery, 1972).
10. *Vernon Review,* op. cit.

10

THE TESTIMONY OF
ONE EYE . . .

The testimony of one eye is naught — he may lie. But when it is corroborated by the other, it is good evidence that none may gainsay. —Gilbert and Sullivan, *The Yeoman of the Guard.*

In evaluating a UFO sighting, the question invariably comes up of whether the witness is reliable. This reflects the commonsense assumption that human testimony falls more or less into two clear categories: reliable, and otherwise. If a witness is *reliable,* the assumption goes, his testimony fairly accurately depicts actual events. The testimony of an *unreliable* witness is held to be probably tainted by fantasy and exaggeration. Yet how distinct are these categories?

Many judge a person's presumed reliability as a witness in much the same way as we estimate his socioeconomic status. College education and respectable careers are a strong plus for reliability, especially in the case of doctors, scientists, and pilots. The testimony of unskilled and uneducated individuals is not found to be so convincing. Our assignment of "reliability" to various persons' testimonies generally reflects society's hierarchies. However, the notion that social status does in some way ensure accurate observation and reporting seems to rest on little more than conjecture.

Just how reliable is "reliable"? When we have obtained a first-hand narrative from an apparently credible source, can the facts of the case be considered reasonably well established? A quick glance at the inconsistency of courtroom testimony bids us to be cautious: in thousands of trials, whether for a traffic accident or for murder, there are as many different accounts as there are eyewitnesses. Since virtually the entire body of evidence for the existence of UFOs stands or falls on the factual accuracy of the testimony of credible persons trying to describe an object *whose identity is* not *known,* let us attack the problem by seeing the degree of accuracy of eyewitness testimony describing an object whose identity *is* known:

In the year 1860, long before *UFO* had become a household word, some U.S. Army officers reported a most remarkable celestial phenomenon. The noted astronomer Simon Newcomb was traveling across Minnesota, returning from an eclipse-viewing expedition that had taken him two thousand miles across the wilderness — only to be clouded out. When they arrived at Fort Snelling the following occurred.

> Some of the officers were greatly surprised by a celestial phenomenon of a very extraordinary character which had been observed for several nights past. A star had been seen, night after night, rising in the east as usual, and starting on its course to the south. But instead of continuing that course across the meridian, as stars invariably had done from the remotest antiquity, it took a turn toward the north, sunk toward the horizon, and finally set near the north point of the horizon. Of course an explanation was wanted.
>
> My assurance that there must be some mistake in the observation could not be accepted, because this erratic course of the heavenly body had been seen by all of them so plainly that no doubt could exist on the subject. The men who saw it were not of the ordinary untrained kind, but graduates of West Point, who, if anyone, ought to be free from optical deceptions. I was confidently invited to look out that night and see for myself. We all watched with the greatest interest.
>
> In due time the planet Mars was seen in the east making its way toward the south. "There it is!" was the exclamation.
>
> "Yes, there it is," said I. "Now that planet is going to keep right on its course toward the south."
>
> "No, it is not," said they; "you will see it turn around and go down towards the north."
>
> Hour after hour passed, and as the planet went on its regular course, the other watchers began to get a little nervous. It showed no signs of deviating from its course. We went out from time to time to look at the sky.
>
> "There it is," said one of the observers at length, pointing to Capella, which was now just rising a little to the east of north; "there is the star setting."
>
> "No, it isn't," said I; "there is the star we have been looking at, now quite inconspicuous near the meridian, and the star which you think is setting is really rising and will soon be higher up."
>
> A very little additional watching showed that no deviation of the general laws of Nature had occurred, but that the observers of previous nights had jumped at the conclusion that two objects, widely apart in the heavens, were the same.[1]

Newcomb observes that he has always remembered this experience as "illustrative of the fallacy of all human testimony about ghosts, [spirit] rappings, and other phenomena of that character." It tells us something about UFO testimony as well.

In a more recent example, there is the "fleet of dazzling UFOs" that "raced silently across the night sky of Rio de Janeiro" on the morning of March 12, 1978, witnessed by thousands, including pilots, a professor, and military personnel. Colonel Rui Guardiolo, a pilot in the Brazilian Air Force, observed the event in the company of his wife and two friends. "It was coming straight down on a crash course upon the Campo dos Affonsos Air Force Base," said he. But just as the UFO squadron reached an altitude of about 2000 feet, it leveled off, enabling him to see "two main mother ships . . . followed by rows of smaller vessels."

Lygia Pape, a professor of art at a university in Rio, was on the beach that night with some friends. Suddenly someone shouted for everyone to look at the sky. "There was an enormous object that approached from the north," she recalled. "Around each of the four large ships was a grouping of five smaller ones . . . There was a kind of vibration. I did not hear it but I felt it. It was so extraordinary that I still get goose bumps to think of it."

In the city of Belo Horizonte, a retired military policeman, Colonel Waldyr Foureaux, declared, "It was flying at the altitude of about 500 meters" (1500 feet). "It was flying so near the mountain range that I thought it would crash. To fly so low, it had to make very accurate mathematical calculations. There had to be something commanding the ship." In Sao Paolo, the phenomenon was witnessed by Francisco Simonelli Crusiero, a private pilot. "The object was flying horizontally," said he. "It was about the size of a jumbo jet. It had white lights around it like fluorescent lamps . . . It was not a satellite and it was not a meteor. It was a UFO." Mr. Crusiero's drawing of the object he reportedly saw clearly depicts a cigar-shaped craft, sporting a row of portholes along its major axis.

Unfortunately for science, what all those worthy people reported was *not* the UFO event of the century. It was an extremely rare and brilliant fireball meteor or *bolide,* duly noted and recorded by the Smithsonian Institution's Scientific Event Alert Network *Bulletin.* Reports received from astronomers at the Brazilian *Observatorio Nacional* leave no doubt whatsoever as to its true identity. Yet these highly skilled and presumably reliable observers attributed features and behavior to the object that can only be described as highly fanciful. The pilot in the Brazilian Air Force imagined that the object was about to crash on his airfield. The retired military policeman believed the object to be within a few thousand feet—nearly qualifying as a close encounter—and maneuvering under intelligent control. In reality, it was one hundred miles or more distant, following a natural ballistic trajectory. The other pilot fancied that he saw a row of more than a half-dozen evenly spaced portholes on the main object. Surely these people meet every prima facie criterion for being "reliable witnesses." Yet were we to take their testimony at face value, as many UFO researchers are wont to do, we would be led into serious error.[2]

In Aurora, Illinois, just west of Chicago, a dramatic multiple-witness close encounter of the second kind was reported on the evening of April 29, 1978. The incident was reported to CUFOS by Mr. and Mrs. S. of Aurora. (Having submitted their report in confidence, their name has not been published.) Driving home that evening, they stopped to observe a brilliant unidentified object in the sky. Two unrelated groups of bystanders were also pointing to the object and shouting. Sketching the object later, both husband and wife depicted a saucer-shaped body, with a dome on top, surrounded by lights. The lights were reported by all witnesses to rotate around the form, "twirling like a carnival ride," in the words of one witness.

Continuing home, Mr. and Mrs. S. allegedly saw the UFO pass over their car at treetop level; they reported that it had to angle upward to avoid hitting the trees. Its size, they reported, was as big as a football field. Other witnesses, however, estimated the UFO to be only twenty-five feet across. Arriving home, Mr. S. was so agitated that, going to a neighbor's house to alert him to the object, he tore the door off its hinges! The neighbor reports that he still "gets chills" thinking about it; "You want to cry but you're still too shocked." In yet another neighbor's family, an eleven-year-old child hid behind the back seat of the car.

Not only was the Aurora UFO close-in and terrifying but it also reportedly produced electromagnetic effects, which is generally taken as one of the strongest possible indications of an "authentic" UFO. One neighbor of Mr. and Mrs. S. reported that his TV set went blank for two minutes while the UFO was in the vicinity. There were also power failures in Aurora, which likewise seemed to indicate the presence of a UFO.

The Aurora close encounter seemed destined to become a "classic" of UFOlogy. Multiple independent witnesses, physical effects, profound emotional impact upon the observers: "How could such a case be considered anything but a true UFO?" mused Allan Hendry, managing editor of CUFOS' *International UFO Reporter*. But Hendry noted certain similarities between the Aurora close encounter and some previous incidents occurring in that area, which prompted him to follow up on a hunch. It paid off. Hendry discovered that the Aurora UFO was in fact *a misidentification of an aircraft towing an advertising display, operated by Ad Airlines of Chicago.* The aircraft never descended to "treetop" level as the witnesses reported, it was not "saucer shaped" with a "dome" on top, it did not blank out TV pictures or cause power outages, and it did not "follow" anyone's automobile. *Yet all of these effects were reported* by witnesses whose veracity Hendry, as well as other investigators, saw no reason to doubt.

Hendry, who is certainly no UFO debunker, wrote a thought-provoking analysis of the incident for the *International UFO Reporter,* explaining why the study of incidents such as this is of great importance to UFO research. He observed: "In the three hundred calls that IUR has dealt with that were based on confirmed ad planes at night, 90 percent of the witnesses described *not* what was perceptually available, but rather that they could see a disc-shaped form *rotating* with 'fixed' lights; many of these people imagine that they see a dome on top and, when pressed, will swear that they can make out the outline with confidence."[3]

In short, 90 percent of the witnesses, perceiving the string of lights of an advertising aircraft, reported seeing a rotating saucer shape, often with a dome on top—*a shape that existed only in their imagination.* The implications are obvious.

The following case from the U.S. Air Force Project Blue Book is an excellent illustration of the inaccuracies in perception and recollection that can creep into UFO observations. Because the accounts differ so strongly, obviously they cannot both be right; yet it is impossible to determine which account is closer to the truth. It seems impossible that both witnesses could be describing the same object:

	Witness "A," minister's wife	Witness "B," college history student
Date of incident:	June 26, 1966	June 27, 1966
Time:	8:00–8:30	8:50
Sky conditions:	clear sky	heavy clouds
Brightness:	bright as a car headlight	same as bright star
Did object appear to stand still at any time?	no	yes
Did object appear to speed up and rush away at any time?	yes	no
Did the object flash or flicker?	yes	no
Did the object move behind something at any time?	no	yes
Did the object move in front of something at any time?	no	yes
Angular elevation at which object first appeared:	55°	25°
Angular elevation at which object disappeared:	90°	30°
Sketch of object's path:	straight line	90° turn

It would seem that two more different sightings could not be imagined. *Yet each witness cites the other as a corroborating witness.*[4] Regardless of what the original object may have been (it is carried by Blue Book as a "possible aircraft"), the gross inconsistencies indicate that at least one of these accounts (more likely both) contain some very serious errors of observation that make the task of identifying the object next to impossible. Both of the witnesses, however, answered all questions in a perfectly coherent manner. Both of them are active in community religious affairs, and by all indications appear to be solid citizens. Which report -- if either — contains a more or less accurate description of the object they saw?

Witnesses of supposed UFO events are not the only ones who cannot be relied upon to give an accurate description of what they actually saw. Investigators of aircraft accidents face the same problems as UFO investigators. Stephen Barlay, in his book *Aircrash Detective,* notes that "the more time witnesses have to think and talk about what they have seen, the less accurate their memories become." This may explain why many UFO stories, like fish stories, improve with age.

In general, eyewitnesses to aircraft disasters do *not* correctly relate the sequence of events accurately enough to be of assistance in determining the cause of the tragedy. Barlay observes that, in the wake of an aircraft accident, supposed witnesses to the event often step forward who, it later turns out, could not possibly have seen the accident from the point where they were standing. These people were perfectly willing to "describe" the event in great detail nonetheless!

Perhaps the best-witnessed accident in history occurred in 1952 at the Farnborough Air Show in England. A de Havilland 110 fighter jet was in the process of performing a supersonic dive, to thrill the crowd with a powerful sonic boom, when without warning the aircraft began to break apart. Falling debris killed thirty people and injured dozens more. The accident was witnessed by approximately *one hundred thousand people,* including many devoted aviation enthusiasts and eminent experts. The authorities appealed for statements from eyewitnesses, evoking a tremendous response. The cause of the accident was subsequently established by researchers and confirmed by wing-stress tests performed by the aircraft manufacturer. How accurate had the many thousands of accounts of these eyewitnesses been? Astonishingly, "There was only *one letter* which was of some use and there were fewer than a half-dozen people who captured to some extent the true picture of events. Most witnesses 'got the split-second time-sequence of disintegration [as finally proved by the research] backwards, filled in bits with imagination, and preferred theories to reports.' "[5] Is there any reason to presume testimony on the subject of UFOs to be significantly more reliable?

Investigators who attempt to determine the location of meteorite impacts through eyewitness reports face similar problems. Dr. Frank D. Drake, the originator of Project Ozma (chapter 13), summarized the results of efforts of National Radio Astronomy Observatory astronomers to locate meteorites:

The first fact we learned was that a witness' memory of such exotic events
fades very quickly. After one day, about half of the reports are clearly erroneous; after two days, about three-quarters are clearly erroneous . . .
it became clear that later they were reconstructing in their imagination an
event based on some dim memory of what happened.

Drake goes on to note another amazing fact: "In the old meteor literature, with almost every fireball recorded, something like 14 per cent of the
witnesses report the simultaneous crackling sound, which should be
physically impossible. How does the sound get there as fast as the light?"[6]
Brilliant fireballs are typically many dozens of miles from the observer,
and the speed of sound is just one-fifth of a mile per second. Thus the sound
of an exploding fireball will arrive one or more *minutes* after the explosion
is seen. Yet one witness in seven imagines hearing a sound where no sound is
physically possible.
It is not only laymen whose observations can be inaccurate because of
preconceived ideas. Even professional observers of many years' experience,
including noted astronomers, have shown themselves to be as fallible as the
rest of us mortals. Professor E. E. Barnard was, at the turn of the century,
one of the most respected astronomical observers, a specialist in precision
measurement of the position of stars and planets. In the year 1898, using
what is still the largest refracting telescope in the world, the 40" Alvin Clark
refractor at the Yerkes Observatory in Wisconsin, Professor Barnard
obtained a series of measurements that continue to astound astronomers to
this day: he obtained the parallax of the Andromeda nebula.[7]
This may not seem too astonishing unless you have studied a little astronomy. The parallax of an object—its apparent displacement due to the
earth's motion around the sun—is a means for determining the distance of
nearby stellar objects. The method breaks down as we approach one hundred light-years, because the parallax angle becomes too small to be measured (or even detected). The reason that Barnard's measurement continues
to astonish us is that the giant reflecting telescopes of the twentieth century
have established beyond any doubt whatsoever that the Andromeda "nebula" is not a nebula at all: it is the Andromeda *galaxy,* a "twin" of our own
Milky Way. Its distance is approximately two million light-years, twenty
thousand times too distant to show any parallax displacement at all. Yet
Professor Barnard, who believed it to be a gaseous nebula that was quite
nearby, convinced himself (and the editor of the *Astrophysical Journal,*
George Ellery Hale) that a parallax had been observed, suggesting a distance of twenty light-years or less, making the Andromeda galaxy one of the
nearest objects outside our solar system. A more incorrect conclusion could
not possibly be reached. Yet Professor Barnard, discoverer of Jupiter's fifth
moon, of the famous Barnard's star, and many other objects, believing the
"nebula" to be nearby, believed that he had "measured" (using scientific

equipment that could hardly be improved upon even today) a parallactic effect that simply does not exist (but which *would* exist if Barnard's theory were correct).

Also around the turn of the century, the American astronomer Percival Lowell made a series of drawings of the planet Mars, based upon many hours of painstaking observation through his telescope. He paid special attention to the supposed canals of Mars, which he attributed to a race of intelligent beings. Lowell mapped dozens of canals in great detail: he and many others "saw" these same canals, night after night, in their telescopes. Yet with just a few possible exceptions, *the so-called Martian canals existed only in the imagination of the observers.* NASA's Mariner and Viking spacecraft have extensively mapped the Martian surface from close range and have found no surface features whatsoever to correspond with the "canals" mapped by those early Mars observers.

The most amazing (and significant) feature of the illusory Martian canals is that they did not turn up sporadically and randomly across the planet: they were "seen" in the same place by many observers, night after night, year after year. UFO enthusiasts like to point to worldwide similarities in UFO reports, supposedly proving that these accounts must have some basis in fact. But, as the decades-long myth of the Martian canals clearly demonstrates, when the mind knows what it is "supposed" to see, it will often use fantasy and imagination to fill in any necessary details that do not happen to be there, without any suggestion of conscious fabrication.

The planet Mars was not the only one whose surface professional astronomers covered with imaginary features. The great Italian observer Schiaparelli, "discoverer" of Mars's canals, thought that he could see enough detail on Venus's cloud-covered surface to establish a rotational period of approximately two hundred days. Astronomers Niesten and Stuyvaert of the Brussels Observatory made careful drawings of that planet over a nine-year period and "found" that a rotational period of twenty-three hours fit so well that they could even draw up a map of Venus's surface markings.[8] The supposed "rotation," and indeed the very surface markings, observed in both instances must have been wholly imaginary, because recent radar observations establish that Venus has a rotational period of 243 days, but in the *opposite* direction from the other planets.

The planet Mercury was for years believed to have a "captured" rotation, always keeping the same side to the sun, as the moon does to the earth. Numerous maps of the hard-to-observe surface markings of Mercury were drawn up, based on this assumption. The entire "daylit" hemisphere of Mercury was mapped in great detail.[9] But once again, recent radar findings reveal that Mercury does *not* keep one side constantly facing the sun. How could the astronomers who mapped the supposed features of Mercury's "sunlit" side have failed to notice that those features were *not* stationary, but rotating with respect to the sun? Once again, the a priori notion that such features were "supposed" to be fixed in longitude on the "sunlit" side enabled even professional observers to see them that way for decades on end.

UFO enthusiasts ceaselessly suggest that the many similarities in unrelated UFO reports indicate the existence of a real phenomenon. But psychological experiments have shown, time and again, how a witness's testimony can be dramatically altered through asking leading questions (something many UFO investigators, being "true believers," are wont to do). In fact, the research of Dr. Elizabeth Loftus, a psychologist at the University of Washington in Seattle, reveals that the memory of the witness can be distorted merely by the wording of the questions asked. Test subjects were shown a movie of a traffic accident in which a barn does not appear. Asked, "Did you see a barn?" only 2.7 percent answered yes. But of those who were asked, "Did you see *the* barn?"—a leading question—17.3 percent, *more than one in six,* responded in the affirmative. Furthermore, these erroneous ideas persisted long after the question had been asked. "Memory itself undergoes a change as a result of the type of question asked," Loftus concludes.[10]

Since witnesses in major UFO cases are typically subjected to hours of interrogation by enthusiastic UFO proponents, who may consciously or not yield positive reinforcement to statements that increase the "strangeness" of the incident, it is little wonder that the same themes continue to recur in case after case. Thus the "missing hours" and the "animal reaction" aspects to the Hill case were not "discovered" until the Hills had undergone many long hours of interrogation by dedicated UFO believers. In a famous "UFO abduction" case in Kentucky in 1976, the witness did not recall seeing anything extraordinary after a UFO supposedly made a close approach to her car. Some APRO and MUFON members helpfully provided a drawing, showing supposed UFO creatures reported in other incidents. "Is this what you saw after you mentioned the light coming into the car?" Leonard Stringfield of MUFON asked. Not surprisingly, her memory immediately began to improve: "Yes, I can see the face now," she responded. She was unable to recall anything about the creature's body, arms, or legs; perhaps this is because the drawing supplied to her extended only to the shoulders. Stringfield, a member of MUFON's Board of Directors, rates this case as "possibly the most fact-rooted abduction case on record."[11]

Another psychologist who has conducted in-depth studies of human eyewitness testimony is Dr. Robert Buckhout, director of the Center for Responsive Psychology at Brooklyn College of the City University of New York. Reporting his findings in the respected *Scientific American,* Dr. Buckhout writes:

> An observer is less capable of remembering details, less accurate in reading dials and less accurate in detecting signals when under stress; he is quite naturally paying more attention to his own well-being and safety than to non-essential elements in the environment. *Research I have done with Air*

Force flight-crew members confirms that even highly-trained people become poorer observers under stress . . . time estimates are particularly exaggerated. [Emphasis added.]

Since sighting an object that the observer believes to be a UFO does, in many cases, cause the observer to feel stress, Buckhout's quotation should be printed in red ink in every UFO investigator's handbook. Stress can be an especially significant factor when the UFO observer is flying an airplane or driving an automobile, because of the knowledge of the ever-present danger of accident, seemingly made worse by the UFO's supposed proximity.

As for the question of whether a "multiple-witness" UFO sighting adds any assurance of authenticity ("I do not assign a Probability Rating greater than three to any report coming from a single reporter," says J. Allen Hynek), Buckhout notes that while one might expect two, or ten, witnesses to be more reliable than one, "similarity of judgement is a two-edged sword, however: people can agree in error as easily as in truth. A large body of research results demonstrate that an observer can be persuaded to conform to the majority opinion even when the majority is completely wrong."

Thus a multiple-witness UFO sighting gives no guarantee of greater reliability. In fact, the opposite may be true: Buckhout's experiments revealed that, comparing single-witness accounts with those of witnesses in groups, "the group descriptions were more complete than the individual reports but gave rise to significantly more errors of commission: an assortment of incorrect and stereotyped details."[12]

One of the most influential thinkers in history, philosopher David Hume, considered the problem of eyewitness testimony more rigorously than perhaps anyone else before or since. Hume titled his 1748 essay "Of Miracles." While sightings of UFOs and Loch Ness monsters were not in fashion during his day, accounts of religious miracles were legion. Hume observes:

> It is experience only, which gives authority to human testimony; and it is the same experience, which assures us of the laws of nature. When, therefore, these two kinds of experience are contrary, we have nothing to do but subtract the one from the other, and embrace an opinion, either on one side or another, with that assurance which arises from the remainder.

Hume reminds us that the body of experience establishing the laws of nature appears quite persuasive, while the experience to suggest near-infallibility of eyewitness testimony is sadly lacking. He argues that we could only accept the testimony of a miracle if we weighed the possibility of the witness lying or being mistaken and found it to be even more implausible than the narrative that the witness relates. Hume concludes:

> No testimony is sufficient to establish a miracle, unless the testimony be of such a kind, that its falsehood would be more miraculous, than the fact,

which it endeavors to establish; and even in that case there is a mutual destruction of arguments. . . . The many instances of forged miracles, and prophecies, and supernatural events . . . ought reasonably to beget a suspicion against all relations of this kind . . . the knavery and folly of men are such common phenomena, that I should rather believe the most extraordinary events to arise from their concurrence, than admit of so signal a violation of the laws of nature.[13]

Have we found any answers to the question "How reliable is 'reliable'?" It is clear that the answer sometimes is: not reliable at all. Indeed, considering what we have seen in the preceding instances and considering the public's strong interest in extraterrestrial life and space exploration, *it would be surprising if we did not have reports of UFOs,* regardless of whether or not any genuinely mysterious objects are in our skies. Suppose, for the moment, that "genuine" UFOs did once exist but have now departed. We would still continue to receive UFO reports, accounts of close encounters of the various kinds, stories of abductions and impossible maneuvers, *simply because of the propensity of human testimony to become "garbled."*

Most proponents of the reality of UFOs admit that at least 90 percent of the reports are worthless. They are sightings of objects that are readily identifiable. But it is the remaining 10 or 5 or 1 percent that is held to be of great significance. Those who argue in this manner, however, act as if they are unaware that *every* channel of communication contains a certain amount of "noise" within it. Whether the channel is radio, microwave, audio, optical, or anything else, there is always a certain amount of residual noise, which can be minimized but never eliminated. Hi-fi buffs are all too familiar with the problem of noise in their sound systems, which they ceaselessly struggle to keep at an absolute minimum.

When the communication channel is human eyewitness testimony, the "noise" factor can sometimes be extremely large. UFO reports will be generated as a consequence of the "noise" in the system, just as are false characters on a noisy telecommunications line, *regardless of whether or not any "authentic" UFOs exist.* Given an inherently "noisy" instrument—the human perceptual/memory system—and given the ample number of stimuli in the sky available for misperception, it is inevitable that reports of UFOs will be generated. Because of distortions that creep into the narrative, it is in principle no more possible to raise the 95 percent explanation rate to 100 percent than it is to build a communications device in which the noise is zero. There need not be *any* "genuine" UFOs for seemingly perplexing "high-caliber" UFO reports to arise.

Thus the existence of a small residue of UFO reports seemingly without explanation *tells us nothing at all about the true nature of UFOs.* We cannot either prove or disprove the existence of UFOs because of the reports. Of course, if the proportion of apparently unsolvable cases were large, and if the documentation supporting them were overwhelming, our conclusions would be different. But the present number and caliber of UFO sightings can be adequately explained by the fallibility of human testimony, without need of hypotheses that posit "authentic" UFOs.

This neither confirms nor refutes the existence of UFOs. *But the existence of "authentic" UFOs has become an unnecessary hypothesis.* To illustrate the point, we can explain the action of the tides by invoking gravitation, or by gravitation on the weekdays and angels on weekends. Similarly, we can explain the existence of "unsolved" UFO reports by invoking inaccurate perception and reporting, or by inaccurate perception and reporting in the great majority of cases and "genuine UFOs" in a very few.

We can't, of course, prove that "genuine" UFOs do not exist, any more than we can disprove the existence of witches, fairies, or dragons. But Samuel Johnson's argument against the existence of ancient Irish epics is as sound as any disproof of their existence could possibly be: "We do not know that there are any ancient Erse manuscripts; and we have no other reason to disbelieve that there are men with three heads, but that we do not know that there are any such men."[14] We likewise have no other reason to disbelieve in the existence of "genuine" UFOs, but that we do not know that there are any such things.

NOTES

1. Simon Newcomb, *The Reminiscences of an Astronomer* (Boston: Houghton, Mifflin, 1903), pp. 93–95.

2. *National Enquirer*, October 17, 1978, p. 2; Smithsonian Institution Scientific Event Alert Network *Bulletin* 3, no. 3 (March 31, 1978):9.

3. Allan Hendry, "The Case for IFO Study: A Recent Example," *International UFO Reporter* 3, no. 6 (June 1978); see also Hendry, *The UFO Handbook* (New York: Doubleday, 1979).

4. U.S. Air Force Project Blue Book files, Pecos, Texas, August 1966.

5. Stephen Barlay, *Aircrash Detective* (London: Hamish Hamilton, 1969), chapter 9. Quote from *Sunday Times* of London, March 11, 1963.

6. Frank D. Drake, "On the Abilities and Limitations of Witnesses," in *UFO's—A Scientific Debate,* ed. Sagan and Page (Ithaca, N.Y.: Cornell University Press, 1972).

7. *The Astrophysical Journal* 9 (March 1899):184.

8. *The Observatory,* August 1891, p. 290.

9. A map of Mercury's "sunlit side" is found on p. 184 of the *Larousse Encyclopedia of Astronomy* (London: Hamlyn, 1959; revised 1966).

10. Elizabeth Loftus, *Psychology Today,* December 1974; Trotter, *Science News* 108 (October 25, 1975):269.

11. Leonard Stringfield, *Situation Red: The UFO Siege* (New York: Fawcett, 1977), pp. 228, 235.

12. Robert Buckhout, "Eyewitness Testimony," *Scientific American,* December 1974, p. 23; J. Allen Hynek, *The UFO Experience* (Chicago: Regnery, 1972), chapter 4.

13. David Hume, "Of Miracles," *An Enquiry Concerning Human Understanding,* 1st ed., 1748 (Chicago: Regnery, 1965), pp. 119, 122, 132, 134.

14. James Boswell, *Life of Johnson,* 1st ed., 1791 (New York: Random House, 1967), p. 238.

11

UFOs AT EXETER

Two policemen and a youth crouch behind an automobile, reportedly watching a mysterious craft hovering just a hundred yards away and flashing its lights in a regular sequence. Two other youths are terrified as a strange object reportedly flies in from the ocean and follows their car. A silvery light is seen on several occasions by highly credible observers, always hovering ominously over the high-voltage power lines. These are some of the remarkable UFO incidents that are *reported* to have occurred in the vicinity of Exeter, New Hampshire, in the fall of 1965 and which are chronicled in the book *Incident at Exeter* by John G. Fuller.[1] This book, which has sold more than 500,000 copies, has made the Exeter UFO flap one of the best-known of all the waves of UFO sightings, and the reports surrounding this incident are generally considered to be among the most unexplainable and authentic UFO cases on record.

Author Fuller is a former playwright and editor of the *Saturday Review*. His interest in UFOs, the paranormal, and the anti-nuclear crusade slowly grew over a period of years, and today he is one of the best-known writers on these subjects. Fuller has recently written *The Ghost of Flight 401,* in which he asserts that one major airline has managed to fill some of the empty seats on its jumbo jets with spirits from the Beyond.[2] According to the publisher's publicity blurb, Fuller actually "made apparent contact with the dead flight engineer" (via a Ouija board).

The most dramatic reported UFO encounter occurring during the Exeter flap took place during the early morning hours of September 3, 1965. Young Norman Muscarello had been hitchhiking to his home in Exeter. As he passed an open field between two houses, he reportedly saw a remarkable flying object coming directly toward him. He estimated its diameter to be about eighty to ninety feet. Muscarello frantically waved down a passing car and was driven the few miles to the Exeter police station. An hour later, he returned to the site of the incident accompanied by Patrolman Eugene Bertrand.

They saw nothing upon their arrival; so they parked the police cruiser and began walking through the field. When they were a hundred yards from the road, some horses and dogs on the other side of a nearby fence reportedly became alarmed (possibly by their presence?), and suddenly Muscarello shouted, "I see it." Patrolman Bertrand claimed to see it too, a brilliant object that reportedly bathed the entire area in a brilliant red light.

They were unable to discern the object's shape, because it was so brilliant. It hovered in the same position for several minutes, reportedly rocking back and forth on its axis and beaming its lights from left to right, then back again from right to left. Patrolman David Hunt arrived on the scene at about this time and he, too, reported seeing the object, rocking on its axis, moving erratically, and darting about rapidly. Within a few minutes the object was reportedly no longer visible between the trees, and the witnesses returned to Exeter. Later, officers Bertrand and Hunt both told NICAP that they had previously read UFO literature, although Fuller fails to mention this interesting fact.[3]

Other sightings reported during the Exeter wave were equally remarkable. Mrs. Jalbert and her four teenage boys claimed to have repeatedly sighted a brilliant, silvery object hovering above the power line near their home. The object reportedly had flashing lights in many colors and was so brilliant that one could read a book by the light it gave off. They said that, when the object appeared, an airplane frequently came out and "chased" it. Two youths at Hampton Beach reported seeing an object fly in from the ocean and follow their car at a very low altitude, despite their attempts to shake it. A Mrs. Blodgett said she saw a "bright, blinding" ball of light, only a hundred yards away, hovering above the treetops and spinning rapidly. Dozens of these dramatic sightings are found in Fuller's *Incident at Exeter*. If even a small percentage of these reported sightings are factually correct, then the Exeter phenomenon is truly one of the great mysteries of our age.

Fuller leaves the reader with the impression that for a period of several months, some eerie, almost mystical occurrences continued to plague that tiny New Hampshire town. Time and again he darkly hints that the Air Force knows considerably more about the Exeter UFOs than it is telling. He quotes a number of witnesses who claim that, at the time of their UFO sighting, an Air Force plane was seen chasing the unknown object, always without success. Fuller himself, in the presence of news photographer Bob Kimball and Mrs. Lillian Pearce, a housewife who sees UFOs so frequently that she got "sick of telling [the Air Force] about it," claims to have sighted a reddish-orange disk, smaller than the apparent size of the full moon, keeping just ahead of a fighter plane that was "moving as if in hot pursuit." An Air Force pilot, whose identity was not disclosed, reportedly told Fuller that he and his fellow pilots had been ordered to "shoot down any UFO they came across," but they were unable to bring any down because, not only were these supposed craft highly maneuverable, they were "apparently invulnerable."

Reflecting on the colossal magnitude of the implied cover-up that would permit the Air Force to successfully conceal these remarkable events from the public, Fuller observes that "the censorship of the political powers in the Air Force seems to be exercising authority far beyond the powers assigned to it by the civilian control under which it is supposed to operate." If Fuller is correct, not only must we worry about these unknown beings who have us under surveillance for unknown reasons, but our government's sinister policy of silence should give us equal cause for alarm.

In many of the reported UFO sightings in *Incident at Exeter,* the object reportedly hovered over high-voltage power lines, a theme that keeps recurring throughout the book. One UFO witness speculated that the object he saw was hovering over the power lines to "recharge its batteries . . . taking all the electricity from the wires," blissfully unaware that such a power drain would be noted by the utility company within seconds (although some might insist that the power company is cooperating with the Air Force in its sinister cover-up of flying saucers). On November 9, 1965, less than a month after the sightings at Exeter began to trickle off, millions of Americans were suddenly plunged into darkness by the famous failure of the Northeast Power Grid, which Fuller describes as "one of the biggest mysteries in the history of modern civilization." Fuller recounts a number of UFO sightings that reportedly occurred just as the power failed, attempting to establish a cause-and-effect relationship that would seem to be plausible, in view of the Exeter UFOs' reported affinity for hovering in the vicinity of electric power lines.

Reading *Incident at Exeter* for the second time, I was drawn to a curious fact that might have been only coincidence. The sighting by the Hampton Beach boys of the object that reportedly flew in from over the ocean occurred one month before Muscarello's first UFO sighting, which also reportedly arrived from the same direction. But the Hampton Beach sighting occurred two hours later at night than the one a month later. Two hours a month is the rate at which a clock keeping sidereal time (star time) gains on a clock keeping ordinary standard time. The sky is in the same position on August 1 at 4 AM as it is on September 1 at 2 AM, and indeed one might venture to say that *an object whose arrival time advances at the rate of two hours per month is following the timetable of an astronomical body.*

In the 1930s, radio engineers first noticed a strange, unexplained source of radio signals that seemed to peak at a certain time of the day, suggesting that some effect of the daily cycle of sunlight heating the earth's atmosphere may be responsible for the phenomenon. But when the peak strength of the signals began arriving four minutes earlier each day, two hours earlier per month, it became clear that the source of the signals must be an astronomical body, and the science of radio astronomy was born.

Could the Exeter sightings likewise be generated by the appearance of some astronomical object? If so, which object could it be? Two points on a graph cannot establish anything: more information would be needed. Thus I set out to scan the book once again, noting the reported time of the appearance of *all* of the nocturnal UFOs in the Exeter area during the three months of the flap, all of those that appeared to come in from the direction of the ocean (east or southeast).

Unfortunately, this was not an easy task. Many of the sightings described do not include such essential information as the date and time of the incident. In most cases, all we learn about the date are recollections such as, "I'd say two to three weeks ago," or "just about two or three weeks after the officers here saw this object." This lack of hard data severely hampers efforts of serious investigators to dig more deeply into the sightings, introducing uncertainties into the positions of astronomical bodies, and making it completely impossible to check up on the weather conditions at the time of the sighting. Even more uncertain is the direction in which the object is seen. Only rarely did a witness specify the direction, and Fuller seems to never have asked about such details. But it is sometimes possible to determine the direction of the object from such statements as "toward Hampton," provided that one consults a detailed map of the area.

After examining all the nocturnal UFO reports described in Fuller's book occurring in the Exeter area from August through October 1965, only seven could be identified as involving an object appearing in the east or southeast. (In most cases, the direction was determined by the description of "from the ocean"). East is, of course, the direction in which the sun, the moon, and all other astronomical bodies appear to rise. Was there any brilliant object that had recently risen? Both the first Muscarello sighting and the Hampton Beach sighting occurred about two hours after the planet Jupiter had risen. I plotted this information on a graph, adding the other sightings, and obtained a rather striking result. (See Figure 1.)

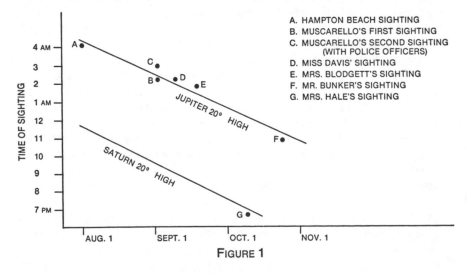

A. HAMPTON BEACH SIGHTING
B. MUSCARELLO'S FIRST SIGHTING
C. MUSCARELLO'S SECOND SIGHTING
   (WITH POLICE OFFICERS)
D. MISS DAVIS' SIGHTING
E. MRS. BLODGETT'S SIGHTING
F. MR. BUNKER'S SIGHTING
G. MRS. HALE'S SIGHTING

FIGURE 1

Even though in some of these cases we are not certain of the exact date, it *is* apparent that as the Exeter sightings continued the mysterious object that reportedly came in from the ocean began arriving earlier in the night. Thus the appearance of the mysterious craftlike object that was frequently reported as coming in from the ocean *closely follows the timetable of the planet Jupiter.* The conclusion suggested by this relationship is that *the UFO was that brilliant planet.*

Of course, no astronomical body can ever perform the intricate maneuvers or close approaches that the Exeter object was *reported* to do. But time and again the serious UFO researcher encounters reports of an object, supposedly at close range, performing remarkable maneuvers, which later turns out to have been a hot-air balloon or a satellite re-entry. Witnesses have been known to "hit the deck" to avoid being struck by an object later determined to be an airplane more than a thousand feet above them, and "close encounters" have been reported with meteors more than a hundred miles away.[4] Subjective impressions of an object's distance and behavior are totally dependent upon the observer's state of mind, so that a distant planet may indeed by perceived as a nearby hovering craft, especially if one has heard that UFOs are reportedly in the vicinity.

At the time of Muscarello's third and final sighting, a woman whom he awakened by his frantic pounding at her door reported seeing the object high in the sky, "smaller than the moon but not as small as a star. The boy [Muscarello] said, that's it, I know it is, because just a few minutes before he had seen it flying low." Her description of the object clearly suggests that Muscarello was looking at some bright celestial object, possibly Jupiter, and imagining it to be coming "in close."

Another Exeter UFO witness, whose name is not given (the time and date of her sighting are also unspecified), described the object that reportedly swooped down "right in front of her car" as disappearing "up in the sky, we lost it, it just diminished. As it goes up, it diminishes and they go so high up they seem to become stars. But not really stars, because they come down, and then up again." This likewise plainly suggests that excitement generated by the UFO flap was causing many residents of the area to mistake ordinary bright celestial objects for strange craft coming in at close range and then quickly retreating. Needless to say, had any UFOs actually been hovering in the sky over Exeter, camouflaging themselves as stars, they would have been recognized immediately and reported by the many amateur astronomers who have been active throughout New England for decades. Despite these many reported "close encounters" with the object that follows Jupiter's timetable, that giant planet remained more than 400 million miles from the earth throughout this entire period.

The evening sky in the autumn boasts fewer brilliant stars than at any other time of the year, and in the autumn of 1965 Mars was a relatively inconspicuous evening star. But Venus was a brilliant object low in the southwest after sunset, shining like a beacon at magnitude -4. Because of the planet's low elevation, due to the southward slant of the sun's path at that time of year, scintillations in the atmosphere would have made Venus appear to be sparkling and dancing much more than it would had it been high in the sky. Scanning *Incident at Exeter* once again, we find that there are indeed many sightings occurring in the one-and-a-half-hour period when Venus was visible. Although there are many sightings that I *suspect* to be Venus, only in a very few cases do we learn the date, time, and direction of the sighting, which are necessary to permit us to make a definite identification.

One sighting occurred just after sunset, "about seven o'clock" (date uncertain), when several people reportedly saw "a red ball of fire," with a jet plane supposedly in hot pursuit. (When a bright star or planet is seen at a low angle of elevation, it usually appears reddish or orange in color, just as the setting sun appears red.) Was this poorly described object Venus? Probably, but we can't be certain. Another witness, Bessie Healy, claims to have repeatedly sighted an object that always hovers over the power lines (probably because the power lines lie to the southwest, though their direction is not stated). When she saw it on October 19, at about 6:15 PM (shortly after sunset), the object reportedly "was really close," with "silver things coming down from it." Red-orange in color, it quickly "moved away as fast as it could go," as soon as her husband came out to see it. An airplane reportedly "was flying around, looking like it was trying to get it."

This object almost certainly was Venus. It was sighted just as Venus first becomes conspicuous, on an evening that the weather records show to have been cloudless, and it was reported to slowly lose altitude, as Venus indeed does when setting. So here we have another "close encounter" with a UFO reported by responsible adults, which supposedly reacted to their presence and was pursued by an airplane, yet turns out to have been a planet more than 80 million miles distant! Discrepancies such as this should serve to caution the serious investigator against taking UFO testimony at face value.

One of Fuller's best UFO witnesses is Mrs. Jalbert, who with her four teenage boys lives outside of Exeter, near the power lines of the Northeast Grid. She and her boys often stood watching by the power lines at dusk, waiting for the UFO to make its appearance. The object reportedly hovers "really close," sometimes moving quickly, then slowly, sometimes bobbing up and down. It "always seems to be somewhere near the lines," occasionally hovering so close to the ground as to actually be "even with the power line." Frequently, Mrs. Jalbert reports, an airplane "comes out and chases it." On some occasions, "windows" were supposedly visible on the object, and it is said to have given off enough light "so that you could have read a book." Fuller was extremely impressed by the credibility of these witnesses, describing the youngsters as "exceptionally intelligent, as was Mrs. Jalbert in her quiet and unassuming way." If their account of these sightings is essentially correct, there is no object known to science that can account for it.

Yet these sightings are almost certainly misinterpretations of the planet Venus, because the time of the object's appearance and departure almost exactly match the time when that planet is visible. The object always appeared just as the sky was getting dark, about 6:45 to 7:00 PM. Venus becomes conspicuous at this time. But the real clincher is Mrs. Jalbert's statement that "by quarter of eight it's gone." Venus was setting at about eight o'clock, so it would in fact disappear for most observers at about "quarter of eight." When an object appears repeatedly on different nights at about the same time, always in the same part of the sky, there can be little doubt that it is an astronomical body. When that same object is shown to keep the precise timetable of the brilliant evening star, its identity is scarcely in doubt any longer.

This case provides us with another excellent illustration of how a description of an object by seemingly competent and reliable witnesses can bear little or no resemblance to that object's true appearance. After interviewing Mrs. Jalbert, Fuller returned that evening in hopes of seeing the UFO himself, but he was disappointed to find the sky overcast and hazy. Joseph Jalbert remarked, "We almost never see them on nights like this," which should come as no surprise, because while UFOs that were genuinely at tree-top level might be seen in any weather, bright planets can only be seen in clear skies.

Further evidence that many of the reported UFOs were bright stars or planets is suggested by an examination of the weather conditions at the time of the sightings. Of the dozens of sightings occurring in the Exeter area during the months of August, September, and October 1965 that are mentioned in *Incident at Exeter,* only in eleven cases do we know the exact date of the sighting. (If I were to restrict this sample further to a requirement of knowing the approximate time, or the direction of the object, the sample would be so small as to reveal nothing.) The weather data was compiled from the Local Climatological Data sheet published for Boston. If a given day was more than 50 percent cloudy, based upon the published observations at three-hour intervals, I designated it as a "cloudy" day. If the cloud cover was 50 percent or less during the twenty-four-hour interval, I designated the day as "clear." During the three-month period, out of a total of ninety-two days, forty-three were "clear" days, and forty-nine were "cloudy," making 47 percent of the days "clear." Of the days when UFOs were sighted, eight out of eleven were "clear." *Thus, although only 47 percent of the days were "clear," 73 percent of the identifiable UFO sightings occurred on "clear" days.* The great majority of sightings occurred on that minority of days that were less than 50 percent cloudy. Because of the small size of the sample, however, this result is not statistically significant. There is about a 20 percent probability that this result is due to chance alone.

This does not *prove* that the sightings were of astronomical objects, although it does suggest that such sightings seem to be most frequent on nights when the planets are visible. Of course I am not suggesting that *all* of the Exeter UFO sightings were of astronomical objects. Many of them may well be due to misinterpretations of aircraft, balloons, birds, and similar phenomena. In fact, one of the sightings that originally led me to the Jupiter hypothesis *may* not have been Jupiter after all. When I received the weather records from Pease Air Force Base, I discovered that they show overcast conditions prevailing at the time of the youths' sighting in Hampton Beach, suggesting that the object was not an astronomical body. But it is also possible that a small rift in the clouds permitted Jupiter to peek through unexpectedly for a brief period (surely everyone has on occasion been surprised to see the moon suddenly appear between the clouds on an otherwise moonless night). This seems especially likely considering how well the time and direction of this case fit the Exeter pattern.

If this explanation of the Exeter sightings is accepted, it has serious implications for the way one interprets the entire phenomenon of UFOs. If apparently sane and rational people can mistake a distant planet for metallic craft at close range and imagine it to be under intelligent control, then no UFO report can be taken at face value unless substantiated by indisputable physical evidence. Like the famous Gestalt illustration, which changes from a vase to two profiles as the viewer changes his interpretation of figure and ground, the Exeter sightings either establish or demolish the validity of the entire UFO phenomenon, depending on which the reader is inclined to view as the more fanciful: the reported sightings or the proposed explanation. Surely, it seems, when Fuller cites two rational adults reporting a craft as large as a jet plane, complete with dome and square windows, which "play[s] tag" with their car, shining its "floodlights" on the road, this cannot by any stretch of the imagination be a misinterpretation of a celestial body. *Yet the pictures they took of the supposedly brilliant object did not come out.* This suggests that they grossly overestimated its brightness; it probably *was* the planet Jupiter, which requires an exposure of several seconds to be recorded on film.

Although the Exeter area was buzzing with UFO sightings, if one or more mysterious craft were in reality lurking in the area for several months wouldn't it have been seen by more than a few scattered witnesses? Would not dozens or hundreds of people see it at the same time? Wouldn't several independent photographs of it be obtained? Not all of the Exeter residents were as eager as was Fuller to believe these remarkable tales. One man went so far as to determine the volume of traffic on Route 101 at the time of night a woman had reportedly been followed "from Epping to the Exeter line" by a UFO. He told Fuller that he went out the following Tuesday about midnight on Route 101, and parked. At no time, he says, was there a greater span of time than three minutes that a car did not pass. "Tell me, why didn't another car observe this thing if she was followed all the way to Exeter?" Why do no UFO sightings anywhere ever report seeing a mysterious craft at treetop level *following someone else's car?* Why are all such stories first-person accounts? I suspect that it is for the same reason that the viewer always perceives the moon or the rainbow as sharing in *his or her own motion,* and not someone else's. A detailed study of the Exeter phenomenon will enable science to gain much valuable insight into the psychology of human perception. But it will teach us nothing about nonterrestrial civilizations.

NOTES

1. John G. Fuller, *Incident at Exeter* (New York: Putnam, 1966). In paperback (New York: Berkley, 1974).
2. John G. Fuller, *Ghost of Flight 401* (New York: Berkley, 1978).
3. Raymond Fowler, *Report to NICAP on the Exeter UFO Report*, September 15, 1965.
4. Philip J. Klass, *UFOs Explained* (New York: Random House, 1974), pp. 17, 42.

12

BEFORE THE YEAR IS OUT . . .

It is a widespread belief in UFO circles that the government knows far more about UFOs than it is willing to reveal. Such a belief is not only exciting but also impossible to disprove, and with those two strong points in its favor the theory of a "government cover-up" of UFOs has become firmly entrenched on the current UFO scene. A moment's reflection would seem to be enough to place the question of such a massive cover-up in its proper perspective. The U.S. government has always found it difficult to prevent glimpses and snatches of its secret operations from leaking out. Many civil servants in Washington talk rather freely about their work. This enables the patient investigator to carefully paste together, from both public and private sources, a glimpse of the shadow world of government activity that is not visible to the public eye. A look at the history of recent government security leaks reveals several things.

- Many of the secrets revealed have been extremely embarrassing to some of the most powerful individuals and groups in Washington. The reputations of several presidents, the FBI, the CIA, and powerful congressional bosses have been damaged by the public disclosure of certain information. All their potent political clout seems to have been unable to stem the tide of embarrassing revelations.

- Once a story begins to leak, the pace of the revelations becomes quicker and quicker, until eventually the dam bursts and the full story is out, such as happened with Watergate. If a UFO cover-up really does exist, we should expect to see the dike slowly crumble, as the stories of suppression of UFO evidence become substantiated. But this is not happening.

- In recent years the entire legal mechanism for prosecuting violations of the government's secrecy codes appears to have broken down. Even when national security information is leaked to the press (and thus to the Soviets), in defiance of espionage laws and signed agreements of confidentiality, experience has shown that, if the offender mutters only a few words about feeling a "higher obligation" to tell the public everything he knows, he is unlikely to suffer any legal penalties. Thus fear of prosecution no longer serves to keep anyone from publicly revealing *any* secrets he may feel inclined to leak.

In those cover-ups we know about, how long has the government succeeded in keeping its secrets under wraps? The Watergate cover-up was leaking badly before the first anniversary of the break-in. Daniel Ellsberg leaked the Pentagon Papers to the press before the Vietnam war had ended. America's atomic secrets began leaking to the Soviets while World War II was still in progress. Thus we see that *if* a UFO cover-up exists, it has already lasted a great deal longer than any other cover-up we know of, since claims of government suppression of UFO evidence go back at least thirty years.

One of the best-known promoters of the "UFO cover-up" story has been Stanton T. Friedman, the self-proclaimed "Flying Saucer Physicist" (who actually makes his living by giving UFO lectures and making radio/TV appearances). On a radio talk-show on KNBR, San Francisco (December 19, 1975), Philip J. Klass challenged Friedman to bring forward the "cover-up" evidence he claims to have and present it to the congressional panels that were then investigating abuses by the intelligence agencies: "Come [to Washington] Stanton, and I will put you up in my apartment at no cost, will feed you breakfast and take you out to dinner. I think you owe it to this nation to come here now, while these intelligence investigating committees are in session."

Friedman declined Klass's offer, saying, "The pressure has to come from somebody else other than me." But if the evidence were really there as claimed, the cover-up advocates would not find it necessary to always back down from such challenges.

There is another aspect of the government's activity that argues strongly *against* the existence of a massive UFO cover-up: the space program. If a UFO can reportedly zip from Zeta Reticuli to Alpha Mensae with sufficient ease to establish "trade routes," as Betty Hill alleges, why would we continue to waste money and effort on development of present-day rockets, which are plainly obsolete before they are built, *if* UFOs are real? NASA has spent more than a billion dollars on the Viking project, whose principal mission was the fruitless search for life on Mars. Why would NASA spend so much money to learn something that it supposedly already knows?

Where does all this leave us? The strongest conclusion we can firmly reach is that *the U.S. Government is not acting like an organization with proof that UFOs are real and are a product of some nonearthly intelligence.* This does not, of course, *prove* the nonexistence of a cover-up. The only way to do that would be to conduct an exhaustive search of every last file in the Pentagon and CIA headquarters, and that is simply *not* going to happen.

In truth it must be said that *if* the government is in fact attempting to cover up UFO information, it is certainly *not* doing a thorough or effective job, because the news of hundreds of sightings reaches the various UFO groups each year. An ineffective cover-up is much worse than no cover-up at all, as Richard Nixon and others learned the hard way. If one believes the well-known "classic" UFO cases to be authentic, then one has to attempt to explain why it is that the government permits so much presumably "authentic" UFO information to reach the public, when it is allegedly up to its ears in a massive UFO cover-up.

When all the evidence concerning UFO cover-ups, both for and against, is carefully weighed, we see that the scale tilts strongly toward the negative. Of course, I can't *prove* that there isn't any massive UFO conspiracy, because such things can't be proved. This is not to say that there are absolutely *no* UFO materials in the government files that the public has not seen, for who can say what some secrecy-mad bureaucrat may have decided to toss into a vault? But, taken as a whole, the evidence clearly suggests that if every last scrap of UFO-related information were obtained from all government files, nothing would be found that would in any way alter the overall picture of the UFO phenomenon as we know it today.

The other side of the UFO cover-up mania is the often-stated belief that the cover is about to be removed. Like the various end-of-the-world cults, which suffer no noticeable loss of faith when their appointed deadline for *Götterdammerung* passes without incident, UFO proponents have mercifully short memories when it comes to recalling embarrassing predictions they have made of an approaching end of UFO secrecy. At the risk of ruffling a few feathers, let us recall some of the recent (and not so recent) predictions of spectacular, soon-to-follow UFO events.

Ten "top psychics" selected by the supermarket tabloid *The Star* (October 30, 1979) revealed their predictions for 1980. Among them: "Spiritualist Minister" Reverend Gayle Eaton predicted, "We will make contact with aliens from outer space during 1980." A "psychic counselor," the Reverend Chris McGaughy, added more details: "In late 1980, we will make direct contact with alien space beings. As a result, much will be revealed to us about the lost city of Atlantis."

In the January 30, 1979, issue of the tabloid *National Enquirer,* former NICAP Director Major Donald Keyhoe suggested that "the recent rash of UFO sightings could mean that the aliens are ready to identify themselves to us this year." MUFON's Deputy Director John F. Schuessler observed that "this is the year of the UFO." The supposed aliens "are getting bolder," Schuessler added. "There's a very good chance that this year they're going to say 'hello.'" In the *Enquirer*'s March 13, 1979, issue, it was revealed that eighty-one out of a hundred carefully chosen "seers" predicted "startling contact with alien beings this year."

APRO's Dr. Leo Sprinkle told the *National Enquirer* (January 31, 1978) that "we will learn more about UFOs in 1978 than everything we have learned about this phenomenon in the last 50 years." He expected that year to bring mankind's "biggest step forward" to solving the mystery of the UFO. "Psychic" Shawn Robbins predicted that the first open UFO contact would occur in 1978. "Psychic" Kebrina Kinkade predicted that "we will have actual communications in 1978 from planets like Pluto and Saturn." The famous "psychic" Jeane Dixon predicted (*Midnight/Globe,* April 4, 1978) that "we will have contact with UFOs soon," but she declined to give any specific date.

In the spring of 1977, *U.S. News & World Report* carried the following item in its "Washington Whispers" column: "OFFICIAL WORD COMING ON UFO's: Before the year is out, the Government — perhaps the President — is expected to make what are described as 'unsettling disclosures' about UFO's — unidentified flying objects. Such revelations, based on information from the CIA, would be a reversal of official policy that in the past has downgraded UFO incidents."[1]

Ripples of the *U.S. News* item quickly spread through UFOdom. The editors of *U.S. News,* in keeping with policy, refused to reveal anything concerning their sources for the item. Philip J. Klass offered anyone on the *U.S. News* staff 100-to-1 odds against its happening — an obvious chance for easy money *if* they had confidence in their own story — but Klass found no takers.

Later developments suggested that the *U.S. News* piece was based on a gross misinterpretation of a hasty statement made by Jody Powell, President Carter's news secretary. Powell later admitted his error in saying that the Carter administration was responsible for releasing U.S. Air Force Project Blue Book UFO files to the National Archives.[2] (Some accounts have it that Powell stated that the files *would* soon be released.) The Blue Book files, however, had been opened up at the Archives the previous year by the Ford Administration; Powell had obviously made this statement without being fully informed on the matter.

In the July 1977 *Science Digest* (page 32), we find: "Here at home, reliable sources such as *U.S. News & World Report* and ABC News have recently indicated that our government is expected to make an announcement by the end of the year."

The *Christian Beacon* is a publication of fundamentalist preacher Carl McIntyre's multi-million-dollar religious empire, and the 20th-Century UFO Bureau, directed by Robert Barry, is its official organ for spreading the word on UFOs and their significance to Scriptures. UFOs are piloted by "angels," according to Barry and "Satan's agents [pilot] the demonic vessels, and God also lets extraterrestrial beings pilot their own UFOs." He maintains that Israel's victories in Mideast conflicts are due to the celestial intervention of angels piloting UFOs. In the June 16, 1977, *Christian Beacon,* Barry predicts: "It seems as though this will be the year when those news releases will begin. . . . In discussing this with this Christian gentleman affiliated within CIA circles, I was told he expects the first news release to come at any time."[3]

Mrs. Ruth Norman, founder and leader of the Unarius Life Sciences Center in California, claims to be in mental communication with alien beings on no fewer than thirty-two different planets. Her sizable following, for whom she is "Spacecraft Coordinator" and "messenger of the Space Brothers," takes her stories of celestial communications very seriously. In March of 1976, Mrs. Norman bet $4,000 of her own money with Ladbroke and Company, Ltd., of London, that the "Space Brothers" would land by March 30, 1977. She was given 100-to-1 odds. So many of Mrs. Norman's followers rushed to get in on the wager that the bookmaker lowered the odds to 33 to 1. Then in April 1977, a story appeared on the AP wires stating that Mrs. Norman had wagered $6,000 with Ladbroke that at least one spacecraft would arrive by September 30, 1977. She was given odds of 50-to-1. Her followers were said to have contributed $4,000. "I don't expect to lose my bet," she confidently stated. By September 22, her optimism appeared to be wavering somewhat: "They will come soon. How soon might be a matter of months. Or to the end of the century, but probably this year. They don't give us a date." Yet in 1979, a Ladbroke official noted that Mrs. Norman and her followers made up a "significant part" of the alien wager business, having "invested" about $15,000 during the previous year.[4]

In the *National Enquirer's* predictions for 1977, self-proclaimed psychic Shawn Robbins, who claims to have foreseen the capture of Patty Hearst, predicted: "An unmanned spacecraft from another planet will crash in Arizona, and researchers will gain fantastic new knowledge of space travel." Micky Dahne foresees that "archaeologists in Egypt will discover a spaceship that crashed in ancient times, proving once and for all that earth has been visited by beings from another planet." Supposed psychic Kebrina Kinkade concurs that "the Air Force will reveal it has captured an alien spacecraft and its humanlike occupants." (Other predictions for 1977 include: "Peace will finally arrive in Northern Ireland"; twins for Freddie Prinze; and a "delicate, but successful, eye operation" for Elvis Presley. Both Prinze and Presley died during 1977.)[5]

Jeane Dixon, billed by the *National Enquirer* as "the world's most phenomenal seer," predicted in the summer of 1976 that "aliens — who are really just better-developed humans from a planet on the opposite side of the sun — will begin transmitting their secrets to us no later than August, 1977. They will also land by then."[6]

The well-known UFOlogist Jacques Vallee, in his 1975 book, *The Invisible College,* reports: "There are persistent rumors highly placed officials in the U.S. Government have long had evidence that another form of intelligence was contacting us . . . A former aerospace engineer turned UFO lecturer even believes that at the occasion of the Bicentennial the government will announce that there is life on Mars, and that a meeting between U.S.

representatives and extraterrestrials is imminent!" Vallee does not indicate whether or not he accepts this prediction.[7]

Another voice echoing the Bicentennial date for UFOlogical revelations was that of the alleged psychic Libby Collins Freiberg. Holding a midnight seance on a rooftop overlooking the spot where George O'Barski reported a widely publicized UFO close encounter in 1975, Mrs. Freiberg appeared to go into a trance. She soon began to speak as the voice of Caldon, a "Gropalin," who hails from "another dimension." After giving voice to trite ecological platitudes, Caldon promised to land his flying saucer in the middle of Times Square on July 4, 1976. He has not been heard from since.[8]

The celebrated Dutch-born "psychic" Peter Hurkos, who claims to have contributed to the solution of the Boston Strangler murders and other criminal investigations, predicted in 1975: "Flying Saucers will land in Arizona and New Mexico" sometime between November 1975 and February 1976.[9]

Ralph and Judy Blum, authors of the popular paperback *Beyond Earth: Man's Contact with UFO's* (1974), unambiguously state in the preface: "We predict that by 1975 the government will release definite proof that extraterrestrials are watching us." *Beyond Earth*, which boasts of "new, astounding evidence from outer space, including the silvery creatures of Pascagoula, Mississippi," soon after its publication was placed on the recommended reading list of Hynek's scholarly Center for UFO Studies. "An objective newsman's look at the UFO problem," read CUFOS' endorsement.[10]

In the fall of 1974, the well-known psychic Bernadene Villanueva predicted, "Within the next 18 months we will see absolute, conclusive proof of UFO's.[11]

Syndicated columnist Roscoe Drummond, who presumably earns his living by publishing accurate information, reported in October 1974 that "UFO's are in the news again and with mounting evidence that they are real, not imaginary . . . the time is getting near when the U.S. Air Force will have to abandon its longstanding tactic of concealment or be repudiated by the Department of Defense." Drummond suggests, largely on the basis of a letter received from former NICAP director Major Keyhoe, that the Defense Department is now beginning to "repudiate" its usual skepticism about UFOs, and will soon release heretofore secret information about dramatic UFO encounters.[12]

APRO Director James Lorenzen said in a 1974 interview that "a program has been undertaken that will over the next few months make it obvious that the government has reversed its position" on the existence of UFOs. "My information is that the government will release all its information within the next two years," he stated.[13]

Charles Hickson, who claims to have been abducted aboard a UFO in Pascagoula, Mississippi, in 1973, stated in a radio interview in the fall of 1974, "I think that they [the Air Force] have definite proof that other worlds and beings do exist. And I think that before this year is out, and I say this with some reservation, but I think before the year is out, that our government—particularly our Air Force—is going to come out to the American people and tell them that these things [UFOs] do exist."[14]

Robert S. Carr is a retired instructor of mass communications at the University of South Florida who claims to have proof that since 1948 the Air Force has been concealing at Wright-Patterson Air Force Base in Ohio a flying saucer that crash-landed near Aztec, New Mexico. He claims that the government is also concealing the bodies of twelve humanoid aliens found inside, smaller than earth people but otherwise quite like us, except that their deeply convoluted brains indicate that they were "hundreds" of years old at the time of their death. Professor Carr held a news conference in Tampa on October 15, 1974, at which he stated, "Five weeks ago I heard from the highest authority in Washington that before Christmas the whole UFO cover-up will be ended. There will be public admission that UFO's always have been real, and that for the past 25 years the United States government and the Air Force have known they were piloted by human-like beings."

When *Official UFO* magazine published an article in 1975 refuting Carr's claims about the crashed saucer near Aztec, Carr proclaimed that the refutation "bothers me not in the slightest." In a letter to the editor he was willing to concede that "the capture was made at some other, probably uninhabited, desert spot in the Southwest," and he added: "My latest information, from usually reliable sources inside the anti-secrecy circles . . . is to the effect that last December [1974], when the 'frozen bodies *cum* spaceship' story became too 'hot' for comfort at WP-AFB, Desk Nine of the CIA—the UFO Control Center—ordered the evidence removed to Langley, Virginia, where it now reposes, along with other scientifically priceless artifacts from space, in a fortress-like warehouse out of sight behind the seven-story marble palace that houses the CIA." Carr failed to offer any explanation of why the end of the "UFO cover-up" did not arrive by the previous Christmas.[15]

A popular UFO writer, the late Frank Edwards, discussing the big UFO flap of 1965 in his enormously successful book *Flying Saucers—Serious Business* (1966), wrote that contact with UFOs "cannot be far away": "If the conclusions of the scientists in NICAP are correct, then we are probably witnessing the sixth phase of a seven-phase program of the UFOs . . . the seventh phase—known to the military as 'Overt Landing' or deliberate contact—cannot be far away. If we have, indeed, gone through six phases in nineteen years—then the final phase would seem to be due in the next two or three years—although it could come tomorrow."[16]

The British publication *Flying Saucer Review,* often termed "respected" by UFO proponents, features wild tales about UFOs written in a stilted, academic style. In an editorial in its issue of May–June 1957, *FSR* asked,

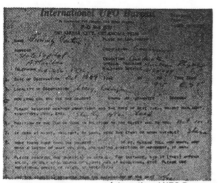

PLATE 1. Jimmy Carter's 1973 UFO report (chapter 2), in his own handwriting. The date of the incident was incorrectly recalled as sometime in October 1969; the date was later determined to have been January 6, 1969.

PLATE 2. The planet Venus as seen in full daylight, taken about noon on June 12, 1977. The thin crescent moon is seen above Venus. 250 mm telephoto lens, f/32, 1/8 second on Kodachrome 64 film. No filters or special processing were used. Venus is often called the "Queen of the UFOs"; no other single object is so often reported as a UFO.

PLATE 3. UFO "abductee" Betty Hill (chapter 5). She is holding a sculpture of one of the creatures that supposedly forced her aboard a UFO. She is also holding one of more than a hundred photographs of UFOs she claims to have taken in recent years. This photograph shows irregular streaks of light such as one might obtain by taking a time-exposure photograph of aircraft using a hand-held camera.

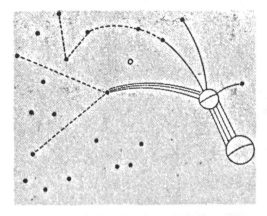

PLATE 4. Under post-hypnotic suggestion, Betty Hill drew an "alien star map" that she supposedly saw aboard the UFO. The heavy lines are supposed to represent trade routes; the thin lines, places they went occasionally; and the broken lines were expeditions.

PLATE 5. The stars of the constellation Pegasus. CTA 102 is a quasar that, when first discovered, was believed by some astronomers to possibly be an artificial radio beacon.

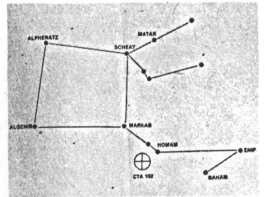

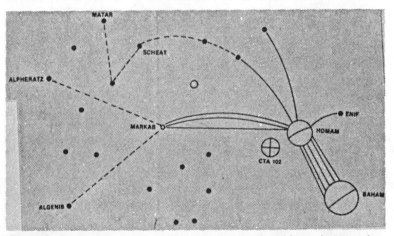

PLATE 6. Betty Hill was struck by the apparent resemblance between her sketch and the stars of Pegasus. This was the first of three proposed identifications of her "alien star map," with the star names supplied by Betty Hill herself. CTA-102 seemed to be a "beacon" to guide the UFOs home from their explorations.

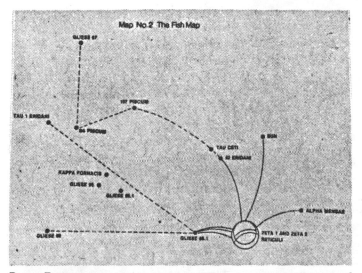

Map No.2 The Fish Map

PLATE 7. The second and most famous proposed identification of Betty Hill's "alien star map," that of Marjorie Fish. While the 15 stars identified are all solar-type stars, and hence presumably favorable for life, 11 stars on the original sketch cannot be identified in this map. The separation of the two giant globes of Betty's sketch is also far too small.

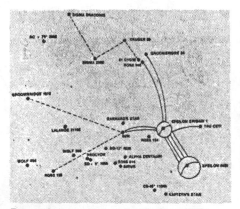

PLATE 8. The third and thus far final proposed identification of Betty Hill's "alien star map," that of Charles Atterberg. While it is the most accurate of the three and accounts for the greatest number of stars, it has never been widely accepted by UFO proponents.

PLATE 9. "Close Encounter of the Third Kind." Sculpture of a supposed UFO creature by New York City free-lance artist George A. Rackus, based upon published descriptions of alleged alien encounters.

PLATE 10. One of the author's authentic-looking photographs of a flying saucer. This one was fabricated from a banana-split ice-cream dish, illuminated by a flashlight in a darkened basement. Modeling clay rounds off the flat top of the dish, with a toothpick stuck at the top to serve as an antenna. Black dots provide us with portholes.

PLATE 11. This authentic-looking flying saucer is approximately 8 inches in diameter. It was fabricated by the author from an aluminum plate, a cottage-cheese container, Ping Pong balls, black tape, and some black dots to serve as portholes. It is similar in appearance to many of the supposedly authentic close-up photographs of UFOs produced by "contactees," such as the late George Adamski. A photograph of this type contains no information whatsoever as to the size or distance of the object being photographed.

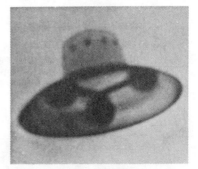

PLATE 12. The two UFOs actually represent a single, small elliptical-shaped light source that was photographed twice in a darkened basement. The camera was then carried outdoors for a time exposure to record the background. The film was not advanced between the three exposures.

PLATE 13. This supposed UFO would probably stand up to the most "expert" scrutiny and become accepted as a "classic" unknown were the author to present it as supposedly authentic. A model UFO fabricated from aluminum plates and Ping Pong balls was tossed into the air at night. As it appeared to pass the vicinity of the moon, it was photographed using an electronic strobe flash, with an exposure setting of one-half second. The extremely brief duration of the flash—less than one-thousandth of a second— "froze" the motion of the model UFO. The shutter then remained open long enough to record an image of the moon, while the model "UFO" sailed invisibly out of the field.

PLATE 14. Lens flares are the result of stray light from a brilliant light source being reflected off the interface between elements of a multi-element lens and onto the wrong spot on the film. Here the author has photographed what appears to be a whole fleet of UFOs but is actually a lens flare from a row of streetlights just beyond the left edge of the camera's field of view.

PLATE 15. This "classic" UFO photograph was taken on board a ship near the island of Trindade, Brazil, in 1958 (chapter 6). Although the photographer was known to be a specialist in trick photography, NICAP nonetheless selected this as one of the four best available UFO photos.

U.S. Air Force Photograph

PLATE 16. A photo from the famous series of UFO photographs taken by Rex Heflin near Santa Ana, California, on August 3, 1965. While the object supposedly flew directly over the crowded Santa Ana Freeway, visible in the distance, no one else seems to have noticed it (chapter 6).

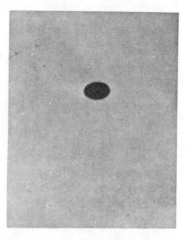

PLATE 17. One of more than a hundred UFO photographs taken by Jorma Viita, the prolific UFO photographer who lives in Denmark (chapter 6). Viita has noted that the UFOs seem only to appear when he is alone, but says he does not know why this is so. This UFO has five geometrically spaced holes on its underside and looks very much like a button.

NASA

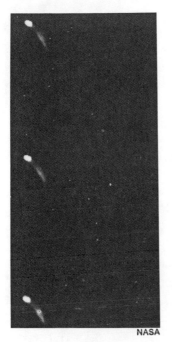

PLATE 18. The "tadpole UFO" movie-film segment attributed to Gemini 4 astronaut James McDivitt (chapter 6). While McDivitt claims to have seen an unidentified object, possibly a portion of the rocket that boosted him into orbit, he has stated that this film does *not* depict the object he saw. This is a film of a lens flare produced by sunlight reflecting off a bolt on the spacecraft window. Nonetheless, NICAP included it among the "four best" UFO photos.

Mr. and Mrs. Paul Trent

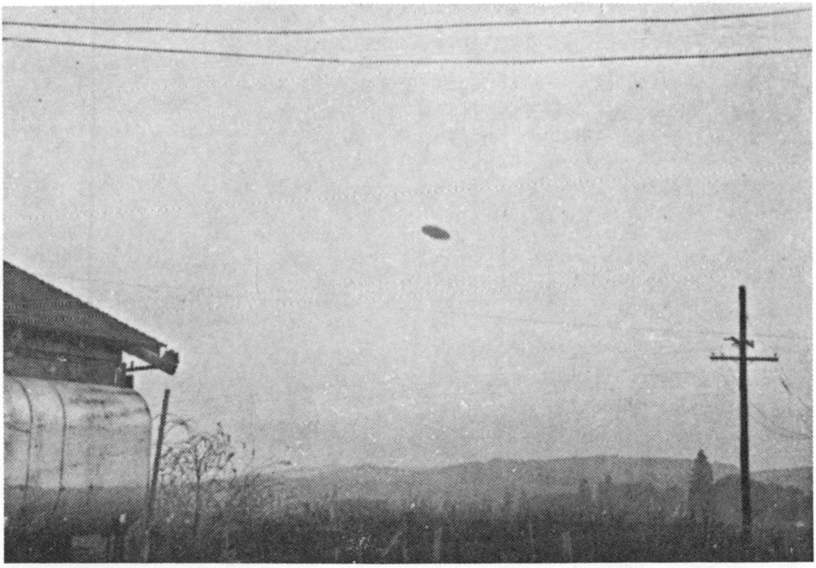

PLATE 19. The famous UFO photograph taken May 11, 1950, at McMinnville, Oregon, by Mr. and Mrs. Paul Trent. While the witnesses claim that the object was seen in the evening at about sunset, the shadows under the garage roof conclusively establish that the photo was taken at about 7:30 AM. The UFO was probably a small model suspended by threads from the overhead wires. Most UFO books crop out these wires.

PLATE 20. The Trent UFO (detail). Note that the peak on the "dome" is off center.

PLATE 21. Joseph Glanvill (1636-1680) was a pioneer in the philosophy of science, a champion of the "new science" of Descartes, Galileo, and Francis Bacon, a Fellow of the Royal Society of London, and the prime proponent of the "scientific study" of witchcraft (chapter 7).

PLATE 22. "Frances and the Fairies," the first of the famous fairy photographs from Cottingley, England, 1917-1920. These photographs were defended as authentic by the celebrated Sir Arthur Conan Doyle and have more recently been at least tentatively endorsed by several prominent UFOlogists (chapter 8).

PLATE 23. Elsie and the gnome.

Plate 24

Plate 25

Plate 26

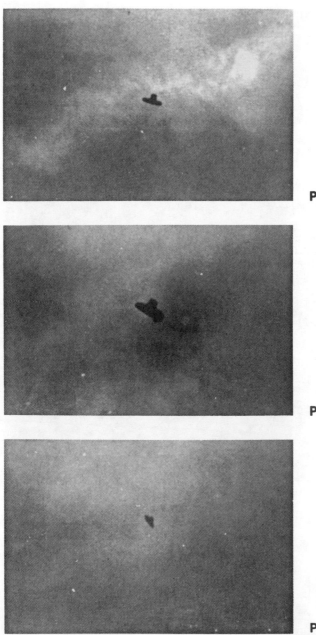

PLATE 27

PLATE 28

PLATE 29

PLATES 24-29. The six UFO photographs taken by 11-year-old David Dorn, of Deerfield, Illinois, in May 1974 (chapter 9). The UFO has a slightly different shape in each of the six photos. The first photo clearly depicts a three-dimensional object, while the other five appear to be two-dimensional, featureless images. The negatives are said to have been accidentally lost. Dr. J. Allen Hynek has endorsed this case as "a real UFO experience." All photographs by David Dorn

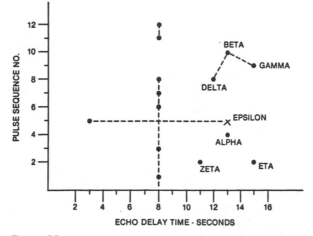

PLATE 30. Duncan Lunan's plot of long-delayed echoes (chapter 13) supposedly produced by an alien space probe, said to prove that the aliens hail from the star Epsilon Bootis. However, the star positions are only approximately correct, and several bright stars in the region have been arbitrarily excluded.

PLATE 31. Apollo 11 photograph of a supposed "unidentified object," as published in *Science Digest* (chapter 14).

PLATE 32. The original NASA photograph from which plate 31 was taken, showing insulation fragment at right. The supposed "unidentified object" is nowhere to be seen.

PLATE 33. *(left)* Gray Barker, author of *They Knew Too Much About Flying Saucers* (chapter 15), which first popularized the supposed "Men in Black"; *(right)* Timothy Green Beckley, UFO writer and entrepreneur, who claims the title "Mr. UFO" (chapter 4).

PLATE 34. James W. Moseley, longtime UFO fan and "middle UFOlogist," is seen here at the 1980 National UFO Conference, which he organized. Moseley was allegedly "silenced" by the Men in Black in 1954 (chapter 15).

PLATE 35. Stanton T. Friedman, who bills himself as "The Flying Saucer Physicist" (chapter 12), selling UFO literature at the 1980 National UFO Conference.

PLATE 36. John Keel, author of *The Mothman Prophecies* (chapter 18).

PLATE 37. Dr. J. Allen Hynek, former UFO consultant to the U.S. Air Force and founder of the Center for UFO Studies (chapter 9).

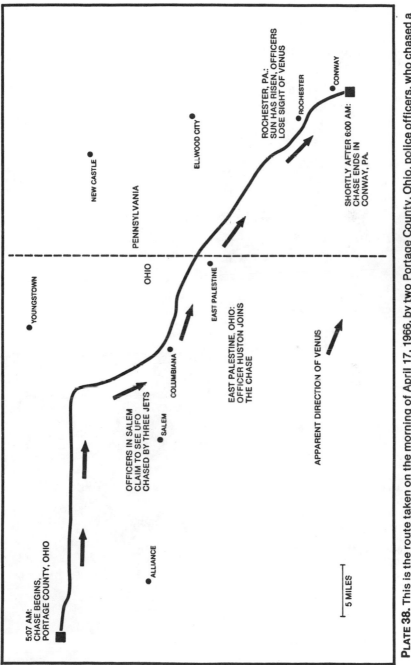

PLATE 38. This is the route taken on the morning of April 17, 1966, by two Portage County, Ohio, police officers, who chased a supposed UFO into Pennsylvania at speeds of up to 103 m.p.h. (chapter 19). The direction of travel of the officers almost precisely matches the apparent direction of Venus, suggesting that they were in fact chasing that brilliant morning star.

Within the figure:

5:07 AM:
CHASE BEGINS,
PORTAGE COUNTY, OHIO

OFFICERS IN SALEM
CLAIM TO SEE UFO
CHASED BY THREE JETS

EAST PALESTINE, OHIO:
OFFICER HUSTON JOINS
THE CHASE

APPARENT DIRECTION OF VENUS

ROCHESTER, PA.:
SUN HAS RISEN, OFFICERS
LOSE SIGHT OF VENUS

SHORTLY AFTER 6:00 AM:
CHASE ENDS IN
CONWAY, PA.

YOUNGSTOWN

ALLIANCE

SALEM

COLUMBIANA

EAST PALESTINE

OHIO

PENNSYLVANIA

NEW CASTLE

ELLWOOD CITY

ROCHESTER

CONWAY

5 MILES

PLATE 39. The late Ray Palmer, one of the "founding fathers" of UFOlogy, in later years promoted the notion that the earth is hollow and that there is a giant, gaping hole where the North Pole ought to be and that flying saucers originate from a civilization inside the polar hole (chapter 20). This photo supposedly "proving" the existence of the hole is a composite of several ESSA satellite photos taken on the same day; the "hole" represents the region where the sun never rises during the winter months.

PLATE 40. A photograph from the U.S. Defense Meteorological Satellite Program (DMSP), showing the Japanese squid fishing fleet (arrow) in its summer fishing area in the Sea of Japan (chapter 21). Each boat carries up to a third of a million watts of incandescent light to lure squid from the ocean depths. As can be seen from the photograph, the total light output from the fleet exceeds that of the city of Tokyo.

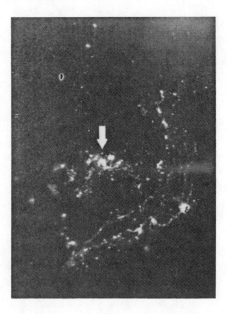

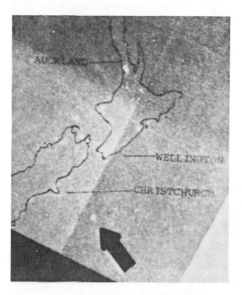

PLATE 41. Another DMSP satellite photograph showing the Japanese squid fishing fleet in its winter fishing area off the coast of New Zealand (arrow). This photograph was taken while the celebrated New Zealand UFO incident was in progress (chapter 21). The total light output of the fleet exceeds both that of Christchurch and that of Wellington.

PLATE 42. Superior mirage of a freighter on Lake Michigan, April 10, 1971, as seen from Evanston, Illinois. An infrequently seen and only rarely photographed phenomenon, the superior mirage is the result of a temperature-inversion condition, when a layer of warm air lies over a cooler layer and remains stable for at least a few minutes. We see an inverted mirage image of the ship directly above the ship itself. A superior mirage can bring into view an object that is normally miles beyond the horizon, accounting for numerous accounts of strange lights or objects sighted just above the horizon. A superior mirage always appears to be within a fraction of a degree of the horizon and is almost never seen except over deserts or large bodies of water.

PLATE 43. The Fata Morgana, a very rare and beautiful type of superior mirage. The image of the object under observation is distorted beyond all recognition (this object is a freighter), appearing as a constantly changing pattern of "palm trees" and "castles-in-the-air." The Fata Morgana, the result of highly complex and unstable layers of warm and cold air, takes its name from fairy lore and is said to evoke in the viewer a profound sense of longing. Photographed over Lake Michigan from Evanston, Illinois, on April 10, 1971.

PLATE 44. The founding members of the CSICOP UFO Subcommittee engaged in painstaking UFO research. From left: Philip J. Klass, Robert Sheaffer, James E. Oberg.

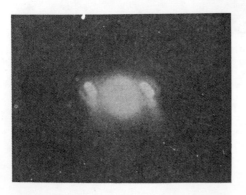

PLATE 45. An "authentic" UFO: a commercial airliner with landing lights on, preparing to land in the fog.

"Is 1957, as Bender said, the year?" Al Bender was the man who "Knew Too Much About Flying Saucers," and as a consequence was supposedly teleported to a secret UFO base at the South Pole by the Men in Black (chapter 15). When in 1953 Bender was asked when the government would end its supposed cover-up of UFOs, he replied, "If not within five months from now, not for about four years." Taking the matter ever so seriously, *Flying Saucer Review* asks, "How did Bender know in 1953 that we should be told about saucers in 1957?" A rumor was discussed that predicted that the first artificial satellites "will be equipped with special electronic equipment which will be used to study flying saucers." FSR concludes, "All this lends credence to the possibility that the authorities may shortly announce that saucers exist and that they consider them hostile."[17]

In the spring of 1950, *U.S. News & World Report* published an exclusive story, featured on the cover, revealing that "flying saucers" are real and that they are secret aircraft of the U.S. Navy. They were said to be a combination of jet aircraft and helicopter, obeying all laws of aerodynamics. Right-angle turns were accomplished by turning off rear jets, while simultaneously turning on those in the front and side. No explanation is given of the techniques that keep the crew of the aircraft from being flattened against the walls. *U.S. News* cautions its readers that the government is likely to keep denying this project for some time. Their prediction has proved to be correct, since the government still has not revealed any such project thirty years later.[18]

Why were the predictions of UFO revelations so especially persistent from 1974 until 1977? One can make a very plausible guess. At the start of 1974 the investigation of the Watergate affair was building up momentum, and as the year progressed it became increasingly evident that the Nixon presidency would soon be coming to an end. When Michigan Congressman Gerald Ford was selected as the new vice-president, UFO buffs were quick to recall that eight years earlier, during the big UFO flap of 1966, Congressman Ford had been highly critical of the Air Force's handling of its UFO investigations and called for a congressional hearing into the matter. From the tone of his statements, it seemed that Gerald Ford was sympathetic to the UFO proponents—if he was not one himself! This man was soon to become president. Those who believed in a massive government "UFO cover-up" felt sure that Gerald Ford, as president, would blow the lid off it. Of course, nothing happened. (One reliable account has it that the *real* UFO buff in the Ford household was the former First Lady Betty Ford, whose enthusiasm for UFOs greatly exceeds her husband's.) The same scenario was repeated shortly before the 1976 elections, when it became evident that Jimmy Carter would likely become president, and it continued into the early stages of the Carter presidency. Carter had himself reported a UFO sighting (chapter 2), and once again the UFO buffs felt certain that Carter as president would finally end the cover-up. But again, nothing happened.

No matter how many years may have elapsed since this book was written, it is a good bet that as you read this "highly-placed sources" will still be predicting that the government will "soon" release its "secret evidence" for the existence of UFOs. No other event except perhaps the Second Coming has ever been so widely predicted and awaited yet has given those who wait so little cause for hope. The belief in a government UFO cover-up will persist for as long as there are believers in UFOs. The UFO rumor machine, driven by the same powerful forces that generate the sighting reports themselves, will undoubtedly continue for as long as anyone can foresee.

NOTES

1. "Washington Whispers," *U.S. News & World Report,* April 18, 1977.

2. "UFO Newsfront," *International UFO Reporter,* CUFOS, June 1977.

3. *Christian Beacon,* June 16, 1977; *New York Post,* August 10, 1977.

4. *Grit,* January 16, 1977; *Washington Post,* April 14, 1977; *Washington Post,* September 23, 1977; *National Examiner,* June 21, 1976; *The Dominion,* Wellington, N.Z., January 2, 1979.

5. *National Enquirer,* January 4, 1977.

6. *National Enquirer,* September 14, 1976.

7. Jacques Vallee, *The Invisible College* (New York: Dutton, 1975), p. 207.

8. *Modern People,* May 9, 1976.

9. *UFO Report,* People Press, 1975.

10. Ralph and Judy Blum, *Beyond Earth: Man's Contact with UFO's* (New York: Bantam Books, 1974); Center for UFO Studies news bulletin, May 1974.

11. *National Enquirer,* November 5, 1974.

12. Roscoe Drummond, *Los Angeles Times* Syndicate, October 30, 1974.

13. *National Insider,* December 14, 1975; see also related comments in *National Examiner,* December 9, 1974, and in *Modern People,* October 13, 1974.

14. WWDC Radio, Washington, D.C., November 14, 1974.

15. *National Insider,* February 2, 1975; *Tampa Tribune,* October 16, 1974; *Official UFO,* February 1976, p. 8.

16. Frank Edwards, *Flying Saucers—Serious Business* (New York: Lyle Stuart, 1966), chapter 13.

17. *Flying Saucer Review* 3, no. 3 (May-June 1957):19.

18. *U.S. News & World Report,* April 7, 1950, p. 13.

13

RADIO MESSAGES FROM SPACE

Most scientists are in agreement that, if and when the first interstellar contact between intelligent civilizations takes place, it will probably be made not by spacecraft but by radio. Radio waves have a number of unique advantages for long-range contact that no nuts-and-bolts vehicle can enjoy. Unimaginably huge amounts of energy would be required to propel a payload to its interstellar destination if it is to arrive in just centuries. (Considerably less energy will suffice if we are willing to spend a few hundred thousand years in transit.) But radio waves require so little energy to generate that we can send out signals to hundreds of different stars at very little cost. Radio waves cannot break down or malfunction en route to their destination, and, most significant of all, they travel at the ultimate velocity—the speed of light—across the unimaginable depths of interstellar space.

In recent years, a number of excellent books have been published on the Search for Extraterrestrial Intelligence (SETI, also sometimes known as CETI, Communication with Extraterrestrial Intelligence).[1] A few scientists at major radio observatories have even begun the tedious, seemingly futile search for artificial signals generated by some extraterrestrial intelligence.

However, there are claims from seemingly credible sources that such radio contact between planets has already occurred. The young Scots spaceflight enthusiast, Duncan Lunan, has recently received worldwide attention by claiming that a robot space probe from a distant alien civilization is now circling the earth. Lunan bases his claim on his interpretation of a few mysterious "long-delayed echoes" (LDEs) of short-wave radio signals first heard by European researchers in the 1920s.

The cornerstone of Lunan's "discovery" is that the echoes recorded by Dr. B. Van der Pol, of Philips Radio in the Netherlands, on the evening of October 11, 1928, can supposedly be plotted to yield a map of the stars of the constellation Bootes.[2] Van der Pol arranged a special short-wave transmission to study the LDEs, which had been sporadically reported across Europe.

Lunan plotted the echoes received by Van der Pol to produce the pattern seen in plate 30. He interprets the points on the right as the stars of the constellation Bootes, which they crudely resemble. The single point on the left is interpreted as a "missing" star, Epsilon Bootis, supposedly indicating the star of the probe's origin. If this point is moved to the right to be equidistant from the vertical line on the other side of it, the picture of the constellation Bootes is "completed," according to Lunan. (How the Booteans learned our arbitrary constellation boundaries is not explained.) The brilliant star Arcturus (Alpha Bootis) is admittedly not in the proper position, but Lunan offers a ready explanation. As Arcturus appears to earthlings to be changing its position much more rapidly than any other stars supposedly on this map, the misplaced star supposedly informs us that the space probe arrived in our vicinity some 13,000 years ago.

Unfortunately, some serious objections can be raised to this tidy explanation. What Lunan has given us is only a crude approximation to the actual stars of the Bootes region, even granting the supposed 13,000-year discrepancy. These inaccuracies are difficult to ascribe to Van der Pol. One would not think it too difficult for an advanced, space-faring civilization to make its interstellar probes capable of transmitting its star maps correctly. Zeta Bootis is supposedly represented by the eleven-second echo on pulse sequence 2. Yet its correct position would not only be one or two seconds later but also *one pulse sequence earlier.* Both Gamma and Eta Bootis would also be closer to their actual places had they been on the previous pulse sequence. If we align the top parts of Lunan's map with an accurate one, the bottom of Lunan's map is wrenched some 20° to the left, but even if we generously bend it back, the stars still don't quite fit.

Even more curious is the way stars are selectively included on the map. The faintest star shown, Zeta Bootis, is only half as bright as other stars that are excluded. Lunan attempts to answer this point by contending that this star may have been brighter in the past than it is now. Even granting this point, not only are several other stars missing that by rights ought to be included, but one of the brightest stars in this region—Alpha Corona Borealis—is conspicuously absent. Could the space people have known in 11,000 B.C. that this star was destined *not* to be included in the star-picture of Bootes the Herdsman? Lunan weakly replies that to include the stars of Corona Borealis would have confused the picture.

However, even if all of these objections could be satisfactorily answered, and if one ignores the absurdity of supposing a probe from another solar system to utilize the *second* as its fundamental unit of time, the Bootes map would still have to be rejected because *Lunan's map does not correctly depict the echoes published by Van der Pol.* Going back to the original source,[3] we find Van der Pol's timings of the fourteen echoes of the evening of October 11. Although Lunan plots the fourteen points on twelve lines, *nowhere does Van der Pol suggest that any multiple echoes were received.* In a previous paper in *Nature,*[4] Van der Pol's fellow researcher, Professor Carl Stormer of Oslo, describes the echoes he himself heard on the *afternoon* of October 11, and adds, "Sometimes two echoes were heard with an interval of about four seconds." Lunan distorts this statement to suggest that "in two cases two echoes were heard four seconds apart," and he applies it to the Van der Pol echoes, even though the statement was made by Stormer. Such doctoring of the data is necessary, because when one plots the Van der Pol echoes exactly as they were published, the resulting pattern looks even less like Bootes than does Lunan's famous map.

Inspired by his exciting "discoveries" concerning the Van der Pol echoes, Lunan soon discovered that other long-delayed echoes could likewise be force-fitted onto star maps. He found, for example, that Stormer's echoes heard on the afternoon of October 24 might be interpreted as some of the stars of the constellations Hercules, Lyra, Serpens, and Corona Borealis, if only one looks at these stars in the correct manner. Lunan boasts that "once again, all the first-, second-, and third-magnitude stars are shown," except for Gamma and Theta Herculis, Gamma Coronae Borealis, and Gamma and Delta Serpentis Captis, which he somehow overlooked. However, three much fainter fourth-magnitude stars were selectively included, two "apparently to aid the identification" of the constellation Hercules, and a third "which helps to identify Alpha and Beta Serpentis Captis." This random inclusion of fainter stars provides Lunan with a powerful tool, since fainter stars can be found at practically any point that can conveniently "aid the identification" of any other stars which happen to be nearby.

But even should we allow this dubious practice, the star map is still quite incorrect. In Lunan's words, "When a tracing of the constellations is laid over the diagram, it proves necessary to rotate it to bring all the star-points successively into alignment," and it is also necessary to make "some allowance for proper motion." This sounds plausible enough until one notices that the amount of "rotation" supposedly required is quite inconsistent for different maps of similar sizes. Even if we are prepared to bend over backward to yield to him on this point too, the intrepid Mr. Lunan is still not home free. Since four points steadfastly refuse to be identified with any stars, they become "reference points." One point supposedly marks the position of the earth's North Pole 13,000 years ago. Two others define a "vector," showing us how far to rotate the map. A fourth point combines with the first to form a supposed pointer to the hypothetical aliens' home star of Epsilon Bootis. It doesn't actually point to it—at least not directly. Since in the course of the required "rotation" the pointer sweeps across nearly half the sky, one might hazard a guess that the vector points not only to Epsilon Bootis but to a lot of other stars as well.

Lunan expanded his Epsilon Bootis hypothesis into a book, *Interstellar Contact* (which appeared in paperback as *The Mysterious Signals from*

Outer Space).[5] Despite the obvious shortcomings in his "star maps," many have cited them as evidence for extraterrestrial contact. Several items about the Lunan "star maps" have appeared in the APRO *Bulletin,* and the popular UFO writer Brad Steiger beats the drum for Lunan in his book *Alien Meetings.*[6]

But even Duncan Lunan is beginning to have second thoughts about the Bootes map. It was not the many internal inconsistencies that caused him to reconsider. A forty-year-old typing error in a star catalog was brought to light, causing the estimated distance to the double star system of Epsilon Bootis to be revised upward from 103 light-years to 203. Not only does this make the hypothetical trip here twice as long, but it also causes our estimate of the two stars' masses to increase, and hence their expected lifetimes dramatically shorten. Lunan now concedes that "both stars (Epsilon Bootis A and B) were apparently too massive and therefore too short-lived for any planets they possess to sustain intelligent life."[7]

This does not, however, cause him to abandon his theory that the radio echoes are produced by some extraterrestrial intelligence. If the map does not depict the stars of the constellation Bootes, then perhaps it is the constellation Cetus, featuring the well-known star Tau Ceti, one of the best nearby stellar prospects for habitable planets. It strikes one as singularly odd that Lunan, who claims to have extracted from various "star maps" a detailed map of the Booteans' home solar system, down to the tiniest moon (even showing the point where the probe's ramjet engine came on), could now so cavalierly jettison all these remarkable discoveries and claim that the Bootes map, which once "fit" so well, represented a different solar system all along, whose sun isn't even double. In a development that cannot help but recall the "UFO star map" of Betty Hill, with its several incompatible "identifications," Lunan cites the Soviet astronomer Shpilevski's interpretation of Lunan's Bootes map, arguing that it in fact depicts the stars of Cetus. "The star map hypothesis just will not lie down," Lunan observes — not incorrectly, for the star-map hypothesis, having fallen on its face, is being unmercifully kicked and prodded, instead of being permitted to die the natural death it deserves.

Interestingly enough, the long-delayed echoes have never been definitively explained. Radio echoes of seconds or even minutes delay are theoretically possible under certain conditions in the earth's ionosphere, when the group velocity of a short wavefront can approach zero. But it has never been conclusively demonstrated that this does in fact happen. Studies show that LDEs have occurred most frequently when the sun is near the earth's geomagnetic equator, suggesting a geophysical explanation. Other researchers have found the presence of LDEs to correlate with certain angles between the stable Lagrange points of the moon's orbit and the observer's horizon. This suggests that particles of cosmic dust and debris may accumulate in these regions, which are free from gravitational instabilities and sometimes reflect radio signals. Research on long-delayed echoes is much more difficult today, since the short-wave bands are far more crowded than they were in the 1920s. Even a small transmitter on the other side of the world might obliterate these rare and very faint echoes.[8]

Other claims of radio contact from space abound in UFOdom. Longtime NICAP director Major Donald E. Keyhoe writes ominously in his book *Flying Saucers: Top Secret* about radio emissions detected by astronomers, emanating from Venus and Jupiter. The study of natural radio emissions from the sun and the planets is, of course, a major tool of radio astronomers for probing our solar system. Keyhoe titles his chapter "Signals from Space," but nowhere in it does he suggest that these radio emissions need *not* be artificial. Keyhoe cautions, however, that the radio emissions from Venus do not necessarily prove the existence of Venusians. "A space race from somewhere else could have set up a base there," he explains. Speculating as to why a certain Ohio State astronomer never followed through his discovery of radio emissions from Venus with a statement tying them to UFOs, Keyhoe suggests that he may have been "silenced" by the Air Force's chief UFO consultant, J. Allen Hynek, who was at Ohio State and was then a staunch UFO debunker.[9]

The relationship between SETI and UFOs (or, more precisely, the lack thereof) is a source of endless public confusion. Invariably, in public lectures and discussions, as soon as it is determined that the speaker does *not* believe that UFOs are the product of some unknown intelligence, the question always follows, "But don't you believe in life on other worlds?" Often the question is set forth with great emphasis and even moralistic condescension, implying that the UFO skeptic must be a benighted and arrogant reactionary who cannot bring himself to open his mind to the rest of the universe. While dishing out such abuse may give the questioner a gratifying feeling of moral superiority, in fact it betrays the acceptance of a common fallacy: that disbelieving in the reality of reported UFO sightings implies a denial of the possibility of intelligent life elsewhere in the universe. When the proposition is stated in this form, its falsehood becomes immediately apparent. Nonetheless, it is a significant, if unstated, pillar of the world-view of large numbers of people, including many who should know better.

This view notwithstanding, when we postulate the existence of extraterrestrial beings on unimaginably distant worlds, *it does not automatically follow that they must be paying us a visit right now.* Such thinking parallels that of theologians of an earlier age, who attempted to prove the existence of God as a "necessary being," independent of any tangible evidence. UFOlogists argue that in all the vastness of the universe, civilizations far more advanced than ours must necessarily exist. Since, given enough time, such a civilization would presumably develop an almost unlimited capacity for space travel, they must be here now. This is nothing more than a restatement of St. Anselm's eleventh-century ontological argument for the existence of God. St. Anselm wrote: "God cannot be conceived not to exist—God is that, than which nothing greater can be conceived. That which can be conceived not to exist is not God."[10]

The UFOlogical version of the ontological argument might be stated: The most advanced civilization in the universe cannot be conceived not to exist—the most advanced civilization is that than which none more proficient in space travel can be conceived. A civilization which cannot easily cross interstellar distances to visit earth is not the most advanced.

In both cases there is an attempt to "prove" the existence of something that has an impact upon our lives, based only upon abstract ideas of what the universe *ought* to contain. Theologians and UFOlogists share more underlying assumptions than either would care to admit.

The ontological argument for the existence of extraterrestrial visitors is nearly always set forth by persons with only a limited understanding of astronomy and physics. They do not understand the astonishing distances between stellar systems and do not realize the unimaginably huge amounts of energy required to accelerate an object to a healthy fraction of the speed of light. The distances between stars in our own galaxy are so vast that even at the speed of light, many decades, centuries, and even millennia are required to traverse them. Even such UFO proponents as J. Allen Hynek freely admit the implausibilities of interstellar travel on a grand scale (which prompts them not to reconsider their thinking but to adopt even more bizarre "new wave" UFO hypotheses).

It should be noted that some of the best-known proponents of the idea of intelligent life elsewhere in the universe are UFO skeptics. Probably no one in the United States has championed the cause of SETI as tirelessly as Cornell University astronomer Carl Sagan. Sagan's evangelizing to promote the scientific world-view that encompasses a universe filled with many intelligences beyond our own has earned him the preeminent claim to the title "Mr. SETI." Yet Sagan is a fellow of the Committee for the Scientific Investigation of Claims of the Paranormal and is quite skeptical about UFOs. "My own view is that there are no cases that are simultaneously very reliable (reported independently by a large number of witnesses), and very exotic . . . we must employ the most critical reasoning and the most skeptical attitudes in approaching such data. The data does not pass such tests."[11]

Another staunch UFO skeptic and CSICOP fellow is Isaac Asimov, whose writings do not exactly suggest that he is a closed-minded, unimaginative person afraid to face up to new ideas. Arthur C. Clarke, whose position on the question of UFOs is slightly more ambiguous, is nonetheless inclined to pooh-pooh the subject. English science writer and SETI proponent Ian Ridpath, author of *Worlds Beyond* and *Messages from the Stars,* is likewise unconvinced. "The field of UFOlogy has failed to produce *one* concrete example of an alien visitation, from any dimension," writes Ridpath in the British publication *New Scientist.* "After a generation of flying saucer stories with no conclusive results, the burden of proof remains squarely on the UFOlogists."[12] My own UFO skepticism notwithstanding, I have written a number of SETI articles for *Spaceflight* and other magazines, which have received favorable comments from the SETI community. Hence, contrary to what some people would like you to believe, UFO skepticism is *not* synonymous with earth chauvinism. In fact, I cannot think of a single major SETI figure who has taken an unambiguous pro-UFO position.

Many UFO believers, on the other hand, take a dim view of SETI. After all, how wasteful it seems to spend millions of dollars in an attempt to contact alien civilizations using radio telescopes if one firmly believes that alien spaceships are cruising our skies every night! In particular, Stanton Friedman has singled out SETI proponents for ridicule. He scornfully dismisses proposals to listen for alien radio transmissions as "job security," mocking what he characterizes as the notion that alien civilizations are endlessly beaming out "Hello Earth! Hello Earth!"[13] When Friedman criticizes the cost of proposed SETI programs, it is probably not out of patriotic zeal for trimming the bloated federal budget, but perhaps from envy that other proposals for discovering extraterrestrial intelligence, via an all-out program of UFO research, have not found a similar degree of support. In actuality, far from being allies, the UFO believers and the SETI proponents have become bitter rivals, since if it is true that the earth's skies are filled with alien spacecraft it is pure folly to reach out across the light-years in an attempt to make the first extraterrestrial contact. The money to be allocated for locating extraterrestrial intelligence, if any, will not go to both camps.

Despite the claims and occasional protestations of the UFO proponents, organized science has given SETI a lukewarm embrace, while all but totally rejecting the supposed UFO evidence. In perhaps a dozen instances, major radio telescopes costing large sums of money have supported astronomers' searches for extraterrestrial intelligence; no comparable amount of scientific capital has ever been tied up in UFO "research."

NASA has recently gone so far as to include a three-million-dollar a year appropriation for SETI in its budget requests. But this appropriation ran into trouble in the Congress. Senator William Proxmire (D–Wis) awarded NASA his "Golden Fleece" for wanting to use taxpayer money for what he termed a "multimillion dollar, long-range program of questionable searches for intelligence beyond our solar system." The scientific community has, however, regarded SETI in a somewhat more favorable light. SETI proponents argue that any equipment built for SETI will also be well-suited for conventional radio astronomy, and hence its value to science will not be limitd to the search for extraterrestrial intelligence. NASA, meanwhile, is finding ways to circumvent congressional disapproval. A low-keyed SETI program is now proceeding, under the name "exobiology," which seems to have escaped Proxmire's attention!

Despite all the criticism and arguments, the age of SETI is already underway, although just barely. It began in 1960, at the National Radio Astronomy Observatory (NRAO) in West Virginia, when Dr. Frank Drake carried out Project Ozma, a search for intelligent signals at the twenty-one centimeter wavelength of interstellar hydrogen. Using an eighty-five-foot radio telescope, Project Ozma examined only two stars, Epsilon Eridani and Tau Ceti.

From 1972 to 1976, also at the NRAO, Dr. Benjamin M. Zuckerman and Dr. Patrick Palmer continued this work, with Project Ozma II. The second Ozma had the use of radio telescopes as large as three hundred feet in diameter, gathering nearly twelve and a half times as much radio energy as an eighty-five-foot dish. Where the first Ozma had just a single radio receiver, Ozma II had 384, each one tuned to a slightly different wavelength in the vicinity of the target wavelength. Project Ozma examined only two stars; Project Ozma II, seven hundred. The rapid progress being made in radio astronomy promises that further significant increases in speed and sensitivity such as these can be expected in future SETI programs.

At Ohio State University, Dr. Robert S. Dixon has been conducting a twenty-four-hour, all-sky SETI survey since December of 1973. No attempt is made to pre-select target stars in advance; the rotation of the earth constantly sweeps the hypothetical beam of the radio telescope across the sky, and hence there are an average of three favorable nearby stars being examined at any moment of the night or day. The Ohio State project is currently being computerized, to eliminate the need for time-consuming manual identification of all the many known celestial sources of radio emissions that turn up in the course of the search. Other SETI programs have been undertaken at NRAO, at the Arecibo radio observatory in Puerto Rico, and in Canada and the Soviet Union.[14]

Encouraged by the rapidly increasing SETI activity in recent years, many people understandably leap to the exciting conclusion that our first radio contact with an alien civilization is just around the corner. While there is no way of knowing for certain when (or if) such contact will take place, we would all do well to keep in mind the tremendous obstacles to early success in the SETI field. Project Ozma's Dr. Frank Drake, long a leader in the SETI field, recently estimated that the total number of combinations of wavelength, direction, bandwidth, and other parameters which must be searched to find the first extraterrestrial signal is on the order of 10^{19}. Assuming this estimate to be correct, if we could search one combination of wavelength, direction, and so forth, each second (we obviously could not), *it would be more than three hundred billion years before the first alien signal was discovered.* Unfortunately for impatient humans such as we, who live less than a century, it's a mighty *big* universe.

Fortunately, there are certain plausible SETI assumptions which, if correct, might make this hopeless undertaking somewhat less than totally futile.

For example, if all intelligent civilizations in the universe realized this problem and adopted some "natural" wavelength—perhaps the prominent twenty-one-centimeter wavelength of interstellar hydrogen—our one-combination-a-second search would find an alien civilization once every thirty years. Whether such time estimates are at all realistic is of course impossible to say. Perhaps Drake will turn out to have been overly pessimistic as to the number of alien civilizations in our galaxy, the strength of their radio signals, and the average distance between civilizations. (Or he may have been far too optimistic.) Perhaps we just happen to be located in a region where we have one or more interstellar neighbors nearby, much closer than the average distance between civilizations. (Or we may happen to be in an exceptionally lonely corner.) In any case, the search for extraterrestrial intelligence is certain to be a long, tedious, and trying undertaking. It will require large commitments of capital, manpower, and scientific expertise for an indefinite period of time, with no guarantee of eventual success.

However, a "counterrevolution" of SETI skeptics is rapidly gaining ground in the scientific community, sponsoring a highly controversial conference at the University of Maryland on November 2–3, 1979. Participating were such well-known former SETI advocates and theorists as Ronald Bracewell, Sebastian Von Hoerner, Benjamin Zuckerman, Patrick Palmer, Freeman Dyson, and Michael Papagiannis. The general theme of the conference was that, using O'Neill-style space colonies as giant, lumbering space-arks to spend centuries crossing interstellar space, it should be possible for a single civilization to colonize the entire galaxy in roughly ten million years—just a tiny fraction of the age of the galaxy. If millions or billions of other civilizations far older than ours are supposedly out there, *why has not one of them progressed to this stage?* The logical conclusion would seem to be that it is because we are alone in the galaxy—perhaps even in the universe. The most pessimistic of SETI skeptics, Michael Hart of Trinity University, told the conference that even the most ridiculously optimistic estimate of the occurrence of life in the universe yields far less than one planet having life in each galaxy. In fact, Hart estimates, at most only *one* galaxy in 10^{31} has any planet with life of *any* kind.[15]

How much more comforting it is than facing up to the cold and lonely facts about the universe to adopt the belief that alien civilizations are filling our skies with flying saucers day in and day out. Not many people are psychologically equipped to live with the many long years of uncertainty and disappointment that any legitimate program for establishing extraterrestrial contact is certain to require. Hence, as long as the need to believe in the reality of alien contact is stronger than the realization of the magnitude of the effort that will be required, the UFO movement will continue to flourish.

NOTES

1. Some books on SETI are *Communication with Extraterrestrial Intelligence,* ed. Carl Sagan (Cambridge, Mass.: MIT Press, 1973); Ian Ridpath, *Messages from the Stars* (New York: Harper & Row, 1978); I. S. Shklovskii and Carl Sagan, *Intelligent Life in the Universe* (New York: Holden-Day, 1966).

2. See Lunan's paper, "Space Probe from Epsilon Bootis," *Spaceflight* (a magazine published by the British Interplanetary Society) April 1973, p. 122.

3. B. Van der Pol, *Nature* 122 (December 8, 1928):878

4. Carl Stormer, *Nature* 122 (November 3, 1928):681.

5. Duncan Lunan, *Interstellar Contact* (Chicago: Regnery, 1975).

6. *APRO Bulletin,* January/February 1973; March/April 1973; May/June 1974; Brad Steiger, *Alien Meetings* (New York: Ace, 1978), pp. 20–21.

7. Lunan, *The SERT Journal* 10 (September 1976):181.

8. Theories about long-delayed echoes are found in Stormer, *The Polar Aurora* (New York: Oxford University Press, 1955); Lawton and Newton, *Spaceflight* 16 (May 1974):181; Sasoon, *Spaceflight* 16 (July 1974):258.

9. Donald E. Keyhoe, *Flying Saucers: Top Secret* (New York: Putnam, 1960), pp. 200–202.

10. *Philosophic Problems,* ed. Mandelbaum (New York: Macmillan, 1967), pp. 686–87.

11. Carl Sagan, *The Cosmic Connection* (New York: Dell, 1975), pp. 199, 207.

12. Ian Ridpath, "Flying Saucers Thirty Years On," *New Scientist,* July 14, 1977, p. 79.

13. Stanton Friedman, lecture at American University, Washington, D.C., October 13, 1976.

14. For more information on current SETI projects, see Sheaffer, *Spaceflight,* December 1975, p. 421; October 1976, p. 343; September 1977, p. 307.

15. *New York Times,* November 4, 1979, p. 12; James E. Oberg, *Fate,* June 1980; Sheaffer, *Spaceflight,* November-December 1980, p. 334.

14

UFOs AND THE MEDIA

All I know is what I read in the papers. —Will Rogers

Like Will Rogers, all most people know about many current topics is what they read in the papers, or hear on radio and TV. But if Will Rogers were alive today and wanted to keep reliably informed on developments concerning UFOs, he would be in trouble, because one of the most disappointing aspects of the entire UFO question has been the treatment of that subject by the mass media.

No one can deny the enormous impact upon modern-day thought exerted by the major magazines and newspapers, radio stations, Hollywood, and, towering above all, the major TV networks. They and they alone decide what is news (as well as what is not), how much attention is to be given to any particular subject, and from what viewpoint it is to be presented. In a very real sense, Walter Cronkite is more powerful and is more of an opinion leader than any recent president. In 1973 President Nixon declared war on the media because they published embarrassing "leaks," and the media responded in kind. The full power of the presidency clashed head-on with the power of the major media. The following year, President Nixon resigned.

Unfortunately, those segments of the mass media that pride themselves on professionalism in news reporting—the major TV and radio networks, as well as leading newspapers and magazines—do not usually carry their professional scruples over into the reporting of UFO stories. Indeed one often discerns in UFO reporting a total blurring of the journalistic distinctions that normally distinguish the "better" publications and TV organizations from their brethren of the yellow paper.

As one example, let us consider the treatment that the highly respected, Pulitzer prize-winning *Washington Post* gave to the Jimmy Carter UFO sighting (chapter 2). In April of 1977, one of their aviation/science reporters chanced upon the fact that I was deeply involved in researching the facts of that incident. He telephoned me asking if it was indeed true that the president had once reported seeing a UFO. I replied that it was, and proceeded to cite references for information about the incident. I pointed out, however, that this was not news, the story having already appeared in the *New York Times,* the *Atlanta Constitution,* the tabloid *National Enquirer,* and various UFO publications. I suggested, however, if he would delay a few days in reporting this non-news event of eight years earlier, I might well have a *real* news story for him—the solution of the incident—since I was at that moment closing in on some documents that would almost certainly reveal the precise date of the incident (which Carter could not recall). The reporter replied that he could not afford to wait on such a hot news item, since he feared that some other paper or reporter would "scoop" him. He followed all my leads and prepared a story, which appeared on the front page of the *Washington Post* of April 30, 1977. It revealed practically nothing about the Carter UFO that had not been published somewhere before.

Just a few days later, I called the reporter back. I now had the solution to the Jimmy Carter UFO sighting. This *was* news, having never been published anywhere. But his response was that he had just run a story on that subject and hence could not insert another one a few days later, even if it did resolve the "mystery." Out of a sense of obligation, I felt, more than any positive enthusiasm, he accepted my findings. They were eventually published, but buried in the *Post*'s Washington gossip column of May 9, 1977, which ran just one and a half column inches. The front-page story ten days earlier had occupied ten times that amount of space, even though it had no real news to report. If the prestigious *Washington Post* had been seriously interested in reporting the news, instead of just titillating its readers in the manner of tabloids, its ratio of coverage would have been reversed.

Nor is the equally celebrated *New York Times* any more immune from inaccurate and sensationalized UFO reporting. Page 23 of the January 14, 1979, issue of the *Times* carried a column with the heading "CIA Papers Detail UFO Surveillance." The staunchly pro-UFO group, Ground Saucer Watch, had for some time been petitioning the CIA under the freedom-of-information act, expecting to obtain shocking evidence of a government cover-up of UFO evidence. What they obtained was remarkably unimpressive: a few new UFO reports, a lot of newspaper clippings, correspondence from UFO buffs, and miscellaneous interoffice memos signifying little. Nonetheless, the *New York Times* was persuaded to run a totally uncritical story that seems to have been based upon taking one of GSW's press handouts at face value. GSW's William Spaulding is quoted repeating "crashed saucer" rumors and asserting that "the government has been lying to us all these years."

The *Times* carried the story without a hint of critical investigation of Spaulding's claims. Spaulding states: "After reviewing the documents,

Ground Saucer Watch believes that U.F.O.'s do exist, they are real, the U.S. government has been totally untruthful and the cover-up is massive." There is nothing in the article to suggest that the CIA or any other government agency was contacted for comment on this potentially earth-shaking story, that any UFO skeptics were interviewed to give their interpretation of these papers, or that the reporter had actually *seen* any of these documents beyond the few that Spaulding chose to quote. A small-town weekly, or even a high-school newspaper, could have reported the story at least as well.

The story in the *Baltimore Sun* on February 5, 1979, was equally uncritical. The piece was headlined "Files Indicate U.S. Is Not Telling All It Knows About UFO's." There is no evidence to suggest that this reporter either submitted GSW's Spaulding to any difficult or penetrating questions, contacted anyone with a differing viewpoint, or viewed any of the documents other than those Spaulding had selected. Journalistic reputations are not built upon stories like these.

While these "revelations" were being reported widely and uncritically by the media, Philip J. Klass, who had filed a matching freedom-of-information request, was carefully perusing the more than nine hundred pages of documents. Although he received the same pages that GSW and others did, his interpretation of them was radically different. For example, Klass found a memo dated July 3, 1953, stating plainly that henceforth the UFO investigation (which had been pursued sporadically for several years) "will be considered as inactive." There is nothing in subsequent years to suggest that any CIA UFO program has been reactivated. Neither Spaulding, Zechel, nor any other UFO proponent reported this "smoking gun" memo, nor did the *New York Times,* the *Baltimore Sun,* or any other "serious" newspaper dig beyond the surface to discover it.

Another memo, dated August 8, 1955, recommends that, since there have been no significant developments in UFOs in several years, "the [UFO] project be terminated and the files thereof be placed in dead storage." No enterprising young investigative journalist or UFO proponent seems to have discovered this fact either. Klass notes that the CIA's collection of UFO reports, clippings, and correspondence, which GSW claims constitutes a "massive" cover-up, amounts to *less than one page of UFO-related material per week.* Several prestigious newspapers somehow failed to notice this fact. Klass prepared a press release under the auspices of CSICOP, refuting the wild charges of proof of a CIA cover-up, and sent it to major newspapers and wire services in the United States. The *New York Times* found it unfit to print, as did every other newspaper it reached. Wild and unfounded claims of a massive UFO cover-up are news, it seems. Reasoned refutations of such claims are not. This incident reveals no real difference between "respected" newspapers and the *National Enquirer* when it comes to UFO reporting.

Nor were any lessons learned from this incident. On October 14, 1979, the *New York Times Magazine* ran a feature story titled "U.F.O. Files:

The Untold Story," which once again uncritically quotes the pronouncements of Spaulding, Zechel, and NICAP on the question of government UFO documents.

Perhaps the worst offender among the major media has been NBC television, which has for several years been feeding the public a diet of sensationalist programs on the subject of the supposed "paranormal." The Committee for the Scientific Investigation of Claims of the Paranormal has engaged NBC-TV in a running feud over the latter's lack of fairness and balance and the gross inaccuracies in its coverage of "psychic surgery" and the paranormal.

In just a single week (admittedly the worst), NBC-TV, which was slipping badly in the ratings and seemed desperate to climb back up, managed to serve up the following sensationalist programs to mislead its viewers.

• "In Search of the Bermuda Triangle" (April 28, 1977), for which the paid advertisement in *TV Guide* summed up the program's theme: "A 'nonhuman' voice broadcasts a warning to Miami: the Bermuda Triangle is an alien test ground. Does this explain the mysterious disappearances of hundreds of ships, planes, and people in the Bermuda Triangle waters?" No attempt was made to present a balanced, objective view of the allegedly mysterious disappearances in the region, whose explanations by Lawrence Kusche and others are readily available, but ignored.[1] So outrageous was this show that I filed a complaint with the National News Council, a private "watchdog" organization for self-policing of the media, charging three specific inaccuracies and also that the program was misrepresented as a documentary—and hence presumed to be accurate—when in fact it was not. NBC, in its defense, stated that the program "clearly was not presented as news or public affairs," but the Council noted that "the manner of its promotion and presentation was an invitation to such confusion." In its conclusions, the Council (whose findings are regularly published in the respected *Columbia Journalism Review*) found that two of my three charges of inaccuracy were "warranted" (a third was inconclusive) and also expressed the judgment "that NBC was lax in its oversight of this program and that this laxness abetted a great deal of confusion as to whether the program was or was not a documentary."[2]

While NBC did preface the program with a brief disclaimer, suggesting that what you were about to see was "based in part on theory and conjecture," the disclaimer was itself disclaimed by the series' sign-off statement, which made the claim that "this program was the result of the work of scientists, researchers, and a group of highly skilled technicians." I have yet to see NBC name the "scientists" who took responsibility for the contents of this "documentary."

• *Mysteries from Beyond Earth* (April 30, 1977), a movie purporting to demonstrate the reality of such diverse "mysteries" as UFO sightings and abductions, the Bermuda Triangle, Bigfoot, Atlantis, psychic energy, and ghosts. As in so many "documentaries" of this genre, the supposed facts presented are at best questionable and at worst totally false. The script of the movie was written by well-known UFO proponents Ralph and Judy Blum, whose chief claim to fame is their prediction that the government would release proof of extraterrestrials by 1975 (chapter 12).

• *In Search of Noah's Ark* (May 2, 1977), a movie purporting to show that the "authentic" Noah's Ark rests intact atop Mt. Ararat in Turkey, but that circumstances have always conspired to prevent "arkeologists", from obtaining proof sufficient to convince the skeptics.

In the NBC-TV documentary "UFOs: Do You Believe?" (December 15, 1974), UFO skeptics Philip J. Klass and Carl Sagan received at least token representation, although we see far less of them than we do of the UFO proponents. When Klass was being filmed for the show in his apartment, he presented a carefully reasoned proposed explanation for one of the principal "unexplained" cases presented on the program. But when the show was edited, Klass's explanation was left out, and the UFO encounter was left "unexplained." NBC's news department obviously considered that, while the supposedly "mysterious" aspect of a UFO case is newsworthy, proposed explanations for it are not.

In April and May 1975, a program was syndicated nationwide, titled "UFOs—Past, Present, and Future." This was a dismal sixty-minute pseudodocumentary narrated by Rod Serling that, I am happy to report, was not picked up by NBC. UFO skeptics did not receive even token representation on this program. "What you are about to witness is based on fact. Some will find it fascinating, many find it frightening, but it is all true! With special thanks to NASA and the Department of Defense for their cooperation." Of couse, those agencies will provide routine, if minimal, cooperation to any filmmaker, but the mere invocation of such names generates the expectation of some dramatic revelation. Unfortunately, what follows this remarkable statement is case after case of sensationalized UFO sightings, leading up to a composite sketch, based upon supposed eyewitness descriptions, of what "the aliens" actually look like.

Publications that specialize in science-related reporting often do little better than the general media in reporting on UFOs and related subjects. Perhaps some of the most glaring examples in recent years are found in the pages of the popular newsstand monthly *Science Digest,* which purports to be a reliable source of scientific information for the layman (and in some subjects it indeed is). That magazine has even gone so far as to claim in its advertising that it covers new discoveries in every field of science from "plate tectonics to pyramid power," boasting of its coverage of ESP and UFOs, yet asserting that its coverage "is always accurate and authoritative" because of its distinguished board of editorial consultants, which includes writer Isaac Asimov and astronomer Kenneth Franklin. (Of course, these consultants do not review the many wild articles on UFOs, pyramid power, and so forth, but their names are used by the magazine nonetheless.)

The July 1977 issue of *Science Digest* contained an article by UFO buff James Mullaney, repeating many often-heard but never-supported claims. He related how "telepathic contact with UFOs occurred at the Pentagon as long ago as 1959."[3] He also claims that "the crew of Apollo 11, during the first moon-landing, reported that their capsule was paced by what appeared to be a mass of intelligent energy," an assertion that is not in any way supported by the transcript of capsule communications for that mission or by any other credible source. James Oberg traces the source of that rumor, reported in *Science Digest* as fact, to a Japanese sensationalist UFO magazine published in 1974, which made its way into this country via Robert Barry's Twentieth Century UFO Bureau (chapter 12). NASA photographs were airbrushed, cropped, and subjected to contrast enhancement to create counterfeit UFOs out of reflections, glare, and other ordinary spaceflight visual effects.[4]

But the most dramatic absurdity from *Science Digest* was yet to come. The very next issue (August 1977) contained an article by longtime NICAP member Don Berliner on the supposed "cover-up" and "censorship" of UFO data by the U.S. Air Force. The "censorship," we learn, consists of deleting the names and addresses of civilian UFO witnesses from declassified Blue Book files, as required by the recently passed privacy act. Berliner sneers that this is only "the official explanation," and hints at motivations far more sinister. The only photograph accompanying the Berliner article (about which Berliner later denied any knowledge or responsibility) allegedly shows an "unidentified object" photographed by the Apollo 11 astronauts, with the earth in the background. James Oberg has pointed out that the nondescript white blob labeled an "unidentified object" does not appear in the original NASA photograph (see plates 31, 32). Where could it have come from?

Science Digest's chief editor Daniel Button vehemently insists that he did not add the spurious "unidentified object" to the photograph, that the "mystery object" was on the photo when he obtained it from NASA headquarters. Then why do *all* other copies of the NASA print, except the one at *Science Digest*, show nothing at all where Button's UFO is supposed to be? I telephoned Button for an explanation. Because *Science Digest* requested the photograph, he said, NASA began to "retouch" the photo so that the UFO no longer appears! "My suspicion is right now that NASA has changed its policy and changed its story and altered its negatives and prints," he stated. He did not attempt to explain how NASA managed to retroactively retouch those prints that had left their office long before they were panicked by the inquiries of *Science Digest*.

Number four of the ten "UFOlogical Principles" set forth by Klass in *UFOs Explained* gives us ample food for thought concerning the media's role in reporting (as well as in generating) UFO sightings. It states: "News media that give great prominence to a UFO report when it is first received, subsequently devote little if any space or time to reporting a prosaic explanation for the case when all the facts are uncovered."[5]

We see this occurring time and again in the UFO field. A report of a UFO incident receives a great deal of coverage in the press—for example, the Jimmy Carter UFO sighting. An explanation usually turns up sooner or later, but it will be almost totally, if not completely, ignored. Klass and Hendry cite numerous examples of this journalistic syndrome, which might be described as "It's sensation I want—don't bother me with the facts."[6] Whenever the excitement of reporting a dramatic UFO encounter (and the obvious commercial value thereof) clashes with responsible journalistic professionalism, it is a good bet that the former will triumph.

It is not immediately apparent why this should be, especially since many of the publications and news organizations that do such a dismal job on UFOs usually apply the highest of standards to "real" news stories and would never consciously stoop to publishing unverified assertions as fact in those stories. Pulitzer prizes are not won in that manner. Allan Hendry suggests that the reason normally responsible news organizations report UFO incidents in such an irresponsible manner is because "the press regards UFO sightings not as news items but as 'human interest' items."[7] I suspect that he is right. It is especially unfortunate that this is the case since virtually all readers *assume* that they are seeing a reliable news item, considering the source. A great deal of misinformation is propagated in this manner.

When you next see a report of a UFO sighting in the newspapers or on radio or TV, keep in mind that you are almost certainly *not* seeing a story that has been subjected to any kind of investigative journalism, no matter how respected the source. In all probability, it is an uninvestigated, unexamined account of some individual's UFO *report,* and it is well to remember that reports often bear little or no resemblance to the object that triggered them. Similarly, when you see a news story or a feature story quoting a well-known UFO proponent stating some astonishing "fact," remember that in all probability the "expert's" claim is simply taken at face value with no investigation whatever, even if the source is a respected publication or news organization. Blunders and unsubstantiated statements that would *never* be tolerated in reporting a political event or a science development occur routinely in reporting UFO stories. Apparently they get away with such sloppiness because no journalistic peer pressure develops to push them toward more accurate reporting.

Should you critically examine a particular UFO incident and detect a serious error in a news report, or find one to be grossly biased by selection or by omission, get involved! Write a letter to the editor of the paper or the producer of the TV show; I know of a few instances where people who pointed out such errors were invited to participate in helping straighten the matter out. If the media moguls in your particular instance are adamantly irrational and unconcerned, perhaps you may wish to file a complaint with the president of the network or newspaper or with the National News Council in New York City, or you might submit your opinion of the coverage to a "media criticism" magazine (various such magazines are published, chiefly for journalism buffs) or to a magazine such as CSICOP's *Skeptical Inquirer,* which reports responsibly on paranormal matters.[8]

Until pressure begins to be felt by the media, either from the public, other journalists, or both, the situation is unlikely to change. When using newspapers, magazines, or television or radio news as a source of information about UFOs, the prudent person must remember: *caveat lector* (let the reader beware). A journalistic reputation earned in covering *real* news stories gives no guarantee that UFO reporting will show any degree whatsoever of critical standards or investigative reporting.

NOTES

1. The best book yet written on the subject is the highly informative work by Lawrence Kusche, *The Bermuda Triangle Mystery Solved* (New York: Harper & Row, hardcover, 1975; paperback, Warner).

2. National News Council Complaint No. 127, Sheaffer against NBC-TV and Landsburg Productions, decided January 31, 1978.

3. This famous incident was critically examined by Randall Fitzgerald in *Second Look,* October 1979, p. 12.

4. James E. Oberg and Robert Sheaffer, "Pseudoscience at Science Digest," *Skeptical Inquirer* 2, no. 1 (Fall–Winter 1979).

5. Philip J. Klass, *UFOs Explained* (New York: Random House, 1974), p. 30.

6. *UFOs Explained,* chapter 3; Allan Hendry, *The UFO Handbook* (New York: Doubleday, 1979), chapter 17.

7. Hendry, chapter 17.

8. *Skeptical Inquirer,* Box 229, Central Park Station, Buffalo, N.Y. 14215.

15

THOSE MYSTERIOUS
"MEN IN BLACK"

> *This much is known about those mysterious Men In Black who show up after almost every important saucer sighting or landing: they do not represent any known government; their basic purpose is to discredit or terrorize eyewitnesses; and they have seized or obliterated all UFO evidence for more than 27 years!"— UFO Annual, 1976*[1]

"Three men in black suits with threatening expressions on their faces. Three men who walk in on you and make certain demands . . . after they got through with you, you wished you'd never heard of the word 'saucer.' You turned pale and got awfully sick. You couldn't get anything to stay on your stomach for three long days."[2]

These are the words Gray Barker used more than twenty years ago to describe the reported visits of the mysterious Men in Black (MIB), who are said to turn up in the aftermath of UFO sightings. They will reportedly stop at nothing in their attempts to keep the UFO subject tightly under wraps. The quote comes from a book titled *They Knew Too Much About Flying Saucers*. It is an exciting, fast-paced account of how several UFO researchers have reportedly stumbled upon the startling *truth* about UFOs, one after another. But, just as they are about to reveal publicly what they know, they are each suddenly visited by three mysterious, sinister Men in Black. After this most unwelcome visit, the formerly indefatigable UFO investigator becomes suddenly unwilling even to *discuss* the subject of UFOs, much less to reveal what has happened to cause him suddenly to become so silent.

Gray Barker currently operates the Saucerian Press from a post-office box in Clarksburg, West Virginia. They carry a complete line of far-out UFO literature, offering for sale such fascinating titles as *We Met the Space*

People, Flying Saucer Revelations, My Visit to Venus, and *How to Contact Space People.* For $6.95, the Saucerian Press will send a long-playing record of contactee Howard Menger playilng "Music from the Planet Saturn." For just $7.95 they will send you *Flying Saucers Close Up,* containing "almost two lbs. of fascinating reading," of which the ad says, "Spacemen Commanded the Author to Write This Book!"

In February of 1975, Barker sent out a "UFO Warning!" to every name on his mailing list. It contained stern advice about the dangers one allegedly encounters by learning too much about flying saucers. "First They Got Bender . . . Then They Got John and Barbara . . . Then They Got Jessup!" Barker proclaims in bold letters on the outside of the folded leaflet. He warns: "If You Are Accumulating Too Much Information in a Certain UFO Subject . . . Better Not Read These Contents!" (ellipsis in original). Barker urged that if the staple securing the enclosure was "molested or broken," the recipient should notify the sender at once. Inside was the usual invitation to purchase contactee-oriented UFO books.

Barker's own book, *They Knew Too Much About Flying Saucers,* could be deemed one of the most important books in the history of the UFO movement, because it was the first book ever written on the subject of the Men in Black; it dates all the way back to 1956. Were the earliest MIB stories, almost a quarter of a century old, as hard to swallow as they are now? As I breathlessly read this book, I learned the *startling truth* about the origin of the legend of the sinister Men in Black.

The story of the Men in Black begins with young Albert K. Bender of Bridgeport, Connecticut, who in April of 1952 founded an organization known as the International Flying Saucer Bureau (IFSB). The group had what we would today call a "contactee" orientation. In the press release announcing the group's formation, Bender described its chief goals. One of them was, "We aim to establish friendly relations with the flying-saucer people." Bender assured the UFO occupants that, when they finally decided to land openly, they could consider the IFSB as their friends, "providing they decide to land on earth with a friendly gesture."[3]

Bender concedes that at that time he already had a reputation around town as the local eccentric, which he says has caused many of his critics to unfairly conclude that he was (to use his own term) "nuts." Bender lived alone with his stepfather in a three-story house. Since he occupied a room adjacent to an especially "creepy" attic, he decided to turn his bedroom into a "chamber of horrors." He decorated it so effectively with skeletons, bats, spiders, and ghosts of all description that the local newspaper ran a feature article on his macabre creations. "I had enjoyed reading fantasy literature," Bender explained.[4]

At the time of the founding of the IFSB, today's familiar UFO groups such as APRO, NICAP, MUFON, and CUFOS were not yet in existence. Bender's flying-saucer group rapidly picked up members and media attention, not only in the United States and Canada but also in England and Australia. Among those joining Bender's organization were Gray Barker, Frank Scully, the writer who first popularized the "little green men in pickle jars" rumor, and Coral E. Lorenzen, who was soon to found a UFO group of her own.

The International Flying Saucer Bureau began publishing a quarterly journal titled *Space Review,* which like all bulletins of UFO organizations contained accounts of reported UFO sightings and news concerning the organization, as well as some rather far-out UFO speculation. In the issue for April 1953, Bender shocked his membership by promising a "startling revelation" about UFOs in the next issue, which was due in July. UFO circles were abuzz with speculation and rumors about what he planned to reveal. Bender guarded the "secret" well; attempts by Barker and others to obtain advance information about the coming "revelation" were unsuccessful.

When the much-awaited July 1953 issue of *Space Review* finally arrived, *it contained nothing at all out of the ordinary*: just page after page of the usual unverified flying-saucer material. The IFSB membership was both surprised and dismayed, as might be expected, but Bender resisted all attempts to ferret out the "mystery."

The suspense deepened when, in September of 1953, word began to leak out that Bender was planning to close down the International Flying Saucer Bureau! When pressed for an explanation by one of the Bureau's chief UFO investigators, August C. Roberts, Bender finally blurted out, "I know the secret of the disks!" But Bender said that he was unable to reveal the secret, because *he had been visited by three strange men dressed in black suits, who had pledged him to total silence!* Bender would say no more.

A short time later, Roberts and Dominick Lucchesi, another IFSB member, visited the tight-lipped Bender at his home in Bridgeport. Barker skillfully dramatizes the critical interview, based on the account of it he received from Lucchesi. One can almost feel one's heart pounding, reading this dramatic confrontation. (Bender later asserted that an invisible extraterrestrial being had been present in the room at the time of the interview, which no doubt must have made things all the more uncomfortable.) Who are the Men? Where do they come from? What do they want? "I can't answer that," Bender solemnly repeated. Question after question followed, about the saucers, their origin, their purposes in coming to earth (the answers to all of which Bender *claimed* to know). But Bender steadfastly refused to give anything more than a few scattered, tantalizing hints as to what he knew about the mystery of the Flying Saucers and the three strange Men in Black.[5]

When the next issue of *Space Review* appeared in October, it formally announced the closing of the IFSB. A form was enclosed for members to use for refunds on the unused part of their subscriptions. The issue also contained a late bulletin:

> A source, which the IFSB considers very reliable, has informed us that the investigation of the flying-saucer mystery and the solution is approaching

its final stages . . . The mystery of the flying saucers is no longer a mystery. The source is already known, but information about this is being withheld by orders from a higher source . . . *We advise those engaged in saucer work to please be very cautious* [emphasis added].[6]

Why do those engaged in saucer work need to be "very cautious"? Bender, more tight-lipped than ever, wasn't saying. All attempts to get him to reveal the solution to "the mystery of the flying saucers" were in vain. Not everyone was convinced of the dire urgency of solving the "Bender mystery," as it soon came to be called. Former IFSB member Coral E. Lorenzen, who along with her husband, James, had just founded APRO, suggested in the APRO *Bulletin* dated November 15, 1953, that Bender may have closed down the IFSB for financial reasons. She is quoted by Barker as saying that the group may have received its initial backing from a "pulp" magazine publisher and that when this sponsor later withdrew Bender invented his preposterous tale to explain why he was getting out. Whatever the reason, APRO certainly could not have been disappointed to see its only major rival close up shop.

News of the "Bender mystery" spread rapidly throughout UFOdom, and soon UFO enthusiasts everywhere were wildly speculating about the identity of the three Men in Black. Gray Barker's potboiler *They Knew Too Much About Flying Saucers,* which came out three years later, abounds with speculative answers. Dominick Lucchesi noted that Bender had once significantly spelled the word "down" in capital letters in one of his UFO articles, suggesting that the saucers are somehow related to the famous "Shaver mystery." The late Richard S. Shaver wrote a number of articles for *Amazing Stories* magazine (edited by the late Ray Palmer, whose name pops up everywhere in the UFO field), concerning a degenerate race of beings, descendants of the survivors of the lost continent of Lemuria, which supposedly today inhabit the caverns of the earth's interior. The first few such stories were published as science fiction, but Shaver then began claiming that all his stories were true. Shaver, a welder, describes how the "mystery" began when he first heard voices hidden in the noise of his welding machine. He says he gradually began to "remember" the distant past of Lemuria by mentally absorbing the "thought records" that were hidden in secret caves. Shaver also wrote at length of the robots constructed by these underground creatures, some of which were helpful to humans (the Teros), while the degenerate robots (the Deros) were responsible for much of the world's misfortunes. James Oberg visited Palmer shortly before the latter's death in 1977. Palmer told Oberg that Shaver had actually been in a mental hospital at the time he claimed to have been underground, but that Shaver's articles caused the greatest deluge of corroborative mail ever to reach his magazine.

Roberts and Lucchesi asked Bender point-blank if the "secret of the disks" was in any way related to the Shaver mystery. Bender gave no answer at all; Barker informs us that Bender "tensed noticeably" when asked this question. Sensing his uneasiness, the interrogators briefly asked him about something else, then returned to the subject of Shaver and his remarkable underground kingdom. Again Bender refused to say anything, and he quickly changed the subject. The Men in Black, Barker suggested, may be the agents of the mysterious creatures who contacted Shaver through his welding machine and have now silenced Bender to keep him from revealing what he knows about the link between the UFOs and the sinister Dero robots.

Another explanation that Barker explores in some detail is the possible relationship between the flying saucers and the alarming build-up of ice at the South Pole. He explains the theories of an electrical engineer named Hugh A. Brown, of Long Island, who has been waging a one-man campaign to alert the world to the certain doom that awaits it, due to the five trillion tons of new ice that Brown says form each year around the South Pole. Barker describes Brown's frustration, "turning over and over in bed at night," because no one in a position of authority will heed his frenzied warnings. "Sooner or later, maybe even tomorrow or next week, or even the next minute," Barker warns, the "zero hour" will inevitably arrive, unless "drastic steps" are taken. When this dreadful event finally happens, the earth, he says, will "shiver, careen over on its side, tipping over like a giant overloaded canoe."

Al Bender had discussed the impending Ice Crisis in his UFO publication, *Space Review*: "The time for the next capsising may be 1953 and from all points of view, the earth is 'pretty wobbly' and that time may be at hand . . . the coming of the saucers may have to do with saving us from our horrible fate."[7] In this supposedly impending crisis, Barker sees another possible explanation for Bender being silenced by the Men in Black: If he were about to reveal to the world the cataclysm it would soon face, the authorities would certainly have to step in to prevent the mass panic that Bender's dreadful revelation would surely incite.

A third possible explanation suggested by Barker was the alleged conspiracy on the part of the world's leading astronomers to cover up what they have seen through their telescopes on the planet Mars. Mars was very close to the earth in the summer of 1954, affording astronomers an excellent opportunity to study the Red Planet. Since Mars at the time of its close approaches is always in the southernmost portions of the ecliptic, many astronomers traveled to the Southern Hemisphere to be able to observe that planet higher in the sky. Barker hints that the astronomers departed for South Africa with "an unnatural urgency," and he openly wondered why the Sunday supplements were not filled with feature articles about Mars. There appeared to be a "blackout on news about Mars," according to Barker, and he suggests that the Men in Black may have had a hand in this.

Of course, since even the giant craters and mountains of Mars are far too small to be seen by any earth-based telescopes under even the most ideal conditions, it is absurd to suggest that astronomers could have detected any signs of intelligent life on Mars, even if it existed (and the Viking missions strongly suggest that it does not). But in addition to his suspicion about a Mars cover-up, Barker alludes to hints that "astronomers had focused their telescopes close to Earth, peering at something that they could not explain." An artificial satellite? he suggests. (This was before the launch of Sputnik.) It was supposedly "hinted" by knowledgeable sources that the supposed satellite had not been placed there by anyone on earth! A Mars cover-up. A mystery satellite. Three Men in Black. Barker skillfully weaves them all together into a backdrop for the great "Bender mystery."

Al Bender was not the only one "silenced" by the three men. Edgar R. Jarrold operated the Australian Flying Saucer Bureau out of his home in New South Wales. Toward the end of 1952, Jarrold contacted the IFSB in Bridgeport, offering to share news and information about saucer sightings. Soon he, too, was supposedly "silenced" by a mysterious visitor. Jarrold's troubles are said to have begun when he was awakened one night, at 2:45 AM, by a violent pounding outside his door, accompanied by an overpowering odor suggestive of burning plastic. But nothing was to be found outside to account for the disturbance. For the next few days the head of the Australian Flying Saucer Bureau appeared to be shadowed by a "mystery car," which was said to glide by in the middle of the night with its lights turned off, often stopping out front, all the time carrying two sinister-looking occupants. Jarrold later reported to Barker that he subsequently received an unexpected visitor, whom he declined to identify. The visitor supposedly told Jarrold things that amazed him "beyond description" but had sworn him to secrecy, and Jarrold refused to divulge anything.

First Bender had been silenced, then Jarrold! Where would the Men in Black strike next? One pulp-magazine story asserts that Edgar Jarrold "disappeared under mysterious circumstances." But even Barker concedes that Jarrold's "disappearance" from the UFO scene implies nothing more mysterious than the fact that he resigned from the Bureau and stopped writing letters to his friends in America. However, not wishing to have anyone conclude that the Jarrold mystery is insufficiently mysterious, Barker passed on to his readers a rumor: Jarrold was finally persuaded to give up his UFO investigations when he was attacked in broad daylight by an invisible corporeal entity, which violently pushed him down a flight of stairs in a department store in downtown Sydney.

The sinister silencers lost little time in striking again. James Moseley was the editor of a small monthly newsletter, *Saucer News.* The October 1954 issue carried an article headlined "The Flying Saucer Mystery—Solved." In it Moseley asserts that just before the issue went to press he had received "irrefutable documented evidence" that conclusively established the answer to the saucer mystery. As there was insufficient time to include this "startling data" in the present issue, Moseley promised that it would be presented "in full" in the November issue.

Barker relates how he reached Moseley by telephone, to attempt to discover the secret that he had long been so eager to learn. But even though the two men were (and still are) good friends, Moseley refused to reveal any details. He asserted that his line was tapped, and told Barker that he would "just have to wait for the November issue."

When the November issue finally arrived, airmail special delivery, Barker opened it "breathlessly," only to find Moseley claiming that "the documents referred to above are no longer in my possession," and that he was not "at liberty" to discuss them. Moseley also pronounced a familiar warning: he urged all flying saucer investigators to be "extremely cautious in dealing with certain phases of the Saucer Mystery." Moseley had been silenced by the Men in Black! One can almost hear Barker gasp out loud as he writes, "Bender, Jarrold, the others—now Moseley!"

If Moseley's supposed "silencing" by the Men in Black is indicative of the quality of work they do, we can all heave a sigh of relief, because Moseley remains one of the most unsilenced individuals in all UFOdom. At the time of this writing, twenty-five years after he was allegedly "silenced" by sinister forces, James Moseley continues to issue his newsletter, which is keenly enjoyed by many for its witty, gossippy, irreverent tone. Having sold the rights to the name *Saucer News,* Moseley continues to publish it under a different name each month: *Saucer Cruise, Saucer Booze, Saucer Jews*—whatever propriety will allow, and then some. As all regular readers of the publication are surely aware, Moseley's sense of humor is almost legendary. One may perhaps label him "the Voltaire of the UFO movement," in view of his perceptive and witty satires. It does not take a Sherlock Holmes to deduce that, by being "silenced," Moseley probably was enjoying another one of his jokes, this one being perhaps his funniest. First he pulled everyone's leg by parodying Bender's promise of a spectacular flying-saucer revelation, then failing to deliver, supposedly because the secret was somehow too terrible to reveal. It is inconceivable that Barker could have overlooked this interpretation of the incident. Yet Barker sent his book off to the printer, squeezing the last drop of "mystery" from Moseley's monkeyshines.

They Knew Too Much About Flying Saucers closes with no firm solutions to the Bender Mystery. A number of additional hypotheses are tossed out: perhaps Bender discovered that our sun was about to explode as a supernova and the authorities stepped in to prevent panic; perhaps he stumbled onto some military secret and was forced into silence; he may have learned too much about a new source of unlimited energy and was silenced by the sinister agents of greedy capitalists. Whatever the answer may be, Barker ends his book with a warning: "They will be at your door, too, unless we all get wise and find out who the three men really are."

However, Barker is too good a showman to leave such a lucrative "mystery" unsolved forever. Six years after the publication of *They Knew Too Much About Flying Saucers,* Barker dropped the other shoe, publishing a sequel, *Flying Saucers and the Three Men,* written by none other than Albert K. Bender himself. In it Bender finally reveals to a breathless world the answer to the mystery: *the three Men in Black are extraterrestrials* who visited Bender to keep him from revealing to the world what he knew about the mission of the flying-saucer people here on earth. This book tells Bender's incredible story in his own words, Gray Barker having been reduced to the role of annotator, introductor, and epiloguer.

In this book Bender relates how, shortly after the founding of the IFSB, he began to have a number of strange experiences in which he felt a disturbing presence of something unknown and sinister. He began receiving messages, "as if telepathically," telling him that he "should not delve into the saucer mystery any further." But the first real confrontation with these sinister forces did not occur until March 15, 1953, on the evening of C-Day.

The IFSB had decided to hold a "World Contact Day" on that date, during which at a specified time every IFSB member throughout the world was requested to telepathically transmit a message of friendship to the space people. The text of the message, which members were expected to memorize, began like this: "Calling occupants of interplanetary craft! Calling occupants of interplanetary craft that have been observing our planet Earth."[8]

Like the other members of the IFSB, Albert Bender retired to his room at the moment for contact to attempt to send a message of friendship telepathically to the space people. But instead of receiving warm greetings from the Space Brothers, as some alleged UFO contactees reported, Bender relates how a sinister, nauseating presence began to manifest itself, warning him "to discontinue delving into the mysteries of the universe," and threatening to "make an appearance should he disobey."

At this point Bender made the notation in the April issue of *Space Review* to expect a startling revelation in July. But the refusal on the part of even the other IFSB officers to believe Bender's story convinced him not to publish his experiences in that issue. Instead, he wrote down an account of the incident on C-Day, with the intention of alerting the authorities in Washington to what was happening. But he claims that the paper mysteriously dematerialized before it could be mailed. One night soon afterward, three mysterious entities reportedly materialized in his bedroom, accompanied by the smell of sulphur, causing him considerable physical discomfort. He describes them as three figures "dressed in black clothes," and wearing black hats. They reportedly had eyes that shined "like flashlight bulbs" as they floated about a foot off the floor. Bender says that the three men told him he was an excellent "contact" for them on earth, and they gave him a small metal amulet, looking something like a coin, to enable him to contact them whenever he wished. They explained that in order to make contact he should clasp the amulet tightly in his hand, turn on his radio, close his eyes, and repeat the word "Kazik."

Two days after this remarkable experience, Bender reportedly attempted to make contact with the Men in Black. He turned on his radio, clasped the amulet, and closing his eyes repeated the magic word, "Kazik . . . Kazik," until he again felt the physical discomfort that was supposed to accompany an alien's presence. He asserts that this time he was teleported aboard a flying saucer, where he spoke with an extraterrestrial. During his visit he learned that the UFOs have come to earth to mine an extremely valuable (but unspecified) chemical from the oceans and that, should the earth people attempt to stop the UFO aliens before their mining operations have been completed, our entire planet will be destroyed. Bender also claims to have seen the aliens in their natural forms, and he describes them as "hideous monsters"; they only assume the form of the Men in Black, he informs us, when they need to appear before earthlings.

Bender reported a number of subsequent encounters with the three men. He claims to have been teleported to the flying saucers' secret base under the Antarctic ice, where he met another alien in his natural form as a "monster." He was even granted an audience with "the Exalted One," who revealed to him many deep mysteries of the universe. Bender describes seeing some of the machinery used in the UFOnauts' mining operations. He also claims that the Exalted One permitted him to see a UFO star map. Betty Hill has of course made a similar claim. Bender includes a sketch of the map in his book, but Marjorie Fish has not yet come up with an identification of the stars on it.

When a number of months had passed after this alleged visit and Bender's teleportation back to Bridgeport, he reported that the UFO aliens signaled him that they had completed their mission on earth. They had left our region of the universe, leaving Bender free at long last to reveal his remarkable story. Since that time, he says, he has seen nothing more of the Men in Black.

The legend of the Men in Black was picked up and expanded by UFO writers John Keel, Brad Steiger, and many others. Today, the story of the Men in Black has become an integral part of flying saucer folklore.

One would expect that serious UFO researchers would give little or no credence to the Men in Black stories, which with little effort can be traced back to dubious beginnings. After all, when one is engaged in legitimate scientific research, as nearly all UFOlogists claim to be, one must always be careful not to accept unsound information, and one should be especially cautious in dealing with stories that originate under questionable circumstances.

But, alas, it is asking too much to expect the "scientific" UFOlogists, who have shown themselves so eager to substitute quantity of evidence for quality, to exercise better judgment in dealing with stories of the Men in Black. The motto of the UFO believers seems to be: "Any story that is repeated often enough must have some basis in fact." Will it surprise the reader to learn that stories about the Men in Black are now being taken seriously by many of the most prominent "scientific" UFO investigators?

The Ohio state director for MUFON, Nils Pacquette, stated that two mysterious men in a black Cadillac attempted to confiscate from him some metal samples that were allegedly from a UFO. He said that a check of the license number of their car supposedly revealed that that number had never been issued.[9] APRO researcher Dick Ruhl reports that one day, when he was getting "evidence" analyzed from a supposed UFO landing site, he found himself being followed by a black Mustang with license plates UFO-35, driven by a man dressed totally in black. Ruhl also relates that he has reason to believe that the MIB are also monitoring his UFO lectures.[10] UFO writer Jerome Clark reports personally witnessing, while outdoors one dark night researching a supposedly paranormal phenomenon, the sudden materialization of "the silhouette of an enormous figure in a cloak."[11] Clark has recently made it clear, however, that he doubts Bender's tales.

Dr. Ron Westrum, a sociologist at Eastern Michigan University, took the stories of the Men in Black seriously enough to undertake a study of their supposed actions, under the auspices of MUFON. Westrum, a MUFON consultant in sociology, informed the MUFON membership that he wanted to hear discreetly from anyone who had ever been "silenced" or in any way threatened by the mysterious Men in Black. "It appears that some MUFON investigators and witnesses they have interviewed have been bothered by harassment of various kinds. It might prove useful to have one committee in MUFON to deal with these [MIB] problems," he suggested.[12] But his study was embarrassingly short; he was unable to find a single individual who had experienced a "classic" MIB visitation. Westrum did, however, receive a number of letters from people wanting to learn about the MIB harassment that his study would supposedly reveal.

Jacques Vallee, a former member of the Scientific Board of the Center for UFO Studies, has few doubts about the reality of the sinister Men in Black. "It's very nice as a science-fiction story," Vallee states, "but apparently it did happen in several verified instances." He is quite convinced that the Men in Black really are part of the overall UFO phenomenon; he told an interviewer for *UFO Report* that "there are too many documented reports of this kind to ignore their existence." (Yet Ron Westrum was unable to find a single one.) Vallee admits that he was once skeptical of all MIB reports but has now seen indisputable evidence that the Men in Black not only have tampered with UFO evidence but also "had knowledge of the case that couldn't be obtained by ordinary means."[13]

The best-known "scientific" UFO researcher in the United States today, J. Allen Hynek, was by 1975 also converted to believing in the Men in Black. Hynek is quoted in the *National Enquirer* describing an MIB incident reportedly occurring in Mexico. Hynek, who at that time was the head of the *Enquirer*'s Blue Ribbon UFO Panel, says that a UFO witness who failed to meet with him for a scheduled interview did so because he had been silenced by the Men in Black. They reportedly forced his car off the road and warned him to be silent about his UFO sighting "if he knew what was good for him."[14]

In a 1976 interview, Hynek tells of a report of another "perplexing" MIB-like incident that was phoned in during the middle of the night over the Center for UFO Studies' hot line. The call was placed by a police officer in a small town in Minnesota, where a UFO flap had been going on for some months. The story concerns an individual in a "big black Cadillac" reportedly behaving very strangely one night. He appeared to be harassing a couple in another car for no apparent reason, repeatedly preventing them from making a telephone call. As they chased the mysterious black Cadillac down the road, to obtain its license number, Hynek relates that "before their eyes, the vehicle in front of them lifted up into the air and disappeared, 'as if it had flown into another dimension.' "[15]

Emphasizing the significance given to MIB reports by CUFOS is the account of Richard Yinger, a sociologist at Palm Beach Junior College in Florida. Yinger traveled to Evanston, where he spent several weeks with Hynek at the UFO Center. In an interview with a Florida newspaper, Yinger repeats the account of the reported MIB incident in Mexico, which he had obtained directly from Hynek. He goes on to say that he had always thought the stories about the Men in Black to be mere sensationalism until his visit to Evanston: "I never took those men in black (MIBs) seriously before—not until I saw how seriously Hynek and the scientists around him consider them . . . to me this is more incredible than the UFOs themselves. I can handle UFOs, but I just can't handle those men in black."[16]

You discover the secret of the disks. But you can't reveal it because you are visited by three strange Men in Black who force you to remain silent. Why have they come? Is it related to the Shaver mystery? Or the Mars cover-up? The impending ice crisis at the South Pole? They soon get Jarrold, and later Moseley. Then at last you are free to reveal the secrets that the Men in Black forced you to hold back: the incident on World Contact Day. The teleportations. The Exalted One. The monsters. The amulet. *Kazik.* The eyes that glow like flashlight bulbs. "I never took those Men in Black seriously before—not until I saw how seriously Hynek and the scientists around him consider them." It all serves to demonstrate how, in wandering through the wonderland of UFOs, a little credulity goes a long way.

NOTES

1. *UFO Report UFO Annual,* 1976, p. 16.
2. Gray Barker, *They Knew Too Much About Flying Saucers* (New York: University Books, 1956), p. 92.
3. Albert K. Bender, *Flying Saucers and the Three Men,* 1962 (Paperback Library, 1968), p. 16.

4. Bender, pp. 10–12.

5. Barker, pp. 128–135; Bender, p. 115.

6. Barker, p. 138.

7. Quoted by Barker, p. 117.

8. Bender, p. 69.

9. *National Enquirer,* September 23, 1975.

10. *Massapequa* (New York) *Post,* November 11, 1976.

11. Jerome Clark, *UFO Report,* July 1977.

12. MUFON *Skylook,* October 1974, p. 15.

13. J. Allen Hynek and Jacques Vallee, *The Edge of Reality* (Chicago: Regnery, 1975), chapter 3; *UFO Report,* April 1976.

14. *National Enquirer,* September 23, 1975.

15. *UFO Report,* August 1976.

16. *Palm Beach Post Times* (Florida), September 14, 1975.

16

UFOs: A JEALOUS PHENOMENON

Is the time of our inquiry always wrong, the place always elsewhere?
— Jacques Vallee[1]

The claim is often made by "scientific" UFO investigators that UFOs are indeed a real phenomenon and that the chronic absence of evidence of their existence is due only to the lack of scientific interest in the subject. According to this view, UFOs are a phenomenon that will someday become an accepted field of scientific study, once our current prejudices on the subject can be overcome.

At first this argument appears to have merit. Perhaps UFOs *are* simply a new and as yet poorly understood phenomenon, as electricity was two centuries ago. But the analogy doesn't seem quite correct—something in it is not quite right. There plainly is an as yet unformulated distinction between a hotly debated subject such as UFOs, and a poorly understood but unquestionably legitimate phenomenon such as superconductivity. Exactly *what* can the difference be?

One dramatic difference is that, unlike legitimate scientific phenomena, UFOs seem to select very carefully just where and when they will condescend to appear. Borrowing a phrase from Theophrastus, I have coined the term *jealous phenomenon* to designate such whimsical behavior. An understanding of jealous phenomena will help us to discover what it is that separates alleged phenomena such as UFOs, ESP, and Bigfoot from many unquestionably genuine but poorly understood phenomena in the real world.

What do we mean by a *jealous* phenomenon? Turning to the single most authoritative reference work on the English language, the twelve-volume

Oxford English Dictionary, we find the following entry under the word *jealous:* "zealous or solicitous for the preservation or well-being of something possessed or esteemed; *vigilant or careful in guarding; suspiciously careful or watchful* [emphasis added]."[2] Doesn't this exactly describe the behavior attributed to UFOs? They are always reported to be exhibiting "suspiciously careful or watchful" behavior in selecting where and to whom they will appear.

Theophrastus was a Greek philosopher and scientist of the fourth century B.C. who studied under Aristotle. Upon the death of that famous scholar, Theophrastus carried on the master's studies and teaching. Although Theophrastus wrote on many subjects, he specialized in biology; he probably knew as much about that subject as any man of his time.

But one must be careful not to confuse Theophrastus' biology with the biology of today. Science in antiquity was a curious mixture of careful observation and frivolous folklore. The biology of Aristotle and Theophrastus was composed of equal parts of descriptive anatomy, animal psychology, and fanciful invention. Hearsay was one of the principal sources to be drawn upon in composing a scholarly work, much as is now done by many "serious" UFO investigators. Thus while one finds much of value in the scientific writings of classical antiquity, there is a constant intermingling of fact and fantasy, of science and superstition. In one of the works of Aristotle we find a masterful description of the day-by-day development of the chick inside the egg, based upon the most painstaking observation, but we also find the assertion that bees carry around stones as ballast to steady their flight on windy days.[3] Pliny, among the greatest of Roman scholars, wrote at length on the behavior of dragons. Aelian, another Roman, asserts that eagles cleverly drop tortoises from great heights onto rocks to crack their shells, this accounting for the untimely death of the great dramatist Aeschylus, whose bald head was mistaken for a stone by a nearsighted eagle. Fact and fantasy, as we can see, mingled quite freely in the writings of ancient science.

Theophrastus composed a "scientific" treatise titled *Jealous Animals.* Since it is not found among the collected works of Theophrastus, one can only surmise that the work did not survive. But fortunately we do know what was said in *Jealous Animals,* because other ancient writers whose texts have survived to the present discuss the work.

Jealousy is, of course, an all-too-human characteristic, but Theophrastus thought he could also discern examples of jealous behavior in animals. Take the elephant, for example. Elephants, he said, somehow know that men hunt them only for their tusks. When one of these tusks falls off from natural causes, does the elephant simply walk away from it, since it is of no further use? No, says Pliny (drawing upon Theophrastus), for the elephant is a *jealous* animal: hence he buries his fallen tusk in the ground. The tusk is of no value whatever to the elephant any longer, but since it *is* of value to humans the elephant reportedly goes to great trouble to thwart them.

The skin shed by a spotted lizard was reputed to be a remedy for epilepsy. But such skins were difficult to come by; according to Theophrastus, as soon as the lizard shed its skin it would speedily devour it, in order to prevent humans from enjoying its benefit. Another jealous animal was said to be the stag, which takes pains to hide its right horn (but not its left), because the stag knows of the great medicinal powers contained therein, which it jealously withholds from mankind.[4]

Today we laugh at the folly of ascribing human motivations to the animal world. But appearing even more primitive and anthropocentric to the modern mind is the ancients' notion that animals should even *care* enough about human plans and wishes to take such pains to thwart them. Are we humans really so important in the scheme of things that even the lowly beasts plan their day-to-day affairs with us in mind? Such a view seems rather conceited to moderns, which of course it is. But this is exactly the viewpoint espoused by those who assert that UFOs, ESP, monsters, and other dubious phenomena not only actually exist but expend a great deal of time and effort cleverly hiding from human observers.

It is a well-known fact that UFOs are supposed to be extremely wary of showing themselves openly. They reportedly have no qualms about flying over a farm in Oregon or buzzing a National Guard helicopter in Ohio, so long as not too many people will see them and the evidence of their visit will not be too convincing. They will not, however, under any circumstances fly low over a crowded vacation site in broad daylight or hover conspicuously over a major city, because the photographic record they would presumably leave behind would be clear and unmistakable. UFOs have reportedly landed from time to time to kidnap for a short time a frightened couple in a deserted region of the White Mountains, or a pair of nocturnal fishermen along the sleepy banks of the Pascagoula River. However, UFOs always seem to take the utmost precaution to see that none of their alleged abductees ever walk away with anything more tangible than an ambiguous "star map" or an improbable tale.

In short, one must conclude that the UFOs' reported behavior is *principally determined by an overriding concern with human thoughts and emotions.* The UFO reportedly hides its presence for the same reason that the elephant is supposed to bury its discarded tusks: both are determined to thwart human wishes. If the elephant of ancient myths was a jealous animal, then UFOs, psychokinesis, psychic surgery, and other questionable phenomena can best be described as *jealous phenomena,* because they are clearly supposed to be "suspiciously careful or watchful" in preserving something far more esteemed—and far less tangible—than mere tusks or herbs: the ultimate unverifiability of their own existence.

Coral and Jim Lorenzen, the founders of APRO, observe that "UFOs are notoriously camera shy."[5] Not *entirely* camera shy, for at least a few genuine photographs of UFOs are alleged to exist. These supposedly genuine photographs are both scarce and unconvincing. UFO believers sometimes debate the question of whether UFOs are "infallible," in the sense that they never crash and leave behind debris and never have to make a prolonged forced landing that would enable unquestionable evidence of their existence to be secured.

Amazing as this is, I do not find this aspect of the UFOs' supposed "infallibility" to be their most incredible feat. Far more impressive is their ability to select, on those rare occasions when they "permit" a photograph to be taken, areas where there is *one and only one photographer* ready to snap their picture. All supposed UFO photographs produced to date have been taken by a single photographer, using only one camera. (I can suggest an explanation, cynic that I am: consistent UFO hoaxes involving more than one camera are exceedingly difficult to pull off.) Such remarkable selectivity these UFOs seem to possess! One camera they permit now and then, but two *independent* cameras, *never*.

A famous series of UFO photographs taken at San Jose de Valderas, Spain, in 1967, showing a strange astrological-type insignia on the object, were reportedly obtained by two separate photographers. But after a detailed analysis, the French UFO investigator Claude Poher informed the Center for UFO Studies that the "two" cameras could not have had their lenses even as much as a few centimeters apart! Poher concluded that only *one* camera was used and that "the photographs are a hoax, produced by using a small model of translucent plastic, on which the insignia was drawn in ink."[6] These photos, however, are still to be found in many UFO books and magazines as "classic" evidence.

The problems faced by would-be UFO photographers have been neatly summed up by John Keel in his book about the Mothman sightings in West Virginia: "Camera malfunctions are remarkably common among would-be UFO photographers, and even those who try to take pictures of the serpent at Loch Ness. It almost seems as if some outside force fouls up cameras when monsters and UFO's are around."[7] I couldn't come up with a better account of a *jealous phenomenon* myself. Another obstacle UFO photographers must contend with are the sinister, mysterious Men in Black, who are reported to turn up frequently at witnesses' homes to confiscate any UFO photos they may have obtained. To those who believe in the double whammy of mysterious camera jam-ups followed by forcible confiscation of the evidence, perhaps it is not so surprising that no UFO has ever been captured on film by two or more independent photographers.

The French UFO investigator Aime Michel sent a letter to the British publication *Flying Saucer Review* that shows him to be acutely aware of the problem of UFOs as a jealous phenomenon. He observes that a wave of UFO sightings then in progress had been continuing for a year. "However," he notes, "in *no case* have we been able to secure the absolute definitive proof that will be capable of convincing everyone . . . bearing in mind the large numbers of cameras and apparatus of all kinds in the world, it is incompatible with the laws of chance that no irrefutable evidence has ever been obtained." After recognizing the chronic and perplexing lack of evidence, however, does he go on to suggest, however tentatively, the most obvious conclusion to be drawn—that UFOs do not exist? Not at all. He applies a sort of Occam's razor in reverse, where one rescues one's failing hypotheses by frantically multiplying their elements beyond necessity. Michel concludes that the UFO phenomenon is "programmed" in such a way that "it shall spread more and more as rumor, but that at the same time it shall elude the human methods of establishing proof, that is to say it eludes science."[8]

But the most interesting question is one that Michel makes no attempt to answer: If we, the inhabitants of earth, are so cosmically insignificant that we are never contacted by the supposed inhabitants of the UFOs, why are we so important that they take such pains to keep us from knowing for certain about their existence? Surely the UFOnauts cannot be afraid that we will attack them, for it is an article of faith among UFO believers that the government and the military *already* have secret proof of the UFOs existence. Hence there is no conceivable motivation for UFOs to conceal themselves from the public at large. Michel's hypothesis again places human beings at the center of the universe, creatures from whose sight UFOs must endlessly flee.

The paradox of UFOs as a jealous phenomenon will be clearly seen when we consider the evidence obtained when an unquestionably genuine flying object makes an unexpected appearance. A remarkable object flew over the Rocky Mountains on the afternoon of August 10, 1972. It was sighted by thousands of people, scattered across a half-dozen states. The object was a brilliant daylight fireball, a meteorite of substantial size that grazed the earth's atmosphere but fortunately did not strike the ground. Had it done so, it would have had the impact of an atomic bomb.

The object remained in the earth's atmosphere for less than two minutes— just 101 seconds. Yet during this brief encounter it left behind more evidence of its existence than have all of the UFOs of the past thirty years combined. Not only was it witnessed by thousands of independent witnesses from Utah to Alberta, but the sonic boom caused by the meteorite was heard by thousands more. Its path was recorded in so many photographs (even though no one knew in advance that it was coming) that there can be no doubt today of the object's reality. At least two separate motion picture sequences were obtained showing the object crossing most of the sky, and a large number of still photographs were taken—many of them dramatic full-color shots, all of them absolutely consistent in size and appearance.[9] For a hoaxer to fabricate and coordinate so many widely scattered photographs without slipping up would be a virtual impossibility. Not only is the photographic record left by this meteorite extremely impressive, but its path was recorded by a satellite-borne infrared radiometer operated by the U.S. Air Force.

Thus it is seen that when a *genuine* object from space entered the earth's atmosphere, however briefly and unexpectedly, it left behind a mountain of indisputable physical evidence confirming its existence, *even though it flew over the least densely populated area of the continental United States.* Given the large number of UFOs that have reportedly been seen throughout the world (including some reportedly bold enough to have landed on the outskirts of both Chicago and New York City and to have hovered for hours off the beaches of Los Angeles), *why has no UFO ever been as widely seen and photographed as the Great Rocky Mountain Fireball of 1972?* Could the reason be that meteors are real but that UFOs are not? If not, how is it that UFOs always manage to ensure that whatever evidence they "consent" to leave behind, whether photographic, physical, or other, will *never* be fully convincing?

Another classic example of a jealous phenomenon is the "psychic" ability to bend a spoon, allegedly without exerting any physical force on it. This is a neat little trick that today is very much in vogue, its best-known performer being the celebrated Uri Geller, the Israeli Cagliostro. One might expect that, if such a power actually existed, it would work equally well in full view of observers as it does when everyone's eyes have been diverted by a momentary distraction. But this is not the case. Those who have studied Geller in action report that he keeps the atmosphere surrounding him in a constant state of turmoil. He is endlessly requesting articles from another room, jumping from one "experiment" to another, getting up to go to the bathroom, and so forth, all of which makes it nearly impossible for anyone to actually *see* a "paranormal" event happen: all one generally sees is the result.

In fact, Professor John Taylor, a noted mathematician at King's College in London, has even gone so far as to coin the term "shyness effect" to describe the metal's apparent unwillingness to perform its psychic miracles under close scrutiny. Professor Taylor notes that the spoon or fork is most likely to bend when "the observer's attention has been shifted from the object he [the "psychic"] is trying to bend. Indeed, this feature of bending not happening when the object is being watched—'the shyness effect'—is very common. It seems to be correlated with the presence of skeptics or others who have a poor relationship with the subject."[10] In other words, it most often occurs in the presence of those who are wise to the tricks being employed by the "psychic" and who are on guard against them. (Taylor has recently repudiated his belief in Geller's powers.[11]) Spoon-bending is thus seen to be another jealous phenomenon. It is "suspiciously careful or watchful" about permitting human observers to watch any spoon in the act of bending. We may see the spoon before, and can examine it afterward, but the "psychic" bending itself only Heaven (and Uri Geller) are permitted to watch.

One could go on to name dozens of other jealous phenomena that have always managed to elude the grasp of science. The Loch Ness monster, dumb beast that it is, somehow always manages to slip away before its "scientific" pursuers can do better than snap a blurred photo of an unconvincing head or an out-of-focus appendage. Certainly one would expect that eventually this slow-moving, dim-witted reptile could be outsmarted by scientists employing sophisticated state-of-the-art electronic detection systems and that unambiguous photographs could be obtained.

Likewise, the Bigfoot of American folklore has succeeded in escaping from every reported encounter with the civilized world, keeping its secrecy, as well as its safety, intact. And, after decades of "scientific" testing, the highly jealous phenomenon of Extrasensory Perception (ESP) has titillated its researchers countless times, and yet has consistently failed to produce any evidence whatever that can meet the rigorous standards of science. The list seems endless. What all these phenomena have in common is an infallible talent for making themselves scarce whenever there is any danger that their reality might be established beyond dispute.

UFOs, monsters, "psychic" manifestations, and similar phenomena seem to play peek-a-boo with the world of objective reality, popping into existence in the company of the credulous, and popping out again when the skeptics arrive. From time to time they "consent" to have their pictures taken, but like a movie star protecting an unflattering profile, these phenomena appear to insist, as it were, that the photographs always be sufficiently blurred, indistinct, or unauthenticated to render them totally unconvincing to all except true believers.

UFO believers often suggest the analogy that UFOs are as unexplainable to present-day science as the Aurora Borealis was to the science of the eighteenth century. Hence the final answer to the UFO riddle will be left to future centuries. If UFOs were an unquestionably legitimate subject for scientific investigation, as are quasars and pulsars, the analogy might well be valid. But it ignores the highly significant fact that UFOs are a *jealous* phenomenon. The Aurora Borealis did and does not play peek-a-boo, hiding itself from skeptical observers and appearing only to isolated witnesses. It shows itself openly, to believer and skeptic alike, and hence its objective existence makes it a legitimate object for scientific study.

A common mistake among UFO theorists is to regard the chronic lack of evidence to be the result of the relative rarity of the UFO phenomenon. But this is not a reasonable assumption. Many natural phenomena, such as tornadoes and brilliant meteors, are both unpredictable and fleeting yet leave behind unambiguous evidence of their existence. Jealous phenomena should not be confused with rare ones. A phenomenon that objectively exists, no matter how rare, will eventually be brought into the open. The gorilla, long a legendary animal, yielded skeletal remains not long after the first European explorers penetrated the African interior. Yet the legendary

Bigfoot, which reportedly inhabits such wild, unexplored places as California, Oregon, and New Jersey, somehow continues to escape the clutches of science year after year.

In the late eighteenth century the French Academy of Sciences committed its celebrated blunder of denying that meteorites do indeed on occasion fall from the sky, a mistake they repudiated thirty-one years later when indisputable evidence was finally presented. Yet UFOs have been in the public eye longer than this, as spiritualism and clairvoyance have been for well over a century, and yet the quality of the proof offered in support of these alleged phenomena is no better today than it was at the very beginning. A jealous phenomenon will continue to play peek-a-boo with the universe of objective reality for decades on end, for as long as anyone is willing to show it proper attention. When its adherents finally tire of it and move on to something else, as did believers in alchemy and spirit-rapping, the phenomenon quickly faded into oblivion, its traces to be found only in the pages of historians' treatises.

In *Incident at Exeter,* a book about a series of UFO sightings in New England in 1965 (see chapter 11), author John G. Fuller attempts to explain why it is that people believe in the existence of certain things that are almost never seen but disbelieve in UFOs. He finds the answer to be the pronouncements of "authorities." Even though only a tiny fraction of the population has ever seen a great white whale or a plover's egg, their existence is uncontested. Fuller says that this is because "authorities have proclaimed them to exist."[12] He suggests that the only reason that UFOs are not also universally accepted is because no authority has yet stepped forward to proclaim their existence.

While this may indeed be an accurate description of the workings of Mr. Fuller's own mind, it clearly does not in any way weaken the case against UFOs, because the UFO is a *jealous* phenomenon. Whales and okapi are uncontested precisely because they are *objective,* have been seen and studied, and hence are not "jealous"—but not because of what some exalted "authority" may have to say on the matter. If I were to proclaim publicly the nonexistence of the white whale, claiming it to exist only in popular folklore, I would very quickly be humiliated by some zoologist, who would send me indisputable proof of that animal's existence. But, although I have been publicly saying for a number of years that UFOs simply do not exist, no UFOlogist has ever been able to make such a demonstration. A jealous phenomenon is just too modest to permit itself to be triumphantly paraded before the unbelievers. When studying phenomena that *are* truly part of the objective universe, a scientist has little need for the pronouncements of any "authority," no matter how venerable.

The noted UFOlogist, Dr. J. Allen Hynek, is well aware of the UFOs' characteristics as a jealous phenomenon. In his book *The Edge of Reality,* Hynek squarely faces up to the matter:

The UFO is what has been termed a "jealous phenomenon." [Hynek fails to mention from whom he has borrowed the idea; I introduced the concept to him when I was a student at Northwestern.] A Boeing 747 is not a jealous phenomenon, an eclipse isn't jealous, anyone can observe it. But a UFO is a "jealous phenomenon" in that it seems to show itself preferentially in a particular area; a UFO seems to be localized in both space and time.[13]

Having recognized the remarkable jealousy of the UFO phenomenon, Hynek then proceeds to go absolutely nowhere with the concept. He does not attempt to explain how such peculiar behavior can be reconciled with his belief that the UFO phenomenon is indeed real and not just a product of overactive imaginations. Nor does he attempt to explain how UFOs are able infallibly to control the amount of evidence they leave behind, to keep it always just short of the amount that would prove their existence unquestionably.

It might appear that a phenomenon such as ball lightning is an exception to the point I am making, that jealous behavior is the earmark of a nonexistent phenomenon. Here we have what appears to be a jealous phenomenon that *is* legitimate (or at least *appears* to be legitimate; I'm still not *fully* convinced). But even granting the legitimacy of the phenomenon's existence, it is by no means clear that the phenomenon is jealous; more likely it is simply rare. Although next to nothing in the way of physical evidence has been produced to substantiate the existence of the phenomenon, given its brief lifetime and the great rarity of its reported manifestations, the scarceness of evidence does not appear to be remarkable or suspicious, as it does for UFOs. Ball lightning is not reported to persist for many minutes, or even hours, as are UFOs, it is not reported to return repeatedly to the same favored individuals, as are UFOs, and it does not appear that there are fifteen million Americans who claim to have seen it—that is the number who have claimed to have seen UFOs. If ball lightning were reported as frequently as UFOs and had as many eager investigators hot on its trail, then it indeed *would* be remarkable that better evidence has not been obtained.

If we wish to sum up our observations by formulating a firmer definition of a jealous phenomenon, we might try something like this: A phenomenon is said to be *jealous* if it is impossible to conclusively establish the fact of its existence even after many years of investigation and if *the evidence for the phenomenon's existence falls significantly short of the degree of evidence that would be left behind by an unquestionably legitimate phenomenon for which there is an equal number of sightings of the same overall character.*

The conclusion to be drawn is obvious: *A Jealous Phenomenon does not exist.* Anything that has been vigorously investigated for as many years as UFOs or telepathy have, and still has yet to be *established,* let alone fully analyzed, has almost certainly eluded its pursuers for a very basic reason: it has no basis in reality. The fact that a phenomenon appears to wink in and out of existence as the skeptics arrive and depart is the strongest possible indication that it exists only in the overheated imaginations of íts investigators.

NOTES

1. Jacques Vallee, *The Invisible College* (New York: Dutton, 1975), p. 166.

2. *Oxford English Dictionary* (Oxford University Press, 1971).

3. Aristotle, *History of Animals.*

4. See Thorndike, *A History of Magic and Experimental Science* (New York: Macmillan, 1929), pp. 75, 238, 234-35; in index, see "jealousy in animals."

5. Coral and James Lorenzen, *Encounters with UFO Occupants* (New York: Berkley, 1976), p. 398.

6. Claude Poher, *Center for UFO Studies Bulletin* (Spring 1977).

7. John Keel, *The Mothman Prophecies* (New York: Saturday Review Press, 1975), p. 37.

8. "Mail Bag," *Flying Saucer Review* 20, no. 3 (1974):28; quoted by Sprinkle, *1975 MUFON Symposium Proceedings.*

9. Luigi G. Jacchia, "A Meteorite That Missed the Earth," *Sky and Telescope* 48, no. 1 (July 1974):4.

10. John Taylor, *Superminds* (New York: Viking, 1976), chapter 4.

11. "News and Comment," *Skeptical Inquirer* 3, no. 3 (Spring 1979):3; Taylor, *Nature* 276: 64-67.

12. John G. Fuller, *Incident at Exeter* (New York: Putnam, 1966), chapter 7.

13. J. Allen Hynek and Jacques Vallee, *The Edge of Reality* (Chicago: Regnery, 1975), chapter 3.

17

LIBERATION FROM REALITY

The "new wave" of UFOlogy represents a distinct break with previous thinking on the subject. For two decades following Major Keyhoe's influential 1950 article in *True* magazine, "The Flying Saucers Are Real," the majority opinion among UFO proponents held that UFOs were nuts-and-bolts spacecraft from some other planet. Skeptics argued forcefully against this view, citing the seemingly insurmountable difficulties involved in transporting any appreciable mass across interstellar distances in time scales as short as decades or even centuries. While the pace of UFO sightings quickened in the mid-to-late 1960s, the tenability of the extraterrestrial hypothesis was gradually deteriorating.

With the publication of physicist William Markowitz's article in *Science* in 1967 titled "The Physics and Metaphysics of Unidentified Flying Objects,"[1] the intellectual respectability of UFOs as extraterrestrial craft seemed to have reached a nadir. Among the many absurdities Markowitz pointed out was that when a spacecraft has been accelerated to relativistic velocities, even the sporadic dust specks and stray hydrogen atoms of "empty" space become lethal: at .99999999999 the speed of light, a collision with a single particle of interstellar dust (which exists in great abundance throughout the galaxy) would be more than three hundred times more devastating than a head-on collision with an automobile traveling at a hundred miles per hour.

While the great majority of UFO proponents were (and are) perfectly content to go on believing in visitations by extraterrestrial spaceships, regardless of the difficulties with that hypothesis, by the late 1960s a few of the more perceptive UFO theorists began to note serious difficulties with nuts-and-bolts explanations. UFOs are frequently *reported* to materialize or dematerialize in a ghostly manner, something that no solid object can do. UFOs appear to be able to slip in and out of controlled airspace without being detected by radar (although UFOs are supposed to be detectable by radar). More puzzling still is the UFO's apparent property of selective visibility—a UFO might reportedly hover above a city like New York or Los Angeles and yet be seen by only one individual.

But what tantalized perceptive UFO theorists the most was the undeniable dreamlike character of so many UFO encounters. In reported encounters with UFO entities, time and space lose the character they hold during our waking hours; even the laws of logic themselves seem to be more characteristic of the dream state than of the real world. "What time is it?" asks a UFO occupant. "It's 2:30," answers the earthling. "You lie—it is 4 o'clock," the creature bluntly replies.[2] Encountering reports of such a character, it is quite obvious that we have passed out of the real world and into the stuff of dreams.

Around 1970 two books appeared that were to be highly influential in shaping the direction of the UFO movement. Jacques Vallee—whose two previous books suggested that he was an orthodox UFOlogist, if an unusually energetic one—went forth in a totally new direction with his *Passport to Magonia* (1969), exploring the realm "from folklore to flying saucers." In it Vallee freely concedes that "the [UFO] entities are endowed with the same fugitiveness and behave with the same ignorance of logical or physical laws as the reflection of a dream, the monsters of our nightmares, the unpredictable witches of our childhood."

Vallee went on to draw a detailed parallel between current reports of UFO occupants and those of fairies in ages gone by. "The modern, global belief in flying saucers and their occupants," Vallee concludes, "is identical to an earlier belief in the fairy faith. The entities described as the pilots of the craft are indistinguishable from the elves, sylphs, and *lutins* of the Middle Ages."[3] Upon first reading this book, I thought that Vallee had reached a *reductio ad absurdum* of the pro-UFO position and was in the process of repudiating his earlier beliefs. But I must confess to being guilty of underestimating the underlying irrationality of the UFO movement. Vallee considered his findings about fairies and witches to be profound and went soaring off to ever-increasing heights of absurdity.

A second influential "new wave" UFO book was written by John Keel, *UFOs: Operation Trojan Horse* (1970). In a style more unabashedly popular than Vallee's, Keel reaches a similar conclusion. Keel emphasizes that the reason the UFO phenomenon *appears* to be absurd is that the supposed intelligences behind the phenomenon deliberately make it so: "If the phenomenon has built-in discrepancies, then no one will take it seriously . . . a large part of the reported data is engineered and deliberately false. The witnesses are not the perpetrators of these hoaxes but are merely the victims."[4] Keel argues ardently in favor not only of UFOs but also of the Men in Black, angels, elementals, Mothmen, spirits, and so on. He views UFO occupants as merely the latest manifestation of a continuum of some metaphysical menagerie containing monsters and beasties of all description.

Today's new-wave UFO theories take many forms, but what they all have in common is the notion that UFOs are "metaphysical," "supernatural," or "interdimensional," instead of extraterrestrial spacecraft. J. Allen Hynek suggests that UFOs may represent an "interdimensional" phenomenon: "I would have to say that the extraterrestrial theory is a naive one . . . we should take into consideration the various factors that strongly suggest a linkage, or at least a parallelism, with occurrences of a paranormal nature." Hynek explains that "if you have these interlocking universes, the chances of going from one to another is extremely small. But also there may be a trick for doing it. A 'mind-over-matter' trick. Out-of-body experiences might be an example. If you can imagine what people describe as 'astral projection' it might be an analogy."[5]

Popular UFO author Brad Steiger takes a position quite similar to that of Keel. In his influential 1976 book *The Gods of Aquarius,* Steiger opts for the view that "what we have thus far been labeling 'spaceships' I firmly believe to be multidimensional mechanisms or psychic constructs of our paraphysical companions." In this book he presents selected writings of other "new wave" UFO theorists. "That UFOs are omnijective and are 'willed' into physical existence seems to be the best explanation for the moment," suggests Michael Talbot. "In an omnijective universe, real and unreal have no meaning." George Wagner states that "reality is plastic . . . that which is simply imagined by one man may, after becoming widely publicized, actually materialize." But Wagner does admit to being puzzled by one difficulty: "the stumper is that nobody has ever reported seeing Mickey Mouse, Donald Duck, or Pinocchio." Steiger soars onward to tie in the supposed "reality game" played by UFOs with Pyramid energy, ghosts, miraculous healing, Uri Geller's magic spoon-bending, and Trevor James Constable's giant infrared amoebae that float invisibly in the stratosphere.[6]

Jerome Clark of *Fate* magazine is one of the most influential of the "new wave" UFOlogists. With Loren Coleman, his coauthor of *The Unidentified,* Clark suggests several "Laws of Paraufology," such as: "the 'objective' manifestations are psychokinetically generated byproducts of those unconscious processes which shape a culture's vision of the otherworld. Existing only temporarily, they are at best only quasiphysical."[7]

For several years, some of the oddest "new-wave" UFO theorizing was to be found in a small, privately circulated newsletter titled *UFOlogy Notebook* (*UN*), put out by Allen H. Greenfield. *UN* has a highly avant-garde flavor, with Greenfield and his friends imagining themselves to be in the vanguard of not only UFOlogy but of an entirely new perspective on the universe. In Greenfield's learned treatise titled "On the Nature of Archetypes and Psychic Projections as They Relate to the Enigma of UFOs," he states, "It is my contention that the UFO phenomenon represents an attempt by the unconscious human psyche to project a collective archetypical symbol into the seemingly 'eternal' (material; non-psychical) environment." In the same issue, Lou Wiedemann reveals "The Truth About UFOs": "There are no such 'things' as UFOs, in that they do not have any existence independent of the mind. The fact is, the human mind has the capacity to project solid images, and these images actually become temporarily real in every sense of the word . . . The government has suppressed this information because of the startling fact that the evidence and scientific proof also proves conclusively that *our entire reality* is made up wholly of projections from the collective unconscious! . . . The real hazard is so immense that it can hardly be conceived . . . if a large enough portion of the population were to understand and/or believe the truth , . . . our world as we know it would cease to exist!"[8]

But if a prize were to be awarded for the most far-out "new wave" UFO theorizing, it would probably have to go to Thomas E. Bearden, an engineer and a retired army officer. While working at the Redstone Arsenal in Alabama on the SAM-D Missile Project, Bearden was (in his own words) "stuffing [UFO] material into the Defense Documentation Center," which makes it available free to defense personnel nationwide at taxpayer expense. Bearden's papers carry high-sounding titles, such as "Field, Formon, Superspace, and Inceptive Cyborg: A Paraphysical Theory of Noncausal Phenomena," and they are crammed full of technical-sounding mumbo-jumbo and impressive-looking mathematics (which generally have nothing at all to do with the subject matter of UFOs and the like). In his papers he claims to derive a scientific foundation for psychokinesis, teleportation, and UFO materializations, working from statements like "the final evolution of the living process is goodness itself, pure being. Unlimited goodness can both be and not be, such is the nature of unlimitedness." Bearden somehow derives that "the UFO phenomena can be fitted to the hypothesis that they represent the prenatal care of the earthman by a linked superbeing, in preparation for the forthcoming linkage of the human species and the birth of another linked superbeing."[9]

One cannot, of course, ever hope to refute even *one* of the "new wave" hypotheses, no matter how bizarre, because they are drawn up so as to carefully avoid the possibility of disproof. Try to prove that somebody did *not* see a "psychic manifestation of the collective unconscious!" Thus the "new wave" deep thinkers have effectively removed their ideas from the realm of critical evaluation (and it does not seem that they are totally unaware of this advantage).

There is one approach, however, that I have used effectively in debate against various "alternate reality" proponents, to show the essential absurdity of their position. The question I pose to them is this: Do you believe in the Easter Bunny? If they do not clam up or go storming out of the room, it is not difficult to force them into saying "yes," because *the existence of the Easter Bunny is 100 percent consistent with every tenet of "new-wave" UFOlogy.* When Hynek speculates that UFOs, absurdities and all, are somehow penetrating into our dimension from some other level of reality, on what grounds could he possibly dismiss a sighting of the Easter Bunny? When Clark, Bearden, and others argue that it is our minds, singly or collectively, that "create" manifestations around us, why is it not possible that we should believe an Easter Bunny into existence in addition to Bigfoot, Mothmen, and UFOs? Certainly there are millions of children around the world who have no doubt at all about the existence of the Easter Bunny. Since many "new wave" believers watch the skies for UFOs, should they not likewise keep vigil over their backyards on Easter morning in the hope of a rare bunny encounter of the third kind? If the "new-wave" ideas are to be taken seriously (as many top UFOlogists insist they must), in no way is the Easter Bunny or Santa Claus or any other absurdity any less "real" than UFOs.

Some recent developments at the time of this writing hold out at least *some* hope that the new "new wave" to follow when the current "new wave" gets old (for nothing gets old as quickly as a high-flying fad) may perhaps turn out to be something less bizarre. Peter Kor (a pen name of Tom Comella) was a seminal figure in the very earliest "new-wave" proto-movement in the mid-1960s. Kor's latest writings on the subject of UFOs are so skeptical that they seem to place him to the right of Klass and Menzel. "The entire saucer mystery and the movement it has spawned are based solely on unsubstantiated claims," Kor now maintains. "Many researchers are afraid of a truly rigorous inquiry . . . they prefer euphoric fantasy to stark reality." As for today's "new wave," Kor calls the idea of alternate realities "ridiculous." He cites Tom Bearden as a classic example of a "pseudo-thinker," arguing "if the laws of logic are invalid . . . then literally no thing, no concept, no argument is what it seems to be. If nothing is what it seems to be, then our theorist literally cannot know what he is thinking or writing about—and the reader literally cannot know what he is reading!"[10]

Even Allen Greenfield has recently stunned his friends in the UFO movement by announcing that he no longer thinks UFOs are "real," except in the sense of a widespread myth. He writes, "Enough cases that I once considered 'good' as evidence for unconventionality have had enough doubt cast on them that, for me, there is enough doubt about the case for the UFO itself to move me into a skeptical stance." Greenfield urges his friends in the UFO movement not to be provoked into a "feeling of despair and loss" by what he has written. "Middle UFOlogist" James W. Moseley adds that he also knows personally "at least a couple of other well-known UFOlogists who have quietly Lost the Faith, but are afraid to admit it publicly—for the same reasons that kept Al Greenfield quiet till now."[11] I met one such individual recently. He is active in several major pro-UFO organizations. He continues publicly to espouse the reality of UFOs, but in private he professes complete skepticism. After so many years in UFOlogy, he does not want to alienate his friends.

Jerome Clark is now beginning to back down from "new wave" UFOlogy as well, but he is *not* moving in the direction of skepticism. He now describes certain parts of his book *The Unidentified* as "inept," blaming his mistakes on a wave of "Ufology's revisionist hysteria."[12] Clark does not now firmly endorse any theory but says that he is "inclined to agree" with the extra-terrestrial hypothesis.

Whether the "newest wave" of UFOlogy will in fact gravitate back toward rationality remains to be seen. As yet, neither the establishments of the "old guard" nor the powerful "new wave" have shown any signs of momentary lapses into being reasonable. But Greenfield and Kor have been in the van-guard of the UFO crowd in the past, and it is at least conceivable that this may be the case today. As for myself, I would like to think that, when you go so far off the deep end that you actually have to start taking the Easter Bunny seriously, you can't go a whole lot farther in that direction. But if I'm wrong, it will not be the first time that I have underestimated the credulity of the UFO movement.

NOTES

1. William Markowitz, *Science,* September 15, 1967, p. 1274.

2. Jacques Vallee, *The Invisible College* (New York: Dutton, 1976), chapter 1.

3. Vallee, *Passport to Magonia* (Chicago: Regnery, 1969), chapters 1 and 3.

4. John Keel, *UFOs: Operation Trojan Horse* (New York: Putnam, 1970), chapters 7 and 10 (in paperback, *Why UFOs?*).

5. J. Allen Hynek, interview in *UFO Report,* August 1976, p. 61; *The Edge of Reality,* chapter 9.

6. Brad Steiger, *The Gods of Aquarius* (New York: Harcourt, Brace, Jovanovich, 1976), pp. 7, 32-33, 232.

7. Jerome Clark and Loren Coleman, *The Unidentified* (New York: Warner, 1977), p. 242.

8. Allen Greenfield, ed., *UFOlogy Notebook* 3, no. 5 (February 1977).

9. Thomas E. Bearden: *Official UFO,* March 1977, p. 8; *Journal of Occult Studies* 1, no. 2 (Winter-Spring 1977-78); paper, "The One Human Problem, Its Solution, and Its Relation to UFO Phenomena" (1977).

10. *Kor's Kosmos,* no. 1 (January 1979).

11. *UFOlogy Notebook* 5, no. 1 (February 1979); James W. Moseley, *Saucer Wit* 26, no. 3 (March 5, 1979).

12. Jerome Clark, *Fate,* August 1980, pp. 109-12.

18

MOTHMEN, WOLF GIRLS, AND TRANSPARENT APES

The dwarfish, large-brained humanoid creatures, which are so frequently reported in supposed "close encounters of the third kind," are not the only types of creatures associated with UFO sightings. The menagerie of other bizarre and implausible creatures includes the Mothman of West Virginia, phantom panthers, robots, Bigfoot and other "hairy monsters," the Wolf Girl, Vegetable Man, and "a little blue man with a tall hat and a beard." Since one could easily devote an entire book to accounts of these creatures in UFO literature, we will have to content ourselves with examining only a few of the more colorful ones.

One of the most widely accepted series of reports of this genre concerns the celebrated Mothman creatures of West Virginia made famous by John Keel in a 1968 article in *Flying Saucer Review* and in his 1975 book *The Mothman Prophecies*. In appearance similar to Batman of comic-book fame, Mothman is said to be a seven-foot-tall manlike creature endowed with Dracula-style wings and big "fiercely glowing" red eyes, "like automobile reflectors." Sightings of Mothman reached a fever pitch during a local wave of UFO sightings in the late 1960s. Mothman was said to delight in chasing cars, and to "have a penchant for scaring females who were menstruating," according to Keel.[1]

Like the other creatures dealt with in this chapter, Mothman is *believed* by some UFO buffs to be associated somehow with UFO sightings. But this does not mean that anyone claims to have actually *sighted* a Mothman creature emerging from a landed UFO. Mothmen, like UFOs, are felt to be *deep* mysteries of cosmic significance, and hence they must in some way be related. Since reported sightings of the Mothmen tended to be highest during a UFO flap, and since the people who reported seeing the creature generally also claimed to have sighted UFOs, the link between UFOs and

Mothmen was considered established. Keel attempts to explain this link by asserting that both the UFO phenomenon and monsters such as Mothman are the work of mysterious "ultraterrestrials"; neither phenomenon truly belongs to what we think of as the real world. (Keel, a leading member of the "new wave" of UFOlogists, regards UFOs not as extraterrestrial space-craft but as some sort of mystical, paranormal phenomenon. From that per-spective, even Mothmen appear to make sense!)

One of the most dramatic incidents in the Mothman saga occurred when some mysterious UFO-like object or force followed a vehicle on a lonely West Virginia road. The driver was unable to shake the entity, which seemed to be preparing to make off with the vehicle, along with its entire cargo: a Red Cross Bloodmobile, filled with a fresh load of human blood!

A Mothman's life may not turn out to be as lonely as one might at first expect, for there have also been sightings of Mothwomen. Keel reports that three U.S. Marines serving in Vietnam in 1969 claimed to have seen a crea-ture that they first took to be a giant bird or bat. When it approached, they reportedly saw that it was a woman—a naked woman—with giant flapping wings, "limber like a bat." Mothwoman reportedly hovered above them for several minutes, the sound of her wings clearly audible in the still air.

At 5:00 PM on December 15, 1967, tragedy struck the area of West Vir-ginia where the sightings of Mothmen and UFOs had been concentrated. The Silver Bridge, which spans the Ohio River at Point Pleasant, West Vir-ginia, was heavily loaded with its usual rush-hour traffic, when it suddenly collapsed with a deafening roar, sending dozens of cars plunging down into the icy waters. Thirty-eight people were killed in the tragedy. Keel claims that for months before the incident he and other UFO buffs had been receiving mysterious telephone calls from unknown entities warning of impending danger. He claims that these entities—which continued to call even after his telephone had been disconnected—had specifically named December 15 as the date of some unnamed tragedy. Keel further claims that these unearthly callers warned in January of 1968 that the Reverend Martin Luther King, Jr., would soon be shot in the throat while standing on a bal-cony in Memphis. Unfortunately, as is so often the case in fortune telling, none of Keel's Mothman prophecies were published until after the events that they supposedly foretold had occurred. Predictions of future events would be far more impressive were we able to read the predictions before the events they foretell had come to pass. When predictions are committed to print months or years in advance, as those of Jeane Dixon and other sup-posed psychics regularly are in the tabloid press, anyone taking the trouble to follow up afterward (which almost nobody does) can see how inaccurate these predictions nearly always turn out to be.

Joining Mothman in West Virginia is Vegetable Man, a strange alien creature that, when first sighted, was mistaken for a bush. The witness, Jen-nings Fredricks, discarded the bush hypothesis upon discovering that (1) the creature had a face with slanting eyes and pointed ears, and (2) what he first took to be branches were in fact arms, which had seized him. Fredricks reports that the creature "telepathically" communicated its friendly intentions to him and its need for "medical assistance," whereupon it used one of its sharp fingers to puncture his arm and to withdraw some of his blood. It then released him and quickly departed. The encounter with Vegetable Man was first published by Gray Barker, who also led the way in raising the public's consciousness about the menace of the Men in Black.[2]

From the vicinity of Delphos, Kansas, where Ronald Johnson and his parents reported a "classic" close encounter of the second kind (chapter 4), comes a series of 1974 sightings of the "Wolf Girl," another creature that seems to follow in the wake of UFO sightings. In fact, one of those who claims to have seen the Wolf Girl is Ronald himself. He described the creature as having wild blonde hair, wearing a torn red dress (even Wolf Girls must preserve propriety!), standing about three feet tall, bent over with a stoop. Ronald says he unsuccessfully gave chase to the creature, who escaped because "when it ran, it got down on all fours and ran away faster than anything human can run." He also claims that, since his 1971 "classic" UFO encounter, not only has the UFO returned to pay him a second visit but he has developed "psychic" powers. The supposed UFO landing on their farm was said to have resulted in virgin births among several lambs that had never mated. Hynek has endorsed the Johnson UFO landing as being of "great scientific interest."[3]

Flying Saucer Review carried a lead article on a sighting of a "little blue man" on Studham Common, near Whipsnade Park Zoo in England. The witnesses were seven schoolboys on their way to school. Described as a "little blue man with a tall hat and a beard," the creature was said to have disappeared "in a puff of smoke" as the boys approached it, only to reappear a few feet away. This reportedly happened several times. Unfortunately for science, this sighting ended prematurely when the boys were called away by the schoolmaster's whistle. When the editors of *Flying Saucer Review,* intrigued by the little blue man incident, began asking around, they succeeded in finding several people in the area who claimed to have seen UFOs and even UFO landings. This was interpreted as further substantiating the sighting of the little blue man.[4]

One of the most fearsome UFO-related creatures on record is what researcher Don Worley terms "UFO-related anthropoids," or "King Kong Junior," for short. In a paper presented at a 1976 symposium sponsored by the Center for UFO Studies, Worley was careful to make the distinction between "the creature" and "the animal called Sasquatch, Big Foot, or Yeti." While this "creature" has the physical appearance of an overgrown apeman, it seems to have a "dual nature," appearing to be "both physical and non-physical," like a ghost. Its presence is said to be correlated with UFO sightings, and it supposedly returns with regularity to the places where it is sighted. In some sightings, the ape-creature is said to be transparent. One witness claimed that the beam of his flashlight became weaker when it fell upon the "creature." Some have claimed that the monster "disappeared in a flash of light," or "disappear[ed] into thin air." Near Derry, Pennsylvania, "a farm was haunted by giant ape-like creatures when UFOs were seen in the sky."[5]

Worley's scholarly paper on transparent apes was presented to CUFOS' by-invitation-only closed symposium in 1976, to which only the cream-of-the-crop of UFOlogy was invited to attend (not a single UFO skeptic was included among them). It is significant that leaders of "scientific" UFOlogy willingly embrace those who prattle about farms "haunted by giant ape-like creatures," but refuse to have anything to do with serious skeptical researchers who present unwelcome conclusions. Were UFOlogy a true science, it would behave in precisely the opposite manner.

NOTES

1. John Keel, "West Virginia's Enigmatic Bird," *Flying Saucer Review* 14 (July–August, 1968); Keel, *The Mothman Prophecies* (New York: Saturday Review Press, 1975; Signet, 1976); *National Insider,* June 1, 1975.

2. *Gray Barker's Newsletter,* March 1976; quoted by Daniel Cohen, *The World of UFO's* (Philadelphia: Lippincott, 1978).

3. *National Enquirer,* May 27, 1973; *Salina* (Kansas) *Journal* feature article (1974, exact date not available); Philip J. Klass, *UFOs Explained* (New York: Random House, 1974), chapter 28.

4. R. H. B. Winder, "The Little Blue Man on Studham Common," *Flying Saucer Review* 13 (July–August 1967):3; quoted by Jacques Vallee, *Passport to Magonia* (Chicago: Regnery, 1970), chapter 3.

5. Don Worley, "The UFO-Related Anthropoids—An Important New Opportunity for Investigator-Researchers with Courage," *Proceedings of the 1976 CUFOS Conference.*

19

A FLYING SAUCER
NAMED FLOYD

We now turn to the story of a famous flying saucer whose name is Floyd. Very few flying saucers can boast of proper names, but that is not the only reason that Floyd is famous. Floyd reportedly was chased by two sheriff's policemen for eighty-six miles through Ohio and Pennsylvania just before sunrise on the morning of Sunday, April 17, 1966 (plate 38). They say it played cat-and-mouse with their car even as they traveled at speeds of up to 103 miles per hour. Several other Ohio and Pennsylvania officers say that they saw the object too.

The late Dr. James E. McDonald, an atmospheric physicist who launched a crusade for scientific recognition of UFOs, considered this case to be one of the most impressive on record and he has endorsed the Floyd papers as "an outstanding contribution to present knowledge of the UFO phenomenon."[1] J. Allen Hynek (dubbed by several national magazines the "Galileo" of UFOlogy[2]), cites this case in his book *The UFO Experience* as the prime example of a "close encounter of the first kind."

Floyd received his name from Deputy Sheriff Dale F. Spaur, 34, of the Portage County, Ohio, Sheriff's Police. He tired of referring to the object he reportedly sighted as "?" and began calling it by his own middle name. Coining this name for the UFO doubtlessly proved to be quite a time-saver, because Deputy Spaur had to repeat his story many times in the weeks following the morning that he and Deputy Sheriff Wilbur Neff, 26, reportedly chased an unknown object.

The number of semi-independent witnesses to this incident (linked only by radio) is truly impressive. If all of these "reported" observations can be verified as *actual* observations, consistent in time, speed, and direction, then the UFO chase that began in Portage County, Ohio, must be regarded as one of the strongest possible proofs for the reality of the UFO phenomenon.

In the weeks and months leading up to the "Great UFO Chase of April 1966," the country was in the grip of a wave of mounting UFO excitement. Sightings had begun in the summer of the previous year, and the momentum was slowly building. The news media had been filled with reports of UFO sightings, gradually leading up to the "incident at Exeter" wave in the fall of 1965 (chapter 11).

During the winter sporadic sightings continued, only to explode in March of 1966 with a rash of sightings in Michigan. Nearly a hundred people, including police officers and college students, reported seeing glowing objects hovering over fields and marshes. Hynek hastened to Michigan, where he reported that "the entire region was gripped with near hysteria" about UFOs. Making the rounds with some police officers, Hynek confessed that "occasionally even *I* thought I glimpsed 'it,'" so heavily UFO-laden was the atmosphere. Police officers excitedly radioed "I see it" back and forth from car to car. Stopping at an intersection, they frantically gestured skyward, indicating a "moving" object, only to have their multiply witnessed UFO shot down by astronomer Hynek as the bright star Arcturus.[3]

On March 25, just three weeks before the Floyd incident, Hynek created a nationwide sensation by proposing "swamp gas" as an explanation for many of the Michigan sightings. Michigan Congressmen Gerald R. Ford and Weston Vivian, outraged by the Air Force's handling of the sightings, demanded a Congressional investigation into the matter, a demand that was widely echoed by journalists and radio-TV commentators. It is against this turbulent background that the stage was set in April 1966 for the Ohio UFO chase.

The major investigative role in this case was played by William B. Weitzel, a philosophy instructor at the University of Pittsburgh. At the time he was chairman of NICAP's Pennsylvania Unit No. 1. The previous year Weitzel had received much attention for his investigation of the famous Beaver County, Pennsylvania, UFO photograph, taken by the Lucci brothers, which Weitzel pronounced to be "one of the most valid of the UFOs on record."[4] (However, three years later, the chief photo analyst for the Condon Report, Dr. William K. Hartmann, had no trouble duplicating these photos by holding a plate on his hand, and illuminating it with a flashlight. Subsequent investigation has left little doubt that the Beaver County photos are in fact a hoax. But there is no record of Weitzel withdrawing his endorsement of them. Shortly after the famous Ohio chase, when Weitzel showed Spaur the as yet unrefuted Beaver County photograhs, Spaur pronounced the hoax UFO in the photos to be "almost identical to the one we saw."[5])

Unfortunately, Weitzel's enthusiasm for the UFO phenomenon caused him to overlook some obvious inconsistencies in the evidence and, worse still, to be blind to significant changes in the witnesses' stories as time passed. Nonetheless, Weitzel's interpretation of the Ohio UFO chase is universally accepted among serious UFO investigators as being the definitive account. Yet before I made my own analysis, no one appears to have taken the trouble to critically examine Weitzel's account of the incident, for if one had one could not possibly have overlooked the highly significant inconsistencies it contains.

On Sunday morning, April 17, 1966, at 4:50 AM, Portage County Deputy Sheriffs Dale Spaur and Wilbur Neff were at the scene of a traffic accident along Route 183 near Atwater Center, Ohio, where an automobile had smashed into a utility pole. The driver had been injured. Spaur and Neff had called in an ambulance and a tow truck, and when these had departed the policemen had remained for a short while to talk with the repairman who was working on the damaged lines. Sunrise was just under an hour away and, even though it was still quite dark, the purple glow of dawn was steadily brightening in the east. The sky that morning was quite clear, and the brilliant planet Venus was shining like a searchlight in the east-southeast. Near its maximum elongation from the sun, the bright morning star was a beautiful and striking sight to early risers.

About 4:50 a report came in over the police radio that a woman in Summitt County, to the west, had reported seeing a strange bright object, "higher than a streetlight but lower than an airplane," reportedly headed east, toward Portage County. (The sheriff's police of the various counties operate a statewide radio linkup, and hence can listen in on reports that do not originate in their own county.)

From the description of the object and from its supposed direction of "travel," it seems quite likely that the UFO the woman reported seeing was simply the planet Venus. Misidentifications of this type are quite common, as UFO proponents readily admit, especially during periods of intense UFO excitement. The three men good-naturedly joked about the reported UFO sighting; the "weird ones" are really out tonight, Spaur observed.

Officers Spaur and Neff then got into their car, Cruiser P-13, and drove off. They started "east" on Route 224, or so Spaur said in his testimony to the Air Force.[6] But he must have meant to say *west,* because he never would have reached the starting point of the chase had he actually gone *east* from the scene of the accident. Spaur confuses east with west a second time when he tells of encountering an old car by the side of the road two miles "east" (actually *west*) of Route 183. This may seem to some to be nit-picking, but the accuracy of Spaur's ability to recall directions is of crucial importance to his later testimony, when he describes the UFO as appearing at nearly every point on the compass. This east-west mixup, made twice and not corrected until a transcript of the interview had been prepared ("I was a little mad at this point" is how Spaur later explained the error; Neff was present, but failed to correct him), demonstrates that we must allow room for error in Spaur's recollection of the reported behavior and travel of the UFO.

Traveling west (not *east*) on U.S. Route 224, the two police officers saw a car parked on the other side of the road. They made a U-turn, and pulled up behind it. Cruiser P-13 was now facing east. Deputy Spaur walked up to the car while Neff remained behind, standing next to their cruiser—standard police procedure.

Scouting the area, Spaur looked behind him—to the west—and reportedly saw a bright object in the sky coming as if from the wooded area on the side of the road. Spaur called out to Neff, who also observed the object. It appeared to be coming toward them. It reportedly passed overhead, making a noise like an "overloaded transformer." In Spaur's earliest written UFO testimony, signed just hours after the chase, he suggests that the humming that was attributed to the UFO "might have come from a power line." But in later versions of his story, all doubt concerning the origin of the sound appears to have vanished. During the chase itself, the object reportedly made no sound whatsoever.

Upon first sighting the object, Spaur was "mildly surprised," according to Weitzel. He mused that this must be the UFO that he had heard so much about. But when the object appeared to come toward them, the two officers became frightened and scrambled back into the car. They reported that the object, large and glowing, had stopped in the east, directly ahead of them.

There is good reason to doubt that the object moving from west to east was as low and as close as the deputies reported, for it was sighted by another witness more than a hundred miles away. The declassified Project Blue Book records contain a report filed by a woman in Vandalia, Ohio, to the southwest of Ravenna, describing a starlike object that "swiftly" crossed the sky, traveling from west to northeast. A possible discrepancy exists in the time of the report, which is given as 5:30 AM, some twenty-five minutes later than the time of the deputies' sighting. But because of the great similarity of the two reports, and their proximity in location and time, it seems likely that both describe the same event.

Apparently a brilliant meteor streaked across the predawn sky, visible over a wide region. It did not pass just over their heads, as Spaur and Neff believed, but was many miles up. Experience has shown that it is impossible for anyone to be accurate in judging the distance from such an object. Witnesses will often report "close encounters" with objects that later turn out to have been many miles away. Klass cites several incidents of this type. One of them involves an experienced airline flight crew that reported a near-collision with an object that turned out to have been a brilliant daylight meteor, *at least 125 miles north of their position.*[7]

So bright was the object, Spaur says, that the entire area around their car was lit up. Since it was now 5:07 AM, less than forty minutes before sunrise, there is no doubt whatsoever that the area around their car was indeed lit up, though not necessarily by any UFO. Only the brightest stars, those of the first (and possibly second) magnitude, remained visible at this time. Venus, however, nearly five magnitudes (ninety times) brighter than a first-magnitude star, was still shining like a beacon in the east. By a remarkable coincidence, this is exactly where Spaur reported the UFO was hovering. *If a genuine UFO had indeed been present, the deputies should have seen two bright objects in the east at this point, Floyd and Venus.* But they saw only one. It is hard to avoid the conclusion that Floyd *was* Venus, at least at this point. The planet Venus does not, of course, zip rapidly from west to east, but there is no compelling reason to believe that a single object was responsible for every aspect of this complex UFO sighting. (In fact, there are some excellent reasons not to believe this, as we shall see.)

The officers had been alerted a few minutes earlier that a UFO was supposedly in the vicinity. Add to this the nationwide hysteria that had prevailed for the past few weeks, and you have the optimum psychological conditions for sighting UFOs. Every planet and every airplane is scrutinized as a potential interloper. The two men must have taken their eyes off the object that moved from west to east as they scrambled into their car. When they looked up and saw Venus ahead of them, they mistakenly concluded that it was the same object they had just sighted. From the time they entered the car, until after they crossed the Pennsylvania line, their attention was riveted to a brilliant object in the east-southeast: unquestionably the planet Venus.

Spaur hit the button on his microphone and radioed back to headquarters that the unidentified object, "the one that everybody says is going over," appeared to be hovering in front of their car. The radio operator asked Spaur if he was carrying his service revolver. He was. "Take a shot at it" was the helpful suggestion. (The radio operator later explained that he thought the object might be a weather balloon, and that a bullet might bring it down.) Spaur decided against that course of action, because he believed the object to be "as big as a house," and he didn't want to risk angering it. After ascertaining that they did not have a camera with them, the two deputies were ordered to keep the object in sight until a camera car could be dispatched to photograph it.

Spaur put the cruiser in gear, inched forward a little, and then a funny thing happened. Floyd appeared to inch forward too. This should not surprise us if we remember that celestial bodies appear to "pace" a moving vehicle. Every child at some point asks his parent why the moon seems to be "following" their car, and it is a wise parent who can explain, in simple terms, that a distant body like the moon or Venus shows no noticeable displacement due to the motion of the vehicle, as nearby objects do, and hence appears to follow the observer. (This explanation, however, appears to be beyond the comprehension of some of the well-known "scientific" UFO investigators, who naively interpret every reported following of a vehicle by a bright celestial body as a "close encounter of the first kind.") No matter how fast Cruiser P-13 approached the object, Floyd appeared to move away at exactly the same speed. Spaur, a former race-car driver, quickly picked up speed and roared after the object. The Great UFO Chase was on.

The two policemen raced eastward on U.S. Route 224 (which later merges with Ohio Route 14) at speeds up to 103 miles per hour. Floyd, ever obliging, appeared to follow this road exactly, reportedly just a few hundred feet in front of their car. For over twenty miles they reportedly chased the object due east, over an almost perfectly straight road. Yet nowhere along Route 14–224 did they report seeing Venus. This was truly a remarkable feat of nonobservation.

Deputy Neff reported that between Atwater Center and Deerfield Floyd kept a bearing somewhat south of east. This exactly describes Venus's position, which was then at an azimuth of about 115°. Meanwhile, a very understandable confusion between Route 14 and Route 14A sent the camera car down 14A, miles away from the position of Cruiser P-13. Had the two police cars actually met, one suspects that the chase might have ended a great deal sooner than it did.

Shortly after passing Atwater Center, Spaur observed that the UFO had "gained altitude," which is exactly what Venus was gradually doing. From the initial sighting at 5:07 AM to the time they reached Beaver Falls, Pennsylvania, at about 5:45, Venus rose from an elevation of 12° to 19°. Anyone watching Venus during this interval would have seen it rise slowly and steadily. This is exactly what Floyd is said to have done during that interval.

At Deerfield Circle, Spaur says that he had to pass between two big trucks: "between a tractor and a trailer" is how he describes it. Yet neither of these drivers seems to have noticed a giant UFO, "as big as a house," which reportedly passed just a few hundred feet over their heads. The two deputies likewise encountered "occasional traffic" (in Weitzel's phrase) between Canfield and Columbiana, around which they had to maneuver at very high speeds. But again we have no indication that any of these other drivers saw anything at all unusual.

Crossing from Portage to Mahoning County, on the bridge over the Berlin Reservoir, the UFO reportedly "picked up probably another 150 feet." (Venus had risen a little too.) Floyd allegedly wavered from the south side of the road to the north side, and then back again as they entered Mahoning County. However, a careful examination of a map reveals that the road curves to the south, then north again, at this point. This will cause an object keeping a fixed bearing to behave exactly as was described. Indeed, every change in direction attributed to Floyd appears to correspond to a turn made by the UFO chasers.

At Canfield, as the deputies turned south-southeast on Ohio Route 14–46, the UFO was reported by Neff to "come across in front of us" over to the left side of the cruiser, then afterwards return to the right side. This again suggests to anyone who examines the map that the object kept a constant bearing. After turning south on Route 183, Spaur reports that the object appeared to be due north. Venus cannot, of course, appear in the north, any more than a policeman driving south at breakneck speed can possibly see an airborne object directly behind him (which, by the way, would then be chasing him, causing one to wonder why, if this account is correct, Spaur did not stop and set up a roadblock). Spaur's mixup of his directions, and his later "improvements" to his original UFO narrative, serve to caution us against taking such reported details too literally. As soon as they made the next turn, and headed east, Floyd promptly returned to his favorite position in the southeast, exactly where Venus ought to have been seen.

It is well known that UFOs are supposed to stop automobile engines, short out headlights, and cause radio equipment to fail, but Floyd displayed none of these disagreeable characteristics. Not only did cruiser P-13 perform like a tiger, cruising smoothly at 103 m.p.h. despite the UFOs alleged nearness, but its radio operated perfectly, so well, in fact, that officers throughout Ohio listened to every detail of the chase. Not surprisingly, many of them looked for the object, and some imagined that they saw it too.

Police Chief Gerald Buchert of Mantua, Ohio, was twenty miles north of where Floyd was reported to be. But when he went outside, he thought he saw it too, and he even managed to obtain a photograph. Afterwards, Weitzel was keenly disappointed to discover that Buchert's supposed UFO photo turned out to be nothing more than a processing defect. Buchert described the position of his UFO with respect to the moon (which was then a thin crescent, low in the sky). It matches perfectly with the known position of Venus. But Weitzel hesitates at concluding that Police Chief Buchert's UFO was in fact Venus, because the UFO was reported to wobble around a little. Floyd, meanwhile, if it really were where Spaur claims it was, would have been more nearly due south and would have appeared to Chief Buchert to be just skirting the horizon if it were visible at all. It would not have been at the 10°-plus altitude he reports.

To the south, in Salem, three police officers drove to the top of a hill in the hope of seeing the UFO, which was reportedly heading directly into their town. They, too, incorrectly believed P-13 to be approaching on Route 14A, when it was in fact nearly ten miles to the north on Route 14–224. But it does not matter that the Great UFO Chase never reached Salem, for these officers claimed that they saw the object too. They reported seeing three jet airplanes, coming from the north, chasing the object at a terrific speed. *Weitzel ignores the obvious absurdity of equating an object supposedly thousands of feet in altitude traveling south at jet-airplane speed, with something reportedly just above the ground, traveling east no faster than an automobile.* Instead, he cites the Salem report as further confirmation of Spaur's observations. Even more improbable is the report coming from police headquarters in Salem, telling of an airplane pilot's voice, loud and clear, which reportedly burst in over the police radio, saying, "I'm going down for a closer look . . . it's about forty-five feet across."[8] The Salem incidents demonstrate the intensity of the UFO hysteria that exploded into a fever pitch in Ohio that morning.

As Spaur and Neff passed Canfield, the UFO reportedly gained altitude once again (as did Venus, the object they have still failed to notice). Outside East Palestine, Ohio, near the Pennsylvania line, Patrolman Wayne Huston was listening to the chase on his radio. He realized that P-13 was not far from his present position and was closing in fast. Spaur told Huston where to look to see the UFO, and Huston duly acknowledged seeing it. Huston reportedly watched the object approach from the northwest—which Venus could never have done—but Weitzel makes this same claim about Pennsylvania Officer Frank Panzanella, a claim I subsequently found to be quite incorrect.

It can be shown, however, that Huston's account of the object's approach is internally inconsistent. Huston claims that he first sighted the object when cruiser P-13 was about five miles away. But he told Weitzel that the UFO appeared to pass overhead in a matter of seconds, leaving him little opportunity to observe the object. If Huston actually did spot Floyd when it and its pursuers were reportedly five miles away and if the object's speed did in fact match P-13's 80–85 m.p.h. velocity at this point, Huston would have had the object in view for at least three and a half minutes. This would give him plenty of time to observe the object carefully and to describe its appearance over the radio, for he was standing outside his police cruiser, extension microphone in hand. But since he reports that the object approached in "seconds," leaving no time to study its appearance, either Huston's account of the object's approach is seriously in error or else he could not have been observing the same "Floyd" that Spaur and Neff were reportedly chasing. Weitzel ignores this contradiction in his search for confirmation, as does Hynek, who considers Huston's account of the object's approach to be the most critical part of the case.

Huston, alone in his cruiser OV-1, joined in the chase as Spaur and Neff roared by. He said that he probably never would have caught up to them if they had not been delayed in traffic on the narrow, winding road. None of the occupants of the cars that slowed them down (who were of course unaware that a wild UFO chase was in progress in the next lane) has ever come forward to confirm the allegation that a giant UFO flew just over their heads, being followed by two speeding police cars.

Coming into Chippewa, Pennsylvania, near Beaver Falls, Huston reports that the chasers were again forced to slow down in traffic, because of a 6:00 AM church service that was about to begin. Not one of these fine and sober early-rising citizens subsequently reported having seen a giant flying saucer, as big as a house, buzzing the top of their church steeple.[9]

Approaching Brady's Run Park, near Beaver, the UFO chasers encountered so much traffic that they were forced to stop. Huston turned on his siren. A Volkswagen had exited from the park, triggering a traffic signal. Three trucks were approaching the traffic light, now red, from the east, and two more trucks waited at the light, ahead of the two cruisers, forcing them to suddenly screech to a halt. (Floyd, ever obliging, was reported to slow down and wait whenever his pursuers were delayed in traffic.) None of these other six drivers seemed to take the slightest notice of the giant UFO which, if the officers' account is to be believed, flew not far over their heads.[10]

Shortly after the three officers crossed the state line, the UFO was reported to have elevated a little more, achieving its greatest altitude of the entire chase. It also became difficult to see. This is not hard to understand. As Venus rises higher in the sky, the sun also rises, making the planet more difficult to see against the brightening sky. When they crossed the state line, the sunrise was only five to ten minutes away.

Venus is bright enough to be seen even after sunrise, but around sunrise the planet becomes much more difficult to see. No longer conspicuous, one must search for a moment in order to find it. Thus at this point in the chase they lost sight of Floyd. Spaur expressed the fear that it had eluded them for good. Spaur was driving in unfamiliar territory. He had to rely on Huston's instructions, telling him where to turn and when to slow down. This left him little time to watch the UFO. "We thought we'd lost it," Spaur later reported. "This will be it, we're going to lose it right here," they thought. The Great UFO Chase might well have ended here. But Floyd (or Fate) had other plans.

A half-hour earlier, around 5:20 AM, Conway, Pennsylvania, Patrolman Frank Panzanella left a restaurant where he had stopped for a cup of coffee after finishing a night's duty. As he drove up the hill on 11th Street in Conway, heading northeast, he reportedly saw an object to his right (in the east) which looked like a "reflection [of sunlight] off a plane." He stopped upon reaching the top of the hill (he was still inside the town) and noted that the object was not moving. Panzanella then turned around, came back down the hill, and parked his cruiser at the Atlantic service station on 10th Street and Route 65, where there were fewer nearby buildings. He watched the object for about thirty minutes. From this position, the rooftop of a nearby house provided an excellent reference that has enabled later investigators to pinpoint the apparent position of the object. Its elevation when first sighted was only about 11°, and it remained just a few degrees south of due east.

Panzanella's testimony is also touted by UFO proponents as an independent confirmation of the observations of the other policemen. After all, he had not been listening to the frenzied UFO chatter over the Ohio police radio channels. But they ignore the fact that the object sighted by Panzanella was reportedly observed to the east of Conway, Pennsylvania, *at the same time that Floyd was reportedly hovering above the hood of Cruiser P-13, which was still in Ohio to the west.* Even the staunchest UFO enthusiast would find it difficult to explain how an object supposedly in Ohio might be seen to the east by someone in Pennsylvania.

Whatever it was that Panzanella saw (a high-altitude balloon is a good possibility), it could not possibly have been Floyd, if Spaur's account of the object's position is correct. This irreconcilable discrepancy poses an obvious difficulty to those who wish to prove that a UFO was actually being chased. How to resolve it? An erroneous statement will do nicely. *Weitzel asserts that Panzanella first sighted the object in the southwest*[11] (he later changed this to "west"[12]), even though the map in his own report to NICAP plainly shows otherwise—east.

Weitzel also claims that Panzanella drove down the hill to avoid a "collision." This seems improbable in light of that officer's April 17 interview with reporter Tom Schley, in which Panzanella said that, when he sighted the UFO from the top of the hill, he "hadn't thought much about it at the time."[13] Weitzel's statements flatly contradict the signed testimony that Panzanella gave to NICAP, which unambiguously indicates the object as being in the east, and makes no mention whatsoever of any near-collision. That a person driving northeast (which is indeed "uphill," exactly as described) could hardly fear a collision with an object supposedly coming from the southwest seems never to have been noticed. Even if we accept the claim that the object did indeed arrive from the west, it reportedly arrived far too soon for it to have conceivably been Floyd, because Panzanella's sighting began when the UFO chasers were still dozens of miles to the west.

That Panzanella's account of the reported direction of the object's arrival should be so grossly distorted in a way that just happens to better fit in with Spaur's account casts strong doubt upon the similar testimony—arrival from the northwest—attributed to Huston. It also raises some very interesting questions: Who is responsible for these misrepresentations, the investigators or the witnesses? Did the witnesses actually change their stories, or were they altered without their knowledge or consent? Did Panzanella perhaps gradually change his story with each retelling, subconsciously wishing to please those persons who were conferring celebrity status upon him? Or was it deliberately misrepresented to make it fit better with the "known" facts? This incident provides an excellent example of how the accounts of UFO sightings to be found in even the most respected and supposedly reliable UFO sources are often grossly in error. When all of the facts appear to fit together so well, it may be because some of them have been reshaped.

Near Rochester, Pennsylvania, UFO chaser Dale Spaur had finally lost sight of the object. The sun had just risen, and Venus faded meekly into the sunlit sky. But after emerging from a series of bridges and tunnels, first Huston, then Spaur claim to have seen Floyd once again. But it wasn't the *same* Floyd: *"it had lost probably half its altitude,"* Spaur reported.[14] This is most significant. When Venus faded to near-invisibility, *the UFO chasers transferred their attention to some other object,* almost certainly to the same object that Panzanella, now only about five miles away, was watching. At this time Venus had an apparent altitude of about 20°. If Floyd-Venus were to lose "half its altitude," that would put it near the 11° apparent altitude of the object reported by Panzanella.

The Great UFO Chase passed through Freedom, Pennsylvania, and entered Conway. Spaur's cruiser was running low on gas. They spotted Panzanella sitting in his cruiser, parked at a gas station on the other side of the road. The two automobiles made U-turns, parked behind Panzanella, and the three men got out. Panzanella at first was hesitant to admit that he'd been watching something unusual, until Huston exclaimed, "We've been with it all the way from Ohio!"

The four policemen watched the object, and later sketched its position with respect to a nearby rooftop TV-antenna, the thin crescent moon, and Venus, which was still faintly visible. Hynek and other UFO proponents make much of the fact that Floyd was reportedly seen at the same time as Venus, implying that the object being chased could not possibly have been that brilliant planet. But they neglect to mention that the simultaneous sighting of the two objects did not occur until the very end of the chase, after the UFO had reportedly "lost half its altitude." Prior to this time, Venus was supposedly not seen at all; only Floyd was visible. This, of course, is absurd. Why should Venus only be spotted after it had faded to near-invisibility after the sunrise and be totally ignored at the beginning of the chase, when it was the most conspicuous object in the heavens?

Another compelling reason for believing that the deputies were chasing Venus is seen when the path they chose is plotted on a map (plate 38). As a result of the UFO chase, Spaur's cruiser P-13 ended up forty-nine miles east and twenty-five miles south of its original position. This corresponds to an average direction of travel of 117° (to the east-southeast). The average apparent azimuth of Venus was 115° during this same interval. Thus we see that *the UFO chasers followed a route exactly as if they were chasing Venus*; approaching an intersection, they would turn onto whatever road took them closest to the apparent direction of that brilliant planet.

What was the object to which the UFO chasers transferred their attention after Venus faded from prominence? The overwhelming probability is that the object was a high-altitude research balloon launched by some university or research agency. Such balloons can travel many hundreds of miles, and they can be almost impossible to trace. The accounts of the object almost perfectly describe the appearance of such a balloon. Upon first seeing it, Panzanella said he thought the object was a reflection of the rising sun off an airplane; reflections from a balloon look quite the same. The period of maximum visibility of such a balloon is, of course, just before sunrise or just after sunset, when the balloon is in direct sunlight because of its altitude but when the sun is below the horizon for ground-based observers. On several occasions I have seen high-altitude balloons under these circumstances, and their appearance is nothing short of dramatic: a dazzlingly brilliant star, shining by reflected sunlight in a bright twilight sky. Panzanella's observation that the object slowly increased in altitude exactly describes the familiar behavior of a balloon being warmed by the rays of the rising sun; the gases inside gradually expand, causing the balloon to rise slowly.

Deputy Spaur later told the Air Force investigators that, as they stood watching Floyd from the gas station in Conway, Panzanella reached the radio operator in nearby Rochester. He requested that the airport be contacted to see if a jet interceptor were available to take a closer look at the object. When the response came back that two planes were supposedly going to be sent up (they never were), the UFO reportedly accelerated straight upward—as if it had heard what had been said—and quickly disappeared. "When they started talking about fighter planes, just as though that thing heard every word that was said, it went (psshew) straight up. And I mean it didn't play no games, it went straight up," Spaur reported.[15] This of course strongly suggests that the object was under intelligent control and did not wish to be closely examined.

Weitzel, Hynek, and Blum have accepted as fact the claim that the object shot "straight up" in this manner.[16] If this is true, it would appear to rule out any natural explanation for the object. *But this claim directly contradicts the testimony given by all three of the officers available for interview immediately after the sighting,* Neff having gone "into seclusion." This contradiction has been ignored by all of the "scientific" UFO investigators, even though this information is readily available in the NICAP files. Indeed, one of these interviews was conducted by one of Weitzel's key UFO collaborators, Tom Schley of the *Beaver County Times.* In three separate newspaper interviews, which must have taken place within hours of the end of the chase: (1) Spaur said that they watched the object at Conway for about twenty minutes. It was still visible when he and the others went inside to make a telephone call. When they came back outside, they were unable to find it.[17] (2) Huston said that when the police officers left, "the object was still hovering."[18] (3) Panzanella said that the four of them stood watching the object until it was "barely visible" after it had risen higher in the sky.[19] Furthermore, Spaur and Neff, in filling out a UFO sighting report, were asked, "Did the object disappear while you were watching it?" Both men answered no.[20]

Thus we see that this extremely significant original testimony, strongly suggesting that the object was a balloon, has been carefully ignored by UFO proponents. They prefer to have us think that the object behaved as if it were under intelligent control and contained a sophisticated propulsion system, when in fact it faded into invisibility exactly as a balloon does when the sun rises higher.

Here we see a second major instance in which a witness in this case appears to have altered his original testimony, or has had it altered for him. It is significant that the testimony is always changed in such a way *as to increase the strangeness of the object.* This incident should serve as a warning against accepting any UFO testimony too uncritically, especially after it has been repeated many times. Stories told by UFO witnesses, like fine wines, tend to improve with age.

After the UFO had faded from view, the four officers stopped at the police station in Rochester, where they spoke briefly with an Air Force officer by telephone. Spaur, Neff, and Huston then returned to Ravenna, the Portage County seat.

The stationhouse was bombarded with phone calls and reporters. Although no announcement of the chase had been made, apparently some reporters who cover police beats had been listening on the radio, and the story was quickly picked up by the wire services. William Weitzel arrived later that same day, as did a number of other UFO investigators and newspaper reporters. Interviews were obtained with each of the principal witnesses except Neff. (Neff was quoted in a Pittsburgh newspaper article, however, which also stated that the object "greatly interested Deputy Neff, who reportedly believes in flying saucers."[21]) Spaur was obviously exhausted, yet he was anxious to cooperate with the investigation. There can be little doubt that Spaur and the other witnesses at this phase were quite sincere in their account of the sighting. They plainly believed that they had indeed been chasing a giant UFO.

In 1966 the Air Force was on the UFO hot seat. There was nothing they would have liked better than to ignore the Great UFO Chase and indeed forget about the whole UFO business, but this was impossible. The great public clamor for answers to the UFO enigma caught the Air Force squarely in the middle. Many persons had accused the Air Force of covering up the supposed truth about the reality of UFOs. The demand for a congressional investigation into UFOs—and the Air Force's handling of them—grew daily. Hardly anyone had a good word for the Air Force on the subject of UFOs (and perhaps deservedly so). They were criticized by some for being too negative about UFOs and by others for even bothering with such things in the first place. And criticism is the one thing that a bureaucracy—whether military, government, or otherwise—simply cannot live with.

It is the very nature of the bureaucratic animal to do its utmost to keep popular dissatisfaction with it to an absolute minimum. It knows that when the situation gets too "hot" somebody must be sacrificed, a scapegoat to be offered up in an attempt to placate the public furor. Criticism jeopardizes not only promotions but next year's budget as well. Thus all controversies must *appear* to be resolved, all questions must *appear* to be answered, regardless of the actual facts. This is the real reason for the Air Force's often hasty investigations of UFOs, for its practice of grabbing at the first explanation for a UFO sighting to come along, regardless of whether it fits the facts. The U.S. Air Force was not attempting to explain UFOs, to cover them up, or to do anything except get out of the spotlight.

The day after the sighting, Spaur received a brief, low-keyed telephone call from Major Hector Quintanella, Jr., head of the Air Force's Project Blue Book. According to Spaur, the conversation began with Quintanella requesting him to "tell me about this mirage you saw."[22] Quintanella appeared to be unfamiliar with many of the significant details concerning the incident, although the story of the chase had been widely reported in the papers and on radio and TV; certainly one would expect the Air Force's chief UFO investigator to keep himself at least reasonably well informed on such significant developments. Spaur was disappointed at what he felt was the brevity and superficiality of Quintanella's telephone interview.

Several days later, after an almost negligible investigative effort, the Air Force released its conclusion: the deputies had seen the Echo satellite and had then transferred their attention to Venus, which they then "chased" into Pennsylvania.[23] While this hypothesis appears to be at least partially correct, as the present analysis shows, Quintanella had based his conclusion upon a superficial analysis of a very complex UFO sighting, and he was unable to defend his analysis when it was challenged. In fact, the Blue Book file on this case actually contains a "Memo for the Record" that states, "Definitely not Echo I or Echo II. They were over the southern hemisphere at the time of the sighting." Blue Book was unable to establish the presence of any bright satellite over Ohio at that time. The superficiality of the Blue Book investigation is further revealed by their half-hearted attempt to determine the position of the Pegasus satellites. They gave up after two phone calls, convinced that the information was not available.[24] Yet James Oberg was able to locate these records for me without difficulty some ten years later. Neither Pegasus nor any other bright satellites had been visible.

Weitzel and the other UFO proponents correctly jumped all over Quintanella for the many aspects of the sighting he had ignored, for example, the alleged changes in the object's direction and the simultaneous sighting of Floyd and Venus. There was in principle no reason that Quintanella could not have launched an in-depth investigation into the sighting, and after a period of weeks or months he might have produced an entirely satisfactory explanation for every major aspect of the sighting. But the news media pressure was on. The Air Force didn't need the correct answer in six months, when all the headlines would have been forgotten and the crisis would be past. They needed an answer in a hurry, any answer: Congress was beginning to stir!

After chatting with Spaur for a few minutes on the telephone, the Air Force would have been perfectly happy to let the incident die right there: superficial investigation, superficial conclusion. But the pro-UFO forces, led by William Weitzel, were stirring up a storm. Ohio Congressman William Stanton began to pressure the Air Force for a re-evaluation of the incident, and he was joined by a number of other prominent local citizens. Political clout, the only force capable of prevailing against bureaucratic inertia, began to work its magic: Quintanella would travel to Ravenna to interview the witnesses.

It seems that *both* sides intended to play silly games with this interview. Quintanella came only because he had to, out of concern for the Air Force's public image. He did his best to "snow" Spaur and the other deputies with impressive scientific facts and figures that sounded none the less convincing for being absurd and incorrect. Spaur, meanwhile, had evidently been carefully "coached" by the pro-UFO forces. (Weitzel and several of his UFO colleagues were in the building at the time, but they were not permitted to be present at the interview.) Someone else clearly must have prepared little speeches for Spaur, which he recited in singsong fashion, and not very successfully at that. The ensuing interview, recorded by Weitzel, reveals the depth to which the "science" of UFOlogy can sink when it degenerates into a game and is played by partisans who are more interested in scoring points than in evaluating hypotheses.

"Venus, Venus," muttered Quintanella as he rattled some papers, "Venus today rises at 02:49 in the morning, and it rises at 110° azimuth and 25° elevation." This is absurd. On the morning of the chase, Venus rose at about 4:00 AM, at 100° azimuth; the figures he cites are not correct for the day of the interview either. The Major also seems to have forgotten that, by definition, everything always rises at exactly zero degrees elevation! Quintanella was obviously putting on a show to impress the deputies. "It doesn't have to rise low on the horizon," he added knowledgeably, "it can rise high. But it's on the ecliptic, yes, it's always on the ecliptic." Spaur was snowed. "Okay, so it's on the ecliptic," he meekly conceded. (I wonder if either of the two men could have defined the word *ecliptic*.) Score one for Quintanella.

But Deputy Spaur was not prepared to give up without a fight. He had been provided the ammunition that (it was hoped) would permit him to demolish the satellite-Venus hypothesis, if he could only deliver it without slipping up. "First of all," Spaur boldly began, "as I understand it, a satellite orbits at about seven thousand, three hundred and some miles an hour, to seven thousand, five hundred. I may be wrong." He is. Spaur had rattled off the numbers admirably, but he had accidentally left out a syllable throughout his recitation: satellites orbit at seven*teen* thousand miles an hour not seven thousand. But no matter, because Quintanella didn't know the difference. Score one for Spaur.

"Second of all," Spaur continued, any satellite that came as low as Floyd reportedly did would quickly burn up in the atmosphere. This is true, but totally irrelevant, since UFOlogical experience clearly indicates that there is little relationship between the estimated altitude of an unidentified object and its actual altitude.

"Second of all," continued Spaur (he meant "third of all"), "our satellite doesn't stop and go, and go up and down." "No, they zig-zag," Quintanella soberly stated. The Major paused for a moment and realized what an idiotic thing he had just said. A correction: they only *appear* to zig-zag, he somewhat sheepishly restated. Score another for Spaur.

"Second of all" (by now Spaur should have reached "fourth of all"), "I'm under the impression that Venus rises out of the east as the morning star.

Now this is probably another thing that's wrong, I'm not sure." Spaur is quite correct, but he should have stuck to his guns: he who equivocates is lost. "Depends . . . depends," Quintanella slyly asserted, "Sometimes it'll rise right over you." That is ridiculous, of course, but Spaur was defeated; his pro-UFO allies were not present to come to his rescue. "Oh, okay," he reluctantly conceded. Score another for Quintanella.

In the end, the interview counted for nothing. No minds were changed because none were open for an impartial examination of the evidence. Both NICAP and Quintanella stubbornly held to their previously stated positions, each of them refusing to take note of the serious inconsistencies in their own analyses. We are fortunate, however, that the Great UFO Chase has afforded us an unparalleled opportunity to observe both the Air Force's Project Blue Book and the pro-UFO forces in action and to note the shortcomings of each.

Although the Air Force happened upon a substantially (though not completely) correct hypothesis to explain the sighting, they did not assemble enough information to justify their conclusions. Hence they were incapable of defending them when challenged. It must be conceded that even though the NICAP forces led by William Weitzel had reached an erroneous conclusion and defended it vehemently, there is no question that the thoroughness of their investigation was more impressive than the slipshod work done by the Air Force on this case.

Even the aftermath of the Great UFO Chase was suitably dramatic. Six months after the incident, on October 9, 1966, the Associated Press issued a story by John De Groot that was widely carried in newspapers from coast to coast. It alleged that the flying-saucer incident had changed Spaur's life into a "nightmare." In it we read that his personal life was shattered by the publicity and ridicule that descended upon him in the wake of the Great UFO Chase. "He is no longer a deputy sheriff. His marriage is shattered. He has lost forty pounds. He lives on a bowl of cereal and a sandwich each day." Spaur was depicted as living in a lonely motel room, estranged from his wife and children, having literally no money left from his meager paycheck as a painter after he paid for his motel room and court-ordered child support.

And he blames everything on Floyd: "Saucer . . . ##@@!" Spaur said bitterly. If he could change any or all of his past life, he reflected, only one thing would need to be changed: "the night we chased that damned thing."

I do not claim to have any inside information concerning the private life of Dale F. Spaur, either before or after the UFO chase. Nonetheless, it does seem to me that it is all too convenient for a lonely and bitter man to blame all of the troubles in his life on a flying saucer. It cannot be denied that the publicity following in the wake of such a famous UFO incident may well prove to be difficult and upsetting. But to suggest that such an incident alone could be responsible for turning an otherwise healthy family life topsy-turvy is exactly the sort of psychological crutch to which a person in a difficult situation might well cling. There are too many instances in which reports of famous UFO sightings do *not* cause such disastrous upheavals in the witnesses' lives to lead one to believe that the UFO incident was the only reason for this unhappy outcome. (Spaur's personal difficulties in the wake of his UFO sighting appear to be the inspiration behind UFO-buff Steven Speilberg's portrayal of the Neary family breakup after the father's UFO sighting in the movie *Close Encounters of the Third Kind*. Another scene in this movie, where several police cars chase a UFO across a state line, is also an obvious dramatization of Spaur's experience.)

Daniese Spaur filed charges of assault and battery against Dale on August 2, but when the case came to trial on October 17, it was dismissed by the prosecutor, with the costs to be paid by the complainant: Daniese wound up paying $14.90 in court costs. The results of the "divorce" proceedings are even more curious. Daniese Evonne Spaur vs. Dale Floyd Spaur, Court of Common Pleas, Ravenna, Ohio, October 21, 1966: "The court finds that no common-law marriage existed between the parties. Therefore it is adjudged and decreed that this case be dismissed at plaintiff's cost." Apparently Dale and Daniese had never actually been married![25]

Following publication of the De Groot story, Spaur appears to have completely vanished. In 1972 the *Dayton Daily News* attempted to locate him for a follow-up story, without success.[26] Spaur reportedly turned up at a meeting of a UFO organization in Cleveland in February of 1975. He claimed to be earning a living as a professional race-car driver in Erie, Pennsylvania. He was still hoping for a re-evaluation of his UFO chase.[27] The most recent accounts say that Spaur is now living in a small town in West Virginia. (Weitzel had earlier noted Spaur's racing experience, which reportedly "paid off" during the chase. Spaur's enthusiasm for automobile racing might go a long way toward explaining the zest with which he pursued a supposed UFO at speeds of more than a hundred miles an hour.)

Such is the story of the flying saucer named Floyd. It is a classic sighting. It is also full of holes. Dr. J. Allen Hynek rates this case as a "strong unidentified." Hynek writes, "I have presented aspects of this case in some detail because although it is just one of a great many similar cases, it is a fine example . . . of a Close Encounter of the First Kind."[28] Hynek's evaluation of this case is especially perplexing. During March of 1966 he witnessed first-hand the "near hysteria" (his own words) over UFOs in Michigan, as police officers imagined celestial objects to be brilliant "moving" UFOs. But when the same scenario was reported a month later in Ohio, Hynek, who was not present this time, reached the conclusion that the policemen must indeed have sighted a genuine UFO!

The late Dr. McDonald considered the evidence assembled in support of this case to be "outstanding." Yet none of these recognized UFO authorities seemed to take the slightest notice that Spaur was revealed in the De Groot piece to be a UFO "repeater," a clear sign that a person's UFO testimony had best be taken with a grain of salt. It is remarkable how readily such well-known UFO "experts" can be misled by inaccurate data, inaccurate reporting, and a powerful will to believe.

NOTES

1. James E. McDonald's endorsement was given to NICAP, October 30, 1966.

2. J. Allen Hynek was called the "Galileo of UFOlogy" by *Newsweek,* November 21, 1977, p. 97; the "Galileo of UFO Studies" by *Oui,* April 1977, cover.

3. Hynek, "Are Flying Saucers Real?" *Saturday Evening Post,* December 17, 1966, p. 20.

4. *Flying Saucers* (New York: *Look* Special Publication, Cowles Communications, 1967), p. 39.

5. Edward U. Condon, *Scientific Study of Unidentified Objects,* Case 53; supplement to *Ravenna Record Courier,* April 18, 1966.

6. Spaur and Neff's interview with the Air Force's Project Blue Book was taped by William Weitzel, and copies were widely distributed.

7. Philip J. Klass, *UFO's Explained* (New York: Random House, 1974), p. 42.

8. William Weitzel, "Into the Middle of Hell," *UFO Reports,* October 1967, p. 45.

9. *East Liverpool* (Ohio) *Review,* April 18, 1966. Interview with Huston.

10. Weitzel, *Report of NICAP Pennsylvania Unit No. 1,* April 8, 1967.

11. Weitzel, *Report to NICAP,* June 23, 1966.

12. Weitzel, *UFO Reports,* October 1967, p. 41.

13. Tom Schley, *Beaver County Times,* April 18, 1966.

14. Project Blue Book interview, May 10, 1966.

15. Project Blue Book interview, May 10, 1966.

16. Hynek, *The UFO Experience,* chapter 8; Blum, *Beyond Earth,* chapter 9.

17. *Cleveland Plain Dealer,* April 18, 1966.

18. *East Liverpool Review,* April 18, 1966.

19. *Beaver County Times,* April 18, 1966.

20. U.S. Air Force Project Blue Book files.

21. *Pittsburgh Post Gazette,* April 18, 1966.

22. Weitzel, *UFO Reports,* October 1967, p. 44.

23. Weitzel, *UFO Reports,* p. 45.

24. Memo for the record, Project Blue Book files.

25. *State of Ohio* vs. *Dale Spaur,* State Case No. 62775; Court of Common Pleas, Case no. 34849.

26. *Dayton* (Ohio) *Daily News,* May 26, 1972.

27. Joseph Wittemer, personal correspondence.

28. Hynek, *The UFO Experience,* chapter 8.

20

WHAT ARE UFOs?

Everyone interested in the subject of UFOs seems to be promoting some theory that is supposed to satisfactorily explain all aspects of the UFO phenomenon. The public at large thinks that the only two hypotheses about UFOs are: (1) They are all hoaxes and misperceptions. (2) They are spacecraft from another planet. While these are indeed the two hypotheses that have received the greatest popular attention, they are by no means the only explanations popular in UFO circles today. A vigorous debate is now being carried out between proponents of the various hypotheses, attempting to answer the questions: What are UFOs? Where do they come from?

The extraterrestrial hypothesis is both the oldest and the best known of all the pro-UFO hypotheses. While it has been losing ground in recent years to other hypotheses, it still appears to be the most widely held. In the early 1950s it was widely speculated that UFOs originated somewhere in our own solar system; one of the most popular hypotheses designated Mars as the planet of origin.

Prior to the Mariner and Viking space probes of the 1960s and 1970s, the planet Mars had an aura of great mystery. Sufficiently earthlike to hold promise of harboring life as we know it, there appeared some reason to believe that life, perhaps even intelligent life, did indeed exist there. Astronomers observed seasonal changes that were widely attributed to the growth of vegetation. The celebrated "canals" of Mars (which, like all jealous phenomena, not everyone could see) seemed to many as if they *might* be massive engineering projects on a planetary scale. But the Mariner photographic reconnaissance of Mars in 1965 revealed not domed cities and lush Martian forests, but a barren, cratered surface surprisingly like that of the moon. After the historic Viking landings of 1976, which transmitted to earth close-up photographs of the barren, rocky, inhospitable surface of that planet and thereby confirmed scientists' estimates of the extremely low Martian temperatures and atmospheric pressures, even the most ardent proponents of Martian life were forced to admit that Mars appears, at least during the present epoch of its planetary evolution, to be incapable of supporting any life except perhaps the most hardy microorganisms. UFOlogists reluctantly abandoned Mars as a potential home base for UFOs.

Even the moons of Mars had been endowed with mystery. The fact that these two tiny moonlets — just a few miles across — were not discovered until 1877 caused some speculation that the moons are artificial and had not been launched until shortly before they were observed. Of course, the extreme faintness of these two tiny moons, Deimos and Phobos, and their close proximity to the bright disk of Mars makes them all but impossible to see even today, except under the most favorable conditions through large, high-quality telescopes. Earth-based telescopes cannot directly measure the size of the Martian moons, although estimates of their size can be made from their observed brightness. These estimates appeared to pose a serious dilemma, because the small size estimated for Phobos appeared to be inconsistent with the tiny, yet measurable, decay observed in its orbit.[1]

The Soviet astronomer I. S. Shklovskii, who is coauthor with Carl Sagan of the SETI classic *Intelligent Life in the Universe,* proposed a startling explanation for this discrepancy: the Martian moons have high orbital drag because they are far larger than has been assumed, suggesting that they are of artificial construction and are *hollow.* Shklovskii's hypothesis does indeed explain the discrepancy, but since the scientific method dictates that hypotheses should be constructed so as to involve the *fewest* possible speculative elements, the "hollow Martian moon" hypothesis generated considerably more enthusiasm *outside* the scientific community than it did within. Proponents of the hollow-moon hypothesis were placed on the defensive when Mariner 9 photographs revealed Phobos to be an irregular-shaped object with a heavily cratered surface. The orbital discrepancy appears to have been resolved when analysis of the Viking Orbiter data revealed that the two Martian moons are larger than estimated but have the *lowest* surface brightness of any known objects in the solar system; the assumption of a higher surface brightness caused their size to be underestimated. Hence there is no longer any reason to believe these moons to be hollow.

Venus was next to Mars in favor as the origin of UFOs. Contactees who flourished in the 1950s, such as George Adamski, were fond of claiming that the wise and benevolent Space Brothers, with whom they claimed to be on the closest terms of friendship, hailed mostly from Venus. Popular writers speculated that beneath the Venusian clouds lay a warm, steamy planet, very much like the earth at an earlier stage of its evolution. Science-fiction writers covered that planet with lush jungles, dinosaurs, and many other ex-exotic trappings. Again, it was too good to be true. Space probes from the United States and the USSR sent back data that presents an unambiguous picture of that planet's surface: temperatures hot enough to melt lead and a poisonous atmosphere of carbon dioxide of crushing density and very high corrosive power. Venus, like Mars, had to be eliminated as a potential home for UFOs.

Some UFO theorists have even suggested the moon as the point of origin for UFOs, although the lunar hypothesis was never as popular as those advocating Venus or Mars. Adamski claimed to have circled the moon in a flying saucer years before the Apollo astronauts arrived. He claimed to have seen on the moon's back side (which no one had yet seen) not the craters and mountains that everyone expected, but flowing rivers and prosperous cities inhabited by the Space People! Fortunately for Adamski, no high-resolution photographs of the moon's unseen side were taken during his lifetime, because although nearly 100 percent of the moon's surface has now been mapped in great detail, not a single river or city has yet been noted. Nonetheless, many UFOlogists continue to take the tales of Adamski very seriously. James McCampbell, director of research of MUFON, wrote in his 1973 book *UFOlogy* that, since the UFO occupants described by George Adamski "thoroughly anticipated numerous unrelated events around the world for two decades . . . his writings certainly deserve to be scrutinized for information about UFOs." McCampbell does not consider the possibility that all of these subsequent reports may have been *inspired* by Adamski's well-publicized tales. Hynek endorsed McCampbell's book as "an implied treasure chest of knowledge which could prove of monumental benefit to mankind."[2]

One would think that the Apollo expeditions to the moon would have finally put an end to oddball theories about lunar inhabitants, but these theories have adapted themselves well to the new information. Donald Wilson has recently written a book titled *Our Mysterious Spaceship Moon,* purporting to demonstrate that the moon is not a natural member of our solar system. It is actually, he says, a giant hollow sphere of artificial construction that was placed in orbit around our planet by some unknown alien race.[3]

It is not difficult to demonstrate that Wilson's hypothesis is utterly absurd. Newton's law of gravitation allows astronomers to calculate the mass of the moon exactly, and just as one can easily discern an empty eggshell from an uncracked egg by weighing them, we can state with no uncertainty whatsoever that the moon is not hollow. Wilson picked up his "hollow moon" theory from an article published in a Soviet magazine by Vasin and Scherbakov, whom he calls top Soviet scientists.

Unfortunately for Wilson, James Oberg took the trouble to consult a computerized bibliography of the world's scientific literature, and he found no scientific papers written by Vasin or Scherbakov. He did learn from other sources, however, that Vasin is a popular Soviet journalist who had written his "hollow moon" story tongue-in-cheek as a satire upon Shklovskii's now-discredited theory that the Martian moons are artificial and hollow. A truly excellent satire, we might add, for the joke is not only on

Shklovskii, but on Wilson as well, and on the many thousands of his readers in the United States who were all too ready to abandon themselves to such "lunacy."

Another writer who claims to detect an alien presence on the moon is George Leonard, who in 1976 wrote *Somebody Else Is on the Moon.* Mr. Leonard's favorite practice is to obtain from NASA's photo services many photographs taken from lunar orbit, which he scrutinizes for signs of alien activity. In these photos he claims to be able to discern evidence of large-scale lunar construction projects. He asks his readers to see giant cranes inside the craters, as well as roads and ramps and other evidence of intelligent activity. James Oberg has noted that no matter what the resolution of the photo may happen to be—whether the smallest object visible is miles across, or blocks, or just yards—these supposed lunar construction projects are always *precisely* at the limit of resolution. They are never clearly and unambiguously seen. Thus alien lunar construction sites are another example of a jealous phenomenon, obligingly shrinking themselves or expanding, depending on how acutely they are being observed. Leonard charges that top NASA scientists keep these alien activities under close surveillance but that a massive government conspiracy conceals the startling truth from the public.[4]

Unfortunately for Mr. Leonard, the prints he has used to make these startling discoveries are not NASA's highest quality, but are mass-production second- or third-generation copies. Oberg obtained a few first-generation prints from NASA's photo archives in the Johnson Space Center to show to Leonard. In these clearer prints the supposed "alien construction projects" are plainly seen to be natural lunar features. But Leonard was not convinced. After meeting with Oberg, he considered it far more likely that all the NASA prints were retouched and that Oberg is some kind of MIB-like disinformation specialist than that he himself was wrong in concluding that the moon is covered with platforms, ramps, cranes, and other construction paraphernalia.

Having eliminated Venus, Mars, and the moon as possible points of origin for UFOs, the proponents of the extraterrestrial hypothesis found themselves rapidly running out of planets in the solar system where UFOs might originate. UFO contactee Truman Bethurum and "psychic" Jeane Dixon have suggested that UFOs originate on an earthlike planet on the other side of the sun; this supposed planet, which has been given the name Clarion, would never be visible from the earth. However, the celestial mechanics of such an orbit makes no sense at all. Even if such a planet did exist at this moment, the perturbations of its orbit by Venus and the other planets would be such that in just thirty years Clarion would become visible during total eclipses of the sun. Furthermore, its effect on the orbit of Venus would be noticeable within three months.[5]

That leaves only the giant planets of our solar system, Jupiter, Saturn, Uranus, and Neptune, as possible points of origin for the UFOs. (We may safely rule out Mercury and Pluto as being too hot and too cold, respectively.) But even the giant planets seem to hold little hope as abodes of intelligent life. The atmospheres of the giant planets are extremely cold and consist of poisonous gases such as methane and ammonia. While there is reason to believe that warmer temperatures may prevail deep inside Jupiter's crushing atmosphere and Carl Sagan has suggested that there may be types of organisms that could adapt to some sort of existence in the ceaseless convection of the turbulent Jupiter atmosphere, even the most fervent proponents of the extraterrestrial hypothesis generally concede that the giant planets of our solar system do not seem a likely point of origin for UFOs.

Having eliminated all major bodies in our solar system from consideration, the extraterrestrial proponents are forced to take the terrifying plunge into interstellar space to find a home for their UFOs. While it currently takes several years for our space probes to reach the nearest of the outer planets, Jupiter and Saturn, no one seriously doubts that a technology more advanced than ours could make the trip in months, weeks, or perhaps even days, given more advanced propulsion systems and more efficient sources of energy.

But the distances to even the nearest stars are so overwhelmingly greater than this—a trip to the nearest star, Alpha Centauri, is more than 60,000 times as far as a trip to Jupiter—that travel speeds approaching the speed of light become necessary if we wish to reach our destination within a single *human* lifetime. If our top speed is just one-tenth the speed of light—sixty-seven million miles an hour—it will require more than eighty years for a round trip to even the nearest star. Even if we could travel at 99 percent of the speed of light, it would still require almost forty years to reach Zeta Reticuli, the star where many believe Betty Hill's UFO abductors live. (Those on board the spaceship traveling at such a velocity would of course have aged much less than this. But when they returned, eighty years would have elapsed back home.) The ability to reach such phenomenal velocities appears to pose insurmountable problems, not only to existing technologies but to any conceivable technology as well, because accelerating to near-optic velocity requires phenomenal expenditures of energy. *Even if our propulsion system were 100 percent efficient in turning matter into energy—* something that no existing mechanism can even remotely approach—*we would still need prohibitively large supplies of fuel to send even a small payload on a round trip to the nearest star.*

Suppose that we have somehow perfected a propulsion system that utilizes the most efficient energy source possible with 100 percent efficiency: the mutual annihilation of matter and antimatter. (Do not ask where we will get the antimatter, how we will store it, or how we will control the rate at which it reacts with matter.) Harvard physicist Edward Purcell calculates that even under this most favorable set of circumstances, to accelerate to 99 percent of the speed of light and then slow down again upon reaching a destination would require us to carry 196 tons of fuel for every ton of pay-load. And this will not even get us home! Unless we can count on there being a convenient matter/antimatter filling station at our destination or unless we do not intend to return home, we shall have to carry 40,000 tons of matter/antimatter for every ton of payload.[6] These limitations are not mere technical problems that can be overcome but are fundamental laws of physics; they apply to *all* civilizations, no matter how advanced.

Some popular writers are fond of speculating about the use of black holes — stars that have collapsed to an unimaginable degree — as "tunnels" through space. It is speculated by some theorists that it may perhaps be possible to pop into a black hole at point A, and emerge instantly at point B, many light-years away. Even if this is true, however, it does little to solve the problem of interstellar travel. Assuming that one finds a suitable black hole conveniently nearby, how does one go about determining where (or if) one will reappear? Do we just plunge in and hope for the best? And assuming that the black hole takes us where we're going, how do we arrange the return trip?

We must also contend with the matter of tidal forces: as a person approaches the black hole, the acceleration of gravity tugging at his feet becomes overwhelmingly greater than the force on his head, causing him to be stretched out like taffy. Perhaps we should build our spaceships out of rubber to allow for this expansion. We must also face the problem that black holes appear to be dozens of light-years apart, at a minimum. Even if we could pop into black holes and pop out again as easily as we take a ride on the subway, we would still need to develop and perfect interstellar travel merely to reach the nearest black hole, and to travel from the exit hole to the destination planet.

Because of the many obvious difficulties with the extraterrestrial hypothesis, UFO believers have lately become prolific in formulating other equally bizarre hypotheses. One such hypothesis is that UFOs are actually secret devices manufactured right here on earth. While a few UFO sightings might be attributed to tests of secret military projects, no earthly technology could conceivably exist that in any way matches the astonishing feats that UFOs are *alleged* to perform. Right-angle turns at thousands of miles an hour, antigravity powers, and magic healing radiation have all been attributed to UFOs. If such reports are true, no secret military project anywhere in the world could possibly explain them. But UFO proponents have never been known to let mere facts stand in the way of an interesting theory.

While the Soviets, the Chinese, or the Spanish are sometimes given credit for constructing such devices, the American CIA is most often named as the party responsible for UFOs. In fact, a UFO fan-magazine recently published an analysis by Dr. Leon Davidson, a longtime UFO-conspiracy buff, supposedly proving once and for all that the CIA is the secret originator of Unidentified Flying Objects. How does he prove this? He analyzes the insignia that was reportedly seen by Lonnie Zamora on a landed UFO at Socorro, New Mexico, in 1964. By a sequence of partial rotations and interchanges, Davidson discovers that the insignia can be made to plainly spell out the letters *CIA*. He goes on to observe that just one more small interchange within the insignia yields the letters *AD,* the initials of former CIA director Allen Dulles. If UFOs really were built and flown by the CIA, one would hope that their ever-so-secret agents would be more careful than to put identifying symbols on the craft.

Another possible terrestrial origin for UFOs that has been suggested is that a secret enclave of Nazis that supposedly fled to Antarctica upon the fall of the Third Reich are manufacturing them. Christof Friedrich of Toronto, Ontario, operates Samisdat Publishers, Ltd., which sells a book titled *UFO's: Nazi Secret Weapon?* As summarized in an article in the tabloid *National Spotlite,* the book reveals that the flying saucers being sighted today are advanced models of Nazi aircraft that were being developed at the close of World War II. "Adolf Hitler, now in his eighties, is blind and needs a seeing-eye dog—but he's still running the show," *Spotlite* reports. The Samisdat Press also offers for sale a "Nazi flying saucer spotter identification chart," showing some three dozen of "the better known German U.F.O. prototypes." It also sells an "Official UFO Investigator Pass," which conveniently contains bilingual questions "to ask [the] UFO crew," such as *Was ist ihr Antrieb?"* ("What is your method of propulsion") and *"Sind sie bewaffnet?"* ("Is your craft armed?").[7]

If we are unable to find a plausible location on the earth's surface where UFOs might originate, this does not mean that we must abandon the terrestrial hypothesis, because there exists a small but vocal group of UFOlogists who believe that UFOs originate *inside* the earth. Our earth is *hollow,* they insist, just like the two Martian satellites and our mysterious spaceship moon. Giant, gaping holes are said to be located at the North and South Poles, "not more than 285 miles in diameter—and not less than 50," which lead into the inner region. A "Great Central Sun" is said to illuminate the interior, creating a climate that is Mediterranean. These holes-in-the-poles are said to have been explored by Admiral Byrd during his polar expeditions. However, the government is said to be covering up all of Byrd's remarkable discoveries, including prehistoric animals and an underground race of "supermen."

While the idea of an underground race living inside a hollow earth is found in occult literature going back many years, the foremost proponent of these hypotheses in recent times was the late Ray Palmer, who operated the Palmer Press in Amherst, Wisconsin. Palmer ranks as a truly major figure in the history of UFOs, one who is often underestimated. We met Palmer in chapter 15, and recall his role in promoting the cult of the Great Shaver Mystery, with its Dero and Tero subterranean robots. Around 1970, Palmer became obsessed with the notion of a hollow earth and devoted many pages of his monthly magazine *Flying Saucers* to promoting it. No matter how powerful the objections some readers might raise to his holes-in-the-poles ideas, he would gaily waltz around them, to his own satisfaction at least. In a move suggestive of the widely reported Men in Black, he implies that certain financial reverses he recently suffered as a result of a court decision were intended to harass him for having dared to print the truth about the secret holes-in-the-poles.[8]

Palmer's proudest "evidence" was a NASA photograph that he describes as "the most remarkable photo ever made" (plate 39). It was taken by NASA's ESSA-7 satellite on November 23, 1968. Palmer boasts that "we do not see any ice fields in a large circular area directly at the geographic pole. Instead, we see—*The Hole!*" Not only is the earth hollow with openings at either pole, says he, but Mariner photos of the planet Mars show a "perfectly circular and inexplicable black circle at the exact geographic pole." Mercury appears to be hollow too.[9]

The ESSA-7 photo, as well as others he published, does indeed *appear* to show a perfectly circular opening at the North Pole. But let us consider the time of the year at which it was taken, November 23. As everyone knows, the poles experience a six-month-long "night" during which the sun never rises. On the 23 of November, the sun passes overhead for observers 20° south of the equator, meaning that for observers at north latitude 70° or more the sun never rises at all. Hence within 20° of the North Pole, there is total darkness on that date. We note something else that is strange about the picture: except for the area around the pole, no part of the Northern Hemisphere appears to be experiencing night. That, of course, is impossible. The ESSA photograph is a *composite* of many images of portions of the Northern Hemisphere, each one taken around the time of local noon. The "hole in the pole" is simply the region above 70° that was experiencing darkness, even at noon.

Yet no matter how many readers of Palmer's magazines raised this obvious and insurmountable objection, Ray Palmer would respond with some astonishing non sequitur and then pat himself on the back for having so cleverly answered the "platitudes" of those who denied the existence of the holes in the poles. Palmer compared his critics to those in the court of Queen Isabella who argued against Columbus's expedition. He insisted that the ESSA photo was a composite made up from photos taken during *a single orbit* (which it plainly is not), and he claimed that the satellite's camera was using *infrared* film, which can see in the dark, and hence no night is apparent. The only reason, he concludes, that the North Pole was dark is that it lies at the center of a giant, gaping hole! If this were true, it should be possible for Palmer to produce an identical photograph taken during the summer months. But the "hole" could only be seen in his photographs from January or November. No "hole" in the North Pole is to be found in the satellite photograph taken in June. (The hole was hidden by clouds in that one, Palmer asserted.) Palmer even went so far as to challenge his critics to explain why, as we approach the pole, "the ocean begins to slant to the north."[10]

It is of course possible for astronomers to determine the mass of the earth, as they do the moon, on the basis of its gravitational effects on other members of the solar system. As a result, we are just as certain that the earth is not hollow as we are that the moon is not. Yet no evidence of any type could cause Ray Palmer and the other holes-in-the-poles buffs to doubt that the earth is hollow. One would expect that, if the present-day UFO movement were indeed as scientific as some would have us believe, it would repudiate such obviously kooky hypotheses in a loud, unmistakable voice. But precisely the opposite is happening.

Brinsley LePoer Trench, founder of the "respected" *Flying Saucer Review,* has recently written a book titled *Secret of the Ages: UFO's from Inside the Earth,* which champions Palmer's holes in the poles. (LePoer Trench sits in the British House of Lords as the Eighth Earl of Clancarty, where he organized the 1979 House of Lords UFO debate.) The influential John Keel lauds Palmer as "the man who deserves the most recognition in the UFO field . . . more than 20 years would pass before the UFOlogical establishment would catch up with him."[11] At the 1977 International UFO Congress in Chicago, which included such well-known speakers as Hynek, Harder, Lorenzen, Clark, Vallee, and Friedman, one of the most popular and best-received talks was the one given by Ray Palmer. As Keel said, the UFO establishment is gradually catching up to Palmer's unconventional theories.

Since so many well-known UFOlogists are now beginning to appreciate the difficulties in those theories that assert either a terrestrial or an extraterrestrial origin for UFOs, one would expect that a few of them might begin expressing doubts about the validity of the UFO phenomenon in general. If so, one has overestimated them, for instead of edging back toward a healthy skepticism, the leading UFOlogists seem to be fighting each other to see who can come up with the most outrageously bizarre theory about UFOs. If the existence of UFOs as solid, "nuts-and-bolts" objects does not seem tenable, then perhaps UFOs really do exist but are ghostlike in substance. This enables UFO theorists to reconcile the existence of the UFO phenomenon with any conceivable present or future observation, the maxim being: When a UFO report appears to make no sense at all, it is common sense that must be suspect, not the observation. As Hynek explains, "There are other planes of existence — the astral plane, the etheric plane, and so forth."[12]

In chapter 17 we encountered some of the more outlandish theories about "nonmaterial UFOs." There are at least as many problems associated with metaphysical explanations of UFOs as there are with nuts-and-bolts ones. If UFOs are an ethereal phenomenon, how could they show up on radar and in photographs? How could they kidnap Travis Walton and Betty Hill?

UFOs must be sometimes physical and sometimes not. But by this reasoning we have complicated our hypothesis, thereby diminishing its scientific merit; we are no better off than the nuts-and-bolts advocate attempting to explain how UFOs can infallibly *avoid* unambiguous detection.

Occam's Razor is the cutting edge of scientific decision-making. This celebrated principle, which has been a cornerstone of the scientific method since it was first articulated by William of Occam in the fourteenth century, dictates that when there are two or more competing scientific hypotheses, we should adopt the one that contains the *fewest speculative elements.* "Entities are not to be multiplied beyond necessity" is the formulation of Occam's Razor best known to us today.

To understand how Occam's Razor is applied, let us examine two possible explanations for the phenomenon of lightning and thunder. One hypothesis states that it is the result of discharges of static electricity in the atmosphere; the other holds it to be the work of the gods in Valhalla, emanating from the blows of Donner's magic hammer and Wotan's mighty spear. Both hypotheses satisfactorily explain the phenomenon. But the latter hypothesis contains considerably more speculative elements than the former. While we are quite familiar with electricity from its role in many other phenomena, present-day science has not as yet encountered any phenomenon that can be explained most economically in terms of Wotan and Valhalla. Thus while we cannot *prove* that thunder is not caused by the gods of Valhalla, Occam's Razor dictates that we reject that hypothesis in favor of simpler, more prosaic ones that do not require us to posit the existence of an entirely new order of beings merely to explain the phenomenon.

How do "psychic" explanations of UFOs fare under the scrutiny of Occam's Razor? About as well as explanations involving the gods of Valhalla. By postulating the existence of an as yet unproven "psychic world" as an ad hoc explanation for UFO reports, we have formulated one of the most complex hypotheses imaginable; it is as absurd as attributing the energy crisis to a realm of invisible oil-drinking angels! Even the extraterrestrial hypothesis would be preferred to the "psychic" hypothesis for UFOs. Were these the *only* two hypotheses available (they plainly are not), we should have to choose the extraterrestrial hypothesis as being the less complex, since the idea of space travel involves fewer speculative elements than the idea of insubstantial but most convenient "psychic" ghosts.

What exactly is meant by asserting that UFOs are a psychic phenomenon, or that they originate in "alternate realities" or "interpenetrating universes"? Do these terms have any meaningful content? Are there any known observable properties of an "alternate reality" — *or are these just convenient names that have been made up to obscure the fact that the psychic proponents still have given us no real explanation?* The hypothesis that UFOs are a psychic phenomenon is rightfully scorned by any scientific body, for it defines no properties of the phenomenon, it does not integrate UFOs with other existing bodies of knowledge; it merely substitutes an ill-defined word in place of a meaningful explanation.

The Aristotelian scholars of the Middle Ages, for whom the greatest scholarly achievement was to write yet another commentary on some treatise of antiquity, were especially adept at substituting name for substance. Empty words were all the explanation that the scholarly world wanted or needed for centuries. Today's "scientific" UFOlogists seek to impose a new Aristotelianism upon the world of science by inventing a scholarly sounding term devoid of all meaning and then pretending that it tells us something about UFOs. Until they can define with scientific precision what an "alternate reality" is supposed to be, list its observable properties, clearly state what future observations it does and does not imply, and formulate some mathematical representation of the difference between an "alternate" reality and the ordinary kind, we may safely infer that their hypotheses are lacking any real substance.

Yet another difficulty with the "psychic" explanation of UFOs is that the hypothesis is so broad that it is consistent with any observation whatsoever. No matter what may happen in the future, the statement "UFOs originate in an alternate reality" runs little risk of being proved false. In fact, it is impossible to refute such a nebulous statement. *Consequently, it is not a viable scientific hypothesis.*

The distinguished philosopher of science, Sir Karl Popper, has developed at length the concept of *falsifiability* as a means for distinguishing a scientific from a pseudoscientific hypothesis. A scientific hypothesis must at least in principle be falsifiable: it must be entirely clear just how the hypothesis could be proved false. A hypothesis need not be true to be scientifically meaningful. For example, the "holes in the poles" hypothesis is indeed falsifiable; we need only fly over the North Pole and discover no hole there. Hence the hypothesis is meaningful, although quite wrong. But should we hypothesize that the earth is populated by invisible dragons who do not interact with their surroundings in any way, we have clearly formulated a nonscientific hypothesis, since there is no way in which the existence of intangible, nonmaterial dragons could ever be disproved.

How does one attempt to falsify, even in principle, the statement that UFOs are a psychic phenomenon? Since we do not know exactly what a psychic phenomenon is supposed to be, how could we definitely establish that UFOs were *not* to be included among them? How would one attempt to show that UFOs do *not* originate in "another space-time continuum"? *If there is no way to disprove such statements, they cannot be considered legitimate scientific hypotheses.* Imagine the chilly reception that would have greeted Einstein's theories had he predicted that the increase in mass of a moving object was a "psychic" increase in "meta-mass" and hence could not be measured. Yet we are expected to hail nonsense such as this about UFOs as if it were the scientific breakthrough of the century!

The "scientific" UFOlogists need not imagine themselves to be persecuted because orthodox science refuses to take them seriously; they need only look as far as their own hypotheses to see sufficient grounds for this rejection. Newton's law of universal gravitation stands in danger of being refuted by the discovery of a single apple, anywhere, that would indisputably fall away from the ground. But "psychic" explanations for UFOs are consistent with any observations whatsoever (for is there anything that a "psychic phenomenon" clearly cannot do?), and hence they are not in any sense meaningful, let alone scientific.

In addition to extraterrestrial, terrestrial, and "psychic" explanations for UFOs, many other hypotheses have been proposed that have failed to gain widespread acceptance. In a letter in *Science* in 1952, Dr. Edgar F. Mauer, M.D., proposed that flying saucers were probably *muscae volitantes,* "flittering flies," or "spots before the eyes."[13] He observes that the erratic motions attributed to the saucers are characteristic of this phenomenon. While there is little doubt that "spots before the eyes" can account for at least some single-witness UFO sightings, the hypothesis is plainly too narrow in scope to provide a full explanation for the UFO phenomenon, which includes supposed UFO photographs, Mothmen, radar sightings, humanoid occupant reports, and abductions. It is difficult to imagine how anyone could be abducted by a spot before his eye!

Another innovative theory was suggested by Donald H. Robey in a *Saturday Review* article in 1959. He hypothesized that flying saucers were related to comets. In 1947, when widespread UFO sightings began, the earth's vicinity was, he says, visited by more comets than ever before. Robey states that calculations have shown that a cometary ice-fragment twelve inches in diameter would still retain half its diameter after having passed through the earth's atmosphere. Since it would be rounded and smoothed during its rapid plunge through the atmosphere, possibly causing it to flatten into a disk, Robey speculates that the cometoid would acquire temporary lift from jets of air or from vaporization on its underside. Very peculiar motions are to be expected, he says, due to these irregular forces. Robey further suggests that since solar outbursts, which are accompanied by powerful magnetic fields, appear to have effects on comets, they may affect cometoids as well, and perhaps may explain the UFOs reported magnetic effects.[14] Neither UFO debunkers nor believers seem to take much notice of Robey's cometoid hypothesis.

Another explanation for UFOs is that the phenomenon is in some way related to ball lightning, a little-understood phenomenon in which a basketball-sized globe of light appears to hover or float erratically. It can reportedly singe hair and clothing and disappear instantaneously in a blinding flash. The ball-lightning explanation for UFOs was proposed as early as 1952 by Malcolm Thomson of the Thomson Laboratory, General Electric Company, who suggested in a letter in *Science* that ball lightning, bead lightning (which looks like a chain of luminous beads that slowly fade away), and luminous clouds may account for a large number of flying-saucer sightings.[15]

It was the idea that UFOs might represent a phenomenon similar to ball lightning that drew Philip J. Klass into the realm of UFOlogy. Having no previous interest in the subject, Klass happened to read John Fuller's book *Incident at Exeter* and was struck by the apparent resemblance between the reported characteristics of the UFOs and a plasma-type phenomenon akin to ball lightning. Especially remarkable seemed to be the UFOs' reported affinity for hovering over power lines. Plasma UFOs as postulated by Klass went considerably beyond the recognized scope of the ball-lightning phenomenon; he hypothesized a type of brilliantly glowing plasma that not only could be formed independent of any thunderstorm but also could last far longer than was believed possible for any plasma in the atmosphere.

Several years after the publication of this explanation in *UFOs Identified* (Random House, 1968), Klass began to rethink his appraisal of the UFO phenomenon. He now explains that when he first became interested in UFOs it did not seem to him to be possible that apparently sane and sober persons would mistake a distant planet or a hovering hot-air balloon for a huge, brilliant object just hundreds of feet away. But the experience of years of investigating UFO reports convinced him that such misperceptions are not only possible but in fact often happen. Klass now believes that the phenomenon of ball lightning plays only a minor role in the overall UFO picture.

The existence of such a wide range of theories about UFOs can be, of course, a healthy sign, because competition between differing theories is at the heart of the scientific method. However, this may also be indicative of total confusion, a clear sign that no one really has *any* reliable information on UFOs. Perhaps UFOlogy, like medieval theology, has no more substance than angels' wings. This would explain why no clear consensus on any theory has ever emerged.

A successful theory not only accounts for all known facts at least as well as any other competing theory but predicts effects not yet observed, which, if subsequently encountered, will provide compelling evidence in favor of the theory's validity.

Unfortunately, none of the pro-UFO theories yet proposed has proved to have any predictive value whatsoever, which is one of the principal reasons that scientists have not jumped aboard the UFO bandwagon. Einstein's theory of relativity triumphed because it not only accounted for puzzling observations like the Michelson-Morely experiment, which seemed to be saying that the earth was standing still, but also went on to predict the results of observations that were not yet made, such as the curvature of light rays in a gravitational field and the measurable slowing of time for an object accelerated to speeds approaching the speed of light. When these effects (and a good many others) were subsequently observed, there was virtually unanimous agreement among physicists that Einstein's theories represented a significant advance in our understanding of the universe.

Yet the hypothesis that UFOs are extraterrestrial spacecraft—or any other theory that holds UFOs to be both real and puzzling—does not lead to any clear and unambiguous predictions. Those who proclaim UFOlogy to be an infant science—if they are sincere in their beliefs and if they understand the methodology of science—should begin at once to take steps to confer predictive value upon their hypotheses, for without it UFOlogy will remain forever outside the realm of science.

One of the few UFOlogists to attempt to make any definite predictions is Dr. David R. Saunders, a psychologist and statistician who is the author of the book *UFO's Yes!* Saunders was the member of the Condon Committee who leaked to the press embarrassing papers of that committee, causing him to be fired by an angry Dr. Condon. Based on his computerized catalogue of many thousands of reported UFO sightings, Saunders has noted what appears to be a cycle of approximately five years in the peak concentration of UFO reports. He believes he has also discovered a pattern in the geographic location of sightings as well. Based upon these observations, Saunders confidently predicted that a major UFO "flap" would occur in the Soviet Union, starting in December 1977. However, it never happened.[16]

For different reasons, Philip J. Klass predicted in August of 1977 that there would be a strong upsurge in UFO sightings starting in December, occurring not in the Soviet Union but in the United States, because of the publicity surrounding the release of the much-hyped movie *Close Encounters of the Third Kind.*[17] There was a significant 46 percent increase in UFO sightings from January through September 1978, compared with the same period a year earlier, according to the figures published by CUFOS. But CUFOS' Allan Hendry has not as of this writing published the figures for the final three months of 1978, despite proddings from Klass. Hendry and CUFOS continue to insist, however, that no significant UFO flap was caused by the movie publicity. Yet CUFOS' J. Allen Hynek wrote in a bulletin sent to the Center's investigators that CUFOS' new Coordinator of Investigations, Robert Runser, who took the job in April 1978, "has been very much snowed-under by the mass of cases which were received following the showing of the film 'Close Encounters of the Third Kind.'" CUFOS continues to claim that these were mainly reports of *old* cases and that Klass was wrong in predicting a UFO flap, but CUFOS still has not released the figures for the months in question.

Another difficulty in the pro-UFO hypothesis is that the hypothesis that UFOs are real and are puzzling *is itself unfalsifiable,* at least in the form that the belief is promoted at present. For how do you falsify, *even in principle,* the hypothesis that UFOs exist? Not by providing explanations of any number of "classic" unexplained UFO sightings; when explained, they simply become IFOs, Identified Flying Objects, and hence they were presumably never UFOs in the first place. By definition, no genuine UFO sighting can ever be explained. So how could anyone even attempt to show that

UFOs don't exist? Suppose we set up automatic cameras in many places, leave them on all night, and after many years no UFOs turn up. Wouldn't this be at least some proof that UFOs do not exist?

Well, this has in fact happened (for example, the Smithsonian Prairie Camera Network), but "scientific" UFOlogists don't view the remarkable lack of evidence as significant in any way. "Maybe UFOs can make themselves invisible to the cameras," they'll say. "Maybe the UFOs know where the cameras are and avoid them. Maybe they slip away into other dimensions. UFOs are, after all, a jealous phenomenon. Maybe they fly straight up and down, not horizontally, and hence never cross the paths of any cameras." A million evasions can be (and are) used to avoid facing up to the astonishing lack of any real UFO evidence. No matter what evidence is or is not obtained, there is no way in which the existence of UFOs can ever be disproved or even made to seem less likely. The UFO hypothesis, as it now exists, is 100 percent unfalsifiable. Hence it is pseudoscience.

The same situation arises in parapsychology and other "paranormal" fields. How could one ever prove, or even show to be probable, that ESP does not exist? Suppose we test a hundred people and find no evidence of anything unusual. "That just means you tested only people who have no ESP." Suppose we find very serious flaws in a "classic" experiment, one of the cornerstones of psychic research. "That only proves that the one experiment is faulty. It doesn't refute the rest." ESP is another completely unfalsifiable hypothesis: all possible facts in the universe either are favorable to the hypothesis or are irrelevant. Hence it is pseudoscience.

What, then, can UFOs be? We have examined all of the popular hypotheses and some not so popular ones as well: visitors from space, secret earth technologies, a supercivilization inside the holes in the poles, psychic phenomena, spots before the eyes, cometoids, plasma balls, and so forth. Every one of them has serious flaws, either in terms of being able to explain the observations or on philosophical grounds, or both. Can we suggest any hypothesis that will successfully meet all these objections? We are not being excessively demanding, since *every hypothesis in every legitimate scientific field is able to satisfy these requirements.*

It is indeed possible to suggest a hypothesis about UFOs that suffers from none of the observational objections that can be raised against the various "nuts and bolts" hypotheses, or the philosophical objections that compel us to disregard the so-called psychic explanations of UFOs. It is the familiar null hypothesis, the cornerstone of statistical analysis; UFOs, as a phenomenon distinct from all others, simply do not exist.

Note how well the null hypothesis explains all of the phenomena that cause the other proposed explanations to stumble and fall. How do UFOs always manage to slip away before the evidence becomes too convincing? Simple. There is no evidence to be found, because the phenomenon exists only in the imagination of the observer. Why do UFOs occasionally seem to show up on radar but the great majority of the time go undetected? Because radar sightings of "UFOs" are due to relatively infrequent conditions of anomalous radar propagation combined with misinterpretation of the data. How do UFOs, when they occasionally permit themselves to be unambiguously photographed, always make sure that there is one and only one photographer present, even if the incident occurs in New York City, Chicago, or Los Angeles? Because the unambiguous UFO photo is a hoax, the work of a lone prankster.

How do UFOs sometimes manage to disappear all at once, like the dematerialization of a ghost? Since UFOs are often just distant lights that are grossly misperceived, the light can be instantaneously rendered invisible by being obscured by atmospheric changes, or by being moved or turned off at its source. Why are UFO sightings strongly concentrated in waves? Such behavior is characteristic of all instances of mass hysteria; see Charles Mackay's classic nineteenth-century book, *Extraordinary Popular Delusions and the Madness of Crowds,* for numerous examples of other such waves throughout history.[18] No other hypothesis is so successful as the null hypothesis at explaining the highly subjective character of the UFO phenomenon, the way in which the sightings appear to be uniquely localized in space and time.

The philosophical objections that cripple the "psychic" explanations of UFOs pose no problems to the null hypothesis (which dictates that, until the data proves otherwise, we consider the sample under observation to be no different in any way from what we ordinarily expect to encounter). The hypothesis does not seek to hide behind nebulous terminology; "hoaxes" and "misperceptions" are clearly defined and clearly understood terms. It is eminently falsifiable; all we need is to have one bona fide UFO land on the White House lawn, and the null hypothesis could plainly be refuted. And it stands up extremely well to Occam's Razor, since it involves creating absolutely no new or speculative entities of any kind. UFO reports can be entirely explained, it says, in terms of other known phenomena. Indeed, the null hypothesis is itself a corollary of Occam's Razor; it directs us *not* to create a new theoretical entity, the "authentic UFO," until the data unambiguously indicates that there is no other reasonable course of action.

I maintain that we have found the answer to the question "What are UFOs?" through a rigorous application of the scientific method. As an unexpected dividend, we find that we have also obtained the answer to the same question that might be raised about ESP, Bigfoot, the Loch Ness monster, "psychic" spoon-bending, and other dubious (that is, jealous) phenomena. Our answer must be that UFOs do not exist.

This answer is certain to disappoint many people who are eager to find that our galaxy (or "our space-time continuum") is populated by all manner of exotic and exciting creatures. No one would be happier than I should it actually be discovered that our earth is playing host to strange creatures from some unknown planet or universe. But wishing will not make it so. And so long as we wish to adhere to the scientific method (that is, to make factual statements about the real world, as opposed to seeking subjective mystical insight), we are forced to face up to the conclusion that UFOs as real and distinct entities simply do not exist. Those who continue to insist otherwise are openly proclaiming their allegiance to a different world-view, one which, although popular, is incompatible with the world-view of science.

NOTES

1. Carl Sagan, *The Cosmic Connection* (New York: Doubleday, 1973), chapter 15.

2. George Adamski, *Inside the Space Ships* (New York: Abelard-Schuman, 1955), chapter 13; James McCampbell, *UFOlogy* (Belmont, Calif.: Jaymac, 1973), p. 116, back cover.

3. Donald Wilson, *Our Mysterious Spaceship Moon* (New York: Dell, 1979).

4. George Leonard, *Somebody Else Is on the Moon* (New York: McKay, 1976).

5. Condon, *Scientific Study of Unidentified Flying Objects* (New York: Bantam Books, 1969), p. 30.

6. Edward Purcell in *Interstellar Communication,* ed. Cameron (W. A. Benjamin, 1963), chapter 13.

7. Samisdat Publishers, Ltd., 206 Carlton St., Toronto, Ontario, M5A 2L1 Canada; *National Spotlite,* July 1975.

8. *Flying Saucers,* Palmer Publications, March 1971, pp. 2, 3.

9. *Flying Saucers,* June 1970, pp. 2-6.

10. *Flying Saucers,* September 1970, pp. 24–40.

11. Brinsley LePoer Trench, *Secret of the Ages* (New York: Pinnacle Books, 1977); John Keel, in *UFO Report,* June 1977, p. 12.

12. J. Allen Hynek, *Fate* magazine interview, June 1976.

13. Edgar F. Mauer, letter in *Science,* December 19, 1952, p. 693.

14. Donald H. Robey, *Saturday Review,* September 5, 1959, p. 51.

15. Malcolm Thomson, letter in *Science,* December 5, 1952, p. 640.

16. David R. Saunders' prediction was discussed at the 1976 CUFOS conference, Lincolnwood, Ill.

17. Philip J. Klass's prediction was made at a press conference of CSICOP, Biltmore Hotel, New York City, August 9, 1977.

18. Charles Mackay, *Extraordinary Popular Delusions and the Madness of Crowds,* 1841 (New York: Noonday Press, 1932).

21

THE NEW ZEALAND UFO FILMS

We're on exactly the same route taken by Captain Powell when he encountered those mysterious objects . . . naturally we'll be looking out for anything unusual. —Newsman Quentin Fogarty, in an aircraft off the New Zealand coast, 12:10 AM, Dec. 31, 1978.

There's a whole formation of Unidentified Flying Objects behind us. —Quentin Fogarty, twenty minutes later.

A December 1978 incident in New Zealand promises to provide the best UFO evidence to date. It is a radar-visual-photographic encounter—to my knowledge the only one of its kind—and the photographs are not just run-of-the-mill pictures but are among the half-dozen or so motion picture films offered as evidence for the UFO. Radar/visual cases are uncommon, as are "good" photo cases. Motion pictures of supposed UFOs are extremely rare. To encounter a UFO case that promises to be not just a radar/visual/photographic case—the only one of its kind—but a well-documented radar/visual/ motion picture incident is unprecedented in UFO annals. Little wonder that J. Allen Hynek has stated, "The film raises this whole area above buffoonery and ridicule, and is by far the most impressive evidence we have examined in more than 75,000 reported UFO sightings."[1]

The most famous incidents of the 1978–1979 New Zealand UFO flap are of course the two UFO movies, especially the one taken from an aircraft by Quentin Fogarty and David Crockett in the predawn hours of December 31, 1978 (New Zealand time). But the drama of the New Zealand incident actually begins ten days earlier, on the night of December 20–21, 1978, on a routine newspaper delivery flight round-trip from Blenheim, New Zealand, to Christchurch. Our examination of the incident must begin there.

Shortly before midnight, officers at a Royal New Zealand Air Force base near Blenheim, near the northern tip of South Island, reported seeing three orange and white lights low in the eastern sky, looking like the lights of a freighter heading into Wellington. (Dr. William Ireland of New Zealand's Department of Scientific and Industrial Research (DSIR), who wrote a paper evaluating the entire series of UFO incidents, argued that one object sighted was probably Jupiter, since the positions appear to closely match. Bruce Maccabee of MUFON/CUFOS/NICAP, whose evaluation of the McMinnville UFO photos was discussed in chapter 6, challenged this identification, principally because the lights were *reported* to wander at times far from Jupiter's position.[2]) At about this time, the radar at Wellington began to see targets from the vicinity of the Clarence River, nowhere near the lights reportedly sighted from Blenheim.

At about midnight, Captain John Randle and First Officer Keith Heine took off from Blenheim, flying in Safe Air Limited's Argosy I, a four-engine turboprop freight aircraft. They headed south toward Christchurch. Not long after takeoff, still over land, the crew reportedly saw an airborne object, giving off an "intense white light, too intense to be a vehicle's head-lamps," according to Randle. "Besides, it was airborne," he stated, "and I could see land features lit up underneath as it passed." Randle was only "mildly curious," according to newspaper accounts, and made no radio report of the object to air traffic controllers. As Argosy I neared the Clarence area, where the UFOs were reportedly visible on radar, the crew could not see anything. "Nobody was terribly excited because occasionally radar does register some odd things," explained radar controller John Cordy. He also observed that one of the targets that had stopped moving remained in view even though the radar's moving target indicator (MTI) was engaged. "Theoretically, it should have disappeared," Cordy explained.[3] A stationary target should not have been visible if the radar was functioning normally.

A second aircraft, Argosy II, took off about three hours afterward, around 3:00 AM, also bound for Christchurch, piloted by Captain Vern Powell and his copilot Ian Perry. Argosy II had been forewarned that UFOs were supposedly in the vicinity and hence undertook the flight in a frame of mind receptive to UFO sightings. "Going to Woodbourne in the crew transfer bus we were talking about UFOs," Captain Powell stated. "When we gave our flight plan to the control tower we were told we might be asked to investigate some unidentified radar returns."[4]

Powell and Perry were not disappointed. Soon after takeoff, Wellington radar advised them that a UFO was reportedly in the vicinity. Unfortunately, they were unable to see anything. However, a second target was reportedly seen as "an intense white light that sometimes changed to a reddish thing. It was much bigger and brighter than any star I have ever seen," said Powell. As they approached Christchurch, Argosy II's weather radar reportedly detected an object streaking across the flight path. A flashing object was visually sighted, which "shot past our bow at breakneck pace" in about five seconds. Since this reported incident occurred in a "blind spot" of the Christchurch radar, it "remains an unconfirmed sighting," in the words of *The Australian*. Meanwhile, Argosy I took off from Christchurch, headed north toward Auckland, in the northern part of North Island. After passing the southbound Argosy II heading in the other direction, Captain Randle reported spotting what appeared to be three large surface vessels, very close to the shore of South Island. While some sources suggest this to be another supposed bizarre UFO incident, Captain Randle's comments clearly indicate that he perceived this only as unusual activity on the part of fishing boats. "One of them seemed to be in shoaling waters. The whole thing was strange because you couldn't consider that stretch of coast safe for any kind of shipping in any circumstances . . . you have to wonder what legitimate purpose ships could have for being there. [Could they be attempting to cheat on New Zealand's two-hundred-mile fishing limits?] I have no idea whether they were Russian, American, or whatever," Randle stated.[5]

While the events of December 20–21 are noteworthy in their own right, they are now remembered chiefly as a prelude to far more dramatic events ten nights later. Unfortunately, no one has yet performed the in-depth analysis required to obtain a complete understanding of the December 21 events; perhaps some enterprising reader in New Zealand would like to undertake this (but never underestimate the magnitude of your task!). A few facts, however, should be noted. The numerous, swift-moving targets on radar on the morning of December 21, 1978, strongly suggest the occurrence of anomalous radar propagation (or "radar angels"), and the radiosonde readings from Christchurch seem to bear this out,[6] although the propagation of radar signals cannot be rigorously determined from radiosonde readings. We should keep in mind that false radar returns are most frequent in mid-summer and that December is a summer month in the Southern Hemisphere.

Also significant is the fact that during the month of December the Japanese squid fishing fleet had been building up in the coastal waters of New Zealand. These boats employ powerful incandescent lights—up to 360,000 watts *per boat*—to attract squid from the ocean depths. Satellite photographs clearly show a concentration of these brilliantly illuminated boats in and near the Tasman Bay, not far from the Cook Strait, which separates the north and south islands of New Zealand. As December passed into January, the boats were gradually moving through the Strait from the west to the east coast of New Zealand. It is very probable that some of the lights sighted are attributable to these fishing boats. Plate 40 shows the Japanese fleet in its summer fishing area in the Sea of Japan. Notice that the total output of light from the main concentration of fishing boats exceeds that of Tokyo. Since the horizon for an airplane flying at 10,500 feet extends over 130 miles, even boats on the other side of New Zealand's South Island would become visible between the mountain peaks.

The rapidly moving object reportedly seen by Argosy II near Christchurch sounds very much like the description of a brilliant meteor: a "bright, flashing white light, almost like a strobe." The predawn hours are the peak time for meteors, and the disintegration of an object in the atmosphere can cause it to appear to rapidly change brightness. Perhaps the most significant comments on the incident are those of Captain Randle, who, unlike Captain Powell, is not convinced that he witnessed anything truly out of the ordinary. "There was nothing I saw that could not have been reproduced by the Air Force with an Iroquois helicopter," he said. "It would have been completely possible for a Japanese or Russian whaling fleet to do these things. The real mystery is not how, but why, these things should happen."[7] Maccabee states that there were no helicopters in the area. Captain Randle's skeptical comments have been, to the best of my knowledge, totally ignored by the news media and UFO groups here in the United States.

Newsman Quentin Fogarty of Melbourne's Channel O (the letter "oh") was on vacation in New Zealand for the 1978 Christmas holidays, when he received a telephone call from his boss, producer Leonard Lee. Fogarty was told to cut short his vacation in order to obtain some news footage on the Randle/Powell incident of a few nights earlier. "We were short of news over the Christmas and New Year's period," producer Lee later explained on a Washington, D.C., TV program.[8]

Fogarty arranged to fly on one of the Safe Air Argosy flights from Blenheim to Wellington to Christchurch, then back to Blenheim, essentially duplicating the route of the earlier flights of Captains Randle and Powell. With him were camerman David Crockett and Crockett's wife, Ngaire, a sound recordist. At the controls were the pilot, Captain Bill Startup, and the copilot, Robert Guard. The Safe Air Argosy turboprop transport (designated Safe Alpha Echo, or S.A.E., in its air-to-ground communications) was on a regularly scheduled newspaper distribution run, bringing the Sunday morning papers into Christchurch.

The principal source of information for what follows has been Dr. Bruce S. Maccabee. Being a well-known analyst of UFO photos who is not generally skeptical about the UFO question, Maccabee was invited to travel to New Zealand and Australia at the expense of Channel O to further investigate the incident and to assist them in the preparation of their stories and documentary films about it. Fortunately for everyone, Maccabee is a most unusual UFOlogist—he does not attempt to "hide" certain UFO facts while promoting others. Whether Maccabee is right or wrong, at the very least he is consistent in his close adherence to the principles of science. It is through the cooperation of Bruce Maccabee that the New Zealand story can be pieced together. Because of space limitations, only the highlights of the extremely complex incident can be presented here.

The brief fifty-mile flight from Blenheim to Wellington, across the Cook Strait, was uneventful. After picking up a load of newspapers, S.A.E. took off from Wellington at 11:46 PM New Zealand Daylight Savings Time, December 30, 1978 (10:46 AM GMT, Dec. 30), heading south. Fogarty's stated aim was to obtain film footage of the inside of the aircraft, to be used in his planned here-I-am-on-the-spot news item. "We're on exactly the same route taken by Captain Powell when he encountered those mysterious objects," Fogarty stated as he began his "stand-up" narration for the camera in the loading bay of the aircraft. "It's a beautiful clear night, and naturally we'll be looking out for anything unusual." This seems to have been a news "hype" on the part of Fogarty, since neither the news crew nor the flight crew claims to have expected to see anything. But nonetheless, if something happened to turn up, he would be ready for it.

During Fogarty's narration, about ten minutes after midnight, as the plane was approaching the region where the previous UFO sighting had been reported, the pilot and copilot allegedly saw unusual bright lights appearing and disappearing in the direction of Kaikoura, but this is not clear from the transcript of their radio conversations. The pilot radioed Wellington to ask if there were any unidentified radar targets in the vicinity of the Kaikoura Penninsula. The controller had reportedly seen several unidentified radio targets about thirteen miles from the plane, in the 1:00 position (just to the right of straight ahead), "appearing and disappearing" in a random manner typical of anomalous radar targets (radar "angels"). "If you've got a chance would you keep an eye on them?" S.A.E. requested.

About a minute afterward, radar reported a target in the 3:00 position, right on the coastline. The crew made no mention of seeing it. A target then briefly appeared in the aircraft's 12:00 position. Captain Startup now claims to have seen it, but made no mention of it at the time. A strong target then popped into the radar scope in the 11:00 position. It disappeared in the next sweep of the radar, without having been visually spotted. "Target now at just left of 9:00 at about two miles"; still nothing visible. One and a half minutes later, a "strong" target popped into the radar scope twelve miles away at the 10:00 position. "S.A.E., we have a TV crew on board. They're trying to record this," the pilot said, proposing to do a left orbit (360 ° turn) to look for it. At about twenty-two minutes after midnight, another target then popped into the radar scope on the plane's left, just two miles away. Again, nothing was seen. The only unusual lights that had been seen thus far, according to the record of the Air Traffic Control tape, were the supposedly very bright lights that were reportedly seen above the city lights of Kaikoura.

Soon after the first radar contact, Captain Startup called the news crew up onto the flight deck and pointed out the lights. After watching for about five minutes, Fogarty recommenced his taped narration. It is "hard to describe my feelings" at the moment, he stated, "but we've seen six or seven or even more bright lights over Kaikoura." "We are now turning around once more to get a better view of these objects," said Fogarty during the first orbit. The objects "are airborne," said Fogarty. "If they weren't, Wellington radar would not be picking them up." However, Maccabee reports that the Wellington radar can "see" down to the surface in this region.

During this portion of the trip south, the camerman obtained three separate film segments of a few seconds each in which a brilliant blue-white light appears and disappears. The precise time and location at which the photographs were taken is not known. One of these lights appears to have been to the right of the plane, which would be to the west, toward land, if the plane were on its direct course to Christchurch, or could be any direction at all if the plane were still finishing up its orbit. The other two segments carry no information as to the direction the camera was pointing. No details are seen in the light, and no objects are visible in the background.

There is about a five-minute break in the Air Traffic Control tape at this point. When it resumes, the aircraft confirms seeing an object with "a flashing light" dead ahead at three miles, also sighted on radar. This is the first apparently consistent radar/visual incident of the flight. At this point the Wellington Control Tower telephoned Christchurch. "S.A.E. is UFO hunting with me," Wellington explained. Fogarty's narration at this point proclaims that the UFO lights were so bright that they seemed to be "lighting up the sky of the town," and the other witnesses agree that the unidentified lights were brighter than the town lights. However, the film taken of the area around the city does not appear to confirm this. Maccabee says that the witnesses' observations may be confirmed by a different segment of the film shot about this time that appears to show a row of faint lights fading in and out of view. To me, these look like lights on the shoreline badly underexposed. Fogarty proclaimed himself to be a "firm convert" as of that moment.

As the plane turned toward Christchurch there were radar targets behind the aircraft at a distance of ten to fifteen miles; because of their position, it is not known whether anything was there to be seen. Shortly afterward, a radar target appeared one mile behind the plane. Fogarty asserted that the object was "following" them, but Wellington radar said no such thing; the target seemed to be stationary. (Stationary targets should not be seen on properly-functioning MTI scopes.) A second radar target popped into view at a distance of four miles, while the first target then disappeared. Once again, the object was not seen; Maccabee says that this is because nobody bothered to look for it. Fogarty continued his filmed narration with great flourish, proclaiming that it was "really getting a bit frightening" up there in the aircraft. A "whole formation" of UFOs was behind them, this newsman flatly asserted, demonstrating that astonishing lust for sensation that almost invariably characterizes the media's treatment of UFOs. Fogarty complained that it was unfortunately next to impossible to film these UFOs, however, because by the time the cameraman could focus in on them, they would disappear.

Wellington then reported "a strong target right in formation with you; could be left or right. Your target has doubled in size." However, nothing was seen. Meanwhile, the previous target vanished. About forty seconds later, Wellington reported that the aircraft target had reduced to normal size. The copilot then reportedly saw a faint greenish light above and to the left of the green wingtip light. Fogarty described it as looking like a "very faint star" that flashed with a very bright white and green light. According to Fogarty, this object, like many others, could not be filmed because it would just "appear and disappear"; Maccabee adds that it was too far to the right to be filmed unless the cameraman climbed into the copilot's seat. Wellington radar did confirm this target in the plane's 3:00–4:00 position, at a distance of about four miles.

By this time, Safe Alpha Echo had traveled into the Air Traffic Control zone of Christchurch. The radar operators at Wellington and Christchurch were now in regular telephone contact, revealing an interesting discrepancy; while peculiar radar targets had been seen popping in and out of existence all night by the Wellington scope, Christchurch saw virtually nothing, despite the fact that some targets were within its 100-mile range. Wellington saw a target in the aircraft's 5:00 position at ten miles. "No, nothing," Christchurch responded. Wellington described its motion. "Not a thing." If the UFOs that were reportedly pursuing the aircraft were in fact real objects and above about 7000 feet elevation (as they seemed to be), they would have been detected at the same time, in the same place, by both radars, and moreover would have coincided with the positions of the lights reported by the observers.

Unfortunately, the Wellington tape did not record the last twenty-six minutes of the flight to Christchurch, and the Christchurch Air Traffic Control tape is no longer in existence, so we must rely upon individuals' memories in reconstructing this segment of the incident. Fogarty stated on his tape that the Christchurch radar had picked up a target about six miles behind the plane. At that time Wellington radar also showed a target behind the plane, but it was at a distance of fifteen miles. The plane made another orbit, but nothing was seen. Shortly before landing, copilot Guard reportedly saw a light pacing the aircraft at what appeared to be a lower altitude, which appeared to be flashing regularly. Because of his duties involving the landing, he was unable to watch it continuously. He thought that it might be the headlights of a vehicle traveling on a road along the coast, until it reportedly crossed a river without slowing down, although a highway bridge might make it possible to achieve such a feat. Christchurch radar reportedly had a target in this position.

Just before landing, Fogarty recorded that Christchurch radar had warned them that six UFOs were "coming straight towards us." No one else recalls hearing such a statement. Fogarty's UFO narration was frequently exaggerated and sensationalized. It has been said in his defense that he, unlike Crockett, was not wearing headphones, and thus could not clearly hear what was being said on the aircraft radio. But if he did not know the facts of the matter, he seemed not to care, recording for future broadcast a curious mixture of information and misinformation.

After the landing, while discussing the UFO events with the crew, the Christchurch radar controller attributed the final target to a "side lobe" problem, which may be a satisfactory solution, even though according to the copilot the side lobe was reported to have continued inland after the plane landed. When interviewed by Maccabee six weeks later, the controller would neither confirm nor deny any anomalous Christchurch targets, but "whatever he saw was unimpressive to him," according to Maccabee.

While on the ground at Christchurch, Fogarty reportedly saw a bright orange-yellow light that appeared to fade and pulsate, "similar to the lights we had seen on the downward trip." The ground crew, who worked there every night, said that it was just the light on a radio tower. But Fogarty did not accept this explanation and insisted it was a real UFO. Startup also reported seeing "a big bright light similar to the ones we saw at Kaikoura" while on the ground at Christchurch and was incredulous when told that it was a light on a radio tower. Several months later, William Ireland visited the Christchurch airfield and photographed what he says was the same "UFO" reported by Startup and Fogarty; a light atop a radio tower.

S.A.E. remained on the ground in Christchurch for approximately an hour and a quarter, to allow its cargo of newspapers to be unloaded. Quentin Fogarty says that he had originally planned to remain in Christchurch with his friend, fellow newsman Dennis Grant, who was meeting him at the airport. But Ngaire Crockett, the sound recordist, had apparently seen enough UFOs for one night. Upset by the night's events, she decided to remain in Christchurch until the next day. (Fogarty notes that she was afraid of flying, even when no UFOs were supposedly in the vicinity.) Her husband, David Crockett, returned to Blenheim aboard S.A.E. Because there was now a vacant spot aboard the aircraft, newsman Grant opted to make the return flight with his friend Fogarty.

At 2:17 AM, S.A.E. was airborne once again. Approximately three minutes after takeoff, the aircraft climbed above a low cloud cover that blanketed the land (the sky over the ocean was quite clear). Almost immediately, they reportedly spotted a brilliant light about 20° to the right of the aircraft's heading, or east-northeast of Christchurch. On closer inspection, it appeared to be two lights, the brighter one on top with a fainter one below it, as if a reflection on the ocean. "This is quite incredible, really," Fogarty exclaimed. "We've only been flying for three minutes, and we've already picked up two unidentified flying objects."

Captain Startup had the impression that he was seeing the full moon without any features (the moon was not visible that night). Copilot Guard described it as a "squashed orange"; Dennis Grant, as a "Ping Pong ball"; Quentin Fogarty, as a "very, very bright star." The light sporadically disappeared behind clouds and was reported to be so bright that it lit up the clouds around it. David Crockett succeeded in photographing the light, his film showing it to fade in and out. The plane's radar was switched on, and it reportedly showed a sizable target whose position coincided with that of the object, roughly twenty to twenty-two miles away. The object was out of range of the Wellington radar. Christchurch radar, however, could have picked up the object, but did not. According to Maccabee, this indicates that the object was below 3,000 feet in altitude, in the Christchurch radar's "cone of silence."

The events that transpired next are both the most crucial and the most confused of the entire flight. As they headed north, the object seemed to move further toward the right. The line of sight estimated for this object when it was first seen, while the aircraft was flying a straight path defined by radio navigation aids as the "MOTO track," was about the same as the line of sight to the main body of the Japanese squid fishing fleet, some 155 miles east and slightly south of Christchurch, although some estimates place the line as much as 25° north of that position. Unfortunately, we have no accurate measurements of the object's position angle, and the estimates of the various witnesses disagree by as much as 20°. The conflicting values result in an uncertainty of many tens of miles in the position of the object. Later, just before the aircraft left the MOTO track, the line of sight fell off to the right as one would expect for a stationary object, but the witnesses' estimates now place the UFO to the south of the fleet, which was then putting out more light than the entire city of Christchurch. Yet none of the witnesses said anything at the time about seeing the fleet, at least as far as is shown by the air traffic control tape and Fogarty's tape (they afterward claimed to have seen the fleet). They did not photograph the lights of the fleet, nor did they use the overwhelming brilliance of the fleet as an obvious reference point for their supposed UFO, which was at most just 20° away. All they photographed, all they remarked about seeing, was that extremely brilliant UFO. When I spoke with Fogarty in July 1980, he said that he could not recall seeing *any* boats or lighthouses at this point in the flight, only UFOs.

However, there are problems with the hypothesis that the witnesses saw the main body of the squid fishing fleet, some 145 miles away (plate 41). Because of the plane's altitude, the elevation of the lights above the sea, and the glow of the lights in the atmosphere, the lights would have been quite visible at that range, even in the absence of any mirage. Captain Startup afterward claimed to have seen the squid fishing fleet at the same time as the object: "We saw the squid fleet that night. It was nowhere near where we spotted the lights." Yet Maccabee's charts show that the line of sight to the fleet was in the same general direction as the supposed UFO. Captain Startup has ridiculed the idea that they may have seen the fishing fleet, saying, "It was unlikely that a squid boat was fishing at that altitude."[9] Yet if the UFO were actually airborne above 3,000 feet and moving, as alleged, it would have been picked up by the far more powerful Christchurch radar, which was seeing a blip for the aircraft but not for the UFO. On the other hand, the estimated angle of the object below the horizon is incompatible with a truly distant object. However, since the plane was at various times climbing and banking, it seems likely that horizon angles could be seriously misjudged, especially since the aircraft was over a dark ocean with no visible points of reference (and since Fogarty was interpreting every motion of the plane as the UFO moving up or down).

Captain Startup decided to turn toward the object for a better look, flying 90° east of the MOTO track for perhaps twelve miles. Crockett mounted a telephoto lens in his camera, obtaining more footage showing only a brilliant, overexposed light. Much of this footage was out of focus, which does not seem to have harmed its commercial value. The large, grossly out-of-focus "beach ball" image is the most frequently seen still frame of the entire footage. The witnesses estimated that the line of sight to the UFO was as much as 40° to 60° south of the line of sight to where the fleet must have been. They claim that the UFO passed between the plane and the Banks Peninsula, although the brilliant lighthouses on that peninsula do not appear on the film. Maccabee originally concluded, based on all the testimony, that the plane flew directly over the UFO, and that the crew's failure to observe the separate lights of a fishing boat proved that a boat must be ruled out. Later, Maccabee obtained additional data, which this time "proved" that as the plane turned to the right the UFO did also, keeping the same relative distances, like two dancers on a dance floor (or like a car being "followed" by a distant celestial object, which will appear to recede if you approach it).

After several minutes, Startup reportedly lost sight of the object due to it being blocked by the nose of the aircraft, although copilot Guard must have been able to see it. Even though the film crew was still watching the mysterious UFO, Startup called off the chase and brought the aircraft back to the MOTO track. Who can say what discoveries were denied to science by his sudden loss of curiosity? The precise distance they traveled off the MOTO track is not known, nor is the precise heading they took afterward. There are certain irreconcilable difficulties in attempting to determine the precise schedule and sequence of events at this point, working from Fogarty's tape and the tape of the Wellington control tower.

After the left turn, the object was apparently once again on the right of the aircraft where Crockett could film it. However, Startup reportedly saw the object reappear to the *front-left* and apparently above the aircraft. At first, Maccabee argued that Startup saw the UFO that the plane flew directly over; but when the object was "moved," in subsequent writings he argued that a second UFO briefly appeared, seen only by Startup on the left of the plane, while everyone else was still watching the first object on the right. However, only one UFO was reportedly detected by the aircraft radar, and none on Christchurch radar. William Ireland has suggested that Startup saw the planet Jupiter to his left, which was shining brightly in that part of the sky. Maccabee does not accept this, however, because Startup's estimation of the brightness and motion of the second object, if accurate, would not be consistent with Jupiter.

Maccabee rejects the hypothesis that the brilliant object photographed here was a fishing boat (or boats), largely because the reported position of the objects seems incompatible with a totally stationary object. However, the reported visual positions of the object were never accurately measured or recorded, and the witnesses' accounts were sometimes mutually inconsistent. (For example, Dennis Grant wrote "2:30, directly ahead," but the flight crew insists that the object was nowhere near that position.) The object's initial position on the aircraft radar is nowhere near the final visual position of the object, which would suggest rapid motion, *if* the same object is indeed the cause of both. It is next to impossible to report accurately the motion of a luminous object against a black background from an aircraft moving around the axis of pitch, yaw, and roll. It is known beyond any doubt that there were dozens of fishing boats off the east coast of New Zealand's South Island at the time and that each of them carried up to 360,000 watts of incandescent light to lure their prey from the ocean depths.

Measurements of the brightness of the object on the film made by Maccabee suggest that the object *could* possibly have been a fishing boat in the position indicated by the aircraft radar before that object was lost when the aircraft turned.[10] Ireland argues that this is what it was.[11] A boat on the surface would escape detection by the Christchurch radar, as did this supposed UFO. The main counterargument is that, while it would reportedly have been perfectly legal for a boat to fish in that position *if* it reported its position to the government, no boat did. (Are boats of some nations in the habit of fishing illegally?) The argument against the bright light being the distant fishing fleet is Maccabee's calculation that at this distance the fleet would not have been as bright as the object on film. This is, however, mainly based upon the measurement of a single frame that shows a peculiar anomaly, but the measurement may be in error, although Maccabee says that it seems to fit in well with other measurements on the film. Philip J. Klass suggests that they may have photographed one of the two brilliant lighthouses near the reported position of the object. The main argument about this is that the lighthouses display a flashing pattern while the UFO, though apparently fading out occasionally, had a steady bright light most of the time.

To me, the least credible aspect of this phase of the sighting was the witnesses' total failure to describe seeing any fishing boats at all! Startup *now* claims to have seen the squid fleet. "It was nowhere near where we spotted the lights," he said, contradicting what we know must be true. But at the time, they saw *only* UFOs, reported only UFOs, and somehow missed the obvious opportunity to use the brilliantly lit, stationary squid boats as reference points for the UFOs, whose only now-known reference frame is the body of the moving aircraft. If only the crew had said "the UFO is about twenty degrees to the right of the fishing fleet," it would have removed the suspicion that the UFO *was* the fishing fleet.

Continuing the flight northward to Blenheim, about ten minutes afterward Wellington radar reported a target twenty miles from the plane, six miles north of Kaikoura. Maccabee reports that it "may" have been seen on the plane's radar (no one is sure) but nothing was seen visually. Wellington soon reported two more radar targets at heading 11:00, distance fifteen miles. Again nothing was seen. "We don't appear to be picking it up quite so easily on this leg," Captain Startup replied. "We had them very bright southbound, but, uh, seem to be a little less active, visually anyway."

Then there was still another radar target, heading 9:00, distance eight miles; once again, no report that it was seen. Quentin Fogarty recommenced his commentary, stating that there had been "no further activity . . . I've had quite enough of UFOs for one night," he added. Maccabee notes that while Captain Startup reported nothing at the time, he allegedly told the other witnesses just after the flight that the plane's radar picked up targets whose positions appeared to match those reported by Wellington. However, he too had apparently had enough UFOs for one night and said nothing about them; hence the existence of these targets on the aircraft radar cannot now be confirmed.

Fogarty afterwards was to claim that during this segment of the flight "something equally strange happened inside the plane." After becoming aware of a light coming up the stairwell from the cargo hold, Fogarty relates, "I felt a presence in the back of the plane. I turned to look down the stairs and my eyes met Dennis's. We said nothing." Not only was their aircraft being pursued by squadrons of UFOs, but it apparently was haunted as well! Perhaps stranger still, since Maccabee has noted serious inconsistencies in attempts to reconstruct the time sequence of the previous "close encounter" segment, Fogarty and Crockett are now suggesting that the plane entered a "time warp"[12] when it left the MOTO track and lost several minutes, citing Maccabee as their source. While not denying making that statement, Maccabee says that the occurrence of a "time warp" cannot be proven, since the discrepancy may also be due to an error in one of the accounts.

Having passed Kaikoura and now on the final leg of the trip back to Blenheim, the crew asked Wellington if the radar showed a target in the 12:00 position. "Affirmative. I have a strong target at 12:00 to you at twenty miles," came the reply. Startup reported that he had "that one" on radar, and "quite a good visual display" as well. Crockett succeeded in capturing a rapidly flashing light on film. Other flashing lights were seen, in a direction indicating that they were apparently on or over land. "It looks like an aircraft beacon" said Fogarty about one of the lights. To determine whether it was, Wellington Air Traffic Control called Blenheim, asking that the rotary beacon of the flight service at Blenheim be shut off. When it was, one of the most prominent UFOs disappeared. Maccabee observes that the object captured on film here was not the Blenheim beacon, since it does not match the color or periodicity of this or any other beacon. Unfortunately, no one aboard the aircraft seems to remember having seen the UFO captured on film. The flashing light *does* seem to have the right periodicity to be an aircraft anti-collision light, as Philip J. Klass has noted. The Wellington Air Traffic Control, however, has reportedly stated that there was absolutely no other traffic in the area at the time. It may be possible that the aircraft's own anti-collision light was photographed, reflecting off the propeller blades or some other part of the aircraft body. The color, however, seems to be not what one would expect. Maccabee speculates that they photographed a flashing UFO that actually went "off" at about the same time as the beacon. Almost any object on the ground, such as an emergency vehicle, could conceivably be responsible for the UFO that was captured on film but not noticed at the time.

Wellington reported four more radar targets about a mile off the coast. One or more of these "may have been seen," according to Maccabee. Another target appeared directly ahead of the aircraft, just two miles distant. "No sighting of that one." The crew reported seeing a bright light that appeared to be behind Blenheim airfield. "Nothing showing over there at all," Wellington radar responded. A minute later, the crew asked Wellington if there were any targets in the 2:00–3:00 position. "Nothing showing up," was the reply. Wellington had a target in the 9:30 position; the passengers "may" have seen something there, Maccabee reports. Captain Startup reported seeing lights, like the cabin lights on fishing boats, in the Cook Strait shortly before landing at Blenheim. Wellington saw just one boat, although the crew saw many. These were almost certainly squid fishing boats, moving from the western coastal waters to the eastern coastal waters of New Zealand. As the plane circled near Cape Campbell to lose altitude, the crew asked if there was a target over Picton. "No. No targets at all," Wellington replied. That was the final UFO of the night. The plane landed safely at Blenheim a few minutes thereafter.

Did the radar targets represent genuine UFOs? "At all times on Saturday night there were at least one or two UFOs on the screen," said Wellington radar operator Geoff Causer, indicating either that some very strange radar-propagation conditions were occurring or else that an entire squadron of alien craft were buzzing New Zealand's South Island.[13] Since several apparently stationary targets turned up on a radar that supposedly showed only moving targets, one might be pardoned for surmising that something was amiss. But the most convincing anti-UFO evidence was the behavior of the radar targets themselves, popping in and out of existence, here for one radar scan, there for another, with no clear direction or pattern of motion. Sometimes separate targets merged into one and the size of the target sometimes varied. This Alice-in-Wonderland behavior is typical of radar "angels" (spurious targets) caused by certain meteorological conditions. Angels have been the bane of radar users ever since the earliest days of radar during World War II; and even today, with many kinds of radar units in use throughout the world, scientists still continue research into the subject of radar propagation. It is a question of great importance, both for military and commercial purposes, and the final answers are far from established.

It *is* known, however, that radar angels in temperate regions occur most frequently in the middle of the summer. In New Zealand, December is a summer month. A chart published by the Naval Research Laboratory showing the regions where anomalous radar propagation most frequently occurs, shows that in the Southern Hemisphere summer the east coast of New Zealand has at least a 30 percent chance of experiencing anomalous radar propagations at any given time.[14] Furthermore, New Zealand weather records indicated the presence of at least two, if not three, separate atmospheric layers of anomalous propagation at that time. Two temperature inversion layers (where the temperature increases with altitude, the opposite of normal) were detected by a radiosonde balloon, as well as what appears to be an extraordinarily strong "superautoconvective layer," the opposite of a temperature inversion (the temperature decreases with height, but much faster than normal), which also plays havoc with radar.

The New Zealand meteorologist who prepared my chart wrote on it, at that point, "This feature is most unusual but the radiosonde trace has been checked and seems correct." However, later charts prepared by that same office show this feature crossed out on the suspicion that the reading may have been erroneous, so unusual is this superautoconvective layer. When I wrote for an explanation, I was advised that some of the radiosondes used during this period had experienced failures, and it was suspected that the apparent superautoconvective layer may have been due to an equipment malfunction. The readings may, however, be quite legitimate, and the question cannot now be definitively answered. In any case, the existence of the two inversion layers has not been challenged.

Temperature inversions also cause visual mirages, resulting in objects that are normally far beyond the horizon becoming temporarily visible, usually inverted, and often distorted almost beyond recognition. Plates 42 and 43 are among the few photographs published that clearly show superior mirages, the result of one or more temperature inversion layers.[15]

Maccabee, using the formulas given in Section 6 of the *Condon Report,* has calculated a Refractive Index Forecast (RIF) for radar, apparently showing that despite two or even three inversion/superautoconvective layers, no anomalous propagation did occur on that night. However, the Naval Research Laboratory research report referred to previously states that "the radiosonde is a slow-response instrument that measures temperature, pressure, and moisture content of the air while being carried aloft by a lighter-than-air balloon . . . A RIF, however, requires both accurate and fast-response measuring instruments, especially for the vapor pressure and temperature parameters. Therefore, the use of radiosonde data seriously limits the ability to detect accurately the significant refractive index gradients needed to obtain a reliable RIF."[16]

Thus while Maccabee's mathematical approach to this question is indeed correct, the only data available to work from—readings from a slow-response radiosonde—are not sufficiently accurate to allow a reliable RIF to be computed. They only show the broad features; we know that there were at least two, if not three, separate layers of abnormal radar (as well as optical) refraction present, but the data concerning their size and extent gives us only a rough picture of the true conditions that prevailed in the upper atmosphere on that night. The Wellington radar technician, however, says that he performed a test that should reveal anomalous propagation, and found none.

In any case, in the great majority of instances, the reported directions and distances of the radar UFOs do not correspond to those of the visual UFOs. In many cases, one is seen when the other is not noted. Maccabee's figures show that in twenty-one separate instances involving possibly simultaneous radar/visual sightings using the Wellington radar, in only five do the direction and distances of the objects appear to correspond even approximately. Thus in 76 percent of the instances, the radar and visual targets do *not* correspond; and in only 24 percent, they do. (We are eliminating those instances in which the direction of the visual target is not known.) Even totally unrelated events will appear to match up a certain percentage of the time, due to chance, although in the great majority of instances they will not. If genuine unidentified flying objects had been present, the radar and visual aspects of *every* genuine sighting would correspond quite well. Since in 76 percent of the cases they do not, the evidence seems to be saying that there was really nothing out of the ordinary present.

Almost as soon as the aircraft had landed at Blenheim, the sensational story of the flight and its film burst into the headlines in New Zealand, and soon the story was making news around the globe. Three nights later, the Royal New Zealand Air Force, acting no doubt in part to quell public concerns about alleged mysterious craft having penetrated New Zealand's airspace, sent out a squadron of Orion aircraft to look into the situation. In their seven-hour UFO hunt, they checked out fourteen unexplained radar targets showing up on the Wellington and Christchurch radars. In the positions of most of these targets, there was nothing at all to be seen. In some positions, the radar targets disappeared before the plane arrived, and they found pockets of severe clear air turbulence. In the position of one of the targets, they found a ship at anchor. While the aircraft made three passes over the ship's position, the ground-based radar plotted the ship in three different positions, "moving" at 50 km/hour. "The odd thing was that between the ship and the radar was a 920 meter [3,000 foot] mountain," said aircraft squadron leader Ray Carran. "Since radar beams theoretically travel in a straight line, I cannot explain how this came about—but I think they should check the radar." The New Zealand Air Force flyers also observed the main body of the Japanese squid fishing fleet, about 160 miles off the coast. "It is turning out an incredible amount of light power," said Carran. "When we were flying equidistant between the fleet and Christchurch, the glow from the fleet was much brighter than that from the city."[17]

As news of the Fogarty/Crockett film spread around the world, explanations for it proliferated as rapidly as did newspaper headlines. Most of the explanations were totally absurd. Sir Bernard Lovell, the famous British astronomer, dismissed the incident as "most probably" meteors that failed to burn up on entering the earth's atmosphere. He should have known better. The duration of the incident, and the relatively low angular velocity of the objects, make the meteor explanation absurd. Noted British amateur astronomer and science writer Patrick Moore suggested the phenomenon was a balloon or an unscheduled aircraft. But this, too, does not fit the reported parameters of duration, distance, and relative motion.

David Mabin, head of New Zealand's Mount John Observatory, first said that the film almost certainly showed Venus. His explanation might have carried more credibility if Venus had risen by the time the film was taken. After seeing the film, he decided it showed Jupiter. A New Zealand physicist, Professor N. Barber, rejected the Venus explanation but for the wrong reason. "Venus is at present crescent-shaped, and these [frames from the film showing the object] were round," he said, betraying total ignorance of the relative angular size of the crescent Venus and the resolution of a hand-held lens. MUFON's representative in New Zealand, Harold Fulton, had even a better "proof" against the Venus hypothesis: "You couldn't get a picture with a telephoto lens with Venus 37.5 million miles away."[18] The sun is nearly three times this distance, yet has overwhelmed many a photograph.

Mr. G. Harrow, a bird-watcher from Kaikoura, ventured the explanation that the objects sighted visually and on radar were "mating mutton birds," reflecting the lights from squid boats off the Kaikoura coast. Dr. J. A. Webb, senior lecturer in electricial engineering at Canterbury University, suggested that the sightings may have been due to car lights "bouncing off" air layers. Mrs. Eru Pilcher of Kaikoura suggested that the UFOs seen were just her cabbages "reflecting off the clouds or something. I've got nearly a quarter of an acre of them—they are big beauties, and their leaves shine in the moonlight."[19]

But perhaps the most intriguing explanation for the objects filmed is that of Australian amateur astronomer Lanigan O'Keefe. He made videotape copies of the film from his TV set and ran them through a "line scan analyzer," which supposedly proved that the object filmed was the planet Jupiter. It even revealed, he says, Jupiter's four bright moons in exactly the correct positions.[20] However, the reported azimuth of the UFO does not usually match that of Jupiter, and the altitude does not match either, although it is possible that Jupiter may have played a minor role in the incident. Worse yet, Mr. O'Keefe originally got a "match" for the positions of Jupiter's moons using the wrong time for the photo; when he later inserted the correct time, it still "matched." This sounds too close for comfort to the "matching" star maps of Marjorie Fish, Charles Atterberg, et al. O'Keefe interprets what is unquestionably an out-of-focus image of the "UFO" as an in-focus image of Jupiter perfectly enlarged by an "atmospheric lens," showing surface features such as equatorial bands and the Great Red Spot—all photographed through an aircraft window, using a hand-held camera!

UFOs became a hot topic in New Zealand, and some local journalists were embarrassed that an Australian TV station, 1,500 miles away, grabbed what seemed to be the story of the century from their own home turf. (New Zealanders must be the first to exploit New Zealand's natural resources, including UFOs!) Thus New Zealand's TV-1 sent a film crew to the Clarence River area near Kaikoura on the morning of January 3, three nights after the Channel O films were obtained. As might be expected, they too were successful. Their UFO was first spotted at 3:15 AM, which corresponds amazingly well with the time of Venus's rising, and its direction matches that of Venus as well. According to reporter Terry Olsen, the object reportedly remained more or less stationary, moving slowly to the left and up, exactly like a celestial body viewed from the Southern Hemisphere. It remained visible even after sunrise: "It appeared to be a silvery star after all the other stars in the sky had fled."

MUFON's Harold Fulton analyzed this film and reported that "the dark spot in the middle of the ball of light is actually the UFO, and the whiteness around it is radiation."[21] Yet one could not hope to find a better description of Venus than that given by the film crew.

J. Allen Hynek obviously agreed, judging from the questions he posed to Terry Olsen on ABC-TV's "Good Morning America" show on January 5, 1979: "I am wondering whether he actually saw Venus at the same time?" An excellent question. "I can't recognize Venus," Olsen replied, "I'm not an astronomer." We thought so. Do you know if the large, circular object photographed was actually in focus? Hynek asked. We have no way of knowing, said Olsen, "the camerman had never operated [this lens] before." Several other penetrating questions by Hynek ascertained that the Clarence River TV-1 film's UFO looked and acted exactly like Venus. However, asked by the show's host for an evaluation, Hynek waffled, muttering that further study was needed. He dared not even whisper the word *Venus*! Elsewhere, however, Hynek had freely conceded that the TV-1 film almost certainly shows Venus. But appearing before several million viewers on live network-TV, Hynek was unwilling to give aid and comfort to the enemy by suggesting that this dramatic-looking UFO film depicts nothing but Venus badly out of focus.[22]

The selling of the saucer films began in earnest almost as soon as S.A.E. returned to Blenheim. The story was first broken by Dennis Grant, and by late morning "the Christchurch radio was going crazy over our story," said Fogarty.[23] Channel O ordered Fogarty to leave for Melbourne later that same day; he had not slept at all the previous night, nor at any time since the morning of Saturday, December 30. Arriving in Melbourne on January 1, Fogarty worked all night on what he modestly described as "the story of the century." So relentlessly did he push himself in the preparation of this superhot news item and in battling Channel O's management concerning copyrights, that by January 2 he admitted himself to a hospital, suffering from nervous exhaustion. He had gone without sleep for fifty hours.

Almost as soon as the Crockett film had been developed in Melbourne, rights to the footage were being aggressively hawked to news organizations throughout the world. Fogarty's scoop was shown Monday night, January 1, in Australia. Twelve hours later, Monday night in North America, the films were shown in the United States on the CBS Evening News. The rights had been sold to the BBC in England and to Hong Kong TV, as well as to CBS, for "undisclosed sums." The tapes in Hong Kong were offered for international syndication through the UPI-ITN news-film network, on offer to any bidder.[24]

Even the TV-1 film, which was unquestionably Venus, suddenly became hot commercial property. Since CBS had bought the rights to the first New Zealand UFO film for its newscasts, ABC quickly grabbed the second, as did the BBC, Japanese, and Hong Kong TV stations as well. "We could make tens of thousands of dollars, maybe more," TV-1 director Doug Eckhoff gleefully exclaimed. In another interview he said, "I won't say what we've been selling it for—but the prices have been very high."[25] No one, least of all ABC–TV, seemed to care that it was just an out-of-focus film of Venus rising. Apparently, when journalistic ethics come into conflict with the profit potential offered by Barnum-style promotional humbug, even "responsible" news organizations almost invariably shed their pretensions without a moment's hesitation.

Before the films were two weeks old, Channel O's producer Leonard Lee was in the United States appearing on television programs and negotiating with publishers for photo rights to the UFO film. His trip was paid for by the tabloid *National Enquirer*. Bruce Maccabee met with Lee many times and later traveled to New York City from his home near Washington, D.C., to participate in Channel O's press conference at the plush Essex House hotel. While in New York, Lee negotiated with representatives of media mogul Rupert Murdoch's publishing empire, which includes the tabloid *The Star*.

Lee apparently enjoyed more success there than in his negotiations with the *National Enquirer. The Star* published a series of articles promoting the film, quoting various experts, including one in which Maccabee states, "So much of our work ends up in shooting down turkeys. This is one turkey that deserves the closest possible research." They also published a photo of Leonard Lee in bed in his hotel room, with a briefcase supposedly containing the film handcuffed to his arm. The headline read, "Sensational UFO film arrives here amid incredible security measures."[26] This was pure hokum.

I appeared on a TV show over WJLA–TV in Washington, D.C., along with Leonard Lee and Bruce Maccabee, taped on January 18, 1979 and aired on January 28. Off camera, Lee was as polite and refined as could be. But when the cameras started rolling, he attempted to interrupt my opening statement. When this did not succeed, the cameras remaining on me, he fixed his gaze upon me, stared daggers, and made a frightful face, hoping to unnerve me and destroy my composure while I was still on camera. When this also failed, given his turn to speak, he scornfully dismissed my discussion of temperature inversions and their effect upon radar and distant lights as the latest tomfoolery that the know-nothing debunkers were throwing at him, and he went through the list that included "mating mutton birds" and other such lunacy. He apparently feared that I was threatening his extremely lucrative commercial property. After the filming was over, Lee became congenial once again.

A few months afterward, Leonard Lee became mixed up in yet another bizarre incident. In July 1979, NASA's Skylab satellite, a helpless giant whose final hours were completely at the mercy of the vagaries of the upper atmosphere and storms on the sun, had almost the entire earth on a "Skylab alert" for falling debris. When it finally made its fiery reentry to earth, pieces of Skylab fell harmlessly into the Indian Ocean and the deserts of western Australia. Soon afterwards, a wild rumor began circulating in Australia that the Skylab, space home to three different astronaut crews, was actually engaged in a secret espionage mission and was deliberately brought down by NASA "near" the Pine Gap maximum-security satellite tracking command in Australia so that it could be whisked away to the United States.

Leonard Lee soon began to make hay of this yarn too. He claimed that NASA had known in advance exactly where Skylab would land and that Channel O broadcast this top-secret information, but a .U.S. government official had asked him to "drop it." "I told him I had no intention of doing so," Lee explained. Lee afterward attended a NASA team's Australian press conference concerning Skylab's reentry. "When we asked questions about Skylab and Pine Gap, the NASA spokesman was visibly shaken and his hands shook," Lee claimed. "The question was asked three times. The only reply was that no mention was to be made of Pine Gap."[27]

On April 20, 1979, Timothy Green Beckley, head of Global Communications, the publishers of *UFO Review,* held a press conference in New York

City to promote the Channel O film, in cooperation with the Australian Broadcasting Commission. Beckley, UFO exploiter extraordinaire, is regularly the sponsor of many wild and woolly UFO ads, such as "Yes! Aliens Walk Amongst Us — But Are You Prepared to Meet Them?" Maccabee once again traveled to New York to assist in the presentation. Beckley's press release stated, "Because of the one-of-a-kind nature of the film, Global Communications is seeking a $2-million package deal for publishing, TV and motion picture rights." Informed observers doubt that Beckley squeezed two million dollars from the photos, but no one knows for sure just how much he made.

Writer Harry Lebelson was commissioned by *Omni* magazine to do a story on the New Zealand film. Lebelson, working from New York, in January 1979, contacted Quentin Fogarty by telephone in Australia. "The reporter stated that he would not reveal any aspects of the story unless he was paid the sum of $500," Lebelson writes. Unfortunately, instead of refusing payment on journalistic principle, *Omni* haggled about the price. But Fogarty's stated price was firm: there was no interview. Lebelson told Fogarty that the inclusion of his story in a major national magazine would give it legitimacy. "I don't care about legitimacy or illegitimacy," Fogarty replied, "I want to wash my hands of the whole thing." Fogarty subsequently quit his job with Channel O to work on a book about his experience. This is certainly strange behavior for a man who wants to wash his hands of the whole matter. In addition, Captain Startup has written a book on his experience, and David Crockett visited the United States, giving six lectures a day at $2.50 a head.[28] With such financial incentives, objective reporting is likely to take a back seat.

It is doubtful whether the questions about the Channel O film taken the last day of 1978 will ever be settled to everyone's satisfaction. The UFO proponents have rapidly built it into a major "classic" case. The case would have been far more impressive if all of the anomalous radar targets had actually matched the positions of the lights reportedly seen by the witnesses; if the radar targets had not popped in and out of existence like so many gremlins, exactly in the manner of troublesome radar "angels"; if the waters around New Zealand had not been filled with Japanese, Taiwanese, and South Korean squid fishing boats, putting out a quarter to a third of a million watts of incandescent light power *per boat*; if the objects captured on film had shown some clearly discernible structure instead of just a featureless blob of light; if it had not occurred in a place, and at a time, when anomalous radar returns are common; if there had not been two, or even three, different layers of anomalous radar and visual propagation at the time of the incident; if the three radars involved — Wellington, Christchurch, and the aircraft's — had shown unknown objects in the same place at the same time; and if the principals involved in the incident had not immediately plunged into a program of commercial exploitation.

When Hynek says that the Channel O film is "by far the most impressive evidence we have examined in more than 75,000 reported UFO sightings," it shows how weak the supposed evidence for UFOs must actually be.

NOTES

1. J. Allen Hynek, quoted in *The Star* (a tabloid), April 17, 1979.

2. William Ireland, "Unfamiliar Observations of Lights in the Night Sky," New Zealand DSIR Report Number 659, December, 1979; Bruce Maccabee, unpublished comments on Ireland's paper.

3. *The Australian,* January 3, 1979; Channel O News Documentary, January, 1979.

4. *The Dominion,* New Zealand, January 2, 1979.

5. *The Australian,* January 3, 1979.

6. Bruce S. Maccabee, "What Really Happened in New Zealand," unpublished paper, 1979, pp. 38–40. Adaptations of this paper have been published by several UFO groups; see MUFON *Journal,* June and July 1979; GSW Bulletin, Summer and Fall, 1979.

7. *The Dominion,* January 2, 1979.

8. Harry Lebelson, "UFO Update," *Omni,* May 1979, p. 32.

9. *Auckland Star,* New Zealand, January 3, 1979.

10. Bruce S. Maccabee, "Photometric Properties of an Unidentified Bright Object Seen off the Coast of New Zealand," *Applied Optics* August 1, 1979, p. 2527.

11. William Ireland and M. K. Andrews, comments on Maccabee's paper, *Applied Optics* December 1, 1979, p. 3889. See also Maccabee's reply to their comments, *Applied Optics,* June 1, 1980, p. 1745.

12. Fogarty's comments about a time warp are in *Australian Playboy,* August 1979. Crockett's are in an interview in the *Honolulu Advertiser,* July 26, 1979.

13. *The Dominion,* January 2, 1979.

14. Purves, "Geophysical Aspects of Atmospheric Refraction," Naval Research Laboratory Report 7725, June 7, 1974, p. 14.

15. The best account yet published of mirages and related phenomena is found in *The Nature of Light and Colour in the Open Air* by the Dutch astronomer M. Minnaert (Dover Books, 1954).

16. Purves, p. 38.

17. *Auckland Star,* January 3, 1979.

18. *New Zealand Herald,* January 3, 1979; Associated Press story, January 3 (*Omaha World Herald,* p. 13); New Zealand *Evening Standard,* January 3.

19. *Christchurch Press,* New Zealand, January 4, 1979; *The Dominion,* January 3; United Press International, January 4.

20. *Auckland Star,* January 5, 1979.

21. *New Zealand Evening Standard,* January 4, 1979.

22. For more information on the TV-1 film, see Sheaffer, "The New Zealand UFO Flap," *Skeptical Inquirer* 3, no. 3 (Spring 1979), p. 5.

23. *Australian Playboy,* August, 1979.

24. *The Dominion,* January 3, 1979; *Washington Star,* January 2.

25. *The Dominion,* January 4, 1979; *The Australian,* January 4.

26. *The Star,* January 30, 1979.

27. "Perth, Western Australia." Newspaper name uncertain, September 2, 1979.

28. Lebelson, "UFO Update"; Crockett, *Honolulu Advertiser,* July 26, 1979; Bill Startup, *The Kaikoura UFOs* (Auckland: Hodder and Stroughton, 1980).

22

THE UNIVERSE OF
THE TRUE BELIEVER

*If we turn away from science, our civilization will collapse. Scientists
must convince people that it is dangerous to accept irrationalisms . . .*
—Isaac Asimov[1]

If the preceding chapters demonstrate anything, it is that the "scientific"
proponents of UFO research have little in common with genuine scientists.
Despite their lofty rhetoric and pretensions of scientific objectivity, the irrationalisms embraced wholeheartedly by various segments of the UFO
movement—"alternate realities," the Men in Black, Mothmen, Wolf Girls,
and countless other absurdities and hoaxes—clearly identify the UFOlogists
as brothers under the skin with other irrationalists of present and prior ages:
astrologers, aura-readers, theosophists, pyramid-energy promoters, Bermuda Triangle enthusiasts, and others too numerous to mention.

A universe populated by such fabulous creatures and forces as these has
little in common with the world-view of modern science. Such a view seems
vaguely familiar to all of us; we have plainly encountered it somewhere
before. Indeed: it is the universe of the young child, where goblins magically
pop into existence under one's bed, where monsters dwell in the closet as
soon as the light is put out, and no amount of logic suffices to dispel the
fantasy.

If the reader thinks that this judgment is too harsh, consider a few of the
claims taken seriously by some of the recognized and widely applauded
leaders of the UFO movement. Jacques Vallee has written in a very serious
vein about the Red Meu and the Black Meu, creatures reportedly seen only
by his three-year-old daughter, which live in "haunted houses" and play
with "ghosts." "At least I *thought* those were fantasies," Vallee *meu*sed

several years afterward, deeming the mysterious Meu worthy of three pages of discussion in his book, *The Edge of Reality*. John Keel claims in his *Mothman Prophecies* that one night, while out UFO watching, *the moon simply failed to rise,* as if something the size of the moon could leave its orbit and not be missed. Allen H. Greenfield, during his "true believer" phase, cited Keel's nonrising moon as an example of a "reality alteration" associated with UFOs.[2] I looked into the matter, and found that it proves nothing more than that Keel must have misread an almanac. Soon after Greenfield published my letter pointing out that the moon was not expected to be readily visible at 3:30 AM, the exact time Keel reported it to be missing, I received a letter from Keel containing heretofore unpublished details that stretched the yarn still further; never mind the failure to consult an almanac correctly, says he, the moon was *still* missing at 6 AM.

"Emotionally, I find myself militantly antitechnological. Emotionally, I want to condemn science," says UFOlogist and witch Margot Adler, approvingly quoted in Brad Steiger's *Gods of Aquarius*.[3] Given the fact that UFOlogists invariably close ranks when challenged by skeptics, each defending the other's right to be irrational, there can be no reasonable doubt that the UFO movement as a whole represents a regression to prescientific modes of thinking. UFOlogy is not the only place that creatures like Mothman and Bigfoot pop effortlessly in and out of existence, where a flying craft is visible to a handful of people in a major city at noontime and invisible to hundreds of thousands of others. Such bizarre beliefs are part of the daily life of preschool children, who populate their universe with trolls and goblins and invisible animals. However, unlike today's "progressive" UFOlogists, normal children soon outgrow such juvenile patterns of thinking.

Most significant of all in establishing the true frame of orientation of the UFO movement is the way that all UFOlogists, from the most imaginative contactee to the most conservative there-may-be-something-to-it hedger, always see the enemy in the direction of science. *"Pas d'ennemi à gauche"*— no enemies on the left—has for years been the principle under which French Marxists from the most moderate to the most radical have operated, and analogously present-day UFO proponents almost never see danger in any views more extreme than their own.

When someone sets out to write on "scientific" UFOlogy, the general thrust of the work invariably is that the scientific community has been excessively skeptical on the subject of UFOs. The obvious and undeniable fact that science has quite correctly questioned the vast majority of UFO "research," whose methodology is seriously flawed, is either just glossed over or ignored altogether.

A scientific UFOlogist would, of course, reserve his criticism for those whose sins against science have been greatest—and that undeniably lies on the side of UFO belief. An objective book on the subject would have to be, at a minimum, 90 percent "debunking," because the field of UFOlogy certainly contains not less than 90 percent "bunk." However, when someone like Hynek or Friedman begins to criticize a specific researcher, it is nearly always the work of a skeptic such as Klass, Menzel, Condon, Oberg, or myself that is held up for scorn. How often have "scientific" UFOlogists — Hendry, Maccabee, Hynek, Saunders — publicly criticized Gray Barker, Timothy Green Beckley, Major Donald Keyhoe, or Brad Steiger? All of the latter are purveyors of the most absurd and sensationalist UFO nonsense, but all are members in good standing in the UFO movement. The principal "enemy" is always preceived to be in the direction of reason; he is never among those more credulous than I; he is an outsider and is not part of the pro-UFO movement. UFOlogists are all brothers and sisters under the skin, and anyone who loudly ridicules John Keel's Mothman or Betty Hill's UFO landing-site menaces others as well, by bringing the harsh gaze of critical scrutiny directly upon the subject. (Thus bibliographies compiled by UFO proponents generally cite even highly unreliable pro-UFO books but seldom books by UFO skeptics.) Once the light of reason is trained upon the most obvious inanities in the UFO movement, who can say where the destruction of cherished beliefs will end? Might not something sacred to *me* also tumble?

Thus we see that UFOlogy as a powerful social movement *is fundamentally a reaction against science and reason.* The emotional foundation of the movement, the way it forces everyone to choose sides between "us" (any and all UFO proponents) and "them" (any and all UFO skeptics) clearly shows that UFOlogy is more comfortable with the purveyors of outrageous nonsense than with scientific skeptics. The former are felt to be largely harmless, if not downright progressive (for example, UFOlogy's belated laurels for "hole in the pole" Ray Palmer), while the latter are felt to threaten UFOlogy's very existence. If UFOlogy were a true science, its attitude would be precisely the opposite. Indeed, were a young science such as cosmology to embrace or even tolerate such bizarre groups as the Velikovskians or the flat-earthers, the discipline would be in far greater danger from its friends outside the scientific community than from its enemies within it. The preference for eccentrics who incline toward one's own beliefs over scientific critics who challenge them — this is the true litmus test of irrationality.

But even granting that the advocacy of UFO beliefs is irrational — in what way is it harmful? Many people hasten to tell us that UFO myths and other paranormal beliefs are harmless aberrations. So what if people believe in psychic powers, or in creatures cruising the skies in celestial crockery? What harm does it do?

It is because of scientific and technological advances — sanitation, preventive medicine, high-technology agriculture, and similar developments — that the rapid world-population growth of the past few decades has been made possible. Today, the voice of antiscience has gained the upper hand in many fashionable and "educated" circles. Psychic insight is deemed superior to scientific research; the way to solve the energy crisis is to turn back the clock (to outdoor plumbing and oxcarts); and the answer to food shortages is to return to nature (that is, 80 percent of the population existing at a subsistence level on primitive collective farms, using horse-drawn ploughs). It is a sad commentary on present-day educational facilities that platitudes such as these pass for "advanced" thinking today.

But reality clearly dictates otherwise. The world's population has mushroomed to its present level because of modern medicine and high-technology agriculture. Should these advances be repealed, the iron hand of reality will swiftly and inevitably reduce the world's population to what it was in preindustrial times, through starvation, pestilence, war, or a combination of the three. Every paranormal cultist who proclaims that "free energy" can be obtained by nonmaterial means, every "no growth" advocate who strives to turn back the clock to a pre-industrial "paradise" that never really existed, is as great a threat to human life as the anti-Semitic advocate of Aryan supremacy. All are promoting an ideology that, if carried to its logical conclusion, can only result in megadeaths. It is modern science and technology that have made it possible for the world to support a population of four billion for the first time in its history, and if these people are to survive at all (let alone grow and prosper), the scientific outlook and the scientific method must be preserved. To advocate "paranormal" or other irrational solutions to the exceedingly complex problems facing the present age is a crime against our children and their children, yet unborn.

The universe of the True Believer is not a newly discovered realm about to burst forth in unheralded splendor. It is actually a return to a very old world, in which goblins and dragons and witches (or the Men in Black and psychic monsters) are every bit as real as the rivers, trees, and mountains we see around us. It is the world in which all of us dwelt in our earliest years, and which people in primitive preindustrial societies inhabit even today. In such a world, monsters materialize behind one's back whenever the room is in darkness, and even the most fundamental tenets of rationality—for example, that a hanging towel or drapery, or whatever, remains what it is when the light is turned off and does not transmogrify into a ghost—are seriously called into question. There are many today who wish us to adopt once again such an irrational outlook—and worse yet, who would have us label it "progress." After so much has been sacrificed to achieve the gains that we all take for granted today, it would be a travesty of history to lose it all to the rising irrationalisms that threaten a new dark age.

NOTES

1. Quoted in the *Christian Science Monitor,* March 6, 1978, p. 19.
2. Jacques Vallee and J. Allen Hynek, *The Edge of Reality* (Chicago: Regnery, 1975), chapter 5; John Keel, *The Mothman Prophecies* (New York: Saturday Review Press, 1975), pp. 132–33; Greenfield, *UFOlogy Notebook,* October 1976.
3. Brad Steiger, *Gods of Aquarius* (New York: Harcourt, Brace, Jovanovich, 1976), p. 64.

INDEX

PAPERBACKS AVAILABLE FROM PROMETHEUS BOOKS

SCIENCE AND THE PARANORMAL

____ 12.95 Ancient Astronauts, Cosmic Collisions   *William Stiebing, Jr.*
____ 11.95 The Bermuda Triangle Mystery—Solved   *Larry Kusche*
____ 13.95 ESP and Parapsychology   *C. E. M. Hansel*
____ 11.95 Flim-Flam!   *James Randi*
____ 12.95 The Fringe of the Unknown   *L. Sprague de Camp*
____ 12.95 The Gemini Syndrome   *Culver and Ianna*
____ 11.95 The Loch Ness Mystery Solved   *Ronald Binns*
____ 16.95 Paranormal Borderlands of Science   *edited by Kendrick Frazier*
____ 13.95 Psychic Paradoxes   *John Booth*
____ 13.95 The Psychology of the Psychic   *Marks and Kammann*
____ 15.95 Science Confronts the Paranormal   *edited by Kendrick Frazier*
____ 16.95 A Skeptic's Handbook of Parapsychology   *edited by Paul Kurtz*
____ 13.95 The Spiritualists   *Ruth Brandon*
____ 10.95 The Truth About Uri Geller   *James Randi*
____ 11.95 UFOs: The Public Deceived   *Philip J. Klass*
____ 13.95 The UFO Verdict   *Robert Sheaffer*

PHILOSOPHY

____ 11.95 Animal Rights and Human Morality   *Bernard Rollin*
____ 10.95 The Art of Deception   *Nicholas Capaldi*
____ 17.95 Business Ethics   *edited by Snoeyenbos, Almeder, and Humber*
____ 17.95 Contemporary Analytic and Linguistic Philosophies   *edited by E. D. Klemke*
____ 17.95 Contemporary Readings in Social and Political Ethics   *edited by Brodsky, Troyer, and Vance*
____ 16.95 Decisions in Philosophy of Religion   *William B. Williamson*
____ 13.95 Esthetics Contemporary   *edited by Richard Kostelanetz*
____ 16.95 Ethics and the Legal Profession   *edited by Davis and Elliston*
____ 17.95 Ethics and the Search for Values   *edited by Navia and Kelly*
____ 9.95 Ethics Without God   *Kai Nielsen*
____ 10.95 Exuberance   *Paul Kurtz*
____ 11.95 Good and Evil   *Richard Taylor*
____ 14.95 An Invitation to Philosophy   *edited by Capaldi, Kelly, and Navia*
____ 17.95 Journeys Through Philosophy (Revised)   *edited by Capaldi, Navia, and Kelly*
____ 15.95 Latin American Philosophy in the Twentieth Century   *edited by Jorge J. E. Gracia*
____ 3.95 On Liberty   *John Stuart Mill*
____ 10.95 Philosophy: An Introduction   *Antony Flew*
____ 15.95 Philosophy and Science Fiction   *edited by Michael Philips*
____ 16.95 Philosophy and Sex (Revised)   *edited by Baker and Elliston*
____ 4.95 The Politics   *Aristotle*
____ 4.95 The Prince   *Niccolo Machiavelli*
____ 11.95 The Problem of God   *Peter A. Angeles*
____ 5.95 The Republic   *Plato*
____ 3.95 The Second Treatise on Civil Government   *John Locke*
____ 3.95 The Subjection of Women   *John Stuart Mill*
____ 9.95 Thinking Straight   *Antony Flew*
____ 11.95 The Worlds of the Early Greek Philosophers   *edited by Wilbur and Allen*
____ 11.95 The Worlds of Hume and Kant   *edited by Wilbur and Allen*
____ 11.95 The Worlds of Plato and Aristotle   *edited by Wilbur and Allen*

POPULAR SCIENCE

____ 12.95 In the Beginning   *Chris McGowan*
____ 12.95 The Magic Numbers of Dr. Matrix   *Martin Gardner*
____ 11.95 The Roving Mind   *Isaac Asimov*

SOCIAL SCIENCES AND CURRENT EVENTS

_____ 11.95 Thomas Szasz: Primary Values and Major Contentions   *edited by Vatz and Weinberg*

HEALTH ISSUES

_____ 9.95 Caring for An Aging Parent   *Avis Jane Ball*
_____ 9.95 Handle With Care: A Question of Alzheimer's   *Dorothy S. Brown*
_____ 10.95 Out of Our Minds: How to Cope With the Everyday Problems of the Mentally Ill   *Sascha Garson*
_____ 17.95 Psychiatry and Ethics   *edited by Rem B. Edwards*
_____ 9.95 The Smoke-Free Workplace   *Weis and Miller*
_____ 13.95 The Therapeutic State · *Thomas Szasz*
_____ 11.95 Vitamin Politics   *John Fried*
_____ 10.95 You, Your Parent and the Nursing Home   *Nancy Fox*

NEW CONCEPTS IN HUMAN SEXUALITY

_____ 14.95 The Complete Guide to Sexual Fulfillment   *Cauthery and Stanway*
_____ 10.95 Having Love Affairs   *Richard Taylor*
_____ 9.95 How to Stay Two When Baby Makes Three   *Dorman and Klein*
_____ 15.95 Pornography and Censorship   *edited by Copp and Wendell*
_____ 12.95 S & M: Studies in Sadomasochism   *edited by Weinberg and Kamel*
_____ 11.95 Sex and the Bible   *Gerald Larue*
_____ 15.95 Sexual Practices and the Medieval Church   *Bullough and Brundage*
_____ 12.95 Sex Without Love   *Russell Vannoy*

LITERATURE, CRITICISM AND BIOGRAPHY

_____ 12.95 Election Day 2084   *edited by Asimov and Greenberg*
_____ 15.95 Mark Twain: Selected Writings of an American Skeptic   *edited by Victor Doyno*

FRONTIERS IN EDUCATION

_____ 13.95 Excellence in Education   *edited by Altbach, Kelly, and Weis*
_____ 14.95 Higher Education in American Society   *edited by Altbach and Berdahl ·*
_____ 13.95 Paradigms and Promises: New Approaches to Educational Administration   *William Foster*

THE SKEPTIC'S BOOKSHELF

_____ 10.95 The Age of Reason   *Thomas Paine*
_____ 15.95 An Anthology of Atheism and Rationalism   *edited by Gordon Stein*
_____ 10.95 Atheism: The Case Against God   *George H. Smith*
_____ 8.95 The Atheist Debater's Handbook   *B. C. Johnson*
_____ 12.95 Bertrand Russell on God and Religion   *edited by Al Seckel*
_____ 13.95 Judaism Beyond God: A Radical New Way to Be Jewish   *Sherwin T. Wine*
_____ 11.95 The Mystery of the Kingdom of God   *Albert Schweitzer*
_____ 15.95 The Origins of Christianity   *R. Joseph Hoffmann*
_____ 12.95 Some Mistakes of Moses   *Robert G. Ingersoll*

HUMANISM

_____ 11.95 The Best of Robert Ingersoll   *edited by Roger E. Greeley*
_____ 7.95 The Humanist Alternative   *edited by Paul Kurtz*
_____ 12.95 Humanist Ethics   *edited by Morris B. Storer*
_____ 6.95 A Humanist Funeral Service   *Corliss Lamont*
_____ 2.95 Humanist Manifestos I and II
_____ 3.95 A Humanist Wedding Service   *Corliss Lamont*
_____ 10.95 In Defense of Secular Humanism   *Paul Kurtz*
_____ 2.95 A Secular Humanist Declaration

The books listed above can be obtained from your book dealer or directly from Prometheus Books. Please check off the appropriate books. Remittance must accompany all orders from individuals. Please include $2.00 postage and handling for first book, .75 for each additional book (4.50 maximum). (N.Y.S. residents please add applicable sales tax.)

Send to _____
(Please type or print clearly)
Address _____
City _____ State _____ Zip _____
Charge my □ **VISA**   Amount Enclosed _____
         □ **MasterCard**
Acct. _____   Phone orders (outside NYS) call toll free: 800-421-0351.
Exp. Date _____ Tel. # _____   In NYS: 716-837-2475
Signature _____   Please allow 3-6 weeks for delivery

PROMETHEUS BOOKS
700 E. Amherst Street, Buffalo, NY 14215